COLLEGE READING
AND WRITING

COLLEGE READING AND WRITING

ROBERT E. YARBER and J. BURL HOGINS

San Diego Mesa College

The Macmillan Company, *New York*
Collier-Macmillan Limited, *London*

Library of Congress catalog card number: 68–11852

The Macmillan Company, New York
Collier-Macmillan Canada, Ltd., Toronto, Ontario

Printed in the United States of America

A WORD TO THE STUDENT

Although this course in English may be required, you would agree that a workable knowledge of your language is desirable: desirable because this working ability will help you in your other studies; desirable because your social life depends in large measure on your ability to handle language well; desirable because good ideas are formed only within the structure we call language; and desirable because most job opportunities center around language ability. Therefore, whatever reasons motivated you to come to college in the first place are the very same reasons for studying language.

This text was written for you—a person with zest for living, enthusiasm for success, and desire to become an educated person. We have selected thirty-six essays that cover a wide range of interests—from the need for a college education to sex in Sweden. The essays themselves will serve as models for writing your own work and as stimuli for discussion.

In addition to using good essays as models, we have written introductory material for twelve parts in the text. They are meant to help you in developing an idea, limiting your subject, emphasizing your major points, and using effective diction. You will definitely experience marked improvement in your writing by following the advice offered you in these parts.

Additional suggestions are given toward the end of the book: how to use a dictionary and how to develop a better vocabulary. People everywhere recognize the necessity of a good vocabulary, hence the emphasis here is on the fundamentals of vocabulary building. A part is included on improving reading skills and reading habits, employing once again the practical aspects of good reading.

Finally, this book offers a list of 100 theme topics—in case you run low or need an idea to get you started—along with a list of good books and stories you can check before you become dismayed at the question, "What shall I read?", and a glossary of rhetorical terms, i.e., words and phrases used by writers to express the concepts of good writing.

This text, then, is meant to be a practical guide for the student who wants help in learning to use his language more effectively.

R. E. Y.
J. B. H.

CONTENTS

APPENDIX   485

I. ORGANIZATION: THE MAIN IDEA

If you are to write something you think is worth saying to a specific audience, you must have a reasonably full grasp of your subject. You need to be alive intellectually—not vegetating on old clichés and prejudices; you need to have lively experiences in reading and in living; you need to admit pet aversions and prejudices, as well as all kinds of personal opinions—and be willing to write about them. Your paper doesn't need to be profound, but you must be interested in what you are saying, and have a *single* main idea in mind. A few people may be interested in "Freedom in the World Today"; but "Eighteen-year-olds Should Be Able to Vote" will certainly have a wider appeal to college students, may produce a better theme on freedom, and will probably afford you greater security in expressing yourself. So, stay out of vacuums—it's hard to breathe in them. You have no right to bore your reader, and the best ways to avoid boredom are: (1) choose a subject that interests *you*, (2) select one specific idea, (3) gather and offer supporting material, and (4) clearly organize what you have to say.

Have you ever asked these questions, or had someone ask them of you: "What's the idea?" "What are you driving at?" "Why don't you get to the point?" "What do you mean by that?" If you anticipate these questions before you start writing, sticking to one idea is much easier. You need to center your thinking on a single idea, a single purpose, or a single impression. A flashlight won't light up a 40-acre field, but it does well in a small closet. A broad idea can't be covered in a thousand words or even a thousand pages, but a carefully selected, specific one can be covered, and covered well, within the assigned length.

Focusing your attention on a specific subject that you know and like is the best way to approach a writing assignment. How can you know a subject thoroughly? You can know a subject if you have read a great deal about it, heard a great deal about it, or had intense personal experience with it—and given it serious thought.

How can you "spotlight" or limit a subject? Think about the subject until you can write in *one sentence* exactly what your theme is about. This one sentence is called by many names—thesis sentence, guiding sentence, theme sentence, main-idea sentence—but its function is more important than its name: It gives specific purpose and direction to the entire essay.

Let's test the inverted pyramid game: Start broad, narrow down, and come to a one-sentence statement of purpose—come to the point.

Education   *Too broad*
Education is better to-   *Better, but still too*
day than yesterday.   *broad.*
Grades in college should be   *That's it! That's the point.*
abandoned, because they   *Some will disagree, but at*
don't reflect what a student   *least we have a point of*
really learns.   *view.*

Once you have concentrated your main idea into one sentence, you are ready to search for supporting material. To find the kind of material for a short paper (350–1500 words), search your own mind for personal experiences, read an article or two in the library, ask several knowledgeable people for information. Throughout this *search for evidence* keep notes to refer to when you write.

After you have found evidence to support your main idea, you will find that it can best be arranged in one of the following ways: It can serve as an example, as a basis for comparison and contrast, or as a definition. These methods of development are treated in later chapters of this book.

But it is not enough to have a good, clear idea, with evidence to back it up; you must present the idea, with its evidence, in an organized paper which your reader will find interesting and clear. Your papers will usually follow one of three organizational patterns: chronological (time), spatial (physical), or logical.

The chronological order is generally used to narrate a series of events in time. It shows the passage of time—yesterday, today, tomorrow; the order of events—1, 2, 3; or the relationship of a sequence—first, second, third. As a help in giving direction to your reader, use such key words in your paper as *first, second, then, after that,* and *finally.* For a more detailed treatment of the idea of transition, read Part X.

Spatial order is used to describe a place, such as your room or even the glove compartment of your car. It is descriptive, and therefore should not be used for more than a paragraph at a time. Most of us get bored when pure description runs on and on and on. (Remember Dickens?)

Logical order refers to the arrangement of *ideas* in the writer's mind. Did you notice that in chronological and spatial order that the "order" is in areas the author has no control over? After all, we can't make our sun stand still. But in logical arrangements we *can* control the sequence. Therefore, we begin with a topic sentence in a paragraph; then we develop that logical idea. Notice how the second, third, and fourth sentences in the paragraph below serve to expand the topic sentence.

> In the early years of her development, a girl must strive to accomplish what one psychiatrist has called the four tasks of adolescence. She must separate herself from her parents—that is, become emotionally free of them without rejecting them. She must establish a value system for herself, deciding on the moral principles and value judgments by which she will live. She must choose her life goal, which will eventually enable her to be independent of her parents' financial support. And finally, she must determine and accept her sexual role, which means discovering what it means to be a mature woman and accepting not only the joys but the responsibilities of her sexual nature.*

In seeking an appropriate arrangement for your raw materials, then, you will come to see that any one of a number of methods might fit your paper. You should not forget such matters as time order and spatial arrangement; you need to think of your material in terms of definition, comparison, contrast, and example; you must determine whether to use, for instance, development that goes from the general to the specific or from the specific to the general.

A word of encouragement: The highways you drive on are not built a mile at a time, but by inches. Similarly, your writing development will not be smooth and fully developed in a week, or even a month—but you can learn to write an interesting and clear paper by going at it carefully and deliberately. Your writing will improve if you follow this advice: Write on a subject you know and are interested in; think out the subject until it can be stated in one sentence; gather supporting material; and write in a clear fashion, arranging your material according to time, space, or logical order.

* Mary Calderone, M.D., "How Young Men Influence the Girls Who Love Them," from the July, 1965, issue of *Redbook* magazine, copyright © 1965 McCall Corporation.

1. HOW YOUNG MEN INFLUENCE THE GIRLS WHO LOVE THEM *

MARY CALDERONE, M.D.

1   Rare is the young man who is fully aware of the important part he inevitably plays in the life of every girl with whom he has a close personal relationship. He is indeed the exception if he has any real understanding of his role in the evolution by which a girl becomes a woman. For no woman is truly a woman until a man has participated in and completed the process that makes her one.

2   But because it is a *process,* the subtle, complex evolution of a young girl into a woman occurs over a substantial period of time and cannot be explained by any single act or any single relationship. The French word for it, *épanouisse-ment,* which has no exact English translation, conveys the idea of "becoming," and includes such nuances as growth, development, unfolding, flowering and, most particularly, fulfillment. Often the completion of a girl's coming of age will occur as a consequence of her relationship with the one young man who proves to be *the* man in her life. But in maturing into womanhood, she will be influenced by her involvements with all the men to whom she becomes emotionally attached, including friends, teachers, relatives, brothers and especially her father.

3   A girl's development is also influenced by her associations with other women, and profoundly so by her relationship with her mother. And a boy's evolution into manhood is similarly influenced by the girls and the women he chooses to like or love. But I am concentrating here on the impact of men on

* Mary Calderone, M.D., "How Young Men Influence the Girls Who Love Them," from the July, 1965, issue of *Redbook* magazine, copyright © 1965 McCall Corporation. Reprinted by permission of the author.

5

the life of every young girl with whom they share an emotional bond. In my experience, men are generally unaware of the extent of this impact—or unconcerned about it. As a result, their behavior is all too often irresponsible. My hope is that in sharpening their awareness of how a girl grows up, I may increase both their concern and their sense of responsibility.

4   In the early years of her development, a girl must strive to accomplish what one psychiatrist has called the four tasks of adolescence. She must separate herself from her parents—that is, become emotionally free of them without rejecting them. She must establish a value system for herself, deciding on the moral principles and value judgments by which she will live. She must choose her life goal, which will eventually enable her to be independent of her parents' financial support. And finally, she must determine and accept her sexual role, which means discovering what it means to be a mature woman and accepting not only the joys but the responsibilities of her sexual nature.

5   Similar tasks must be accomplished by the adolescent boy. But our society has not made equal demands of boys and girls, especially in terms of their acceptance of the joys of sex as contrasted with the responsibilities. Boys have always been encouraged to develop their healthy drives toward sexual manhood, but little has been demanded of them in exercising responsibility. The opposite has been true for girls. Even in this day of the emancipated female, girls are hardly encouraged to express their sexual nature, but they are still expected to bear the burden of responsibility for all heterosexual relationships. In a changing society, however, as women increasingly share with men a healthy enjoyment of sex, so men should increasingly share the burden of its responsibilities.

6   There are two sides to responsibility, and they are equally important. One is responsibility to ourselves, and this includes the need to know what is right and healthy and nurturing *for us;* and then there is responsibility for the other, the need to try to understand, to the limits of our ability, what may be best *for the other person.* In the latter sense, a young man can hardly be counted on to assume responsibility for the well-being of girls he dates if he lacks any real understanding of what happens to a girl as she slowly matures into womanhood. There is much that he needs to know.

7   He needs to know, for example, that she has in her unconscious an image of the ideal male that has been built up through her relationships with the men in her family and the men she has come to know up to this point in her life. She has also been influenced by our culture with its constant emphasis on sex—in newspapers, magazines, comic books, novels, television, plays, movies and, perhaps worst of all, the commercial advertising that exploits sex for profit.

8   From this vast flow of experience the girl distills her image of the ideal male. No matter what the character may be of a boy she meets, she tends to see her ideal image reflected in him because of her eagerness to find in the flesh the

one male she seeks. Thus a first-love relationship is full of possibilities for misunderstanding, as when a girl who has been reared in a family dominated by a harsh father turns to a boy because he appears sensitive and thoughtful. If he is what he seems to be, he will reinforce her image of the ideal male. But if in reality he is a passive, selfish boy, sooner or later this will become apparent and disillusionment may force the girl to reject that image and accept harshness as the mark of the man.

9   We certainly cannot expect a young man, who may himself be relatively inexperienced in life, to comprehend fully the nature of a young girl's unconscious image of her ideal male. But it is not uncommon for a boy to sense the girl is looking for certain traits—firmness, perhaps, or sensitivity, or tenderness—and for him to assume these characteristics as a short cut to sexual conquest. If he succeeds in his strategy and then abandons the girl afterward, as often happens, it is because he is unaware of—or unconcerned about—the extent of his irresponsibility. Apart from having consciously deceived the girl, thereby diminishing her trust in all men, he no doubt will have permanently altered for the worse her image of the ideal male.

10   A young man must therefore be prepared to face the fact that whether he likes it or not, and whether it is for better or for worse, a responsibility rests on his shoulders when he initiates a sexual relationship with a young and inexperienced girl. Often, however, he is in a poor position to assume such a heavy responsibility, since he, no less than the girl, is floundering in a sea of uncertainties and is himself not entirely sure of the ways in which love is related to sex.

11   Both the boy and the girl are seeking love and sex, but their needs are somewhat different. For the sake of clarifying the point, we can say the girl plays at sex, for which she is not ready, because fundamentally what she wants is love; and the boy plays at love, for which he is not ready, because what he wants is sex. We must understand that in reality both the boy and girl seek love *and* sex, tenderness *and* passion, but that in the early years their drives are rarely synchronized. A girl usually has a greater need for a feeling of legitimacy about the relationship before she can give herself to a boy, a legitimacy rooted in her belief that the boy loves her and that she loves him, for it is this belief that frees her to express the sexual side of her nature. Boys rarely require such a belief to free themselves sexually, but they willingly play at love if this is necessary.

12   In truth, the girl as well as the boy "plays" at love. For real love in any form is composed of many elements, one of the most important of which is primacy of concern for the beloved one. And few are the girls or boys who have achieved sufficient emotional maturity to be able to identify the best interests of another person and put them ahead of their own.

13   There is, however, a crucial difference in how the boy and girl play at love.

The boy can do so consciously; the girl cannot. In this sense, the boy can play at love as he would at any game, using strategy to win. The girl plays at love in a more profound and vulnerable way, since the person she must mislead— if she is to obtain what she wants—is herself. She has a need to *believe* in love, a need that the boy, in most cases, does not have.

14 If a young man does use love in this way, as a lure or a weapon, it is usually without his realizing the dangers in doing so, for this gives him the power to arouse the young girl's sexual nature. Whether he has the moral right to do so is, of course, the critical question. I am one of those who believe we need to develop much new knowledge on which to base new moralities adequate to the changing needs of contemporary society. We do not know all the consequences of introducing a psychologically and emotionally immature girl to sexual stimulation. But we do know that in a large proportion of girls, sexual response does not appear spontaneously, as it apparently does in the male, but is learned at one time or another during her development into womanhood. And in this learning, the male plays the obvious lead.

15 We have always known this. Yet we do not shine in our ability to say to our sons: "Before you make love to a girl, you have an obligation to come to a deliberate decision in full awareness that you will be setting in motion powerful forces in that girl. If you are concerned about her as a human being, you must decide whether or not it is appropriate at her age and stage of development to learn sexual response. And you must decide whether she is ready for this. If you think she is, then you should acknowledge that it will certainly affect her life to some degree, and perhaps more profoundly than you can imagine. If you are *not* concerned about her as a human being, then consider what it will do to you—to your sense of yourself as a responsible human being, to your own character and development—to use her sexually for your temporary gratification. These decisions are your responsibility to make."

16 In my experience, few young men hear words of this kind. The plain fact is that we have lost the ability—or, more alarmingly, the willingness—to bring up sons with the strength and self-confidence to assume major responsibility for setting standards and developing the moral values by which human beings must live. What lawyers term the "burden of proof" in establishing the rightness or wrongness of a sexual relationship has for too long been placed entirely on the girl's shoulders.

17 Two years ago, for example, I attended a conference on the sexual behavior of college students, to find that those who had accepted invitations were for the most part deans and counselors at women's colleges. Why shouldn't there have been similar concern on the part of those who are occupied with the sexual behavior of college men? Doesn't it seem almost self-evident that in a society which proclaims the equality of the sexes, men as well as women must come to grips with the question of sexual morality, and that men must at least share the leadership in seeking its resolution?

18   Man cannot have his cake and eat it too. He cannot expect his eventual marriage to be the most enduring of all possible relationships if, prior to marriage, his relationships with women have been almost exclusively physical and transient. He cannot expect his wife to fulfill him in all ways if, before marrying her, he made little effort to learn about a woman's nature and needs.

19   Many young men (and women too, unfortunately) appear convinced that pleasurable sexual attraction is the most important single basis for entering marriage. This belief, like all pleasure principles, does not hold up in practice. In his autobiographical book, the writer Nelson Algren says: "I don't think of sex as just something that happens now and then. . . . Sex is a diffused feeling. It diffuses everything and only once in a while would it be called Sex. Sex is diffused with love and affection, and I don't think you can make things like that happen. . . . It's got to be the big thing first."

20   I believe that every young man needs to know and to accept the fact that because he plays a crucial role in furthering a young woman's emotional maturity, he must also accept the responsibility that goes with it. He must understand that the sexual act for a woman tends to be the ultimate expression of what she feels about life and her belief in it, expressed through her love for and belief in the man with whom she chooses to live the rest of her life. If she engages in sexual experience before she is mature enough, sex may become an end in itself—or the ability to enjoy sexual experience may be crippled forever —and her capacities for a deeper relationship may be arrested.

21   Young men must face these realities. We know that many young people today place their sexual lives beyond the reach of adult authority. But if they also place them beyond the reach of a better understanding of the place of sex in the life of man, they serve themselves and society poorly. We are changing and so is society. If we do nothing to direct the flow of change, negative and destructive forces will determine its course.

22   Of most profound importance to man and his well-being is his own sexuality and the use he makes of it. It underlies his most important relationship, and indeed pervades all his relationships in one way or another. The Reverend Kenneth Greet, of the Methodist Church in Great Britain, puts it this way: "The beginning of understanding is the recognition that sex is not primarily something we do, but something we are. We have been made male and female in order that we can come together in a unique kind of relationship. Marriage is the most vital form of it. The same act which secures, promotes and deepens that relationship can also produce a child. But there ought not to be any child until the relationship is there as the only fitting environment for it. This approach provides us with the right perspective for a fuller recognition of the immense importance and significance of sex. When we begin to accept it, it inevitably means death to the old double standard of morality. . . . It is also the means of quickening those elements of respect and responsibility which are a vital part of love, if it is to be worthy of the name."

23 In my sixties, as mother, grandmother and physician, and from the security of a long and fulfilling marriage, I would like to challenge the young men of this generation to ponder and answer for themselves the profound question: *What is the purpose of sex?*

24 The kinds of answers being given to this question have created the distorted images and concepts of sexuality for which my generation must accept full responsibility. But unfortunately we are not the ones who can resolve the situations. You are. We can't tell you what to do—only that there is something of first importance to be done. Whether or not your generation does it is your choice. How you do it is your business. The standards of morality that must be set for the society in which you will rear your children are yours to define.

25 The truth about human sexuality as a great creative and re-creative force is yet to be acknowledged. The truth about the relationship of man to woman in the world of today as it turns into the world of tomorrow is yet to be discovered. Only from these two truths can be derived the moralities that we must have if society is to survive as a community in which men and women can find fulfillment in enduring love.

Apparatus for: How Young Men Influence the Girls Who Love Them

Vocabulary: *For each numbered word, select the correct definition by letter from the lettered list.*

1. nuances (¶ 2)   _d_

2. emancipated (¶ 5)   _f_

3. synchronized (¶ 11)   _e_

4. primacy (¶ 12)   _a_

5. vulnerable (¶ 13)   _b_

6. transient (¶ 18)   _c_

a. first or fundamental

b. assailable

c. short-lived

d. subtle qualities

e. occurring at the same time

f. set free

Discussion: *Rhetoric*

1. This essay is constructed around one central idea. Where is it stated?
2. What organizational device does the author use in paragraph 4? Is it effective?
3. In paragraph 6, Mrs. Calderone places a topic sentence at the beginning. How does she develop it? How effective or convincing are her supporting statements?
4. What do *flow* and *distill* suggest in paragraph 8?
5. In several places the author refers to "many young people." Is this phrase sufficiently specific to be persuasive?
6. Does the author adequately define *sexuality?* Explain.

1. Middle of ¶ 3

2. Lists the list in importance order. Yes it is effective.

3. flow means the constant emphases on sex distill means holds back

4. No.

5. No

6. Yes,

Apparatus for: How Young Men Influence the Girls Who Love Them

Discussion: *Theme*

1. Do you agree with the author's first sentence? Explain.
2. Why would the French, rather than the Americans, have a word for the process discussed in this essay?
3. How true is the last sentence of paragraph 2? Is it an accurate description of persons you know?
4. Discuss this sentence: "A girl's development is also influenced . . . profoundly . . . by her relationship with her mother."
5. The second sentence of paragraph 9 makes a statement that the author says is not "uncommon." Do you agree?
6. How does sexuality differ from sex?
7. "What is the purpose of sex?" (¶ 23)

1. _____

_____

2. _____

_____

3. _____

_____

4. _____

_____

5. _____

_____

6. _____

   _____

7. _____

   _____

Writing Suggestions

1. *For the women:* Write a paper in which you either agree or disagree with the following statement: ". . . she will be influenced by her involvements with all the men to whom she becomes emotionally attached, including friends, teachers, relatives, brothers, and especially her father."
2. *For the men:* Write a paper in which you either agree or disagree with the following statement: "A young man must therefore be prepared to face the fact that whether he likes it or not, and whether it is for better or for worse, a responsibility rests on his shoulders when he initiates a sexual relationship with a young and inexperienced girl."
3. Write a paper on the differences between "sexuality" and "sex."
4. Answer the following question: "What is the purpose of sex?"
5. Are the attitudes toward sex held by most of your friends healthy? Present your views in a theme.
6. Present your views on the following topic: "Why I Believe (*or* Do Not Believe) in Pre-marital Sex."

2. HOW TO INSPIRE A TEACHING MACHINE*

HALLETT D. SMITH

1   It was sometime early in the 1970's, as I remember, when Caltech developed the teaching machine as we now know it. For a decade before this, there had been a primitive device, invented, or at least exploited, by Professor B. F. Skinner of Harvard. It was essentially a mechanical gadget or box, which led the student through certain logical steps in any subject which is logically organized, allowing him to develop his knowledge and skill sequentially. The most important component of this crude instrument was not, however, anything mechanical—it was, as in most great inventions, a concept. The concept was that learning takes place more rapidly if the student, whenever he gets something right, gets, what they called in the quaint language of that time, "reward," or, as we should say in modern English, "reinforcement." The idea, of course, came from certain psychological experiments on pigeons. You can train a pigeon to discriminate pretty carefully among various shapes and colors of keys when the situation is such that it is only by pecking the correct one that he gets his grain of corn—that is to say, his reinforcement.

2   Now Professor Skinner's great insight was that he saw that students are very much like pigeons—in fact, some of them are indistinguishable from pigeons. His only problem was, What do you give them instead of a grain of corn? You couldn't use candy because all the health authorities of that day insisted that candy was bad for the teeth, the complexion, and usually the cholesterol count. So the Skinnerian group hit upon a wonderful idea, stimulated possibly by their study, in the taverns of that period, of the reaction of

* Hallett D. Smith, "How to Inspire a Teaching Machine." Reprinted from *The Key Reporter*, vol. 28, no. 1, Autumn 1962. Copyright © 1962 by the United Chapters of Phi Beta Kappa. By permission of the publishers.

students to an antique contraption called a pinball machine, which registered the success of the player by flashing lights and the appearance of a high score on the board. No corn, no candy, just a flashing light and a bell which signaled that he was right. Here was the ideal reinforcement. It motivated the student to write a correct sentence just for the thrill of realizing he had written a correct sentence. It was also pointed out by many thoughtful observers at the time that this idea added a new dimension to human dignity, since pigeons would do their lessons only for corn, but people, provided they were young enough, would work assiduously just to get the satisfaction of knowing that they were right. We are really better than pigeons, after all—or to put it in scientific rather than moral terms, primates can accept a more sophisticated mode of learning reinforcement than avians can.

3 During the next decade, that interesting period that the history books now refer to as the Serious Sixties, the teaching machine was widely applied. It was at first most successful in purely logical subjects, like geometry and other branches of mathematics; then it was applied to languages (it has of course been used in psychology all along); and finally it made its way into the teaching of composition, where, after a few false starts and hesitating experiments, it was finally a tremendous success. Even the most hardened skeptics were convinced. I know, because I was one of them. Nothing could have persuaded me that it would work; but it did.

4 Of course thousands and thousands of English teachers were thrown out of work, but they soon got much more highly paid jobs in industry; this increased the Gross National Product substantially and was a real help, as President Goldwater said, in putting us one lap ahead of the Russians in the economic race.

5 Of course there are always sentimentalists who think that the old way of doing things was better. Carlyle and Ruskin and William Morris thought that the Medieval Period was better than the Nineteenth Century; Henry Ford looked back to the days of the horse and buggy and the simple farm environment; some people now dream of the free enterprise system as it was under Franklin D. Roosevelt. But as an old man who has seen both, I should like to defend the teaching machine and show how it is an improvement over the old system, especially in the teaching of writing.

6 First of all, it can correct mistakes in grammar, punctuation, spelling, and usage. I mean it can correct every single one of them and never miss. When my colleagues at Caltech combined the computer with the primitive teaching machine and then transistorized the whole thing so it was no bigger than a student's desk—well, you've all seen them in classrooms everywhere, I don't need to describe them—this made a fantastic difference. The machine gives a grade immediately and the reasons for the grade. It keeps a record of every grade and the reasons for it on file for twenty years and then automatically erases it.

7   The machine is completely objective and consistent. This is a tremendous benefit—the elimination of argument. Some younger people may not believe this, but there used to be lots of arguments about students' ability to write. Complaints came from parents, relatives, college teachers, employers, newspaper editors, congressmen (imagine that!) and of course television commentators, who complain about everything. But this argument died out rapidly when the machine came in: you just referred complainers to the machine, and it had all the answers. It's absolutely no fun arguing with a machine.

8   Furthermore, the machine gets along well with students. It is not the least influenced by moods, illness, overwork, harassment by the principal, or financial worries. The machine does just as good a job no matter how late it was out last night. The machine can do the same thing over and over without getting bored; therefore it never conveys any poisonous boredom to its students. Finally, in the thirty-five years the machine has been in widespread use we have never yet encountered a case in which the student is smarter than the machine; this has eliminated a lot of hostility on both sides.

9   So much in refutation of the sentimentalists who want to go back to the old, handmade, inefficient system of direct human teaching. The machine is here to stay, and we might as well make the best of it. Our programmers are on the whole good; their median salary last year was just over $75,000 for a nine-month year, which seems reasonably competitive with industry. In general, the situation is improving. But I would like to share with you some worries and concerns in the hope that original insights may occur to some of you—insights that so far have eluded us.

10   You remember that one of the essential characteristics of machine teaching is that it is done step by step. The programming for the machines which teach writing took a lot of work, because every single step had to be discovered after exhaustive analysis, trial, and retesting. Our experts kept constantly in mind the words of Dr. Skinner in the scriptures of machine teaching. He said of the programmer, "His goal must be to keep refining his program until the point is reached at which the answers of the average child will almost always be right." This is what our experts did. The English Composition Teaching Machines, or Comptines, as we came to call them, were so programmed that they could lead the most average student in the country through the gradual steps until he had written a correct and perfect theme. The response of the students in those early days to their reinforcement, their enthusiasm over mastering a new skill, was amusing and gratifying to see. I remember observing one high school boy who said, to nobody in particular, after he had finished a lesson on the Comptine and had seen his grade recorded by it, "You mean I've got an A on an English theme? Man, that's real hairy!" But we began to notice after a few years that the new method, although it worked well for poor or mediocre students, did not work so well for the superior ones.

11   Why this should be true was not immediately apparent, but two research

teams were assigned to the problem, and they finally came up with an answer which is satisfying from a theoretical point of view but has never, so far as I know, been tested empirically. The theoretical explanation is that when a superior student writes a correct sentence, or paragraph, in the Comptine, he gets very little reinforcement when the machine indicates that the item is correct—because he already knew he was right. What is lacking is what one of our younger psychologists called the "Gee-whiz Effect." And our programmers, even the most ingenious ones, couldn't think of any way to provide it.

12   The over-all result was that poor writers were developed into good, correct writers, but the good writers did not get any better. In fact, there is some evidence that they got worse, but our means of measuring this are so crude that we are not sure that the figure has any statistical significance. We consoled ourselves with the thought that when everybody writes with the same level of competence, there should be far fewer communication barriers, and for the past ten years a study group has been conducting surveys to find out if this is true. But I suppose I am old-fashioned. It seems to me that it ought to be possible to have some people write better than others. To put it in terms that reflect my conservative way of thinking, there ought to be some way of introducing inspiration into the teaching machine, such as we had in a few of the old human teachers. My psychologist friends laugh at me when I say this, and point out that I can't analyze or define inspiration. I say maybe not, but I can recognize it when it's there. They smile indulgently, and I'm sure they later remark to each other that the old boy is really getting senile.

13   The second worry or concern I have about our present methods of teaching writing is probably one that I should keep to myself, but this may be my only chance, so I am going to take it. The unpleasant fact is this: now that we know how to teach writing efficiently and well, thanks to the machine, nobody who has learned to write seems to *want* to write. I can remember when people who couldn't write well at all kept on writing, and sometimes they got published and occasionally they wrote best sellers. I can show you some of their books which I still have in my library. I realize that I can't put up a very serious defense of incompetent writers continuing to write and get published. But I'm worried all the same that nobody wants to write any more. Personally, I can't see why the machine should produce this effect. Technological improvement doesn't ordinarily depress the demand for a product improved—usually the opposite.

14   I have only one clue to the cause, and I'm not very confident about that. It is a clue that comes from a historical perspective rather than modern scientific research, so I realize that it will be suspect in most of your minds. When I was preparing this paper I had to go back to some long-neglected or forgotten sources in order to make sure I had my facts straight, because the memory of a man as old as I am is not to be depended upon. One of the documents I consulted was a bound volume of the *Scientific American* way back in November,

1961. It was an article by Professor Skinner on "Teaching Machines," which were then, of course, in their infancy. It is fascinating to see the confidence and courage that Skinner felt in those early days. He wrote as follows:

> Some people see machines as a threat to the teacher, which they are not. Some fancy that they will make education a cold, mechanical process. Others fear that they will turn students into regimented and mindless robots. Such fears are groundless.

15   It was confidence like this, in the face of what must have been considerable skepticism, conservative resistance to change, and even hostility, that successfully brought us into the present age of machine teaching. But the clue I spoke of was not in the Skinner article itself; it was in the Notes on Contributors column of the magazine. There I learned that Professor Skinner majored in English in college, and that he had always planned to be a writer. But "shortly after graduation," to quote him directly, "I discovered the unhappy fact that I had nothing to say, and went on to graduate study in psychology hoping to remedy that shortcoming."

16   Now, do you suppose that the reason why students who have learned to write correctly and well from the Comptine actually *don't* write is that they have nothing to say? Do you suppose that our students catch this disease from Skinner and that the teaching machine is some sort of carrier of it? I'm almost ashamed to voice the idea, because I know it isn't scientific, but it is the only one to occur to me.

17   In conclusion I must confess that the title of this article is actually a little fraudulent. I can't tell you how to inspire a teaching machine, the way people who publish papers called "How to Train a Dog" or "How to Make Two Million Dollars in the Stock Market" can really tell you how to train a dog or make two million dollars, whichever one you happen to be interested in at the moment. I can only lay the problem before you and ask for your help. How can we build into our machine or our programming something that will make good writers become better writers, and how can we arrange it so that people who learn to write from our machines go on writing because they have something to say?

18   We are now well into the last decade of the Fantastic Century, the twentieth. Let us hope that by the time the year 2000 rolls around we will have the answers to these questions. It's your problem as much as it is mine.

Apparatus for: How to Inspire a Teaching Machine

Vocabulary: *For each numbered word, select the correct definition by letter from the lettered list.*

1. exploited (¶ 1)   *d*

2. sequentially (¶ 1)   *c*

3. assiduously (¶ 2)   *e*

4. eluded (¶ 8)   ·   *a*

5. senile (¶ 12)   *b*

a. evaded
b. old age
c. consecutively
d. utilized
e. diligently

Discussion: *Rhetoric*

1. What is the tone of this essay? What is the attitude of the speaker toward his subject? Point out specific paragraphs in your answer.
2. What is the advantage for the author to pretend he is writing from the 1990's in order to look back at the 1960's?
3. How is the theme "rounded off"? That is, how does the author summarize his ideas about teachers and teaching machines?
4. Cite some internal organizational features of this essay. Note, for example, paragraph 13.

1. *Informal TPS, 9,10,11, 12, 13, 14, 15,16,17, 18*

2. *Everything is modernizing already*

3. *He puts it to the reader,*

4. *Author's opinion*

Apparatus for: How to Inspire a Teaching Machine

Discussion: *Theme*

1. Do you think machines will seriously threaten teachers' jobs? Why or why not?
2. The author refers to the Sixties as the "Serious Sixties." Is this the way you would describe them? Why?
3. If machines could do the job of correcting grammar, punctuation, spelling, and usage, should we develop them? Explain.
4. What is the meaning of the last sentence: "It's your problem as much as it is mine."?

1. _____

   _____

2. _____

   _____

3. _____

   _____

4. _____

   _____

Writing Suggestions:

1. "Students Are Hardly Pigeons"
2. Write a theme in which you imagine what a classroom situation will be like in 1995.
3. Analyze the idea of "reinforcement" for essays in English.
4. Describe what a superior teacher does that a machine could not do.
5. Describe the most outstanding teacher you had in high school.

3. SUPERSTITIOUS? HERE'S WHY! *

JULIE FORSYTH BATCHELOR AND CLAUDIA DE LYS

1   Light-haired girls are fickle, prove to be false friends, and are preferred by gentlemen. Dark-haired girls are sincere, have better health, and get married. ("Gentlemen prefer blondes, but marry brunettes.") A redhead is emotionally unstable, has a terrible temper, and deserves to be burned as a witch. You've often heard these and other superstitions.

2   Throughout the ages all sorts of superstitions have grown up. For example, some people have insisted that you can judge a person's character by the color of his hair. This superstition has been fostered in spite of the fact that there is no scientific basis for such a belief.

3   Many superstitions about hair probably began because of a belief that "like makes like." Red meant fire to most of our ancestors, and so a redhead just had to have a fiery disposition. The ancient Egyptians, Greeks, and Romans regarded anyone with red hair as very unlucky. It was during the Middle Ages that redheads were called witches and sometimes burned at the stake. But unpopular as red has been in the past, at the moment it is a favorite hair dye.

4   There are other superstitions besides those dealing with shades of hair. A thick head of hair or a hairy body was supposed to be a sign of great strength, which is false. That a girl's long hair saps her strength when she is ill has turned out to be just an old wives' tale.

5   There's an old adage, "Pull out one gray hair and ten will grow in its place." This is impossible, for only one strand of hair can grow from each hair bulb.

* Adapted from *Superstitious? Here's Why!* copyright, 1954, by Julie Forsyth Batchelor and Claudia de Lys. Reprinted by permission of Harcourt, Brace & World, Inc.

Also, that shock or grief can turn hair white in a single night has never been proved.

6   In sun-worship times, offerings were made to the rays of the sun, believed to be its hair. Since it was supposed that the sun, like other fire, could do harm as well as good, men offered their hair to be burned hoping to please the sun god. In certain places today people burn hair combings because of an old notion that a bird may weave them into a nest and so make the owner insane.

7   Have you heard the superstition that a woman with a V-shaped hairline, called a widow's peak, will lose her first husband and marry again soon after? This notion came about through a change in the color of mourning clothes. Black had been worn for centuries, but during the early Middle Ages white became popular (and still is with the Chinese). Then in 1498, young Anne of Brittany decided to wear black upon the death of her husband Charles VIII. The next king, Louis XII, married her soon afterward, making her queen of France for the second time.

8   Hat designers of the time took advantage of the new mourning color to create an attractive V-shaped, or peaked, bonnet of black and white for semi-mourning. This suggested the V-shaped hairline some women have, that came to be known as a widow's peak. Its association with Queen Anne led to the belief in two marriages.

9   Names have always been important to people. When first given to individuals, animals, and places they were chosen carefully with a hope of endowing whatever was named with some sort of magic. It meant a great deal in those days to have the "right" name. It still does now, but mainly because of each person's mental attitude toward his own name. If you like what you are called and if it gives you confidence, it's the "right" name for you.

10   Name superstitions run into the hundreds. It's lucky to have only seven letters in either first or last name. Men with thirteen letters should add one for good luck. No girl should marry a man whose last name has the same initial as hers, for, as the rhyme goes, "Change the name but not the letter, marry for worse instead of better." A girl whose name is Mary begins with a good start in life.

11   Naming a child after a living person was not popular at one time as it was believed this meant death for one person or the other. But as centuries passed, the custom reversed itself. Now it's a fairly popular custom to name a baby after a living grandparent, under the superstition that this name will assure the child a long life too.

12   Modern custom says that when you are introducing two people you should name the more important person first. This custom goes back to early times when the chief of the tribe or king had to be mentioned by name before others. His name was supposed to have supernatural power.

13 The old expression "Laugh and grow fat" leads many to believe that fat people are always happy. One reason for this saying may be that the extra fatty tissue under their skins makes their frowns and worry lines less noticeable. But psychologists claim that overweight people are usually far from happy.

14 Another popular saying is "Fat people are lazy." But we know now that laziness affects fat and thin alike. A fleshy person appears lazy because his movements are slowed up by the weight he carries. Hundreds of lazy people, both thin and fat, have been cured of laziness when fitted with the proper eyeglasses. Others have gained energy after they have had medical care.

15 A third fallacy in regard to fat people is that there are more fat boys than girls, but statistics show the number is about equal.

16 Palmistry is an ancient art; the study of hands has been traced back to around 5000 B.C. It was especially popular during the Middle Ages until the Church frowned on palmistry because of its pagan origin. Then its practice was taken over mainly by gypsies.

17 The left hand is usually the one read, although both may be consulted. Each line, cross, or mount has a meaning, many relating to myths of primitive times. Very few expert palmists can agree as to their exact meanings.

18 Modern science does not recognize palmistry. The reading of mystical meaning into a line, curve, or mark of the hand is considered a very dangerous superstition. Some of the states have laws prohibiting palmistry, teacup reading, and other forms of attempting to foretell the future.

19 However, people still flock to palmists, who are usually excellent readers of character and who sometimes by chance hit on events that do take place. Having someone talk to us about the most fascinating of subjects—ourselves —has a great appeal.

20 Most superstitions go far back in history. Although very few superstitions have a basis in fact, they have been popular through the ages. Today, these notions are still enjoyed, even if most people don't actually believe in them.

Vocabulary: *Using your dictionary, define each of the following words as it appears in context.*

1. fostered (¶ 2)   _sustained_

2. disposition (¶ 3)   _natural tender_

3. adage (¶ 5)   _proverb_

4. endowing (¶ 9)   _enriching_

5. supernatural (¶ 12)   _above & beyond nor_

6. fallacy (¶ 15)   _a false idea_

7. statistics (¶ 15)   _a fact_

Discussion: *Rhetoric*

1. This essay is organized around one main idea. What is that idea? Is it stated directly in the essay?
2. Describe the effectiveness of using so many examples to support the main idea.
3. Paragraphs 13, 14, and 15 deal with "fat people." What words tie these paragraphs together?
4. Other than examples, what kind of material have the authors used to lend support to their central idea? Consider paragraph 7.

1. _Superstition from long ago._
   It is never stated.
2. _To show how many myths_
   there are.
3. _Expression, fallacy, saying_

4. _Facts,_

Apparatus for: Superstitious? Here's Why!

Discussion: *Theme*

1. Are all superstitions necessarily false? Explain.
2. Why do people cling to superstitions in the twentieth century?
3. Do you agree with all of the conclusions in this essay? For example, do you agree with the last sentence of paragraphs 2 and 20?
4. Cite an example of a modern superstition and attempt to account for its existence.

1. _____

_____

2. _____

_____

3. _____

_____

4. _____

_____

Writing Suggestions

1. In a paper of about 500 words, treat in more depth one of the superstitions mentioned in this essay.
2. Write a paper in which you cite superstitions that are regional or perhaps believed only in your area.
3. Use the following sentence as the basis of a theme: "Gentlemen prefer blondes."
4. Write a paper on the uses of color to suggest evil, good, or other traits.
5. Analyze the reasons why you believe in a particular superstition.

II. DICTION:
THERE'S A WORD FOR IT

Every good essay is organized around a central idea; but a good idea is not enough. It must be expressed in the right diction—in words that are exact, interesting, and suitable.

Notice the difference between these two sentences:

a. He walked down the steps.
b. Ebenezer limped wearily down the rickety staircase.

The second sentence is more vivid because the writer has used exact, colorful words. In your own writing, make it a practice to choose the word that says precisely what you mean. In selecting the right word, keep in mind these three principles of good diction: exactness, vividness, and appropriateness.

EXACTNESS

There is more to writing than filling a page with words. The real challenge is to select those words that are likely to mean exactly the same to your reader as they do to you. This often means, in practice, choosing concrete words rather than abstract words. Concrete words name things that are tangible—that is, that can be seen or touched. The words that describe qualities are abstract, and cannot be perceived. Thus, in the phrase *unusual professor,* the concrete word is *professor,* and the abstract word is *unusual.* Concrete words provoke specific pictures in the mind of your reader. Abstract words, on the other hand, are frequently the source of confusion, and, if chosen without care, create images in the mind of the reader quite different from those you intended. Remember, then, the value of concrete words in your writing.

To be exact in your writing, you must also be aware of both the denotation and the connotation of words. *Denotation* is the literal, or "dictionary," meaning of a word. For example, a *flag* is "a rectangular piece of fabric of distinctive design." *Connotation* refers to the reader's emotional response to the word, as well as to its atmosphere of meaning. Thus, *flag* connotes patriotism, love of country, our nation's proud history, and related meanings. Many times a hastily chosen word will create an unfavorable connotation in the mind of the reader, making him antagonistic toward your meaning, or, at least, confused. Because the connotations of many words vary among readers, try to be certain that your context makes their meaning clear.

One of the most common weaknesses in student writing is wordiness (also known as "padding"). The best antidote to wordiness is to make every word count. Be ruthless in getting rid of unnecessary words that merely bewilder or distract your reader. Examine your themes carefully and, when possible, combine short, choppy sentences into compound or complex sentences; reduce clauses to phrases; and try to distill the meaning of phrases into single words.

VIVIDNESS

In order to hold the interest of your reader, you will need to develop a style of writing that is not only exact, but vivid and interesting as well. Use your imagination in choosing your words. By employing figurative language and expressive descriptive terms, you can keep your reader's attention.

The most common figures of speech are comparisons. They are particularly valuable because they give vividness and color to your writing, and can suggest much in a few words, thereby making your writing more concise. A frequently used figure of speech is the *simile,* in which a comparison is usually stated by using *like* or *as.* ("My arms felt *like* lead weights.") Another common figure of speech is the *metaphor,* which makes an implied comparison. ("The leaves were bathed in October blood.")

Here are two warnings, however, about the use of figurative language. First, avoid illogical or mixed comparisons, which actually confuse the reader. Consider the following: "We will march together in victory down the stream." Second, avoid *clichés,* which are worn-out, stale figures of speech. Clichés add nothing to your writing; in fact, they create the impression that you have been too lazy to think, and have merely grabbed the first trite expression that came to mind. When first coined, most clichés had a certain flair. But when you come across such hackneyed phrases as "quiet as a mouse," or "strong as a lion," your probable reaction is a yawn. Try to avoid clichés in your writing. Check your themes carefully, eliminating worn-out phrases and tired expressions. Attempt to express yourself in a style that is original, fresh, and interesting.

APPROPRIATENESS

The classical injunction "There is a time and place for everything" relates to appropriateness. If you came to class dressed in formal evening clothes, the other students would be amused—not because the clothes were humorous, but because they would be out of place, inappropriate. In your writing, the "dress" you put on your essays must be in keeping with your intention. For example, if you are writing a paper for your English class, you ordinarily should avoid slang. In fact, most slang is so short-lived that its freshness will hardly last until your paper is handed back.

In general, three levels of usage exist in America: formal, informal, and substandard. Informal usage is acceptable in most college writing and speaking, most lectures, and most social gatherings. Good informal English means using one's standard vocabulary accurately, and with some degree of liveliness, in your writing and speaking; it is appropriate for your college essays. Formal English is usually written, and it assumes an educated audience, such as readers of *Scientific American* or *Atlantic Monthly*. Do not get the notion, however, that formal English is dull; it is dull only to those who because of their background cannot understand and appreciate it. As for the other level of usage—substandard—it should be avoided completely, at least in writing and in the classroom, because it is below the level expected of a college student. It uses such illiteracies as *ain't* and *he don't*, crude slang, and similar errors.

The task of developing a good writing style seems enormous, and perhaps it is; but when the process is broken down into small, workable portions, the job can be done. And you'll find the benefits are worth the effort.

Remember:

1. Be exact: Choose each word with precision.
2. Be vivid: Search for colorful, imaginative words and phrases.
3. Be appropriate: Use good informal English.

4. LOVE ACCORDING TO MADISON AVENUE *

Morton M. Hunt

1 In studying the love life of the ancient Romans, I have been struck by the fact that some of the sharpest and most illuminating evidence comes not from weighty works of history but from wayward and trivial sources. A lustful *graffito* scratched on a marble column, palpitating for the scarred arms of a gladiator; indecorous decorations on the bedroom walls of a seaside villa; a versified book of cosmetic recipes; a sentimental funeral oration carved on a huge tombstone—these are the real voices of the past.

2 It occurs to me, therefore, that in our own time the sociologists with their ponderous surveys, the psychologists with their dissecting analyses, and the cultural historians with their masses of documentation may be missing the truth and the essence of modern love. Perhaps those who write the contemporary equivalent of *graffiti* come closer. I suggest that the persons who do so are those who scribble on Madison Avenue—not on the building fronts, to be sure, but on typewriter paper, in air-conditioned cubicles in the well-carpeted offices of B. B. D. & O., K. & E., Y. & R., E.W.R. & R., and so on.

3 Certainly they see a number of truths about American love that have never been reported in the scientific literature. For one thing, the ad men apparently perceive more clearly than anyone else just how deeply love has penetrated and colored the ordinary routine of American life until a number of formerly nonerotic objects have become associated with the most tender scenes and the most romantic moments. Eating utensils, for example, are not thought by most cultural historians to have any love-value, and even the Freudians see symbolism only in the knife. But the ad men for Oneida silverware are more acute

* Reprinted from *Horizon*, November, 1959. Reprinted by permission of the author.

reporters of the local scene. In a recent ad in *Mademoiselle* they recorded the spontaneous love-dialogue of two young people examining a teaspoon at a store counter:

SHE: It's a dream come true, Bob. . . . I thought we'd never find it. Now we could almost choose blindfolded—just by following our hearts.

HE: Looks as if both our hearts are set on "Lasting Spring"—it's a "forever thing," like our marriage!

Paolo and Francesca were moved by a poem, Tristan and Iseult by a potion, but with young lovers in America it is the sight of a four-piece place setting at $18 (plus Federal tax) that unlocks the gates of the heart.

4 Similarly, it is the writers of fashion copy who see through the shadows and mists of native puritanism and recognize that the shoe, which traditionally has played no recognized part in American lovemaking, has recently acquired an aura of erotic value such as it has not had since Solomon, or whoever wrote the *Song of Solomon,* sang the finest bit of advertising copy yet: "How beautiful are thy feet with shoes, O prince's daughter!" In a comparably rapturous vein, the Wohl Shoe Company of St. Louis offered young women, via the February 15, 1959, issue of *Vogue,* a pump described as a "dream of a shoe," and spelled out the dream visually: a lovely young miss leaned upon the manly chest of a masked *caballero.* No prosaic considerations of arch support or hygienic insole for her; the shoe is no longer a piece of utilitarian clothing, but a *laissez-passer* to the wondrous fantasy world of romance. Underwear, too, according to the testimony of the Madison Avenue confraternity, has an equally transporting effect. A case in point is a message some of them produced for Seamprufe, Inc. in a recent issue of *Seventeen.* In this instance, the journey took place in time as well as in space: the ad showed a medieval knight in chain mail, mounted upon a white charger, in the act of sweeping up with one arm a damsel improbably clad only in a lace-trimmed slip of nylon tricot. If, indeed, lingerie produces such reveries in American women, one can only be struck with admiration at the strength of character they show in getting past the state of *deshabille* and actually arriving at their jobs or starting their housework.

5 Like shoes and slips, it would seem that many liquids which formerly were thirst quenchers have also picked up amorous overtones in recent years. Coca-Cola was for decades a drink that made merely for a refreshing pause; nowadays, we learn, it is also an accoutrement of teen-age love-trysts. In the April issue of *Seventeen,* for example, a Coke ad shows lad and lass, carrying a bagful of Coke, looking for a picnic spot; finding it, they shed some outer clothes and open a couple of Cokes; this causes them at once to fall tenderly upon each other's bosom, ecstatically guzzling, preparatory to nuzzling.

6 Even more noteworthy is the instance of beer. This drink was once the hearty, indelicate eructative refreshment of the hard-working plebeian male. It has apparently undergone a marvelous metamorphosis in recent years, becoming not only suitable for delicate lips, but acquiring an aura of enchant-

ment and romance. A series of Schlitz advertisements in several major magazines has shown young couples parked by a lakeside at twilight, alone on a snow-capped mountaintop, and so on. Young, attractive, and clearly drawn to each other, they are always drinking beer out of one glass; these lovers, and their circumstances, exemplify the hedonistic exhortation under the picture: "Know the real joy of good living." This, to be sure, could refer either to the romance or the beer; the ad is not explicit. Nor can one be sure whether romance inspired a desire for beer or beer a desire for romance. One thing *is* indisputable: the distinctive odor of hops, now found upon the attractive female, must have been reclassified in the national aesthetic system, becoming a scent rather than a smell.

7   Other procedures, once gustatory, have likewise become amatory, or so it would seem. The smoking of tobacco, long thought appropriate to manly work or solitary reflection, has become almost obligatory at times of flirtation or intimacy. From the ubiquitous scenes of nubile young people igniting their little white tubes, one gains the impression that drawing in a lungful of soot and carcinogens has an amorous value as great as once did the reading aloud of Byron or the strumming of a banjo. Amatory smoking does present one awkward problem, however, since countless ads (not by cigarette makers) report that love is inconceivable unless the mouth and breath are totally unsullied. Once again the problem is solved by a reshuffling of the national stimulus-response bonds, until smoke, on the breath, becomes exciting; the old proverb should really be altered to read: "Where there is smoke, there will soon be fire." Let no one find fault with this or make mock of it. Do not lovers in the Trobriand Islands extract and eat lice from one another's hair, becoming mightily inflamed with love by the procedure? If, in the liberal spirit of cultural relativism, one accepts this and refuses to find it revolting, should he not do the same in the case of the reeking Americans?

8   Still, Americans themselves have not yet altogether succeeded in eroticizing the by-products of smoking, as Madison Avenue itself admits. A remarkably candid ad for Parliament cigarettes recently came right out about the risk to amorous aesthetes: man and girl were shown, heads thrillingly close together, match lit for their cigarettes, while the copy, drawing attention to the recessed filter, promised in a throaty aside, "No filter feedback on your lips . . . or hers." Love in America in 1959 is evidently not for the oaf, but for the thoughtful practitioner of methodology. Ovid himself, that dedicated professor of tasteful dalliance, would have recognized in the Parliament copywriter a kindred spirit, a fellow toiler in the vineyards of impeccable passion.

9   Again and again the admen indicate how easily Americans are aroused to lust or moved to tenderness by formerly nonerotic consumer products. Consider the vitamins offered in *Cosmopolitan* by the Vitasafe Corporation: their effect is plainly amorous, for the middle-aged couple are snuggling happily while the woman confesses, from an overflowing heart, "He made me feel like a bride

again." Consider the electric portable offered by Smith-Corona: a book-laden youth passing a pretty girl looks down at her typewriter with a mooncalf expression, but it is clear that the machine has made him tender towards the girl as well. Consider fudge, of all things: Carnation Evaporated Milk shows a lass plastering it on cupcakes, while a crewcut lad eats one out of her hand, the plain implication being that fudge is an important component of her sex appeal.

10   This point is not spelled out in so many words, but sometimes obscurity is in itself a species of truth. The Marlboro people have been portraying rugged middle-aged sporting types lighting cigarettes for lovely young things; in small type under each such picture is the cryptic text, "The cigarette designed for men that women like." The Delphic Oracle herself might have written it; parse it and puzzle over it as one will, he cannot be sure whether the "that" liked by the young thing is the cigarette designed for men, or the men themselves. But the truth lies not in deciding which one; the answer is that it means *both* of them, for they are blended in her mind and emotions. *That* is the truth the copywriter was conveying—in the prevailing romantic American landscape, the erotic object and the erotic person have become indistinguishable.

11   Precisely the same conclusion may be drawn from Pan American World Airways' appeal to businesswomen in *Mademoiselle*. "Look what Jet Clippers can do for your dreams," it reads, and illustrates what it means: the young businesswoman is seated on a hillside with a morsel of Roman ruin behind her and a dark-haired handsome man beside her. What is the dream referred to— the man or the *mise-en-scène?* Possibly the text gives a further clue. "The fun of new experiences comes faster on Pan Am wings," it says. No help there; that still fits either one. But does it really matter? Not in the least: the trip abroad, the Roman ruin, the handsome man are all inseparable and indivisible. Love and the product are two aspects of a single essence; that is all they know on Madison Avenue, and all they need to know.

12   Within this general picture of American love, as set down by the creative men in the copy and art departments of the major agencies, no detail is more intriguing than the observation that contemporary Americans, though sup- posedly scornful of occultism, rely upon a variety of philters, amulets, talis- mans, potions, and brews, without which love is unattainable.

13   It is, of course, no secret to anyone that the normal exudates of the human body, the wrinkles that come after youth, and such other common character- istics as dull hair, small breasts, plumpness, and blackheads are totally incom- patible with affection and sex, and that no person with any of these defects can possibly find happiness in life. Luckily there is available today a splendid armamentarium of lotions, oils, paddings, pills, cleansers, and paints the use of which obviates the fault and admits the user to the arena of love.

14   But this is only the surface of truth. A closer inspection of advertising art

and copy reveals a far subtler message being set down for all to read who are not willfully blind. If I read it rightly, there would appear to be, in modern love, a mysterious disembodiment of emotion: it is not so much the *beautiful person* who is loved, but the *beautifying instrumentality*. Observe the statement made repeatedly in ads for Coty's "L'Aimant": "Nothing makes a woman more feminine to a man. . . ." What exegesis can there be, except that the femininity is in the bottled liquid, and not, basically, in the woman? And the same brand of metaphysics must lie behind the Lanvin ad which shows a small boy kissing a small girl who, though pleased, admits to herself: "He loves me . . . he loves my Mommy's Arpège!" The artful minx knows the truth; only by virtue of the applied balsam is she a nymphet, and he, willy-nilly, a nympholept.

15   The female of all ages is continually advised that she need only wipe on this unguent, pat on this fragrance, slip on this magical garment, and lo! he sees with new eyes, thinks with a different brain, loses his own purpose and becomes a willing slave. "If he can't make up his mind . . . wear Wind Song," whispers Prince Matchabelli. Lanvin slyly peddles the same kind of bottled powers, offering them with the tag, "How to make him lose the first round!" And let a woman but slip into a marvelous checked suit made by Junior Sophisticates, and, she is advised, "What can he do but surrender. . . ."

16   All this has a disturbingly supernatural sound, yet a hauntingly familiar one. What *is* it all an echo of? What old, well-known, half-forgotten nightmare? So musing, one may recall that there *were* women once who cloaked themselves in borrowed beauty to steal the love of man—sinful women who compacted with Satan to receive unlawful powers, and in return did his vile work for him. Suddenly, certain words and phrases in advertising copy, seemingly harmless, begin to assume an ominous sound. Danskin, Inc., who make a lounging suit modeled after ballet costumes, use the telltale phrase, "for your 'at home' *bewitching* hours" (my italics). For being bewitching, 30,000 women were burned alive during the fifteenth and sixteenth centuries; let the word not go by unnoticed. And Dawnelle, Inc. frankly (or is it carelessly?) harks back to woman's ancient primal alliance with the Prince of Darkness in both copy and illustration. Says the copy: "You're the temptress who wins him, in Dawnelle's handsewn gloves"; the illustration, meanwhile, shows not one, but four gloved female hands offering a fatuously grinning male four ripe apples. (Has Eve grown more arms, or is the Serpent in an arms race too?)

17   And now the most damning fact begins to appear more clearly. In distinct defiance of the overtly approved mores, the entrapment or illusion created almost always operates within a context of illicit connection. The ads for a hundred products hint at it, but those of the perfume makers are practically outspoken. The names of perfumes are in themselves an insidious and deadly attack upon Judeo-Christian morality—e.g., "Tabu," "Indiscrète," "Conquête," "Temptation," "Surrender," and "My Sin"—while the copy strengthens the assault in words such as these:

"danger in every drop"
"the 'forbidden' fragrance"
"provocative as a stranger's smile"
"dare to wear it only when you seek to conquer"
"a whispered invitation for a man to be masterful"

18   One could extract from all this a sinister truth, namely that woman de-
scended of Eve is still borrowing powers and enchantments in order to arouse
man's lusts and thereby satisfy her own, and in the process is performing
Satan's work of dragging man into mortal sin. Six centuries ago the best-
educated men in Europe considered the situation a clear and present danger
and spoke of it in terms like these:

> In the woman wantonly adorned to capture souls, the garland upon her head
> is as a firebrand of Hell to kindle men, so too the horned headdress of another,
> so the brooch upon the breast [of a third]. . . . Each is a spark, breathing hell-
> fire [and] damning the souls God has created and redeemed at such great cost.

Thus spoke John Bromyard, a typical fourteenth-century English preacher and
compiler of sermons, and thus had spoken in earlier times Tertullian, Jerome,
and Chrysostom. Today none but advertising men link the same factors in a
single picture of woman; but whether the ad men are the Bromyards and Ter-
tullians of our era or whether they are agents of the Foul Fiend is not altogether
clear.

19   The seductive female is not the only pattern of womanhood about which
Madison Avenue furnishes an abundance of information. The other and sharply
contrasting pattern is that of the fiancée-wife-mother. The ancient dichotomy
of Woman into Eve and Mary, mistress and mother, witch and lady, apparently
did not disappear with the end of feudalism but lives on still, according to the
evidence at hand.

20   For whenever the female in an advertisement is alluring and beguiling,
whenever her smile is secretive and mysterious, she represents the ancient spirit
of Profane Love and her mystery is, ultimately, nothing but concupiscence.
But when woman is portayed in the role of fiancée, bride, or wife, she possesses
none of these qualities; instead she is feminine in a pure and wholesome sense.
The American Gem Society, addressing an ad to the girl about to become
engaged, portrays her as a dreaming young thing, chin cupped in hands, wide
eyes staring off into the roseate future, guileless face almost completely innocent of make-up, mouth smiling trustfully and a little wistfully. She is Every-
man's kid sister or girl friend, but never his passionflower. The Kinsey crowd
may publish their revolting statistics on the premarital sexual experiences of
American girls, but the advertisements tell a different and lovelier version of
the truth: the girl who gets a diamond engagement ring has not been be-
smirched by sexual experiments or known the indecent hunger of desire.

21   Even in the embrace of her fiancé she preserves a high-minded concen-

tration upon nonsexual matters. A dinnerware ad in *Seventeen* shows a young couple who have ridden in a sleigh out to a secluded field through which runs a purling stream. The lad romantically picks up the girl in his arms and carries her across the virgin snow, while she tenderly and practically murmurs to him, "You get the license . . . I'll get the Lenox." His intentions may have been licentious rather than licensable, but this comment at once purifies and clarifies his mind.

22   Nuptials and honeymoon make no perceptible change in this side of her character; the bride's mood may be yielding, but her blood runs cool. "Isn't this how you want to live?" asks the Fostoria Glass Company, portraying an ideal young marriage: a young wife, holding a piece of crystal stemware near a single burning taper, seems lost in admiration of the glass and the candle, and only vaguely aware of the handsome husband hovering beside her. She is smiling at him, more or less, with her neat, childish little mouth firmly closed —and a generation trained by Marilyn Monroe does not miss the significance of *that*. Not long ago a Heublein Cocktails ad in *Life* featured what seems merely an amusing line—"A wife's warmest welcome is well chilled"; like so many other jokes, perhaps it says more than it intends to.

23   After a suitable time, the wife becomes a mother, but despite this presumptive evidence of sexual activity, she remains thoroughly pure. In a Vigoro ad we see her romping on the lawn with her husband and children; she is tanned, healthy, and essentially *friendly*. In a Johnson outboard motor ad we see her roaring along with her husband and children in a speedboat; she is sunburned, tousled, and essentially a *good sport*. In a G-E ad we see her clapping her hands gleefully as her husband and daughter present her with a dishwasher; she is slim, pretty (in a low-heeled way), and essentially *homey*.

24   We see her in many other situations—cooking, washing, shopping, playing games—and she is almost invariably clean-looking, hearty, efficient, and brightly lit. Dan River Mills recently devoted a spread in *Life* to the modern American family and showed four typical examples. Every one of the four consisted of a handsome young man, a pretty young woman, and two children (between the ages of four and eight), all dressed in cottons by Dan River. In not one picture is the man touching, holding, or even looking at his wife; in three out of four, he is not even standing beside her, but is separated from her by one of the children. The American wife, it seems reasonable to conclude, is a pal, a helpmeet, a kind of older girl friend; she is emphatically not a lover.

25   The children have a double function in preserving the mother-image: they prove her fecundity, but by their very presence they neutralize or purify the erotic overtones of certain situations. Do she and her husband don Weldon pajamas?—in come the kids, in similar pajamas, making everything sanitary and aboveboard. Does she go off for a ride with her man in a Chrysler product? —she tucks a little girl into her lap, and all is sweet, all is sound. Do she and he park their Chevrolet in a secluded woodland spot?—happily, they brought

the dog along, and it is upon the beast that affection is bestowed. Have she and her husband grown cheerfully middle-aged and regained their privacy as the children left home?—the General Motors time-payment plan shows them hugging *two* dogs—one for each. No wonder the dog is called man's best friend—he defends, by his very presence, the purity of the American wife and mother.

26   Certain other aspects of American love, though not so fully portrayed, are illuminatingly touched upon in magazine advertisements. For it is apparent from any careful scrutiny of the ads that Americans require the stimulus of exotic, remote, or uncomfortable surroundings, in order to experience the real transports of delight. Here is an advertisement showing a couple on a wild, chilly-looking beach at sundown (how *did* they get that automobile down there without making tracks in the sand?); here is another couple deep in the forest primeval, smoking cigarettes and hugging each other; here is a third exploring a wild stream bank in their good clothing, undaunted by steep declivity or tangled underbrush. Oasis Cigarettes render continual reports of lovers cozily nestled on a desert cactus, moodily bussing each other in some dim alley of the Vieux Carré of New Orleans, or perching together in a high window overlooking Monte Carlo. They never wax romantic in Middletown, U.S.A.; they never grow fond in a middle-class living room. Wind-swept Alpine crags, the slippery decks of heeled-over yawls, castles without plumbing, streams in the heart of a jungle—these would seem to be the typical loci of love, rather than the sofa, bed, or park bench. How all this may be possible—since most people are forced to spend their lives at or near home—is a nagging question; perhaps the meaning of it all is that love, in the twentieth century, is an actuality for the wealthy, but still only a dream for the poor and the middle class.

27   Likewise tantalizing are the occasional hints of restiveness and impending revolt on the part of modern man. Ensnared and bewitched by the minx, captured and domesticated by the wife, does he begin nowadays to stir in his chains, remembering the olden days? Drummond Knitwear, in *The New York Times,* portrays two sturdy upright chaps clad in knitted shirts, with a luscious female supine at their feet. Can it be mere coincidence that the Cigar Institute of America shows a manly stogy-fancier hefting a caveman's club, while a maiden clad in a leopardskin crouches adoringly at heel? No, it is not coincidence, for here again is Chief Apparel, in *Playboy,* showing us a Bikini-clad morsel sprawled pantingly on the floor beside a gentleman clad in dashing sports attire. But perhaps the significant clue is that in all three advertisements the gentlemen are ignoring the females. Woman is a toy (the admen seem to be saying)—a plaything to be enjoyed when man chooses, and to be scorned when he does not.

28   Finally, and most challenging of all, is the handful of frivolous and irreverent remarks in recent advertisements that may conceivably portend a general

devaluation of love in the near future. Hanes Hosiery in *The New Yorker* shows us a cartoon of a depressed chap clutching a bottle of poison and thinking, "I'd better drink it. All she wants from me is seamless stockings by Hanes." One does not get flippant about God or the Flag; perhaps Love, long the peer of both of these, is losing its position. A Lea & Perrins ad shows a man and woman curled up warmly together, just after dinner; it is the best of all possible times for serious talk, but listen to what she says: "Do you love Lea & Perrins more than me?" Is nothing sacred to woman any longer, that she dares to jest at a time like this?

29   Whatever may be the ultimate meaning of all these things, one must congratulate the cultural historians of the future; a treasure of evidence is awaiting them, if they will but look away from the scientific studies and scholarly theses and pay attention to the scribblings on Madison Avenue.

Apparatus for: Love According to Madison Avenue

Vocabulary: *Match the definition in the right column with the appropriate word in the left column.*

_____ 1.	graffito (¶ 1)	*a.*	sexual desire
_____ 2.	indecorous (¶ 1)	*b.*	produce abundantly
_____ 3.	*caballero* (¶ 4)	*c.*	flirtatious girl
_____ 4.	*deshabille* (¶ 4)	*d.*	lying on the back
_____ 5.	eructative (¶ 6)	*e.*	pertaining to the sense of taste
_____ 6.	plebeian (¶ 6)	*f.*	amorous play or flirting
_____ 7.	metamorphosis (¶ 6)	*g.*	available methods
_____ 8.	hedonistic (¶ 6)	*h.*	dispose of
_____ 9.	gustatory (¶ 7)	*i.*	Spanish gentleman
_____10.	ubiquitous (¶ 7)	*j.*	unseemly
_____11.	nubile (¶ 7)	*k.*	inscription on a wall
_____12.	unsullied (¶ 7)	*l.*	belched forth
_____13.	dalliance (¶ 8)	*m.*	partially dressed
_____14.	*mise-en-scène* (¶ 11)	*n.*	seeming to exist everywhere
_____15.	exudates (¶ 13)	*o.*	turning, rippling
_____16.	armamentarium (¶ 13)	*p.*	foolish in a self-satisfied way
_____17.	obviates (¶ 13)	*q.*	critical explanation
_____18.	exegesis (¶ 14)	*r.*	suitable for marriage
_____19.	ominous (¶ 16)	*s.*	in a play, the set and properties for a scene
_____20.	fatuously (¶ 16)	*t.*	matter discharged gradually
_____21.	concupiscence (¶ 20)	*u.*	foreshadowed by an omen
_____22.	purling (¶ 21)	*v.*	change from one form to another
_____23.	fecundity (¶ 25)	*w.*	pleasureful
_____24.	minx (¶ 27)	*x.*	not marred or dirty
_____25.	supine (¶ 27)	*y.*	pertaining to common people

Discussion: *Rhetoric*

1. How would you describe the level of usage in Hunt's essay—formal or informal? Justify your answer.
2. The language in this essay is exact. Evaluate the author's use of specific, concrete words in paragraphs 1, 4, 8, and 11.
3. Paragraph 17 lends itself very well to a discussion of connotation and denotation. Give examples that would contribute to such a discussion.
4. Paragraph 21 shows vividness in choice of words, particularly in the last sentence. How do the words *licentious* and *licensable* sum up the author's argument at this stage of the essay?

1. _____

   _____

2. _____

   _____

3. _____

   _____

4. _____

   _____

Discussion: *Theme*

1. Why do advertising men incorporate women in their advertising?
2. Discuss the appeal of Cadillac, Volkswagen, and International Truck advertisements, respectively.
3. Has advertising had a harmful effect on the morals of this generation? Explain.
4. Does the federal government have an obligation to control advertising? Why or why not?
5. Is the essay weak in its logic at any point? Explain.
6. From what you now know, are there values being expressed in advertising? Explain.

1. _____

_____

2. _____

_____

3. _____

_____

4. _____

_____

5. _____

_____

6. _____

_____

Writing Suggestions

1. Write an analysis of some advertising program in your town. Consider the local bread company, plumbing contractor, movers, filling stations, or churches.
2. Write an essay defending or attacking this sentence: "Woman is a toy . . . a plaything to be enjoyed when man chooses, and to be scorned when he does not."
3. Develop one of the following phrases into an imaginative theme:
   "Danger in every drop"
   "The forbidden fragrance"
   "Provocative as a stranger's smile"
4. Write a summary of your advice to someone younger than yourself on adopting a healthy outlook toward advertising.
5. Describe your favorite television advertisement. Explain its appeal.

5. WHAT'S HAPPENING, BABY? *†

PAUL C. HARPER, JR.
President, Needham, Harper & Steers, Inc.

1 A short time ago I was standing in a pub in London with one of my colleagues enjoying a beer. The name of the pub was "The King's Head and Eight Bells" and it is headquarters for the local pack of Mods. Four Mods were standing near us, two boy Mods in the new bell-bottom trousers and bee-waist coats—and two girl Mods with hair in their eyes. Then a fifth Mod with both bell-bottom trousers and hair in his eyes walked up and asked casually, "What's happening, Baby?"

2 As nearly as I can reconstruct it, the reply from one of the girls was, "Pip's topkick just gummed his mini. We all think that's fish."

3 After eavesdropping a little more, it became clear that what she was reporting was that Pip's father had removed his driving privileges, which they all thought was very stuffy. The meeting at the pub was a protest rally.

4 The language and problems of Teens are universal.

5 I am delighted to be standing here today for a number of reasons. First, I am glad to be able to pay my respects to this Club, which has achieved such a remarkable record of helping underprivileged young people. I understand the Club's work has been going on for 66 years, and so the Club's usefulness has withstood the severest test of all—the test of time. Second, I am particularly proud that advertising men have done so much to make the Club's program

* Paul C. Harper, Jr., "What's Happening, Baby?" From *Vital Speeches of the Day,* Nov. 1, 1966. Reprinted by permission of the publisher.
† Delivered at the Off-the-Street Club—Chicago Annual Meeting, June 21, 1966.

possible. It speaks well of our profession. And third, the whole subject of youth and its problems is a close one to me because there are six youths in our family, ages 9–18, 3 boys and 3 girls, and three of them teen-agers—and while they do not classify as underprivileged, they do, of course, share in the real problems faced by all the youths of our time.

6   Today let's focus on teen-agers.

7   Dinner-table conversations at our house are not orderly discussions. The talk will be frequently interrupted by cries of rage from the victim of a furtive pinch or by the tinkle of breaking glassware. But the conversations do have a pattern. Sooner or later at the teenage end of the table, one of five subjects almost always comes up:

1. *Money*
2. *Sex*
3. *Automobiles* (*ours*)
4. *Education*
5. *The War*

8   Now you might ask—well, what else is there to talk about anyway? And honestly, I guess I can't think of many other really interesting subjects.

9   But these five subjects are actually an inventory of the problems—the big deals—facing teen-agers today, and for many reasons they're worth taking a look at. It's worth asking the question, "What's happening, Baby?"

10   Many people today say that teen-agers are a different breed from what they were a generation or two, or three, ago. Whole issues of magazines are written about them, books are dedicated to them, and the movies and TV, in their time-honored way, tend to establish teen-age stereotypes, thus separating them still further from the normal everyday world.

11   Now my proposition is very simple, and it has three points:

1. It is just as dangerous to lump teen-agers as teen-agers as it is to lump adults as adults. Each teen-ager is different, and each is following his own unwritten calendar towards maturity. No two teen-agers mature at the same second in time.
2. Teen-agers are the most colorful and persistent faddists in our society, but a fad is a symptom, not a disease. They wear funny clothes, funny haircuts, say and do strange things. But the fads they adopt are not to be confused with the immutable law which rules every generation of teen-agers. This law says, "Thou shalt be different, but for pretty much the same old reason." No matter how odd their behavior, they are responding to the same age-old urge for independence.
3. In spite of all this, we have to face the fact that teen-agers today do face a world that has changed far more between generations than at any time in

history. And this has produced an unprecedented lack of understanding and sympathy between generations.

12 Unless we try to understand these things a little better, we won't do very well as fathers, citizens, or advertising men. These changes get back to the rather basic things discussed at our dinner table. They are:

Money—Teen-agers today have enough money to make them a real economic force.

Sex—Teen-agers are reaching physical maturity at a somewhat earlier age —and there are more sexual stimuli around than ever before.

Mobility—Teen-agers today have a new dimension of independence—the automobile. They can get around. They can get away.

School—Teen-agers today are under more pressure from the educational establishment than ever before.

War—Teen-agers, long-term, like the rest of us, have the bomb hanging over their heads; short-term, they've got Vietnam.

13 And on top of that—Mom and Dad aren't around as much as they used to be. Mom is more apt to be working and Dad is apt to be away.

14 Given the teen-age appetite for kicking up—showing he's adult, when he isn't—showing he doesn't care, when he really does . . . given these leanings, he has today more opportunity for colorful behavior than ever before.

15 So if we are ever to approach closing the gap between generations—and understanding this vast seething mass of highly charged individuals—we'd better take a closer look at each of these points.

16 There are today 25 million teen-agers, with 27 million due in five years. The nation's official median age is 27.9 and declining. Forty-eight percent of our population is under twenty-six. Fifty percent of brides today are teen-agers; more have their first child in their 19th year than any other. Teen-agers represent $13 billion in disposable income. Twenty percent of them own cars.

17 Let's talk first about *money*. A great majority of teen-agers are certainly a reflection of the affluent society they live in. As pollster Louis Harris points out: "High-school Americans have never known drastic economic depression or wartime shortages—they're happy now, and believe the future can only get better." Generally, youth has no worry about the basic necessities—food, clothing, housing. Their new-found wealth is available for luxuries, recreation, and impulse purchases. Recent research indicates that teen-age girls buy 27 percent of the cosmetics sold in the U.S., 50 percent of all records, 20 percent of all cars. They own a million TV sets, 10 million records players and 20 million radios. They buy 45 percent of all soft drinks, 24 percent of all wristwatches, 30 percent of all low-priced cameras.

18 David Yunich, president of Macy's, New York, points out that "there are really two markets—the teen-ager per se and the young marrieds—both with

money in their overstuffed wallets, both at peak periods of spending when they want more, need more, buy more." And Yunich points out that the youth market controls upwards of $30 billion worth of family purchasing aside from its own spending money. The influence of teen-agers on family purchases has by no means been lost on giant manufacturers. Ford Motor Company has based a recent advertising campaign on the approval parents will get from their teen-agers if they bring home a Mustang.

19 Since teen-agers make up the decisive market for so many products— guitars, motorbikes, sports equipment, and movies, for example—and a very lucrative secondary market for countless other categories, they are bombarded with commercial messages. But even without this commercial assault, teen-agers would probably be big spenders. Response to questions on how they feel when shopping reveals that "they're buying not so much material things but adulthood; in their way they are trying to be like grown-ups." Money, to teen-agers, is a liberating force. Spending it is an expression of adulthood. And in spending it in vast quantities they have institutionalized their tastes. We now have a teen-age market.

20 *Sex* is, of course, a subject in itself. It must be if those scientists out in Kansas City could spend five years behind a one-way mirror without getting bored. But I really prefer the remark of the mayor of a little New England town as he addressed a group of aldermen worried about town morals. "Now, gentlemen," he said, "there's always been sex in this town—there's just a new crowd takin' over." Nevertheless some of the data shows real changes in this area too.

21 There is no doubt that there is an earlier and more intense focusing on sex. Dates in fifth and sixth grades are common place. One survey shows that 45 percent of teen-age girls go steady. Teen-age marriages have increased 600 percent since 1940, accounting for half the marriages in the U.S. More than 50 percent are known to have resulted from pregnancy. The Connecticut Health Department estimates that one of six teen-age girls in the state was illegitimately pregnant last year.

22 There has been no large-scale study of premarital sex among teen-agers, and sources differ on its extent. Some indicate that it is on the increase, at least in certain areas and among certain social strata. Others say that the public is confusing the known increases in premarital sex among college students with increased sex in high schools. Mervin P. Freedman, in "The Young Americans," states his opinion that young men and women need to find security in marriage and a family and that this need far outweighs tendencies toward promiscuous sexual behavior. He believes that this is a reaction against the depersonalization of modern life and sees in the trend to early marriage an indication that family ties will be strengthened rather than weakened in the next several decades. And I think this is the key to the matter. Kids may mature earlier. They may get more stimulation from books, magazines, and

movies. But the key fact is that the other pressures he is under force him to seek the security of an intense companionship—the ultimate expression of which is sex.

23   This brings us to my third point, *mobility*. It's no news that teen-agers today live in cars. Cars have become the standard projection of ego and virility for the boy and give him a dimension of independence he never had before.

24   According to *Newsweek's* penetrating essay, "It is a car, not truth, that sets them free, gives them a sense of romance. The automobile is this century's riverboat." Teen-agers own nine percent of all new cars and an estimated 20 percent of all cars. And, of course, a good many family cars are driven, if not owned, by teens.

25   The auto manufacturers are also heavily involved encouraging those little-recognized cultural phenomena of postwar United States: drag racing, stock car racing, and their logical extension, the demolition derby. The brilliant young social critic Tom Wolfe, author of "The Kandy-Kolored Tangerine-Flake Streamline Baby," points out that sports writers have managed to ignore these new automobile sports despite their enormous popularity because "there are too many kids in it with sideburns, tight Levis, and winklepicker boots." Yet he points out that they attract five to ten million more spectators than football, baseball and basketball each year and that stock car racing is now the number one sport in the South. He sees these sports as symbolizing the emancipation of the young people of the lower social orders in the South from the old social order.

26   The title of Wolfe's collection of essays, "The Kandy-Kolored Tangerine-Flake Streamline Baby," refers to the postwar teen passion for customizing cars and/or hopping them up for more speed. He says that thousands of kids before they get married put all their money into this. "Things have been going on in the development of kids' formal attitude toward cars since 1945, things of great sophistication that adults have not been even remotely aware of, mainly because the kids are so inarticulate about it. It is true to say that among teen-agers the automobile has become the symbol and in part the physical means of triumph over family and community restrictions."

27   The fourth big change in the teen-age environment is *Education*—how you get it, how long you go to school, what you do when you get there, what happens to you if you don't get there.

28   With every year that goes by, the long-term penalties for dropping out increase. And the pressures to get into college, and stay there, therefore increase too.

29   Why this pressure? *Newsweek* says, "High school separates the teen-ager's world as cleanly as if the United States were riven by the Grand Canyon instead

of the Continental Divide. On one side are the blessed, who have earned the right to go to college and probably prosperity. On the other are the damned, who drop out, stop short, or, at best, go to vocational training schools and sharply circumscribed earning potential."

30   College is no longer the sanctuary of the privileged, however. The democratization of college through scholarships, the increased ability of more Americans to pay their way, and the general recognition that you need college to get ahead holds out a mighty inducement. Never before have teen-agers been offered such educational opportunities or been put under such pressure to take advantage of them.

31   But the pressure and the increase in the academic pace have made millions of young Americans more thoughtful than they have ever been before. Issues are discussed at our dinner table that two generations ago were reserved for lecture halls and coffee houses. And through the din some pretty penetrating thoughts come through—reflections of real concern with what is going on in the world.

32   And this brings us to our fifth point—*the Bomb* and *the War*. Every generation has faced the prospect of going to war—in France, in Nicaragua, in the Pacific, in Korea. But no generation until the current one has faced the fact that all of society as he knows it, everything he has been taught was worthwhile, can be blown up in 30 seconds. All generations have had to face the possibility of premature death, but this is the first generation to face the possible death of society.

33   This produces deeply religious attitudes in some and impresses others with the absurdity of human life. In a recent poll, more than half the teen-agers interviewed saw the principal problem confronting the nation as avoiding war. Some commentators have read into this a new emphasis on the enjoyment of pleasures "now," but this is belied by the fact that most teens are more interested in their future than ever before. If they were seriously concerned that there will be no tomorrow, they wouldn't be so motivated to succeed in high school, to get into college, to assure themselves of material success in the future. The net effect of the Bomb has been sobering. It has brought a responsible reaction from our youth, not a wild flight from reality.

34   But there is much evidence to support the notion that what the kids are afraid of is not so much the Bomb as the adults who have the power to trigger it.

35   The young are increasingly questioning grown-up goals and purposes. Edgar Z. Friedenberg, professor of sociology at the University of California, says: "Our youngsters do not hate us adults, or even dislike us particularly, and even the most militant of them are not primarily interested in putting us down . . . but they have learned that they cannot trust us, because we have never had any respect for them and very little for the principles by which we pretend to govern our lives and theirs."

36   Parental authority is diminishing because in all too many cases one or both of the parents simply aren't around. The reasons vary. At one end of the economic scale, father may have long since left his family to their own resources. At the other, he may be providing materially for his family but, in so doing, he may be away more than he is home. Absent fathers and mothers can't swing the kind of moral weight they might if they were on the scene.

37   Teen-agers are not unaware of the world around them. They know that many parents who are shocked at car swiping, exam cheating, and teen vandalism are themselves engaging in higher orders of immoral behavior as tax cheating, price fixing, expense padding, and worse. They wonder why parents don't invest the time to discuss the meaningful things of life, counsel them on their education and their future. Instead they get hung up over the superficialities and fads that every generation goes through.

38   Professor Friedenberg says: "Regulations governing dress and grooming may be trivial. What is not trivial is that submission to such regulation teaches students that they have no rights or dignity. The very triviality of the regulations makes them more effectively humiliating. Most adolescents would accept and even welcome adult direction in matters of grave consequence. But I would maintain that the real function of these regulations is to humiliate, to show any adolescents with too much autonomy what happens to wise guys and trouble-makers." The fact is, it doesn't work. It is well known that parental opposition is the surest way to entrench a fad. The fad which starts out as a symbol of identity with the group soon becomes a full-fledged healthy symbol of rebellion against adult authority. The Louis Harris survey shows that almost half the girls and one-third of the boys bought certain clothes against the express wishes of parents. The extent to which this rebellion can go is seen in the current fad for German helmets and iron crosses, the principal function of which seems to be to bug adults.

39   The other side of the coin is the parent who imitates. This is the pitiful spectacle of the adult trying to proclaim that he thinks young by emulating the dress, the language, and the fads of teen-agers.

40   This drive to prove their youthfulness to their children and themselves succeeds in fact in making them look ridiculous to those for whom they should be trying to set an example. There is strong reason to believe that most teen-agers have *enough* peers and may need an honest-to-goodness parent who is something more than pseudo-teen.

41   Teen-agers hold a jealous possession of their folkways. When adults took over the twist, young people dropped it like a hot pizza and moved on to dances that were exclusively their own—at least for a while. There is a dedicated effort to create dance steps so exhausting that no adult in his right mind would try them.

42   The surest way for an advertiser to assure being turned off or turned out

is for him to portray an obsolete fad, dance, or mode of dress. Since these things can change overnight, or at least much faster than advertisers want to change commercials, it's best to avoid these transitory aspects of teen existence.

43 The same is true of language. We may not understand the language and we certainly shouldn't try to make ourselves understood in it. The language is designed for the exclusive use of teen-agers in communicating with one another, similar to the dialects and language variants that such species as lawyers and advertising men create to keep it in the family.

44 Those of us who are required to establish some form of communication with teen-agers had better stick to our own particular idiom of American English, or risk making damn fools of ourselves.

45 It won't work for parents—and it might be disastrous for advertisers—to try to get chummy with teen-agers by telling them that their products are "boss, tough, out of sight, fab, or dyno." Even though "bad" means "good" in teen, it could prove confusing and downright embarrassing for a client to have to say his product is bad.

46 Teen-agers are certainly as susceptible to advertising as the rest of us, but they are good shoppers who want to have a good reason why before they buy. They resent being exploited by the adult world and, according to Fred and Grace Heckinger, "there are signs that sophisticated youths are turning sour on advertising that tries to pull adult rank on them by just calling a product terrific."

47 Another trap into which advertisers, or anyone else who tries to generalize about teenagers, can easily fall is to lump teen-agers as a group. To try to ascribe rigid characteristics to 24 million people in an open society that talks a lot about individual achievement is playing a dangerous game. What is a typical American teen-ager?

48 A boy or a girl? A thirteen-year-old or an eighteen-year-old? A farmer, a surfer in California, a Groton prep schooler, a Negro in a Detroit slum, a Mexican-American in Arizona, a peace marcher, a drag racer, and on and on.

49 It's no wonder that teen-agers resent being classified as a group. To their everlasting credit and despite their instinct for groupness, teen-agers want to be accepted as individuals. Their desire to have a greater say about how their world is run, their questioning of their society, and their rebellion against parents, are all indications that they think for themselves. They are, according to Harvard Professor Jerome Bruner, "the most competent generation we have ever reared in this country—and the most maligned."

50 So—What's happening, Baby? Well, it's a tragedy or a comedy, depending upon how you look at it, but in spite of all the new pressures and in spite of all the new outlets, the teen-ager remains fundamentally the same.

51   None of these influences—*Money, Sex, Mobility, Education* or *the Bomb* —can mature him faster as a whole person. Nature must take its course. It cannot be speeded up. Society is providing teen-agers with many new devices to make them look mature sooner, but basically each one of them has to bumble and fumble his way to adulthood according to his schedule, which applies to him alone and which even he only dimly senses. You can't buy emotional maturity; you can't teach it; and you certainly can't bottle it.

Apparatus for: What's Happening, Baby?

Vocabulary: *Discuss the following phrases taken from the essay.*

1. "pack of Mods" (¶ 1)
2. "gummed his mini" (¶ 2)
3. "furtive pinch" (¶ 7)
4. "impulse purchases" (¶ 17)
5. "the bomb has been sobering" (¶ 33)
6. "pseudo-teen" (¶ 40)

1. _____

   _____

2. _____

   _____

3. _____

   _____

4. _____

   _____

5. _____

   _____

6. _____

   _____

Discussion: *Rhetoric*

1. Although this selection was first delivered as a speech, it reads uncommonly well as a complete essay. The diction contributes to the easy flow of thoughts. Describe the diction in relation to the subject.
2. The introduction ends at paragraph 4. Then begins the main part of the selection. What is the internal organization of the essay? How does the author help us to keep track of his ideas?
3. How effective are the statistics cited by the author? Do they support his basic idea?
4. Where is the thesis of the selection stated?
5. What paragraphs make up the ending of this essay?

1. _____

   _____

2. _____

   _____

3. _____

   _____

4. _____

   _____

5. _____

   _____

Apparatus for: What's Happening, Baby?

Discussion: *Theme*

1. Would you add to or subtract from the list of relevant topics mentioned in paragraph 7? Explain.
2. In paragraph 18, the $30 billion "youth market" is discussed. Just how involved is the teen-ager in the purchases made by his family?
3. Has mobility via the car contributed to a decline in morals among teen-agers?
4. Why do automobile sports attract five to ten million more spectators than do football, baseball, and basketball?
5. How intense are the pressures to get a college education?
6. Why does the Bomb produce a "deeply religious" attitude in some teen-agers while impressing others with "the absurdity of human life"?
7. How contradictory are adults when dealing with teen-agers? See paragraph 37.
8. Do you agree that teen-agers resent adults' taking over the youthful dance steps? Explain.

1. _____

_____

2. _____

_____

3. _____

_____

4. _____

_____

5. _____

_____

6. _____

_____

7. _____

_____

8. _____

_____

Writing Suggestions

1. A Fad is a Symptom, not a Disease
2. Money, Sex, Mobility, School, and War
3. Project some of the influence teen-agers will have in five to ten years. (See paragraph 16.)
4. How is the demolition derby a comment on life?
5. Analyze some of the pressures on the first generation which faces "the possible death of society."
6. What language should adults use when trying to communicate with teen-agers?
7. What do you consider to be the perfect date? In your theme, give specific instances, rather than relying on vague generalities and clichés.

6. SATURDAY NIGHT IN HARLEM
"A MEMOIR" *

CLAUDE BROWN

1   Saturday night. I suppose there's a Saturday night in every Negro community throughout the nation just like Saturday night in Harlem. The bars will jump. The precinct station will have a busy night. The hospital's emergency ward will jump.

2   Cats who have been working all their lives, who've never been in any trouble before, good-doing righteous cats, self-respecting, law-abiding citizens—they'll all come out. Perhaps it'll be their night in the bar, their night in the police station, maybe their night in the emergency ward.

3   They tell me that young doctors really try hard for a chance to do their internship in Harlem Hospital—it offers such a wide variety of experiences. They say it's the best place in the city where a surgeon can train. They say you get all kinds of experience just working there on Saturday nights.

4   It's usually the older folks who practice this Saturday night thing, or some of the younger cats who haven't come out of the woods yet, young cats who drink a lot of liquor, who didn't quite finish junior high school, who still have most of the Southern ways . . . the young cats who carry knives, the young cats who want to be bad niggers. It's usually the guys around eighteen to twenty-five, guys who haven't separated themselves yet from the older generation or who just haven't become critical of the older generation. They follow the pattern that has been set by the older generation, the Saturday night pattern

---

* Claude Brown, "Saturday Night in Harlem." Reprinted with permission of The Macmillan Company from *Manchild in the Promised Land* by Claude Brown. Copyright © Claude Brown 1965.

of getting drunk, getting a new piece of c - - -, and getting real bad—carrying a knife in your pocket and ready to use it, ready to curse, ready to become a Harlem Saturday night statistic, in the hospital, the police station, or the morgue.

5   The intern who comes to Harlem and starts his internship around April, he'll be ready to go into surgery by June. He's probably already tried to close up windpipes for people who've had their throat slit. Or tried to put intestines back in a stomach. Or somebody has hit somebody in the head with a hatchet. Or somebody has come into his house at the wrong time and caught somebody else going out the window. That's quite a job too, putting a person back together after a four- or five-story fall.

6   I suppose any policeman who's been in Harlem for a month of Saturday nights has had all the experience he'll ever need, as far as handling violence goes. Some of them will have more experience than they'll ever be able to use.

7   To me, it always seemed as though Saturday night was the down-home night. In the tales I'd heard about down home—how so-and-so got bad and killed Cousin Joe or knocked out Cousin Willie's eye—everything violent happened on Saturday night. It was the only time for anything to really happen, because people were too tired working all week from sunup to sundown to raise but so much hell on the week nights. Then, comes Saturday, and they take it kind of easy during the day, resting up for another Saturday night.

8   Down home, when they went to town, all the niggers would just break bad, so it seemed. Everybody just seemed to let out all their hostility on everybody else. Maybe they were hoping that they could get their throats cut. Perhaps if a person was lucky enough to get his throat cut, he'd be free from the fields. On the other hand, if someone was lucky enough to cut somebody else's throat, he'd done the guy a favor, because he'd freed him.

9   In the tales about down home that I'd heard, everybody was trying to either cash out on Saturday night or cash somebody else out. There was always the good corn liquor that Cy Walker used to make, and there was always that new gun that somebody had bought. The first time they shot the gun at so-and-so, he jumped out of the window and didn't stop running until he got home—and got his gun. You'd sit there and say, "Well, I'll be damned. I never knew they had all those bad niggers in the South. I always thought the baddest cat down there was Charlie." But it seemed as though on Saturday night, the niggers got bad. Of course, they didn't get bad enough to mess with Charlie, but they got bad. They were bad enough to cut each other's throats, shoot each other, hit each other in the head with axes, and all that sort of action. Women were bad enough to throw lye on one another.

10   Saturday night down home was really something, but then Saturday night in Harlem was really something too. There is something happening for everybody on Saturday night: for the cat who works all day long on the railroad, in

the garment center, driving a bus, or as a subway conductor. On Saturday night, there is something happening for everybody in Harlem, regardless of what his groove might be. Even the real soul sisters, who go to church and live for Sunday, who live to jump up and clap and call on the Lord, Saturday night means something to them too. Saturday night is the night they start getting ready for Sunday. They have to braid all the kids' hair and get them ready. They have to iron their white usher uniforms and get pretty for Sunday and say a prayer. For the devoted churchgoers, Saturday night means that Sunday will soon be here.

11   Saturday night is a time to try new things. Maybe that's why so many people in the older generation had to lose their lives on Saturday night. It must be something about a Saturday night with Negroes. . . . Maybe they wanted to die on Saturday night. They'd always associated Sunday with going to heaven, because that was when they went to church and sang all those songs, clapped and shouted and stomped their feet and praised the Lord. Maybe they figured that if they died on Sunday morning, the Lord's day, they'd be well on their way.

12   Everybody has this thing about Saturday night. I imagine that before pot or horse or any other drugs hit Harlem good and strong, the people just had to try something else, like knifing or shooting somebody, because Saturday night was the night for daring deeds. Since there was no pot out on a large scale then, I suppose one of the most daring deeds anyone could perform was to shoot or stab somebody.

13   Many of the chicks in the neighborhood took some of their first really big steps on Saturday night. Some cats—or as a girl I knew might say, "no-good niggers"—talked many girls into turning their first tricks on a Saturday night just because the cats needed some money. That's how that thing goes on Saturday night. I recall talking a girl into a trick on a Saturday night. She said it was her first, but I like to tell myself it wasn't. If it was, that was okay. She was a part of Harlem, and Saturday night was a time for first things, even for girls turning their first tricks, pulling their first real John.

14   Saturday night has also been a traditional night for money to be floating around in places like Harlem. It's a night of temptation, the kind of temptation one might see on Catfish Row at the end of the cotton season, on the weekend. Most of the people got paid on Friday night, and Saturday they had some money. If they didn't get paid on Friday, there was a good chance that they'd be around playing the single action on Saturday in the afternoon. By the time the last figure came out, everybody might have some change, even if it was only eight dollars—one dollar on the 0 that afternoon. It was still some money.

15   Then there were all the crap games floating around. The stickup artists would be out hunting. The Murphy boys would be out strong. In the bars, the tricks would be out strong. All the whores would be out there, and any decent,

self-respecting whore could pull at least two-hundred dollars on Saturday night in some of the bad-doing bars on 125th Street.

16   As a matter of fact, Reno used to say, "The cat who can't make no money on Saturday night is in trouble." There was a lot of truth to it, because there was so much money floating around in Harlem on Saturday night, if anyone couldn't get any money then, he just didn't have any business there.

17   It seemed as though Harlem's history is made on Saturday nights. You hear about all the times people have gotten shot—like when two white cops were killed on 146th Street a couple of years ago—on a Saturday night. Just about every time a cop is killed in Harlem, it's on a Saturday night.

18   People know you shouldn't bother with Negroes on Saturday night, because for some reason or another, Negroes just don't mind dying on Saturday night. They seem ready to die, so they're not going to take but so much stuff. There were some people who were always trying to get themselves killed. Every Saturday night, they'd try it all over again.

19   One was Big Bill. When I was just a kid on Eighth Avenue in knee pants, this guy was trying to get himself killed. He was always in some fight with a knife. He was always cutting or trying to cut somebody's throat. He was always getting cut or getting stabbed, getting hit in the head, getting shot. Every Saturday night that he was out there, something happened. If you heard on Sunday morning that somebody had gotten shot or stabbed, you didn't usually ask who did it. You'd ask if Big Bill did it. If he did it, no one paid too much attention to it, because he was always doing something like that. They'd say, "Yeah, man. That cat is crazy."

20   If somebody else had done it, you'd wonder why, and this was something to talk about and discuss. Somebody else might not have been as crazy. In the case of Big Bill, everybody expected that sooner or later somebody would kill him and put him out of his misery and that this was what he was trying for. One time Spanish Joe stabbed him. He just missed his lung, and everybody thought he was going to cool it behind that. But as soon as the cat got back on the street, he was right out there doing it again.

21   Even now, he's always getting in fights out on the streets on Saturday nights. He's always hurting somebody, or somebody's hurting him. He just seems to be hanging on. I think he's just unlucky. Here's a cat who's been trying to get himself killed every Saturday night as far back as I can remember, and he still hasn't made it. I suppose you've got to sympathize with a guy like that, because he's really been trying.

22   Harlem is full of surprises on Saturday night. I remember one in particular.

23   I was down on 116th Street. I was going to visit someone, and I decided to call before I got there. I went into the bar on the corner to call. I saw a familiar face at the bar. We had stopped hanging out together when I was

about nine and never started again. We just weren't that tight any more. We'd had our fights. We were all right; we'd speak if we saw each other. I was just surprised to see him in that neck of the woods. I didn't think he ever went anyplace outside our neighborhood. I guess a lot of people had the same idea. It just goes to show how little we all knew about him.

24   I walked up to him and said, "Hey, Dad, how you doin'?" I guess he was just as surprised to see me down there, and I thought he was going to ask, "Hey, son, what you doin' down here?" I was all set to tell him, "I got a friend down here who owes me some money, and I need it tonight, because I got to take this chick out, so I came down to see him."

25   But he didn't say it. He just asked me if I wanted a drink. He didn't act too surprised to see me. He was out, and this was Saturday night. He'd been in Harlem a lot of Saturday nights, and he'd gotten that big, nasty-looking scar on his neck on a Saturday night.

26   Despite the fact that he didn't ask me what I was doing there, I said, "I got to get uptown. I got to call somebody to wait for me. I hope this chick don't stay in that phone booth too long."

27   He said, "No, I don't think she'll be in there on the phone too long."

28   I didn't pay much attention to it. I said, "She looks like one of those who can really talk."

29   He just said, "Yeah," and kind of smiled.

30   I looked at the woman again. She looked as though she might have been about thirty-three, something like that. I would look over there every couple of minutes. She would look over to the bar at me and smile. I just forgot about the phone and started talking to Dad about my job and what I'd done that night, how I was catching hell, how everything I touched just turned to s - - -, sort of halfway crying.

31   It dawned on me that he had been standing there all by himself when I came in, and I'd never known him to do this. I never thought that he would go to a bar by himself, especially some strange bar, just to stand around and drink. He usually brought his liquor home when he wanted a drink.

32   I said, "Say, Dad, you waitin' for somebody down here?" I knew a friend of his who worked with him. Although I hadn't seen him in a long time, I figured they were still friends. I knew his friend, Eddie, lived down there, so I said, "Dad, you waitin' for somebody? Is Eddie around?"

33   He didn't answer the first question, but to the second one he said, "No, I haven't seen Eddie now in about a month."

34   I said, "Yeah? Well, doesn't he still work on the job with you?"

35   He said that Eddie had an injury; some crates fell on him. "It's not too

bad, but he can't be doing that heavy work around the dock, so he stayed off. He's collecting compensation for it. He's taking it easy, the way I hear it."

36 I said, "Oh." After that, I thought about the first question, but I figured it wouldn't be to wise to repeat it. I thought, well, maybe he's waiting for his woman. And I laughed, because I always thought of Dad as the kind of cat nobody but Mama could take. With her, it was just habit.

37 After a while, the woman from the phone booth came up. She said, "Hi."

38 I looked at her and said, "Oh, do I know you?"

39 Dad introduced her. He said, "Ruth, meet my oldest son."

40 She smiled and said, "Hello. So you're Sonny Boy."

41 I said, "Yeah."

42 She said, "I knew it was you the moment I saw you sittin' there next to your daddy on that stool. You two look so much alike. If he was about ten years younger, he could pass for your older brother."

43 I said, "Yeah, that's something that people are suppose' to tell fathers and sons, huh, that they look like brothers?"

44 She threw both of her hands on her hips and looked at me in a sort of defiant way, but jokingly, and said, "Supposin' it is, young man? That's beside the point. I'm telling you that you and your daddy look alike, even if this is what people are suppose' to tell you. Now, you can believe it if you want to. All I'm interested in is saying it, and I said it. You can take it from there."

45 I looked at her and said, "Okay, I believe it." I had the funniest feeling that this woman knew what was going on. I knew this was his woman.

46 I couldn't feel anything about it. I guess I'd just never given too much thought to the idea of Dad playing around. I couldn't imagine anybody else ever wanting him. In the case of Mama, I think, if it had been her, I would have felt good about it. She deserved to get out and get somebody who would treat her like she was something, like she was a person. Because of this feeling about Mama, I suppose I should have felt bad that Dad was being unfaithful, but I didn't. I didn't see any way in the world to dislike this woman. She seemed to be a nice person.

47 Dad asked her if she wanted a drink.

48 She said to me, "What you drinkin', junior?" I told her I was drinking a bourbon and soda with lemon. She said, "Umph. That sounds like something with a whole lot of sting in it. Maybe I'll try one."

49 She moved closer to Dad and put her hand around his waist. She looked at me as if to say, "Well, young man, that's the way it is. So how you gonna take it?"

50   Dad never even looked at me. He just picked up his drink, as if to say, "S - - -, he's old enough. If he's not, f - - - him." He emptied his glass, put it down, and called to the bartender.

51   When the bartender came to bring Ruth one, Dad got another whiskey, straight. We sat there for a while and started talking. The woman didn't seem to be the least bit ill at ease. She seemed completely relaxed, and she looked pretty, in her own way. She was kind of plump, but she looked like she might have been a very nice-looking girl when she was about twenty.

52   I guess she was pretty for Dad. He was forty at the time, so I suppose anything under thirty-five would have been real nice for him. They seemed to have something. He had a patience with her that I'd never seen him show with Mama. I didn't think he was capable of showing this to any woman. She seemed to be able to play with him, and he took more playing from her than I'd seen him take from anybody else.

53   It made me wonder just how long had he known her and just what was going on with them. All I could see was that, whatever they had with each other, they were really enjoying it. I decided that was enough. I didn't feel as though I had the right to judge them or even have an opinion about them. Whatever they were doing, it seemed to me that they weren't doing it to anybody but themselves. Mama would never be hurt, because there was a good chance that she'd never know. New York was a big city, and they seemed so tight that they must have been tight for a long time, a real long time.

54   I asked her, "Pardon me, Ruth. Haven't I seen you uptown? Do you live up around 145th Street?"

55   Dad still never looked at me. He said, "Sonny Boy, I think you better grab that phone there now. The booth is empty. If you don't get it while it's empty, you're liable to be here all night."

56   I got up and went to the phone booth. When I came out, Dad and his lady friend were gone. That was understandable. I guess I really messed up with that question about 145th Street.

57   I didn't feel bad toward Dad. It was just that I had never seen it as being possible for him to pull a chick on the outside, a nice-looking chick like this Ruth. She seemed to be a person with a nice personality, and she didn't look bad for a woman her age. Maybe she did something for Dad too. He acted like a different person altogether with her. Maybe she was the one who made him relax. He must have been a different person. I'd never seen him act like that with anybody. At home he was always shouting and raising hell, threatening somebody, a real terror.

58   I was kind of sorry that I had started prying into the woman's business. I knew I'd never seen her uptown. I suppose Dad knew it too. I was supposed to act as old as he had treated me. One of the things had been to treat the lady

like she was just a friend of Dad's and to be cool behind it. But then I had just gone on and messed over her. I knew this was something I'd never get a chance to do again. I knew I'd never get a chance to say, "Look, Dad, I'm sorry I said that, and I shouldn't have." Because I knew that this wasn't supposed to be mentioned ever, not even to him.

59   The next time I saw him, I would just have to speak first, about something that was far removed from the night at the bar and from Ruth. But I hoped that I would get a chance to let her know somehow that I was sorry that I hadn't played my part properly.

60   I didn't feel as though he was hurting Mama. I felt she didn't know about it, and what she didn't know wouldn't hurt her. Maybe it was just that she wasn't missing anything, because I didn't feel they were in any great love anyway. It just didn't bother me as I might have thought it would. It just seemed to be one of those Harlem Saturday night surprises.

61   I remember the Saturday night when Dad kicked my brother Pimp out of the house and told him not to come back. Pimp had fallen asleep on the toilet with a needle in his arm. I guess he'd taken a light O.D.[1]

62   Mama was telling me about it. According to her, Dad came in and panicked. He opened the bathroom door and saw Pimp halfway on and halfway off the toilet with a needle in his arm. Mama said he just started calling so loud for her to come there, she thought he was dying. Mama tried to make a joke out of it. She said she thought maybe he'd fallen down in the toilet and was having trouble getting out. I tried to laugh, but all I could get out was a snicker.

63   Mama said she tried to slap Pimp out of it. She thought for a while he was dead when she saw him. She just refused to accept that her child was dead from using dope. She ran into the bathroom and started slapping him and calling his name real loud, as though, even if he was dead, he would hear her and come back.

64   She started hollering for the doctor, and she started hollering about an ambulance. Dad said, "No, don't be callin' no ambulance or no doctors around here. We ain't gon have no police coming in here."

65   Mama started hollering, "The boy might be dead! The boy might be dead!"

66   Dad said, "Huh?" He'd stop and say, "He ain't dead. He ain't dead. It's just that old dope." They both panicked.

67   When Mama finally got Pimp to wake up, after so much slapping and calling his name, Dad was convinced that it was time for Pimp to go. I guess he should have been convinced. It must have been a pretty frightening thing,

[1] Overdose.

even for him, though he wouldn't admit it, to come into the bathroom and see his son slumped over a toilet with a needle in his arm, after having heard so much about the junkies dying from using dope, after having been to so many funerals, after having asked so many times about this kid and that kid who came up with his older son and being told that he'd died from dope—it must have been a pretty frightening thing.

68   Pimp had deceived just about everybody in the family for a long time. After a while, we all knew, but I knew before anybody else that Pimp was dabbling. I was the first one to say, "Come on, man. You got to do something."

69   I guess Pimp sort of knew that I suspected him of using stuff. The first time after I saw him high that night in the Low Hat, I took him to a bar. He didn't know that I had seen him nodding. I said, "Come on, let's have a drink. I want to talk to you. Let's sit down and have a drink."

70   I asked him what he'd like to drink. I remembered that he used to like rum. I think he just took a rum and Coke because he knew I remembered it and thought I might get suspicious if he didn't.

71   When he took his first sip of the rum and Coke, he grimaced. He said, "Man, it's like, I'm so tired. I'm so tired, Sonny, this stuff almost knocks me out."

72   I looked at him and said, "Yeah, man. It can do that to you."

73   Then he looked down and started fumbling with his glass, as if he knew I was suspicious of him. The next thing he said was, "Man, you know, I ain't had no good rum in a long time."

74   When he said this, I paid it no attention. I knew he was going to try to bullshit me. I looked straight at him as he went on talking. I said, "Pimp." I sort of quietly shouted it at him.

75   He said, "Yeah, Sonny?"

76   I said, "How long have you been dabblin' in stuff?"

77   He looked at me for a long time. He got kind of quiet, and he dropped his head. He said, "Oh, about four months, man."

78   I said, "How far are you? How much stuff you usin' a day?"

79   He said, "Oh, man, I buy a bag about every other day, but I don't get high every day."

80   "Are you snortin' or skin poppin'?"

81   "Man, I'm just startin', and I can keep a bag two or three days."

82   I said, "Uh-huh. That's good, because now is the time for you to stop. You got to stop now, before you really get yourself into some trouble."

83 He said, "Yeah, yeah." He was glad to hear this. It seemed as though he had heard something that he had been waiting to hear, he had been given some kind of signal. He seemed to feel that all he had to do now was agree with everything I said and everything would be okay. He was going to prevent any violence from taking place by just being agreeable.

84 "Look, Pimp, you got a job, and you're still working. You're doing good now. Now is the time when you can quit, because if you keep on dabblin', man, you're gon actually go to the dogs. After a while, you won't be able to quit, and you won't have anything to quit for, because once you blow your job, your clothes, and everything you've got, it just won't matter that much. You got a nice girl, man. And maybe you'll want to get married or something. But what you're doin', man, you're gon blow everything."

85 "Yeah, Sonny, I know what you mean, man. I've been tellin' myself. I've been planning on stopping this stuff for the last two weeks. As a matter of fact, last week. . . ."

86 I just knew he was lying. He was saying all this so relaxed, and he seemed so pleased with the way he was telling it. But I could tell he was lying. I knew. He didn't know how to lie, not to me anyway.

87 He said that he had bought some Dorphine tablets and that he had taken his first two today. He was going to keep taking the Dorphine tablets and start cutting down on other drugs from day to day, and in a couple of weeks or so, he'd be ready to sign himself into someplace.

88 I asked him if he'd ever heard of Norman Eddie, in the East Harlem Protestant Parish. He said no, he hadn't. I said, "Well, he's doin' a lot of good work with drug addicts, and if you're really interested, I think I can get him to work with you, man. You could kick it now, before it really gets a strong hold on you."

89 Pimp went right on bullshitting me. He said, "Yeah, Sonny, that's what I want to do. You go ahead and see this cat and let me know what's happening."

90 I was crushed. He didn't understand it at all. He just seemed to look at me as if I were someone who was trying to deprive him of something. And he wasn't even going to pretend to defend it, even though he wanted it terribly. He was just going to sit there and say, "Yeah, yeah, yeah, uh-huh. I'll go along with you. You're right; that's so right. I'm going to be doing it, so there's nothing else to talk about when you stop trying to sell me on it."

91 Even though I could see this, I still felt I had to try. He was my brother, and I could make him kick it. He couldn't help but kick it if I was in his corner, if I really wanted him to. I was going to put everything I had into it.

92 When Mama called me that Saturday night and told me what Dad had said

to Pimp, how he couldn't come back in the house any more, and how afraid she was for him, I said, "Look, Mama, he'll be coming back."

93 She said, "No, he ain't gon come back, because he was really hurt. I think he's just gon go some place and try to take enough of that stuff to kill himself or something."

94 I said, "No, Mama, junkies don't kill themselves. They've got something to live for. They got to live for another high, for the next one. He'll probably come down here." I knew he wasn't coming, but that's what I told her. "Mama, he'll probably come down here, and when he does come down, I'll put him up for the night and call you and let you know."

95 Mama said, "He just might go someplace and get himself into some trouble in the meantime, before he gets down there. Why don't you go out and look for him for a little while. He's probably around there on 144th Street. And let me know if you can't find him. Call me and keep in touch with me, because he ain't had a bath all week, and he got on those old dirty pants. That shirt he has on, he put it on day before yesterday, and it was white. It looks like it's black from the dirt and grime. He ain't had nothin' to eat in a long time. I don't know if he even had anything to eat yesterday, and he's probably hungry."

96 I wanted to tell her, "Look, Mama, junkies don't care about eating. They don't care about clothes. They don't care about baths and stuff like that. It just don't matter to them. All they care about is some heroin, and this is the only thing that's gon do them any good, Mama. You got to face the fact that he's at that state where soap and water's not gon do him any good. Clothes ain't gon do him any good. Food ain't gon do him any good. He's just dead, and maybe the thing that'll do him the most good is the O.D., the O.D. that he's waitin' for." But I couldn't tell her that. I just couldn't seem to bring it out.

97 I knew it was no use, but she got me to promise that I'd look for him. She was a woman, and that was her child. I couldn't tell her that many other women had sons and daughters out there dying too. It wouldn't have meant anything to her, because this was the first child that she had out there who was a drug addict. This was the only one out there she was concerned about, the only junkie that mattered.

98 I went uptown to start looking for Pimp. I looked everywhere. I went to all the places where junkies might go, looked in all the dope dens, in all the back-yards where the junkies might sleep. Nobody had seen him or heard about him. Some people hadn't seen him in days. I kept on looking and hoping. When Mama called me, it had been about eight-thirty or nine o'clock. When I hadn't found Pimp or anybody who had seen Pimp by three-thirty, I became a little worried.

99 I started fearing for him. When this happened, I started getting mad at

myself, because I felt myself going right back into the same pattern again. I knew that if I had seen him then and he was in pain or said his habit was down on him, I would have had to give him some money to get some stuff. I probably would have fallen right back into Pimp's trick bag and helped send him to Kentucky and waited for him to come back and start all over.

100   Still, the longer I looked for him, the more worried I became. And the more worried I became, the more angry I became with myself for worrying, for going back on my word, for weakening, for weakening from Pimp and his weakness. This was what he had always played on with me. He'd beg me for my clothes, to pawn them, because he knew I worried about him.

101   He'd intimidate me with my concern for him. He'd tell me he was going to have to go and try a stickup or something like that. Many times, after he'd left, I'd say, "Nigger, go on. Go on and pull a stickup. Go on and do what you want to. Just hurry up and get it over with; like, pull a stickup and get shot, or go on and throw a brick. Rob somebody's house and get thrown out of a window, or just go on and take that O.D. But whatever you do, please do it in a hurry. Please do it in a hurry and get off my back."

102   That was what I should have told him, but I guess every junkie looks pitiful to his brother. Pimp always seemed to be the most pitiful creature in the world when his habit was down on him. He looked so helpless. I knew I could never turn my back on him if I saw him when his habit was down on him. I was almost certain that this morning would be another time like that.

103   There was nothing else to do but go on uptown and tell Mama that I couldn't find him but that we still had Pimp, we still had our problem.

104   When I got there, I hestitated to knock on the door. I felt ashamed to go in there and tell Mama, "Look, I couldn't find him. I couldn't find hide nor hair of him. Nobody's seen him or heard from him."

105   She expected me to bring her some hope. That's why I went out to begin with, because I figured I could bring him back or at least find him and ease her mind. But I had to come back with nothing, not even knowing where Pimp was.

106   When I finally got around to knocking on the door, Dad opened the door. I think he had just come in. Not from looking for Pimp—he had come in from his Saturday night. He looked at me as if he was a little disappointed or something. Maybe he expected the police to come and bring Pimp home or bring his body home or bring the information that he was dead. It was just me, and he seemed to resent the knowledge that my presence brought him: that we still had our problem.

107   Dad went into the bathroom, and I went into the front room. Mama was sitting at the front window. I just came in, walking slowly, and said I couldn't find him.

108 Mama said, "Yeah, he might just be someplace dead, in some strange backyard. Maybe some of those junkies could have taken him and thrown him in some boiler down in the cellar. Like they did around on 144th Street last year, when that boy took a lot of dope and went in that coma. They put him in that boiler, just about cooked him. Yeah, he just might be layin' around in one of them boilers cookin' right now."

109 I didn't say anything, because I knew what Mama was doing. I felt sorry for her. She was trying to prepare herself for the worst by saying all that stuff. I knew she didn't believe it, and she didn't want to believe it. She just wanted to hear herself say it, just in case somebody brought some sad news. If she told herself that this was what had happened to him, and something happened to him that wasn't as bad, it had to be good.

110 Then Dad came in and said, "Woman, why don't you stop all that foolishness? You don't have to be worried about them damn junkies. Them damn junkies take care of theirselves twice as good as you can. You see that they be out there so long, look like they be dying, and they be hanging around there for years. Why don't you stop talkin' all that foolishness?"

111 Mama didn't seem to hear Dad. She looked out the window, saw the daylight creeping in, stroked the cat—about the tenth cat named Tina—and seemed to realize that Saturday night was gone. Mama stroked the cat lightly and looked out the window, greeting the daylight with a question. She said to the dawn, "Lord, where can my child be this mornin'?"

Apparatus for: Saturday Night in Harlem

Vocabulary: *Compile a list of 10 words that are used in an unusual way in this essay. (Examples are* cat *and* trick.*) Define the words as Claude Brown uses them.*

1. _____   _____

_____

2. _____   _____

_____

3. _____   _____

_____

4. _____   _____

_____

5. _____   _____

_____

6. _____   _____

_____

7. _____   _____

_____

8. _____   _____

_____

9. _____   _____

_____

10. _____   _____

_____

Discussion: *Rhetoric*

1. This essay makes unusual use of some common words and phrases. Appreciating the use of these terms will help you to discover *why* he does what he does. Comment on the author's use of words like *nigger* and *Negro* in the same selection.
2. Is the use of details effective in this selection? What is the dominant impression Brown is attempting to create through his details? Notice especially paragraph 4.
3. What is the attitude of the author toward his subject?
4. Why does Brown reflect on the lore of his past, "down home"? Where was "down home"?
5. The level of usage in this essay is very informal, but is it, therefore, weak? In considering your answer, keep in mind the author's intention and purpose.
6. How effective is the long personal anecdote about the author's father and brother?
7. Is the last question, "Lord, where can my child be this mornin'?" a symbolic one? Explain.

1. _____

_____

2. _____

_____

3. _____

_____

4. _____

_____

5. _____

_____

Apparatus for: Saturday Night in Harlem

6. _____

_____

7. _____

_____

Discussion: *Theme*

1. Why are people intrigued by places like Harlem?
2. Does poverty alone produce ghettos? Explain.
3. Do you think the federal programs designed to alleviate socioeconomic depression go far enough? Explain.
4. What can be done for the dope addicts, particularly in the poverty-stricken areas of our large cities?
5. Is it surprising that so much violence exists on Saturday nights? Explain.
6. In what ways were you touched (or repelled) by this selection?
7. Should marijuana be legalized? Why or why not?

1. _____

_____

2. _____

_____

3. _____

_____

4. _____

_____

5. _____

_____

6. _____

_____

7. _____

_____

Writing Suggestions

1. Describe a neighborhood that you know personally. If you wish, model your description on Brown's essay.
2. Write a personal essay that might be similar in its effect to the author's hunting for his brother in this essay.
3. Use this question as the basis for a theme: "Lord, where can my child be this mornin'?"
4. Evaluate the attitude of the father in Brown's essay.
5. In a paper, analyze the use of vulgarity in Brown's essay.

III. SENTENCE VARIETY

One of your major tasks as a college writer is to hold the interest of your reader. All too often, readers are bored or annoyed by a succession of sentences that are flat, predictable, or monotonous. Sometimes such sentences are short, choppy, and childlike; others rely solely on the subject-verb pattern and follow each other in dreary monotony. Still other such sentences are rambling and difficult to follow. By following the suggestions below, you can develop one of the chief means of securing and maintaining your reader's interest: effective sentence variety.

VARIETY IN SENTENCE LENGTH: SUBORDINATION

There is no ideal or "correct" sentence length. A series of short, choppy sentences, however, soon disturbs the reader. Furthermore, such sentences indicate an immaturity of mind, and suggest an inability to sustain anything but the simplest thoughts. By subordination—that is, by putting more important ideas into main clauses, and changing less important ideas into subordinate clauses, phrases, or even single words—you will develop a smoother structure, as well as a more mature style. Note the "jerky" effect of the following passage:

> William Faulkner was an American novelist. He wrote *The Sound and the Fury*. He received the Nobel Prize for Literature in 1949. He died in 1962. *As I Lay Dying* was also written by Faulkner.

Now observe the improvement brought about by combining the short sentences into longer, smoother ones through subordination:

> William Faulkner, an American novelist, received the Nobel Prize for Literature in 1949. The author of *The Sound and the Fury* and *As I Lay Dying,* he made famous the legendary Yoknapatawpha County.

Be careful that in your efforts to rid your writing of too many short sentences you do not end up with the opposite vice: a series of directionless and bewildering long sentences. The best writers vary the length of their sentences according to their purpose—that is, according to what they are saying and the effect they want to achieve.

VARIETY IN WORD ORDER

Because most sentences in the English language follow the subject-verb pattern, inexperienced writers tend to begin every sentence with the subject. A series of such sentences, however, can easily create monotony. By beginning some of your sentences with an appositive or a modifier, you can achieve variety in your sentence structure, and thus avoid such tedium.

Appositive first: A firm but fair teacher, Mr. Jenkins is admired by all of his students.

Single-word modifiers first: Reluctantly, she entered the dentist's office. (*adverb*)
Exhausted, the basketball player slumped on a bench. (*participle*)
Angry and defiant, the mob ignored the orders of the police. (*adjectives*)

Phrase modifiers first: On my desk I found an important letter. (*prepositional phrase*)
Gasping for air, the diver was pulled from the water. (*participial phrase*)

Clause modifiers first: Although Mrs. Davis was on a diet, she could not lose any weight.
After everyone was seated, the orchestra played its first selection.

VARIETY IN RHETORICAL PATTERN

By varying the rhetorical pattern of your sentences, you will give additional diversity to your writing. Sentences may be classified rhetorically—that is, according to their arrangement and effect—into three groups: loose, periodic, and balanced.

The loose sentence is one that begins with the main statement, and follows with details and modifiers. It is relatively informal, and forms the basis of most of our speech and writing. In the following examples, note the position of the main idea and lesser, supporting details.

Women can do as well as men in most jobs, although there is still prejudice encountered in some professions and among some employers.
I intend to vote for John Dover because I believe in his political philosophy and in his statements to the voters.

Although they are used in good writing, loose sentences can often lack emphasis. For this reason, you should occasionally use periodic sentences.

A periodic sentence is arranged so that its main idea is placed at the end. In this respect, it is the opposite of the loose sentence. Because of the location of its main idea, it holds the reader's attention and interest to its very conclusion. In the following periodic sentences, note how the chief idea is withheld until the end:

> Although he was reluctant to disclose his scores on his college entrance examinations, it was obvious that he was very disappointed.
>
> A hobby that has given me much pleasure and satisfaction for the last several years is restoring old automobiles.

But do not overuse the periodic sentence. Too much suspense can weary the reader, and such sentences can be somewhat unnatural or artificial. Use them only when you are deliberately trying to create emphasis or suspense.

A balanced sentence is one in which sentence elements (words, phrases, clauses) of equal value are set off against each other. Thus it is particularly effective for comparisons and contrasts, as well as for emphatic statements. Study the following examples:

> The President wanted an increase in taxes to reduce the national debt; the Congress wanted a reduction in taxes to stimulate business.
>
> *Who* leads us is less important than *what* leads us.

Thus, good sentences are more than grammatically correct. They are varied in length, in word order, and in their rhetorical patterns. As you read the essays in this section, consider the sentence structure of each selection. And as you write your own compositions, apply the techniques for attaining sentence variety that we have discussed.

7. LIFE AND DEATH OF AN OYSTER *

ALAN DEVOE

1   Now is the time of cold—the time when hungry foxes paw desperately at the frozen earth, and the lean hawks sail screaming over the snow-bowed hemlocks in search of hot blood to assuage the hurting in their frost-pinched bellies. The deer are nibbling at any kind of bud or berry now, in the hock-deep snow, and the rabbits have resorted to stripping the tough bark from tree trunks with their sharp incisors. But, in many a bright-lit restaurant and dining room, this is a time of gastronomic rejoicement. For it is the middle month in that season in which the names of all the months contain an *r*. It is the heyday, in short, of the oyster. . . . This is an excellent time for considering what manner of beasts these are, which lie so pleasantly nestled between the lemon slice and the tabasco.

2   Oysters are not a recently discovered food of man, an epicurean delicacy of his latter-day era of civilization. Man has probably been eating them nearly as long as he has been eating anything. It was a slant-browed forbear, with knuckles still horny after the ape fashion, who first cracked open one of the corrugated shells and found that the gobbet of living tissue inside was sweet on his tongue. Vast heaps of empty oyster shells, piled up by prehistoric man and now called kitchen middens, are readily to be found in many parts of the earth—for instance, on the coasts of Florida—and it is safe to surmise that oysters were as popular and common a part of ancient cave-fare as were berries and wild tubers.

3   Within the span of history, the evidence of oyster eating goes as far back as the record. The earliest Greeks and Romans were devoted oyster fanciers;

Pliny has remarked that oysters were being scientifically cultivated in the first century B.C. In the time of the Emperor Augustus, Sergius Orata was making a large income from the professional maintenance of oyster beds at Baiae. There is probably no other animal under the sun which has for so many millennia vanished into the maw of *homo sapiens* in such uncountable numbers as the wide-ranging mollusk called Ostrea.

4   The oyster is an easy prey, for it is one of the few animals that are completely motionless. Even the fresh-water mussel, the clam, can achieve a limited degree of slow, clumsy movement by the rhythmic protrusion of its whitish, wedge-shaped foot. It can bury itself in the ooze or even, in simple fashion, go hunting. But the oyster does not have a foot; it has only its pulpy body and its two-valved shell. Except for a brief period in its infancy, it lives its life as immobile as a fungus.

5   In the shallow ocean not far from shore, or in a sun-warmed estuary or a mangrove swamp, the oyster passes its days attached by its left valve, which is the larger, to a stone, or a shell or a bit of submerged wreckage. The two halves of its shell are connected, and their openings and closings controlled, by a ligament of muscle; and in the forepart of the oyster's cold, moist body there is a rudimentary brain. There are gills—four rows of them—and ovaries and a liver and a heart with brown-colored auricles. There is a toothless, jawless mouth, situated beneath the crinkly fringe of tissue which is the oyster's mantle, and there is a pair of soft motile palps to serve as lips. Although motionless, the oyster is fully equipped to be an animal. It has intestines, whereby to carry out digestion, gills wherewith to breathe, and cilia with which to catch its food and carry it into its mouth; it has an orifice to serve as rectum.

6   The oyster is blind and without ears, but it has a different and equally serviceable kind of sensitive awareness. It is moved, when a shadow falls athwart it, to contract its tough ligamentous muscles and close its shell, and is similarly moved to open the shell again when the looming danger has passed. It is delicately sensitive to touch, and the impact of danger against its cold pulpy flesh is communicated at once to the ganglia of the brain.

7   Motionless, the oyster lives and feeds and breathes and begets its kind. The mussels are divided into sexes, and their breeding ways are not signally different from the breeding ways of birds or mammals. There is an ejection of spermatozoa from the genitals of the male, and an intake of the sperm by the genitals of the female. But the oyster is a hermaphrodite. The sex of the oyster is not fixed, but variable. A young oyster is a male which, after discharging its spermatozoa, may at the age of a year be changed into a female, and may then, having spawned, become a male again.

8   Generally it is in midsummer—along the Atlantic coast, at any rate—that the oysters begin to spawn. The oyster's eggs have been held inside its gills and mantle-fold until considerably matured, for the oyster belongs to the tribe of

creatures called ovoviviparous. When, the water temperature having risen to sixty-eight or seventy degrees, the oyster is ready for spawning time, its larval young ones are ejected as little ciliated spheres. Being equipped with cilia—that is to say, with little movable hairlike appendages—they are capable of swimming. They dart quite briskly through the water, often for several days. Fishermen call them spat.

9 The infant oyster remains a swimmer until it encounters some firm rough substance, a stone or piece of shell, to which it can attach itself. Once attached, it begins its slow development toward adult oysterhood, and never moves again. Usually it requires several years, as many as four or five, before its slow motionless maturation brings it to the point where it is ready to be caught and pried apart and served up on a *table d'hôte* as a prime Lynnhaven or blue point.

10 The oyster's immobile, nearly vegetable life is interrupted now and again by attacks of enemies. The oyster has several of these, but two kinds of creature are especially menacing. One of these is the starfish, the grotesque animated pentagon with tubes for feet, which prowls at night over the ocean floor in lumbering search for prey. The starfish is a carnivore, and is particularly attracted by clams and oysters.

11 When a starfish finds an oyster, the oyster at once closes its bivalvular shell for protection, and there begins a slow, soundless contest of strength. The starfish humps itself over the oyster shell, fastening its strong spiny tube-feet to the sides, and pulls. The strength in its cold muscular arms is very great. It pulls steadily, without jerks. Ultimately the long smooth pressure of that pull is greater than the oyster's muscles can withstand; the closed shell is gradually forced open and the soft body exposed. The starfish is ready to make a meal. Slowly it extrudes its stomach and turns the stomach inside out; it thrusts the organ into the opened oyster shell and begins the digestion of its prey.

12 The constant preyings of the starfish are one reason why oysters must be so prodigiously fecund in order to survive. Contests between oyster and starfish always end in one way, with the starfish creeping away, satiated, over the ocean floor, and no single vestige of flesh or muscle adhering to the empty oyster shell. The unevenness of this warfare might long ago have decimated the oyster beds, were oysters less prolific than they are. A single oyster, in a single season, deposits some 50,000,000 eggs.

13 Besides the starfish there is another creature which attacks the oyster—or which, more precisely, invades it, for this second creature is a parasite. It is a kind of tapeworm, which completes its life cycle inside the bodies of two successive fishes and bores its way deep into the oyster's soft interior flesh. As the larval tapeworm invades the oyster's tissues, it must pass the fleshy flap called the oyster's mantle, that part of the oyster which secretes the iridescent lining of its shell. Bits of the living tissue of this mantle adhere to the burrowing worm. By their activity they surround the worm with layer upon layer of

secretion. Ultimately the worm becomes wholly encased, and there is produced the gleaming worm-coffin called a pearl. . . .

14   Oysters are among the simplest and lowest of the beasts. They have no mind, no movement, and very little loveliness. We think of them, mostly, as only a prelude to an excellent dinner, during the season of the months whose names contain an *r*. But oysters, in their fashion, are not undeserving of remark. "In their way," as Stephen Paget put it, "they are quite as wonderful as poets, saints, and men of science."

Apparatus for: Life and Death of an Oyster

Vocabulary: *Using your dictionary, define each of the following words as it appears in context.*

1. "to *assuage* the hurting" (¶ 1) _ease_

2. "sharp *incisors*" (¶ 1) _the cutting teeth_

3. "*gastronomic* rejoicement" (¶ 1) _the art of good ea[ting]_

4. "epicurean *delicacy*" (¶ 2) _luxury_

5. "many *millennia*" (¶ 3) _thousands of yea[rs]_

6. "sun-warmed *estuary*" (¶ 5) _where the tide m[eets] the river current_

7. "soft *motile* palps" (¶ 5) _moveable_

8. "prodigiously *fecund*" (¶ 12) _fruitful in offspr[ing]_

9. "*vestige* of flesh" (¶ 12) _trace_

10. "*decimated* the oyster beds" (¶ 12) _to destroy a la[rge] part of._

Discussion: *Rhetoric*

1. Describe in your own words the arrangement of this essay; that is, what does the author talk about first, second, and so on. Why does he arrange his ideas in this fashion?
2. Notice the different kinds of sentences in the first paragraph. Check the names of these in the inter-chapter.
3. All the paragraphs in this essay are of approximately the same length. Do you think the author should have varied their length? For what purpose?
4. Is the last sentence a natural outgrowth of the preceding sections of the essay? Or is it merely tagged on?
5. What fact or description is memorable in this essay? Why?

1. oyster eaters' home description

2. loose, periodic, balanced

3. ~~scribbled out~~

4. natural outgrowth

5.

Apparatus for: Life and Death of an Oyster

Discussion: *Theme*

1. Why are certain foods and drinks associated with special occasions—for example, champagne at New Year's Eve, turkey at Thanksgiving, and ham at Easter?
2. How do you account for the fact that oysters are considered a delicacy? Do you regard them as such?
3. Explain the following sentence: "For it is the middle month in that season in which the names of all months contain an *r*."
4. Can you think of any other food items that would serve as the subject of an essay similar to this one? List them.

1. _____

_____

2. _____

_____

3. _____

_____

4. _____

_____

Writing Suggestions

1. If you had a pleasant (or unpleasant) experience with a pet during your childhood, relate the effect it had on your life.
2. Trace the history of the idea concerning eating oysters only during the "r" months. Obviously, this topic will require extended library research.
3. Concentrating only on the pearl-making qualities of the oyster, write a theme about the *process*.
4. In an essay similar to "Life and Death of an Oyster," describe the life cycle of a caterpillar.

8. ASK THE MAN WHO DOESN'T OWN ONE*

JOHN KEATS

1   Automobiles, like women, can be fun, but they *are* expensive. Since I sold the family hag to the knacker, I have not only enjoyed the bachelor's irresponsible freedom but have also become the richer by more than $1000 a year. Moreover, instead of one car, I now have a dozen. On hot summer days, I use the convertible to drive to the shore. When taking guests to the theater, I tell the chauffeur when the limousine will be required. For camping trips, the station wagon is most useful. For parties in suburbia, one of the new compacts usually meets the need; but if my wife and I take another couple with us, we use one of the larger sedans. Meanwhile, I change no tires, put on no chains. Someone does this for me, free of charge. Frozen gas lines, insurance premiums, license tags, state inspections, antifreeze, grease jobs, oil, gasoline, car washings, garage bills, battery checks, and front-end adjustments are but dimly remembered nightmares of the past. I now enjoy happy motoring, and not the least of my driving pleasure is the thought that money is piling up in the bank. In brief, I rent.

2   At this point, it must be said that renting is not for everyone. Simple arithmetic shows that owning an automobile can be economically absurd, but no man can experience the joy of not owning an automobile unless he can fill a bill of three particulars. First, he must live in a city adequately served by various rapid, convenient means of transportation; second, he must be tough-minded about automobiles; and third, he must be willing to deny himself nothing.

3   The first point is almost self-evident. Some 65,000 towns in the United States have no public transportation facilities, and their well-being is predicated on the use of private automobiles. Then there is suburbia, where a man's need to own at least one car is apparent. Finally, not all cities, nor even all city neighborhoods, are well enough served by alternate means of transportation to make not owning a car worthwhile.

4   Moreover, if a man does live in an area where taxis, trains, buses, and rented cars are easily had, he is still not ready for non-ownership unless he is willing to regard the automobile merely as an expensive, two-ton mechanical wheelchair that has no excuse for existence unless he is sitting in it, going somewhere. Sports-car addicts, antique-car buffs, and conspicuous consumers get as much sheer pleasure out of owning an automobile as other men derive from showing Rhodesian Ridgebacks or collecting matchbook covers. Some men imagine that there are appreciable differences among the standard brands of American automobiles and regard their purchase of any particular one as an evidence of wisdom. There is no way to convince such people that all of our standard automobiles are almost exactly alike in all important respects except price, although even the automobile dealers will privately admit that this is the case.

5   Still other men are perfectly willing to pay any amount of money for convenience, although they may well not get it. For instance, many a man locked in a line of commuter traffic nevertheless refuses to think of himself as taking part in public transportation, although he sits in a chair in a line of cars just as if he were sitting in a chair on an inbound train. The difference between him and the train rider is that he has to contend with the traffic, while the passenger idly reads the morning paper and arrives in the city sooner. Convenience, worth, and value are therefore all relative terms, but one thing is clear: it is impossible for a man to live without a motorcar if an automobile means anything more to him than a pile of metal that has no importance when not in actual use.

6   In the last analysis, everything turns on the matter of use. The real question is not whether to drive a car, but when to drive one. For instance, a man would be an ass to drive between Philadelphia and New York City, because the trains run every hour during the day, travel faster than anyone can drive while staying out of jail, and are far less expensive than the cost of motoring. Figuring the cost of turnpike and Hudson tube tolls, and a conservative operating cost of 10 cents a mile, the cost of driving round trip from Philadelphia to New York is $21.40. The round-trip train fare is $8.60.

7   Obviously, the only time it is economical to drive is when a man is carrying passengers for whose train fare he would otherwise be responsible. If I were to take my wife and three children to Manhattan by the least expensive means, I would rent a car and save $21.60 on the price of the train tickets. To consider the cost per passenger mile may sound like haggling, but I prefer to regard it

as being practical. An automobile is the most expensive means of transportation known to man when it contains only the driver—as it usually does.

8 Moreover, at all times that the thing is not in motion, it sits quietly rotting at the curb, running up the bill that represents the cost of aging. When a city man first rids himself of his car, he is likely to think of how much he will save by going nowhere he cannot walk. With masochistic happiness, he jams himself into cheap, crowded buses instead of sensibly hailing expensive taxicabs. This is false economy and defeats the whole purpose of not owning a car. Care must be taken to ensure that non-ownership increases, rather than decreases, the standard of living, if a genuine sense of freedom is to ensue. The rule is, use the most practical, comfortable, and convenient means of transportation to go wherever need or whim commands; if a taxi represents the best way to ply between points A and B, then hail a cab. It is perfectly possible to splurge and save.

9 In these matters, I speak from an experience that began when my station wagon developed a fatal case of cylinder pox. I was grousing to myself about the necessity for buying a new one when a ghostly voice asked, "Why?"

10 "Because you can't live in the automobile age without an automobile," I muttered to myself.

11 Then I remembered a fragment of conversation. A friend had said that one of the reasons he had moved back to the city from the suburbs was to save $2000 a year by getting rid of his two cars, and I began to wonder how much it was costing me to keep my car. The family ledgers showed that I had paid $2604.50 cash for the thing five years earlier. The wagon was now worth precisely $50 as junk, unless I repaired it. If I put the necessary $300 into a new engine, the car would bring $350, at most, as a trade-in, less than that on the used-car market. Depreciation over the last five years had therefore been $520.90 a year. During the twelve months past, I had spent $545 for gasoline and $285.33 for insurance premiums, license fees, repairs, grease, and oil. Unfortunately, I had no record of parking, toll bridge, and turnpike fees, but a conservative estimate for the sake of arriving at a round number was $10.

12 Thus, I estimated it had cost me $1361.23 to own and operate the station wagon in Philadelphia for the year just ended. Checking through accounts dating to the car's purchase, I found it had cost at least $6295.57 to own the car for five years, an average cost of $1259.11 per year.

13 On the other hand, I had driven the thing 60,000 miles, and could therefore consider the cost of ownership to be 10.49 cents per mile, which did not seem an exorbitant price to pay for both transportation and convenience. I went wearily off to bed thinking that my friend must have said that he *spent* $2000 a year to keep two cars.

14 Yet, it was hard to dismiss the notion that a $2600 car could wind up cost-

ing a man $6300 at the end of five years, and the following morning I started poking into automotive statistics. It turned out that the national average annual cost of owning and operating a $2300 automobile was exactly 10.49 cents per mile. The annual average cost of owning a $2400 automobile in Philadelphia was $1215; in New York the figure was $500 higher; in Chicago the cost was more than $1900 a year; and in Los Angeles the average man was spending nearly $2000 to keep up his car, although he probably had no idea where his money was going. Other statistics were even more interesting. A Chicago businessman reported savings of $1000 a year from selling his car and taking taxis and renting cars instead. His bill came to $900 for transportation, and he had used cabs daily and had rented cars on sixteen occasions, in addition to renting one for a two-week vacation. In New York City, a man who reported an annual owning cost of $1771 discovered that non-owning saved him $551 a year, even though he had rented a car every day at hourly rates.

15   At this point, I began to think there might have been something in what my friend was saying. But I was not yet ready to tell the repairman what to do about my station wagon. I first made up a deliberate exaggeration of my family's need for mobility. It included 1000 taxi rides at $1 each; 100 days of auto rentals at a rate of $10 a day and 10 cents a mile for 50 miles each day; 3650 trips on the commuter train to center city; and five round trips to Canada in a rented car, just for good measure. This was a five-year figure, and the cost of all this hypothetical transportation totaled $380 less than we had actually paid to run our car. Whereupon I put down my pencil, went to the nearest telephone, and told the repairman where he could shove that new engine.

16   During the next carless days, I went through the stage of sneering happily at the sound of wheels spinning helplessly on ice, of laughing at the gasoline and automobile advertisements, of feeling smug as I looked down from the commuter train on the line of beetles creeping along what is lugubriously called the Expressway. But all this was whistling in the dark, because not having a car was proving to be far more inconvenient than I had imagined it would. There were times when the rental agency said, Sorry, we don't have a car for you today. There were times when the trains ran late, when I couldn't get a cab, when buses seemed to run only in the rain. At such times it was difficult to remember when the family car had been laid up for repairs, or stuck in hot traffic with its radiator boiling over, or the hours I spent lying in the slush, fitting on chains. It was not until the end of the first carless year that I was able to understand that the inconvenience of owning a bar balanced—at least, for me—the inconvenience of not owning one.

17   Meanwhile, a change came over the family, for not having a car led us to make choices, instead of sliding along the paths of least resistance. The rule to deny ourselves nothing was predicated on two questions: is this trip necessary, and how do we get there? Driving to the shore, for example, had never been a matter for second thought when we had the station wagon. But now we

paused. Was going to the shore what we most wanted to do? If so, we hired a car and went. When we did, we enjoyed the sea in a way we had never enjoyed it when we took going to the beach for granted. If we did not go, it was only because we had discovered something else we would rather do. In either event, we added something to what we did—the quality of conscious choice.

18 We also began to walk. When we had a car, it had not occurred to us that most of our daily business could be carried out much more rapidly and far more conveniently on foot than by automobile. My wife, for instance, had always taken the car to the supermarket, although the supermarket is little more than a block away. She had imagined it was quicker, which was not the case. She imagined it was easier to load the grub into the back seat and drive it home than to push it home in a shopping cart. That, too, was a wrong idea. At rush hours, I found I could walk from office to train far more rapidly than any taxi could push through the traffic. The children had always walked to school, six blocks away.

19 I had wondered how we had managed to roll up 12,000 miles a year, and now I knew; we had used the car for innumerable short hauls around the city, in the course of daily living, and this was one reason for the burned-out engine. For, as any mechanic will testify, start-and-stop city traffic takes more out of a car than the equivalent number of turnpike miles. I will not pretend that walking is always great fun, or that it is always convenient or practical. But if you walk when it is convenient and take a cab when it isn't, you cover the same ground just as efficaciously as if you traveled those miles in your car. And it is far less expensive.

20 We turned to an auto rental agency whenever it made good sense to drive. Once, when the need arose, we became a two-car family, and I assure you it is a far better thing to operate two cars for a day than to own two cars for a year. Moreover, it is a distinct advantage to be able to rent the type of automobile suited to the need, rather than have to make one automobile serve all needs. The crucial advantage in renting, however, is that you pay for transportation only when you are actually being transported. High as rental cost is, it is still far cheaper to pay for an automobile when you use one than it is to own an automobile that is sometimes in motion but is often parked.

21 These advantages are apparent to an increasing number of city residents, as the rental agencies' books show. One large rental corporation reports that residential renting is the fastest-growing area of its business. It is not referring to those who, arriving in town by plane, thereupon rent a car in the city. It refers to rentals within city neighborhoods to city residents. Before World War II such rentals were virtually nonexistent. Today they total more than $4 million a year in this one company alone, and the growth curve leads the company to predict that the figure will reach $20 million by 1965. Looking at the curve, one corporate executive exclaimed, "We may be on the verge of a revolution in urban living!"

22   "Revolution" is doubtless a strong word, but the trend to non-ownership of automobiles is so marked that Detroit manufacturers are now competing for fleet sales to car-leasing agencies. This is not something the manufacturers like to discuss in public, although some Detroit executives privately predict the day will come when no one will own the car he drives. Even now, they say, most of the cars on the highway are not privately owned. They are rented cars, or company cars, or fleet cars leased by companies, or unpaid-for automobiles that still belong to finance companies. Leasing plans have appeared whereby dealers rent new cars to customers on a yearly basis. In return for a monthly sum, the dealer pays all costs of maintenance, including gas and oil. At the end of the year, the old car is turned in and the client leases a new one.

23   Simple arithmetic, rather than considerations of status, led me into the paths of non-ownership. I was therefore surprised to hear a man say, "The guy with more status than anybody is the guy who can afford not to have a car." There is no reason why this should even be imagined. My anticipated saving of $380 over five years was actually in error. I had expected it to be wrong because I had deliberately exaggerated our transportation needs, but not until the end of the first year did I realize how wildly I had exaggerated them. The cost of public transportation and rented cars came to $216.20. Possibly we did not indulge ourselves enough. In any event, the first year of being without a car saved me precisely $1145.03 over what it had cost to own my station wagon the year before, without any loss of necessary mobility.

24   It would be unfair to maintain that all was peaches and cream, however, or to suggest that all city neighborhoods are as filled with goods and services within easy walking distance as our own. There are plenty of Philadelphia neighborhoods that are fairly remote from a variety of means of transportation, and fairly remote from shopping centers as well. In such neighborhoods, own-ership of an automobile is as necessary as it is in suburbia. And certainly, it was often inconvenient for me to be without a car, although the $1145.03 in the bank more than compensated for the inconvenience. Another man, of course, might enjoy fussing over his automobile and think it well worthwhile to pay an additional thousand dollars a year to have his private car always ready at his door. I suppose value is always in the eye of the beholder, but I haven't the time to pursue that philosophical notion here. I must run off to see a travel agent. He is going to tell me how far $1145.03 will go toward a winter vaca-tion in Jamaica.

Apparatus for: Ask the Man Who Doesn't Own One

Vocabulary: *Find a word in the paragraph that means the following:*

1. based (¶ 3)   PREDICATED

2. quibbling (¶ 7)   hAGGliNG

3. pleasure from suffering (¶ 8)   mAsochisti

4. grumbling (¶ 9)   grousing

5. freedom of movement (¶ 15)   mobility

6. very sadly (¶ 16)   lagubriously

7. efficiently (¶ 19)   EFFiCACIOUS

Discussion: *Rhetoric*

1. Why does the author begin his essay with the question, "Automobiles, like women, can be fun, but they *are* expensive"?
2. Comment on the length and variety of the last three sentences of the first paragraph. Find at least four other paragraphs in which effective use is made of sentence variety.
3. How does the author achieve credibility? That is, how does the detailed account of his experiences with non-ownership relate to people in general?
4. Notice that throughout the essay the writer makes references to persons and situations different from his own. What effect does this have?

1. He compares non ownership of a car to being a bachelor

2. _____

3. He is an average man.

4. To show his point is not perfect for all people.

Apparatus for: Ask the Man Who Doesn't Own One

Discussion: *Theme*

1. Do you think it would be possible for you to get along without a car? Explain.
2. This essay was written in 1962. Have any of the predictions come true?
3. Would the rewards of non-ownership be worth the inconvenience for you? Why or why not?

1. _____

    _____

2. _____

    _____

3. _____

    _____

Writing Suggestions

1. Splurge and Save—or Rent, Don't Buy
2. If you own a car, figure your own cost (see paragraph 11) and write it up as a presentation of "necessary spending."
3. The Automobile: Invention of the Devil
4. The Effect of the Automobile on Teen-age Morals
5. What does the automobile symbolize to you? Is it merely a means of transportation?

9. PLEASE DON'T BITE THE POLITICIANS *

JOHN FISCHER

1   This is a plea for tolerance toward our most misunderstood minority: the professional politicians.

2   No other group in America is the butt of so much suspicion, ridicule, and contempt. All kinds of opinion-makers, from editorial writers to night-club comics—people who would never dream of insulting a Negro, Jew, Catholic, or Paiute Indian—delight in slipping their daily needle of sarcasm into the politician. They have even invented a derisive name for him: The Pol.

3   The hard feeling will reach its peak this month, as it does at the close of every Presidential election. Countless people who ordinarily have nothing to do with politics will wake up on November 9 disappointed, angry, and probably overhung. And not only the losers. Many a member of the winning party will have a sour bellyful of disillusionment about the way his Peerless Leaders (from ward chairman to Presidential candidate) handled the campaign. Bitterest of all will be the amateur politicians—the volunteers who have been working for the last four months in uneasy harness with the pros. Most of them will finger their collar-galls on post-election morning and reflect that their worst suspicions are now confirmed.

4   A case in point is an idealistic young artist, whose cartoons probably are familiar to most of you. Recently he developed a deep concern for politics. He wakes up at 3:00 A.M. to worry about Peace; he believes that all men are brothers, especially if they are brown, black, or yellow; he yearns, quite sin-

* "Please Don't Bite the Politicians," from *The Stupidity Problem and Other Harassments,* by John Fischer. Copyright © 1960 by John Fischer. Reprinted by permission of Harper & Row, Publishers.

cerely, to help the poor and oppressed everywhere. So he has been trying to Do Something About It by working with the Democratic club in his Greenwich Village election district.

5   A few weeks ago he showed me a series of cartoons he had just finished about "typical politicians." They emerged as wonderfully funny but sinister buffoons—both sly and stupid, corrupt, hog rich, and all callously indifferent to the Big Issues such as hunger in Asia and The Bomb.

6   This view distressed me because: (a) it is so similar to the conclusions reached by many earnest amateurs after their first contact with practical politicians; (b) it is wildly unfair and inaccurate; (c) it is dangerous. Unless ordinary citizens understand—and respect—the processes of political life, our society isn't going to work very well. And it is inconsistent (it seems to me) for anyone to be so passionate about democracy and yet so cynical about the instruments through which democracy has to work.

7   It also distressed me because I like politicians. Ever since I started work as a city-hall reporter in New Mexico some thirty years ago. I have spent a lot of time in their company—in smoke-filled rooms, jails, campaign trains, shabby courthouse offices, Senate cloakrooms, and the White House itself. Mostly I've been reporting their doings, but on occasion I have served them as speech writer, district leader, campaign choreboy, and civil servant. On the whole, they have proved better company than any other professional group I've had a chance to know well—including writers, soldiers, businessmen, doctors, and academics. Drunk or sober, they are amusing fellows. Their view of human nature is acute, unromantic, and good humored. They are as sensitive as coloratura sopranos. Few of them have much capacity for malice, and except when making speeches they are seldom bores.

8   On the average, moreover, they have seemed to me at least as honest, dedicated, and idealistic as the main run of Americans—including the fastidious who shrink away from the "dirtiness" of politics.

9   No doubt the politicians are themselves partly to blame for the blotchy image of their profession in the public mind. But the rest of us, I think, are more at fault. In our lazy way, we find it easier to accept the cartoonist's caricature than to take the trouble to look at the politician as a breathing, complex human being. And all too often we try (maybe unwittingly) to push him into the mold of the caricature.

10   A realistic portrait of the typical politician would have to begin with his motives. Why is he in this business?

11   Not for money. I have never known a man who got rich out of politics. I have known many who got poor. Nearly all of those who are reasonably competent could have done better financially in some other line of work. It is true that a good deal of money passes through their hands—politics has become

an outrageously expensive business in this country—but, all legends to the contrary, not much of it sticks.

12 Most wealthy politicians either inherited their bank roll (like Kennedy and Rockefeller) or married it (like Senator Lyndon Johnson) or made it earlier in another trade (like Benton and Bowles). Many have sidelines which thrive on political connections—most commonly the law, insurance, contracting, and broadcasting. Nevertheless a political career is quite likely to drain more dollars out of the bank account than it feeds in.

13 My guess is that people usually turn to politics for the same reason actors seek the stage. They need applause.

14 Like the theatre, politics is a great nourisher of egos. It attracts men who are hungry for attention, for assurance that somebody loves them, for the soul-stirring music of their own voices. (Political speeches are not invariably made because the public craves wisdom, but oftener just because politicians love to talk—even when their only audience is other politicians. Note how hard it is for the chairman to throttle down the oratory at that lowliest of all political gatherings, a meeting of precinct leaders.) A main ingredient in the make-up of every successful politician is a thick slice of ham.

15 It follows that politicians, like actors and prima donnas, are abnormally sensitive to slights. For hundreds of political infantrymen, "recognition" is their only reward. They treasure the right to sit at the speaker's table at a fund-raising dinner, to be consulted before the governor schedules a speech in their baili-wick, to ride a few miles on the train of a whistle-stopping Presidential candi-date. Above all they dote on giving advice. The late Tammany boss, Ed Flynn, once remarked that his most tiresome chore was listening to his henchmen report—at interminable length—on "conditions" in their districts. The strategy they suggested, he said, was almost always either obvious or silly; but he had to hear them out. For any affront to their self-esteem could make a mortal enemy.†

16 But vanity alone by no means explains the politician. While I have long since learned that I am not competent to disentangle anybody's mixed motives (including my own), I strongly suspect that most pros are as much moved by a sense of duty as by their thirst for status. If politics is balm for tender egos, it is equally soothing to the inflamed superego. Perhaps more than most people, politicians are prodded by conscience. Certainly the best of them sincerely feel an obligation to perform a public service. And this, I think, is true at all levels —from the housewife who spends her evenings ringing doorbells and compiling

† Sometimes of course this longing for dignity and recognition can degenerate into a simple lust for power. The extreme cases in modern times probably were Huey Long and Joe McCarthy, who seemed to get a sadistic pleasure out of kicking other people. But they represent the pathology of politics; both were products of abnormal times. When our body politic is functioning normally, it usually sloughs off such malignant types before they can do much damage.

card files, up to men like the late Senator George Norris or Mayor Fiorello La Guardia. Both of these were as truly noble characters as anybody you can find in Plutarch.

17   A third motive is usually present too: the fun of the game. Nearly every skillful politician I have ever met enjoyed the subtleties and excitements of his craft just as a tennis player enjoys a well-played match. Perhaps a better analogy is chess—a kind of chess played with thousands of pieces, each different and every one likely to start charging around the board on his own at any moment; demanding luck as well as art; and offering to the winners the highest of stakes, and to a loser oblivion.

18   If the average politician is, as I believe, a reasonably decent man, why does he have such a bad name?

19   This isn't a new problem. As Joyce Cary has pointed out, "almost every great statesman has been described as a crook. Metternich, Cavour, Bismarck, Gladstone, Disraeli, Lloyd George, Roosevelt: history is made up of names at which the moralist holds his nose."

20   Ever since Pericles, the basic indictment has been dishonesty. This can include two counts: (a) he steals money; (b) he is intellectually dishonest—a hypocrite, a trimmer, a promiser of things he can't deliver.

21   How far can these charges be sustained?

22   It certainly can't be denied that some politicians are common thieves. Almost every week the papers report some officeholder whose hand was out for a mink coat, a free vacation trip, or cold cash. I have never seen any evidence, however, that the percentage of petty chiselers is any higher in politics than in any other profession.

23   All of us know of salesmen who pad their expense accounts, business executives who demand kickbacks from their suppliers, doctors who will split a fee, union officers with sticky fingers, disc jockeys who welcome a little payola. The real difference is that the sharp operators in private life seldom break into the news. The politician is under closer scrutiny, and when he is caught with his hand in the till, his partisan rivals make sure that everybody hears about it. A fair verdict on this count, it seems to me, ought to read: Sometimes guilty, but probably no oftener than anybody else.

24   But what about the politician who takes money, not for personal enrichment, but to finance his political career? This is far more common—indeed almost universal. Campaigns cost plenty; so, unless we want to limit public office to rich men, somebody has to put up the cash.

25   At this point the moral distinctions get pretty tricky. Everybody would agree that it is wicked for a candidate to take a contribution from someone who expects a special favor in return—a gambler who wants immunity from arrest,

or a contractor after that new highway job. On the other hand, if the contributor doesn't expect a specific *quid pro quo,* then most people seem to think his money is clean enough. At least so one gathers from the public reaction to Richard M. Nixon's famous Checkers speech, in which he justified accepting $18,000 from wealthy friends on grounds that none of them "ever received any consideration that he would not have received as an ordinary constituent."

26   All they had been promised—according to Dana Smith, who solicited the fund—was that Nixon would "continue to sell effectively . . . the economic and political systems which we all believe in." Presumably that meant lower taxes and a favorable climate for business. But suppose a candidate honestly believes in higher taxes, and a favorable climate for trade unions? Is it then all right for him to take money from union leaders? And how do you judge those Texas Congressmen who are largely financed by oil men desperately eager to protect their special tax privileges?

27   Among such cases, and many others even more shadowy, I don't see how anybody can draw a clear moral line. Ideally, of course, every campaign should be financed only by small contributions from patriotic citizens who expect nothing in return except good government. But these are about as rare as whooping cranes. It is this stinginess—of which we are nearly all guilty—that makes the candidate seek his funds from dubious sources; and it is in this way that we force him closer to conforming to that unjust caricature of The Typical Politician.

28   If we really wanted to mend matters, we could do two things. Individual citizens might become a lot more generous, and disinterested, in making political contributions. Or we might start financing campaigns out of the public treasury, as the late Senator Richard Neuberger suggested. At the moment, both courses sound utopian. So long, however, as we prefer to leave things as they are, it hardly becomes us to point scornful fingers at the politicians.

29   A fair verdict on this charge, then, might read: Guilt, if any, is usually due to circumstances beyond his control.

30   The amateurs in politics may grant all this, and still argue that the professional is an intellectual fraud. What makes their peeve worse is the suspicion (often well founded) that the pro doesn't quite trust them, or wholly welcome their volunteer help.

31   Let's see how this painful situation looks from the viewpoint of a small-time professional: for example, a ward leader.

32   For the last four years (and for several quadrenniums before that) he has drudged away at the dull, necessary chores—seeing that newcomers to the ward get registered, hunting likely candidates for the town council, directing widows to the Social Security office, raising money to pay the clubhouse rent. Few amateurs have ever volunteered to help. But now that a Presidential campaign

has rolled around, they pour in, eager for the fun and busting their seams with enthusiasm. Can you blame him for feeling that they want to eat the icing off the cake he has been baking for so long?

33   But he stifles this resentment and sets them to work running the mimeograph or answering the telephone. A few (usually women) do well; some get bored after a few days and disappear. Still others feel insulted; they didn't come for this sort of scullery work. What they want is to make speeches, counsel candidates, devise strategy—in short, to take over the old pro's job.

34   With what tact he can dredge up, he dissuades them—and not merely to protect his selfish clutch on the levers of power. How to explain that he can't trust them with such assignments? They simply don't know the delicate network of personal relationships which holds the ward together. Being ignorant of the faces that have to be saved, the egos that require an extra oil massage, the ancient local enmities that must be respected, they might tear apart overnight the organization he has been knitting for decades.

35   Besides, these amateurs are mostly idealists, each dedicated to a Cause. To some, racial justice is the most important issue in the world. Others feel just as strongly about penal reform or Zionism, housing or the United Nations. Each expects the ward leader to share this burning devotion, to the exclusion of practically everything else.

36   God knows he tries. He hates racial discrimination as much as anybody, and besides he has twenty-three Negro families in the north end of the ward. But on the East Side he also has a bunch of Poles who don't like either Negroes or Jews; they seem to spend most of their time loathing Russia, and incidentally the United Nations, which tolerates Soviet membership. None of them gives a damn about penal reform, except old Mrs. Kruszwica who has two sons in the state penitentiary. Both Poles and Negroes like low-rent housing, though; maybe they can be pulled together on that, if the other issues are soft-pedaled enough. . . . The real-estate men won't like it, of course, and neither will a couple of good contributors who worry a lot about high taxes. . . .

37   So his thoughts run, through a hundred other remembrances of his constituents' desires, antipathies, and conflicts. After all, his first job is to carry the ward in November. And that he can never do if he comes out with a ringing, clear-cut declaration on every cause which his amateur helpers hold so dear. Indeed, he has to muffle *their* enthusiasm when it gets too strident. Heavenly as their motives may be, he just can't afford to let these angels rush in where any experienced fool would fear to tread.

38   As a consequence, a lot of volunteers will conclude before election day (as my artist friend did) that the old pro is a man of no convictions. He has been lukewarm about their pet issues. He has evaded uncompromising pledges wherever he could. Sometimes his speeches sounded weaselly, as if he hoped

two opposing groups might interpret them in different ways. And how about those rumors that he accepted a campaign contribution from a big realtor? Isn't it plain enough that he is guilty of the grossest kind of intellectual dishonesty?

39   Not to me, it isn't. For my money he looks like a good man, doing a job which is indispensable in any democracy and doing it just as honestly as he knows how. I think he deserves a lot more respect than he usually gets.

40   If you happen to be the other kind of amateur in politics—one of those who have developed some appreciation of the professionals—and if you in turn would like to gain their affection and trust, here is a simple recipe.

41   Go down to your local party headquarters on the morning after the election. It will reek of stale tobacco smoke, mimeograph ink, and cold coffee dregs. Chances are nobody will be there except the ward leader. He will be as tired as a man can get, but he will be making a limp effort to clean up the joint. Help him sweep up the crumpled Dixie Cups, the trampled cigarette butts, and discarded campaign leaflets. Pick up about a million scraps of paper covered with penciled figures; nearly all the people who jammed the room last night were jotting down returns as they came in over a battery of telephones, and doing hasty sums in an effort to convince themselves that we might win yet, if the boys in the third precinct roll up a bigger majority than expected. (They didn't.) Fold up the rented chairs that have to be returned to an undertaking parlor. Call the phone company and tell them to take out the extra phones, and that, yes, the overdue bill will be paid in a day or two.

42   When the worst of the mess is scraped away, offer the old pro five dollars to help cover the campaign deficit. (There's always a deficit.) If he doesn't drop dead from astonishment, he will be your friend for life. For, in all probability, you will be the first volunteer who has ever given him any help *after* an election. And it could be that you have just taken the first step toward becoming a pro yourself.

Apparatus for: Please Don't Bite the Politicians

Vocabulary: *Using your dictionary, give the etymology of the following words.*

1. sarcasm (¶ 2)   SArCASmOS   SPEAK BiTT

2. derisive (¶ 2)   _____

3. callously (¶ 5)   ~~callose~~ = cAllosus - cAllo s·

4. fastidious (¶ 8)   fAST iDiOUSUS - DiSDAiN

5. bailiwick (¶ 15)   Old English - villAge

6. oblivion (¶ 17)   oblivio - TO forGET

7. dubious (¶ 27)   DUBiOSUS - DOUBT

8. antipathies (¶ 37)   AN TiPATHEiA - tosuff

9. strident (¶ 37)   STriDEnS - TO mAKE A GrAT··
                        or CrEAKiN

10. deficit (¶ 42)   DEfiCErE - iT iS wAn +

Discussion: *Rhetoric*

1. This essay makes good use of sentence variety; notice, for example, paragraphs 2, 10, and 13. Point out other paragraphs that combine several kinds of sentences.
2. The first sentence of the essay announces the author's reason for writing: ". . . plea for tolerance toward . . . politicians." How does he develop this "plea"?
3. Why does Fischer punctuate "And not only the losers" (paragraph 3) as a sentence? Find similar examples.
4. How does the author use *better* in paragraph 7? Is this word used in the usual sense?
5. Paragraph 10 begins the main body of the essay. Where does this section end?
6. What kind of evidence does the author use to persuade the reader that politicians are honest, honorable men?

1. _____

_____

2. Shows how politicians are human

3. To show emphasis on not on the "losers"

4. ¶ 11

_____

5. more interesting, more human no. (¶3)

6. He says the pros are humane but there are many amateurs.

114

Apparatus for: Please Don't Bite the Politicians

Discussion: *Theme*

1. What is the attitude of Fischer toward politicians? Do you share his attitude?
2. Are you worried about persons who ridicule politicians? See paragraph 6 for the author's views.
3. Is it enough to expect politicians to be merely as good as the "average" man? See paragraphs 8, 22, and 23.
4. In paragraph 27, the author says that no clear moral lines can be drawn concerning political contributions. Do you agree? Why or why not?
5. On what does Fischer base his arguments? Does he submit evidence, or merely opinions?

1. _____

_____

2. _____

_____

3. _____

_____

4. _____

_____

5. _____

_____

Writing Suggestions

1. Describe your favorite politician. Make clear the reasons for your admiration.
2. What is your attitude toward politicians? Cite specific reasons for thinking as you do.
3. Explain the difference between a *politician* and a *statesman*.
4. Evaluate the process by which a party platform is formed.
5. Consider the following topic: "Political Parties Are Unnecessary."

VI. PARAGRAPH DEVELOPMENT: THE TOPIC SENTENCE

The building block of writing is the well-developed paragraph. Good paragraphs make reading physically easier because the page of print is broken into segments; they help the reader follow the pattern of thought more closely because they treat one segment of an idea at a time; and they help the writer develop his ideas more clearly.

Especially in exposition and argumentation, the paragraph is a unit of thought, with its own integrity; but it is also closely related to the paragraphs before and after it. When we say *integrity,* we mean that a paragraph is a unit by itself, yet contributes to the whole paper. A brick, for example, is a simple piece of building material; yet it is used to make a wall or a house. So is the paragraph used to build an essay or story.

A paragraph is developed around a topic sentence. The topic sentence contains the main idea of the paragraph; the other sentences support or explain it. In exposition and argumentation, the topic sentence is usually clearly stated. But even when the topic sentence is merely implied, as is often the case in narrative or descriptive writing, the reader should be able to pick up the main idea from it.

The following paragraph, taken from "Maps and Territories" by S. I. Hayakawa, is an excellent example of a paragraph that begins with a topic sentence.

There is a sense in which we all live in two worlds. First, we live in the world of happenings which we know at firsthand. This is an extremely small world, consisting only of that continuum of the things that we have actually seen, felt, or heard—the flow of events constantly passing before our senses. So far as this world of personal experience is concerned, Africa, South America, Asia, Washington, New York, or Los Angeles do not exist if we have never been to these places. Jomo Kenyetta is only a name if we have never seen him. When we ask ourselves how much we know at firsthand, we discover that we know very little indeed.

A paragraph should develop the one idea stated in its topic sentence. In this sense, the topic sentence is a small version of the thesis sentence of the entire essay. Indeed, the paragraph itself is a miniature theme; both have a beginning, middle, and end. In the following paragraph, taken from Paul Giddens' essay "The Scramble for College Athletes," notice that the topic sentence introduces the single idea that controls the remainder of the paragraph.

> I have always maintained that college athletics exist primarily for the enjoyment and benefit of students who wish to participate in them, and they should be conducted as an integral part of the educational program. The same is true of all other extracurricular activities—choir, band, student publications, debate, dramatics—which supplement formal classroom learning. They provide outlets for learning by doing, and they contribute to the development of students' special talents and skills. There is little or no justification, educationally speaking, for maintaining intercollegiate athletics, except for the benefit of the players.

Notice that the last sentence of the paragraph restates the first, and adds a new dimension to the basic idea.

Topic sentences should be as direct as possible. In being direct and clear, the topic sentence is an aid to both the writer and the reader. The following paragraph, from "The Peace Corps Volunteer Returns," by David Pearson, begins with a direct statement.

> When the Peace Corps was started early in 1961, a hue and cry was raised by several prominent educators who worried that this new organization would rob America of its teachers. Not only did their fears prove unfounded, but they got a big bonus. Of the first 1,000 volunteers who went overseas, roughly 13 per cent had some prior teaching experience. Today 26 per cent of the first 1,000 returning PCVs have indicated they will follow a teaching career after service.

We have seen that the topic sentence should be supported by the other sentences in the paragraph. The most important ways to give support to a topic sentence, and therefore develop paragraphs, are as follows:

1. amplify by use of details
2. illustrate or give examples
3. compare or contrast
4. show cause and effect
5. give a definition
6. supply reason and evidence

These methods of development are treated in detail throughout the various chapters in this text.

We stated earlier that all paragraphs have a reason for being. The topic sentence is a formal statement of that reason. This statement can be anywhere in the paragraph: beginning, middle, or end. In description and narration, however, the topic sentence is often merely implied. The paragraph by Paul Giddens quoted above is an example of a paragraph that has a topic sentence at the beginning, and a restatement at the end. Here is another example of a paragraph with the topic sentence stated first. (It is taken from the January, 1967 issue of *Changing Times.*)

> Broadcasters are in hot water again over TV ratings. Industry watchdogs charge that the practice of "hypoing" ratings is widespread and getting worse, thus making it impossible for advertisers to know how big an audience stations and programs normally draw. They say it's done this way: A producer finds out when his area is to get a TV audience check. He then schedules a contest or a prize giveaway—anything that will induce listeners to tune in to the station when the survey is to be made. When the ratings are issued, the station or program comes out on top and, presumably, advertisers flock to buy time. Critics charge that the practice can be highly misleading, but thus far neither the National Association of Broadcasters, the rating services nor government agencies know how to squelch it or how to control it.

The topic sentence in the following descriptive paragraph is merely implied, but it is clear. Phrase the topic sentence for yourself after reading the paragraph. (It is taken from *Brave Men,* by Ernie Pyle.)

> The first planes of the mass onslaught came over a little before 10 A.M. They were the fighters and dive bombers. The main road, running crosswise in front of us, was their bomb line. They were to bomb only on the far side of that road. Our kick-off infantry had been pulled back a few hundred yards from the near side of the road. Everyone in the area had been given the strictest orders to be in foxholes, for high-level bombers can, and do, quite excusably, make mistakes.

For a final example of a good paragraph containing a clear topic sentence at the beginning and a restatement at the end, supported by details and examples, here is a selection from Henry David Thoreau's *Walden:*

> Society is commonly too cheap. We meet at very short intervals, not having had time to acquire any new value for each other. We meet at meals three times a day, and give each other a new taste of that old musty cheese that we are. We have had to agree on a certain set of rules, called etiquette and politeness, to make this frequent meeting tolerable and that we need not come to open war. We meet at the post-office, and at the sociable, and about the fireside every night; we live thick and are in each other's way, and stumble over one another, and I think that we thus lose some respect for one another. Certainly less frequency would suffice for all important and hearty communications. Consider the girls in a factory—never alone, hardly in their dreams. It would be better if there were but one inhabitant to a square mile, as where I live. The value of a man is not in his skin, that we should touch him.

Topic sentences serve both the writer and the reader in many ways. They help eliminate unneeded details or random thoughts; they serve to create unity; and they aid in holding the reader's attention. In short, they keep the writer *and* the reader pointed in the right direction.

10. HOW GOOD ARE AMERICAN CARS? *

JOHN R. BOND

1 American cars are highly prized, greatly respected throughout Europe, where competition is extremely keen. Our cars cost anywhere from 50 to 150 percent more there than at home because of duties and discriminatory levies, yet 144,510 American passenger cars were exported in 1963.

2 Why are our cars so popular overseas? Because they run and run and run. Our engines use little oil and ordinarily need no major repairs for at least 50,000 miles, usually much more. The chassis components stand up better than overseas products on bad roads. The bodies do not rattle or corrode. A well-used American car with 100,000 miles on the odometer will still bring a fantastic price—in other lands.

3 Durability and reliability are taken for granted by the American consumer. This circumstance explains why, with the single exception of the Volkswagen, the American public has become so disenchanted with the small imported car. Many of the latter proved to be economical on fuel, but not so economical when repair charges and depreciation were added up at the end of two or three years.

4 Today every American car manufacturer has a large engineering department and extensive acreage devoted to proving grounds. The auto companies have found, sometimes through sad experience, that it is cheaper to test a new design exhaustively than to produce a relatively untried model and face expensive service problems or corrections in the field.

5 A combined total of a million miles or more of testing is virtually standard

* John R. Bond, "How Good Are American Cars?" Reprinted from *The Atlantic Monthly,* July 1965. Copyright © 1965, by The Atlantic Monthly Company, Boston, Mass. Reprinted with permission.

procedure before any new model is introduced. A typical example is Rambler's all-new six-cylinder engine, announced in mid-1964. One test car with the new engine racked up 107,000 miles with no major attention except routine maintenance. At that mileage the oil consumption was still less than one quart per thousand miles.

6 An interesting sidelight of this particular Rambler test was that the company used off-duty Chicago policemen for drivers. American Motors' engineers stated that their regular test drivers notice incipient malfunctions and report them for correction. Policemen drive like most ordinary people and keep going till the car quits. In all, AMC built ten experimental test engines (very expensive) and logged 2 million miles on these and pilot production-line samples.

7 Tests were run also at such diverse places as Phoenix, Arizona, and Bemidji, Minnesota. More than 15,000 hours were logged on dynamometer testing in Kenosha and Detroit.

8 Such thorough procedures as those described for AMC's Rambler "232" engine are not at all unusual; they are typical throughout the American automotive industry. Equally important, such testing is not confined to the power plant.

9 The seats in a five-year-old car, for example, do not fall to pieces as they did before the war. Why not? Every major auto manufacturer in the United States has an extensive testing laboratory, filled with strange and weird-looking machines. Seats are tested by a machine which forces a wooden model of a derriere into the cushion a given distance, then releases it. The process is repeated every three seconds and continues for a million cycles (if nothing fails). Spring sag, spring breakage, and upholstery durability are evaluated accurately.

10 These laboratories perform several functions. Their first and most obvious duty is to test newly designed components for function and durability before production commences. A second duty is to test items submitted by outside suppliers. A simple stoplight switch is a good example. Samples submitted for approval must pass a test of one million cycles without failure. Once a supplier is selected he must expect further checks on the quality of his product; such tests as are required are a continuous process on a spot-check basis. It is not unusual for an entire shipment from a supplier to be turned down because half of a batch of twenty samples failed prematurely.

11 Laboratory tests are of course an important adjunct to the normal road-test program. A shock absorber that will stand up for 500,000 cycles within a week in the laboratory will probably outlast the car in normal use. Engineers call this accelerated testing, and talk of correlation between lab and road tests. Testing procedures are developed so that a week in the laboratory is equivalent to five years or more on the road. This saves time and money—especially important in an industry which has new models almost every year.

12   No part of the car is too small or too insignificant to escape the laboratory. The outside rear-view mirror is a good case in point, and here is a brief outline of the procedure used by the Ford Motor Company.

13   Sample mirrors are given a ninety-six-hour salt-spray bath to test for plating quality. Other samples get a sixteen-hour corrosion-abrasive test, considered even more severe than the salt bath. Qualification details are spelled out in specification sheets, even to the amount of porosity permitted in the die-cast mounting and the quality of the mirror glass. ("First surface" type of glass is specified, the best on the market, in order to avoid double image.) Sample mirrors are also installed on test cars which run on a very rough proving grounds circuit for 40,000 miles, deemed equivalent to 100,000 miles on ordinary roads.

14   Other sample mirrors get an interesting lab test of the ball joint used for the adjustment feature. This joint must not stick or freeze, yet it must also retain its ability to stay put if the car owner wants to make an adjustment. Mirrors are cycled in the lab by a series of special machines which oscillate the mirror back and forth and in two different directions. At intervals during the cycling the temperature is lowered to minus 20 degrees Fahrenheit, raised to 120 degrees Fahrenheit. After 3,500 gyrations the ball joint must still have 70 percent of its original frictional characteristics to pass. As a result of these tests over the years, Ford specifies a special lubricant for the ball joint, which eliminates sticking yet inhibits wear during the cycling test. The testers have also found that stainless steel (rustproof) mounting screws are essential. After pre-production mirrors are approved, samples from every batch supplied by the vendor are checked on a regular schedule to ensure maintenance of quality control.

15   The Delco "Delcotron" alternator adopted by GM cars in 1964 is an excellent example of thorough testing. Delco, as a large supplier for GM, has its own test laboratory. Before this new alternator was ever placed in production, Delco engineers tested various samples and designs for the equivalent of 70 million miles. Other tests included 2.2 million miles on the dynamometer and 25 million actual miles on the road—all this from a supplier. The auto manufacturer has his own additional qualification tests before acceptance.

16   Some tests are more dramatic than others. At Chrysler the writer watched brake hoses on tests. These are the vital connecting links between the hollow steel brake lines and the bouncing wheels of your car; failure of only one of the four flexible lines would mean that you had no brakes. A battery of machines actually whips them to tatters, and this test runs twenty-four hours a day.

17   A few years ago Pontiac introduced a car with a curved or bent drive shaft connecting the engine and the rear wheels. One of the tests involved a laboratory duplicate of the backbone-like chassis: engine in front, the drive shaft inside its backbone-like tunnel cover and the complete rear axle assembly.

A dynamometer replaced each rear wheel. Automatic controls actuated the engine's throttle, and once every thirty seconds the "car" started up from a standstill, raced up to 80 mph at full throttle, then came to a full stop. The curved drive shaft had to take this enormous strain without failure for 100,000 miles. Before the design and material specifications were finally settled, nearly 100 different shafts were tested. Needless to say, Pontiac Tempest's unique curved drive shaft gave absolutely no trouble in service.

18   In 1938 Chevrolet had 13,000 square feet devoted to lab tests; today it has over 100,000 square feet for this purpose, located at the GM Tech Center just outside Detroit.

19   Chevrolet has a test fixture for the front suspension which strokes the two wheels to duplicate driving over railroad ties for a distance of 1,000 miles. This severe test is computed on the basis of 250,000 cycles of the machine. Another test machine at Chevrolet simulates a loading equivalent to a front-wheel side skid. The suspension must not fail in 500,000 cycles.

20   Rear suspension systems get similar abuse. When Chevrolet first introduced its coil-spring system, it took a test car down to the racetrack at Darlington, South Carolina. The car was elaborately instrumented, and the driver made several laps at over 120 mph. Then the engineers took the recorded data back to the laboratory and built a special test machine to simulate the stresses and strains imposed on the rear end at the track. Cornering loads equivalent to 625,000 racing miles were duplicated before the rear suspension was approved for production.

21   Accessories, optional at extra cost, are very popular with car buyers, especially since these accessories are thoroughly engineered by the car manufacturer and built to give long life without the need for attention or repairs.

22   Automatic transmissions are the most popular extra-cost item: 77.6 percent of all cars produced in the United States last year were so equipped. As with engines, these complex assemblies are not redesigned every year. Chevrolet's Powerglide, for example, has been refined in detail, but it has been fundamentally unchanged since it was first introduced in 1949. But as with engines, a new or revised automatic transmission is thoroughly tested for millions of miles before production commences. The value of this policy was amply demonstrated by the Lincoln division of Ford two years ago. At a new-model preview, Ford let members of the press drive one of the new Lincolns, then immediately drive a year-old model with over 100,000 test miles on the odometer. There were some differences, but the average driver would not be able to notice them.

23   Chrysler's durability test procedure for its optional four-speed manual transmission is interesting, and the company says that it is somewhat more grueling than the requirements of competitors. Chrysler specifies a life test of twenty hours in first gear, twenty-eight hours in second gear, and thirty-five

hours in third, under load. The load is varied for each gear and is equivalent to the strain of running continuously on a hill steep enough to force the engine to operate at wide-open throttle. Years of experience with this accelerated laboratory technique have shown it to be equivalent to over 100,000 miles of driving by the average owner.

24 Air conditioning is an optional accessory becoming more popular each year. In 1964 some 1.4 million cars left the factory equipped with air conditioning. The industry expects that the demand will rise rapidly; 76 percent of the three luxury cars produced in 1964 had air conditioning, as compared with only 17.89 percent of all cars produced.

25 The air-conditioning systems are not redesigned every year. The design of component parts is, however, under a continuous process of development, both to improve cooling performance and to reduce costs. A standard performance test is to put a black car out to bake in the sun, windows closed. A test driver then steps in, fires up the engine, turns on the air conditioning, and clocks the time required for the interior to come down to 70 degrees Fahrenheit. One and a half minutes for a drop from 120 degrees to 70 degrees is not unusual.

26 Another critical test for an air-conditioned car is the performance of its engine-cooling system. The A/C system imposes extra loads on the engine and requires a larger heavy-duty radiator. Also, an engine at idle tends to boil because there is no forward movement of the vehicle to provide a blast of air for engine cooling. For this test most manufacturers specify that on a day when the temperature is 110 degrees, the engine must not boil when idling for at least thirty minutes. For durability of the A/C components, they require 40,000 miles over the rough-road route, equivalent to 100,000 miles of ordinary driving.

27 Testing includes many other accessories. For instance, jacks are tested, and trailer hitches also get careful consideration. In fact, nearly all cars are available today with special options designed and tested solely for the benefit of those motorists who pull trailers. The companies even test roof racks, which surprisingly enough have in the past given a lot of trouble. The test load for a large roof rack is usually 250 pounds. Among other things, they test with a loose load at 90 mph, then put on the brakes for a crash stop.

28 Now let us consider some of the criticisms of our cars. It is true that our most popular, so-called standard, cars have grown larger and heavier since the war. This is a simple result of the great American desire to "get ahead." The mass market for post-war cars has proved to be for something bigger and better than just transportation. And there is nothing wrong with this attitude; if the bulk of sales are in what used to be the Buick-Chrysler category, why blame Chevrolet, Ford, Plymouth, and Dodge for supplying products to meet the demand? These four cars, with weights approaching two tons (unloaded), account for more than half of all sales. All four are big cars in the truest sense

of the term, and though gasoline consumption is not nearly so economical as the pre-war standard of twenty miles per gallon, the fact remains that the consumer is willing to pay for more luxury, more performance.

29   As for the compacts, the figures show conclusively that only one out of five buyers is interested in economy. All these cars weigh under 3,000 pounds, and weight is the all-important factor when it comes to economy, whether we are talking about fuel, oil, tires, or even first cost. American compacts are far superior to comparable imports, primarily because they are designed, tested, and built to give genuinely economical transportation. They may not give thirty miles per gallon, but cost-conscious buyers know that the annual fuel bill is not a significant factor in computing the cost of owning an automobile.

30   Forced obsolescence has been much maligned. When production quantities exceed 350,000 units per year, the tooling is worn out anyway. Hence, the technical innovations evolved each year by engineers can just as well be incorporated when tools, dies, and machines are replaced. While Henry Ford may have saved a dollar or two per Model T (by making no important design changes), he spent over 100 million dollars in 1927 to make the change to the Model A. Yet only 4.5 million Model A's were produced before complete retooling was required for the 1932 V-8. From that time on, Ford retooled every year for a new and improved model. Even Ford capitulated to the inexorable march of technological advances.

31   The detractors of the American car like to point out that most major technical innovations come from Europe. This may well be true if one talks of who was first. But it remained for Detroit to produce the soft-riding independent front suspension at a reasonable cost in 1934. It was Reo in Lansing which first offered an automatic transmission in 1933. Duesenberg in Indianapolis pioneered four-wheel hydraulic brakes in 1921. American tire engineers developed the balloon tire in 1924, the extra-low-pressure tire in 1949, the low profile in 1964. Goodyear pioneered the caliper-disk brake on the Crosley in 1949. The supercharger, first used on the Chadwick car in 1908 and later adapted to high altitude flying by GE, helped us to win World War II.

32   Current European cars often abound in technical or novelty features, but it takes American engineering, design, testing, and manufacturing to make these features practical and available to great numbers of people at a cost they can afford.

33   An oft-quoted example of European "leadership" is the widespread use of independent rear suspension. In the United States, we have only the Corvette and Corvair with this system of rear-springing.

34   I have talked with dozens of engineers in and around Detroit on this subject. They all agree that independent rear suspension has some advantages, but they also agree that the ride is not noticeably improved, that erratic handling is difficult to overcome, and that the high manufacturing cost is not justified

by the results. The Corvair would not be possible without independent rear suspension because of its rear-mounted engine. The Corvette needs a similar type of suspension in order to get adequate traction with its tremendous power-to-weight ratio (up to 425 horsepower, weight only 3,200 pounds).

35 Independent suspension gives a much improved ride on small, light cars, but on 4,000-pound American cars the ratio of sprung to unsprung weight, even with solid one-piece rear axle assemblies, is not critical. The latest American development—positioning the rear axle more positively and accurately by means of three or four rubber-cushioned links—gives excellent results at low cost. The links are arranged to negate acceleration squat and brake lift; they give good cornering control and freedom from transmission of axle-gear noise.

36 The typical American car is astutely designed to supply a simple need: comfortable, reliable transportation at a reasonable cost. I regard the modern American car, at well under $1.00 per pound, as one of the best buys in the world today.

Apparatus for: How Good Are American Cars?

Discussion: *Theme*

1. What was the author's definition of "good" in his title? Was the article what you thought it would be?
2. Why did the author skirt the issue of safety?
3. Are American cars as good as the author says? Explain.
4. How do you account for the continuing popularity of European cars?
5. Despite the fact that American cars are built well, why do they have so many critics?

1. _____

   _____

2. _____

   _____

3. _____

   _____

4. _____

   _____

5. _____

   _____

Writing Suggestions

1. Report on Ralph Nader's book *Unsafe at Any Speed.*
2. If you disagree with the author, write a rebuttal to his essay.
3. Why I Own a _____.
4. How to Buy a Used Car.
5. Don't Kick the Tires, Buster.
6. Do you believe that the automobile has affected the morals of today's youth?

11. DO COLLEGE STUDENTS DRINK TOO MUCH? *

BYRON H. ATKINSON AND A. T. BRUGGER

1   Such headlines as "Students in Car Smashup after College Drinking Party" and "Drunken Fraternity Party Brings Police" are altogether too familiar. They merely confirm the belief of many a newspaper reader that all undergraduates drink, that they drink too much, and that little good comes of their drinking. In private, most college officials will readily admit that drinking is a problem on the American campus, except perhaps at such schools as Brigham Young University and Bob Jones University. For the public, the doings and undoings of the college drinker seem to hold a special fascination.

2   If the press alone has not created the stereotype of the hard-drinking undergraduate, it has certainly accepted it. College pranks and misadventures are generally attributed to excessive drink; and when little harm is done, the incident becomes a bit of buffoonery. Some of the most popular writers of our time have created an enduring illusion of college revelry. F. Scott Fitzgerald's preoccupation with drink is second only to his preoccupation with sex. Think of college and you think of flaming youth; think of flaming youth and you think of liquor and sex. Stephen Vincent Benét's sensitive portrayal of college life before the First World War is equally moist. Students in Damon Runyon's short stories are inevitably drunk, as they "shell-road" some chorus girl on the way back to New Haven. And William Faulkner's Southern college man takes his learning lightly and his drinking seriously.

* Byron H. Atkinson and A. T. Brugger, "Do College Students Drink Too Much?" From the June, 1959, issue of *The Journal of Higher Education*, pages 305–312. Reprinted with permission.

133

3   This picture of undergraduate insobriety has been widely accepted. It fits nicely into the folklore surrounding higher education. Every university has a drinking song, and is frequently known by it. Yale without "Whiffenpoof" and Maine without "Stein" are inconceivable. Moreover, the thought persists that college time is a time to sow one's wild oats. To learn to hold one's liquor well is part of the fictional Americana of "growing up." Where can it be better done than at college? Yet student manners have been fashioned, not by headlines, novels, or legend, but by an age-old tradition.

4   During the Middle Ages student drunkenness was rarely dealt with as a university offense. Toward the close of the fifteenth century, the University of Leipzig imposed penalties for throwing water out of windows at passers-by, interfering with the hangman in the execution of his duty, and other waggish enormities; yet not until much later were two students punished for causing a drunken row. At that, punishment was quite mild. Even grave offenses were genially expiated by sconcing—treating the members of the college to a drink or so. For entertaining a suspect woman in his quarters at the Sorbonne, a clark was fittingly fined a "bachelor" of wine. And four gallons of the very best wine were required of a student who cruelly beat a servant—not for the abused domestic, but for the criminal's hale companions. Sconcing continued at English universities well into the present century, and the "beer bust" preserves the tradition, in a pale copy, on the American campus today.

5   For that matter, any college event was occasion enough for revelry. Freshmen were put through a rousing initiation which involved bullying and feasting on "better than ordinary" wine at the newcomer's expense. The custom survived at the University of St. Andrews up to the end of the nineteenth century; but the thrifty Scots were content to stand treat with raisins. Better than ordinary raisins, perhaps. American fraternities have not yet entirely broken away from this pattern of harsh initiation or from the habit of occasionally introducing liquor into the ceremonies.

6   University guilds once observed the close of the academic year by disposing of surplus revenues in prodigious drinking bouts. On feast days, the convivial Masters of Paris promptly spent their stipends at a neighboring tavern after church services. Not many such festive occasions got altogether out of hand, but on the feast day of St. Scholastica in 1354 a bloody town-and-gown brawl broke out at Oxford. The keeper of an inn called the Swyndlestock abused some students with "stubborn and saucy language," and before things came to an end sixty-three students had been killed, the town and the University had been pillaged, and the Chancellor—more brave than wise—had been fired at when he attempted to quell the tumult. Completely amicable relations between the University and the city were, in due time, restored on St. Scholastica Day, 1955, when the mayor of Oxford, a Cambridge man, received an honorary doctorate, and the vice-chancellor of the University was given honorary free-

dom of the city. Cambridge is, even now, thoroughly prepared for any such event, "the only duty of its High Steward being to attend the hanging of any undergraduate."

7   The parallel between this kind of riot and the contemporary forms of student mass disturbance is apparent. The huge "panty-raid" two years ago at Berkeley, the bloody "Trolley March" at Brown in the twenties, the "gang-war" between Occidental and Pomona students in the thirties—these, with dozens of others, are somewhat subdued copies of the medieval student brawl. There is one important difference. Liquor and drunkenness, usually prime causes of such behavior five hundred years ago, play a very small part in the present-day version.

8   Tender stomachs and heavy heads usually signaled the end of examinations in the great European universities. Not only after but before an examination and, indeed, during its progress did the knowing student cater to the thirst of his masters. The custom persisted at Oxford up to the close of the eighteenth century. It was considered good management for candidates to entertain their masters handsomely, "which they commonly do the night before examination, and sometimes keep them till morning, and so adjourn, Cheek by Joul, from their drinking room to the school, where they are to be examined. . . ."

9   We find no American equivalent for this. Indeed, nothing in American college drinking, whether traditional or contemporary, quite matches the European pattern. Yet, toward the middle of the seventeenth century, about fifty students then attending staid Harvard managed to consume two hundred and seventy barrels of beer in one year. A goodly number paid their tuition in malt. And President Dunster contended with the "undoing pressures of monopolies" in his sprightly defense of Vashti Barda, who kept a tavern nearby, though, to be sure, the good woman had previously agreed not to serve students with more than a quart of beer at a time.

10   Apparently the piety of the nineteenth century did not diminish the bibu-lous propensities of the undergraduate: Yale Sophomores had their rum flips, Quaker students at Haverford smuggled sherry into their quarters, and clan-destine liquor parties were held in the dormitories of Delaware. The flavor of the time is perhaps best captured in the diary of William Hammond, a student at Amherst. With a number of companions he turned a temperance lecture into a "jolly row"; and when a close friend was about to be expelled for going on a spree, Hammond, who sounds remarkably like a member of the Class of 1960, peevishly observed that "here as everywhere else, men are punished, not for sinning, but for being found out."

11   The spirited South had rigid rules and stout thirsts. Virginia enjoyed a legendary reputation for probity and alcohol; Georgia students, the worse for liquor, broke up temperance meetings on more than one occasion; and at North

Carolina a number of undergraduates got roaring drunk and rode horses through the dormitory. Even today, in our fine Southern universities, the tradition of "learning to drink like a gentleman" persists.

12   But drinking was not confined to any one part of the nation. It vexed many a faculty and college president; and it was uppermost in the minds of a large— and influential—part of the public. Drinking and college have become a natural association. But is this association accurate portraiture or caricature?

13   Obviously, a stereotype has developed from all of this and, just as obviously, no generalization which attempts to embrace all geographical areas, types of schools, sex differences, and classes of society can be accurate. Straus and Bacon, among others, have pointed up these differences. They found the highest statistical incidence of drinking among men in private, nonsectarian, men's colleges, and the lowest incidence among women in public, coeducational, Southern, Negro colleges.

14   But statistics can be misleading. We were recently called by the dean of men at one of our outstanding local private colleges. "Dean," said he plaintively, "we have just had to suspend one of our men when an inspection turned up a full bottle of beer in his room. He has been advised to apply at your school. I do hope you will accept him because he is a fine boy and when his period of suspension has expired, we will want to have him back." We suspect that this institution's policy on drinking is based more on public relations than on reality!

15   On sectarian campuses the range of opinion and administrative policy is from total abstinence to moderation. One generalization nearly always holds true. In sectarian colleges, those campuses representing the older religions, such as the Jewish, the Catholic, and the Episcopalian, tend to seek and to follow a policy of temperance whereas the younger Protestant churches try to maintain a policy of total abstinence.

16   We know too that family income and economic status have an influence on drinking. Among those students whose family income was $10,000 or more (in 1951), 86 per cent of the men and 79 per cent of the women drank. The other end of the scale shows that from families with incomes of $2,500, 66 per cent of the men, and 30 per cent of the women, students drank. Apparently, the higher the family income, the more likely it is that the student will drink.

17   Geographical location, ethnic differences, degree of maturity in college, and parental drinking habits all have their places in the kaleidoscope, and all warn against the acceptance of a stereotype of the college student. Aside from this, we are sure that student drinkers display the same range of drinking habits as the adult society from which they come, and that this stereotype of *excessive* college drinking must be rejected.

18 Different contemporary societies will produce strikingly different student drinking habits. Beer, to be sure, is the typical and traditional American student tipple. But we do not find in this country, as we do in New Zealand, "Drinking Blues" given for excellence of performance in beer-drinking, universities seriously competing to find their best qualified teams—qualified both in speed and distance! Sparkling and still wines are found served at tables of many of our more sophisticated student societies, primarily as status symbols of an unusual occasion. Where but in France would we find the *vin ordinaire* as a common and natural beverage on the student's table morning, noon, and night, and late at night? Where but in New College, Oxford would we find that even today a moral tutor receives a drink allowance of £20 "to help put his troubled charges at ease."

19 The American student version of the college drinking society has suffered a dramatic decline in recent years. Such illegal organizations as Phi Phi, Kappa Beta Phi (Phi Beta Kappa reversed), Theta Nu Epsilon, formed primarily for group drinking, once had widespread undergraduate popularity. Today they have disappeared from most campuses, and where they do exist they command only a slim following. In our student society, as in our adult society, drinking, when not an abuse, is a social custom. Thus our students' drinking habits are shaped by family background, religious taboos, and contemporary local standards. All too often, however, these local standards are dual in nature, and this is especially true in college or university towns. In her analysis of the Porterfield Study at Texas Christian University, Mabel A. Elliott has pointed out that college men are less likely to be formally charged by the authorities than are non-college men in the same area. The attitude often seems to be that behavior which is criminal in the non-college adult is simply a prank when performed by the college student. Courts of law are similarly sympathetic. But this indulgent attitude is scarcely shared by the prospective employer. Paradoxically, he may have chuckled when reading about the antics of a soused collegian, but he will not hire the man.

20 What do students themselves think about their drinking habits? Our experience is that the undergraduate of the fifties seems not to share the callow admiration of the undergraduate of the twenties for the "interesting drinker." The pale, Byronic drunk, almost an obsession among the young post-bellum literati of the twenties, finds no counterpart in the modern college or university setting. American college students do not count themselves among the "beat generation" or the "angry young men," although they may follow these phenomena with amused interest. The total abstainer, even on a "moderation" campus, is usually respected for his opinions. At an earlier time he might have been an object of ridicule.

21 This change of attitude may stem from the fact that the drinking habits of modern students do not seem to be based upon psychological insecurity, either

real or fancied. While the "lost generation" of students drank and wallowed in self-pity, our modern undergraduate, if worried or insecure, seems much more apt to seek group security through an evangelical movement or psychotherapy. When he drinks, it is usually not for surcease, nor under group pressures, but for the same reasons his adult counterpart does—conviviality, relaxation, and removal of inhibition. If he has an ideal in drinking habits, it is not the heavy drinker, the "interesting" drinker, or the drinker who creates problems for himself or his group by his drinking. It is rather the ideal of sophisticated maturity in drinking which he admires—the man who discourses easily on the "right" drinks at the "right" time, and who uses alcohol as a social ladder and not as a padded club. The "party drunk" may be tolerated and cared for after a night of fraternity-party drinking, but he is not admired or respected.

22 We find evidence, also, of a double standard in sex roles at student parties where drinking takes place. Again, the parallel with an adult society is striking. The female role is often watchful, conservative, analytical, and "Where are the keys, I'll drive home." The male role requires no explanation to the male reader. The double standard may result from a widespread belief among students that drinking is often associated with morally questionable sexual behavior. It is a fact, of course, that alcohol reduces ability to control learned behavior, and it is likely that it also has a capacity to weaken sexual controls. The difference in the sex role in student drinking thus becomes more readily apparent. For the woman, an instinctive conservatism; for the man, a robust wolf-howl! Perhaps our women students should not be given too much credit for this behavior since it may be more instinctive than learned. Anthropologists have pointed out that in primitive societies only the men are allowed to indulge in drinking orgies. The woman's role is to prepare the drink, police the affair, tie up the more troublesome offenders, and in many other ways act as a restraining influence.

23 Straus and Bacon find, however, that only in a very small percentage of cases is the fraternity or sorority house the setting for student drinking. Of men questioned in their survey, 60 per cent state that their usual place of drinking is a restaurant, tavern, or bar; only 3 per cent claim it to be a fraternity or sorority house. The fact that 2 per cent name "private club" as their usual place of drinking leads us to wonder whether the Ivy League schools were well represented!

24 The student drunk is very often, both in literature and in life, a figure of fun. The anecdotes, jokes, and party stories about him are endless, and of course they, also, feed the stereotype. At U.C.L.A. recently, the campus police answered a frantic night telephone call from a house owner complaining hysterically of strange noises and of curious apparitions on top of a nearby fraternity house. After a cautious climb to the roof, the officers confronted an undergraduate wavering from side to side, zipped up to the neck in a sleeping

bag. Vainly attempting to point an admonitory finger through the stifling folds of the bag, he announced in stentorian tones, "Get lost earthlings; us Martians have taken over!"

25 There may be reason to suspect that the student who recently sent us this anonymous post card may also have taken a couple to buck him up:

> Dear Dean:
>   I have never before attended an university where there is an out-and-out effort on the part of its officers to reduce student freedom to a minimum. In addition to the enormous unnecessary conglomerations of laws, rules, and regulations, there is a stupid, scurvy ridiculous bunch of armed guards called police whose sole function seems to be to hound and prey upon students. This miserable institution also offers its students: inadequate housing, no parking, outmoded recreational facilities plus crummy Kerckhoff Hall.

The university seems to have inculcated a desirable attitude of straightforwardness in this individual. One professor, a sponsor of a recent student dance held in one of our large metropolitan hotels, was confronted by a slightly glassy-eyed upperclassman. "Professor," he shouted, "let me buy you a drink. You probably can't afford one on your salary!" Although the young man had a sound grasp of economics, his tact left something to be desired.

26 Most parents and community leaders believe firmly that college administrators, and the policies which they espouse, not only play a part in developing or hardening student attitudes toward drinking but may, in fact, mold them. There is no question that extreme differences in policy and policing exist, but do they have any real effect? The traditional problem of the administrator is that, if lenient, he will get his lumps from the community; if flexible, he will receive the same lumps from the student body, and he may also find that his policy approaches reality about as closely as do the inane hyperboles of the typical college fight song. If he follows a middle-of-the-road policy, he is sure not only to draw fire from both sides but also to be accused by everyone within sight or hearing of being a contemptible, temporising compromiser. The recent student riot at Cornell, which followed the merest rumor that student parties in living groups would be policed to see that there was no drinking of any kind, gives a clear indication of the attitude of students and administrators at that institution. Reports from campuses in the same geographical area, such as Dartmouth and Princeton, indicate that the occasional wild fraternity party is a respected and continuing tradition. It seems clear that a policy of "straightforward hypocrisy" regarding student drinking exists there, as indeed it does in the University of California. Is this better or worse than a policy which forbids student drinking of any kind, is rigorously enforced, and inevitably results in the suspension or dismissal of those guilty of violating its regulations?

27 Colleges and universities bear more responsibility than any other social group for the behavior of the young men and women who are on their campuses. But most of the influences which mold and motivate these young people

do not come from the colleges and universities. Like the public school, they provide the largest and least dangerous target. Many college officers throughout the country have developed a live-and-let-live attitude. They try to avoid problems, to strengthen student government, and, above all, to evade public notice. Their hope is that, like the chameleon, they will blend indistinguishably with the background. They have come to know that there is no formula, and that that policy is best which works at a given place, with given students, and at a given point in time. There is, of course, much which might be done in the way of education and instruction, but, except at the Yale Institute, there is very little evidence that anything is being accomplished. Perhaps the best policy was stated some one hundred and fifty years ago, when the authorities at William and Mary ordained "that the drinking of spirituous liquors (except in that moderation which becomes a prudent and industrious student) be prohibited."

Apparatus for: Do College Students Drink Too Much?

6. _____

_____

7. _____

_____

Discussion: *Theme*

1. *Do* college students drink too much? Explain.
2. How does the behavior of your group differ from that of your parents when they were your age?
3. Would you defend the actions of the students on your campus who wear exaggerated or "faddish" clothes? Or even act a bit peculiar?
4. How normal is it for college students to drink? What would you label as "too much" at a party?
5. Is heavy drinking a symptom of something else? Explain.
6. Do you consider the conduct code on your campus too strict or too lenient? Explain.
7. How much responsibility does your college administration owe to you in terms of directing your behavior on campus or in school-sponsored events?

1. _____

_____

2. _____

_____

3. _____

_____

4. _____

_____

5. _____

_____

6. _____

_____

7. _____

_____

Writing Suggestions

1. I Think College Students Do (*or* Do Not) Drink Too Much.
2. Use the following sentence as the basis of a theme: "The student drunk is very often . . . a figure of fun."
3. Describe a social function that you have attended at which you saw too much drinking.
4. Give reasons why you think college drinking should (*or* should not) be controlled by the school administration.
5. Examine a newspaper account of a college social function and demonstrate how it differs from your own impression. In other words, refute the stereotype of the college party-goer.
6. Prohibition Should (*or* Should Not) Be Enacted on Campus.

12. MAP AND TERRITORY *

S. I. HAYAKAWA

1   There is a sense in which we all live in two worlds. First, we live in the world
of happenings which we all know at firsthand. This is an extremely small world,
consisting only of that continuum of the things that we have actually seen, felt,
or heard—the flow of events constantly passing before our senses. So far as
this world of personal experience is concerned, Africa, South America, Asia,
Washington, New York, or Los Angeles do not exist if we have never been to
these places. Jomo Kenyetta is only a name if we have never seen him. When
we ask ourselves how much we know at firsthand, we discover that we know
very little indeed.

2   Most of our knowledge, acquired from parents, friends, schools, newspapers, books, conversation, speeches, and television, is received *verbally.* All
our knowledge of history, for example, comes to us only in words. The only
proof we have that the Battle of Waterloo ever took place is that we have had
reports to that effect. These reports are not given us by people who saw it happen, but are based on other reports: reports of reports of reports, which go
back ultimately to the firsthand reports given by people who did see it happening. It is through reports, then, and through reports of reports, that we receive
most knowledge: about government, about what is happening in Korea, about
what picture is showing at the downtown theater—in fact, about anything that
we do not know through direct experience.

3   Let us call this world that comes to us through words the *verbal world,* as

opposed to the world we know or are capable of knowing through our own experience, which we shall call the *extensional world*. (The reason for the choice of the word *extensional* will become clear later.) The human being, like any other creature, begins to make his acquaintance with the extensional world from infancy. Unlike other creatures, however, he begins to receive, as soon as he can learn to understand, reports, reports of reports, reports of reports of reports. In addition he receives inferences made from reports, inferences made from other inferences, and so on. By the time a child is a few years old, has gone to school and to Sunday school, and has made a few friends, he has accumulated a considerable amount of second- and third-hand information about morals, geography, history, nature, people, games—all of which information together constitutes his verbal world.

4   Now, to use the famous metaphor introduced by Alfred Korzybski in his *Science and Sanity* (1933), this verbal world ought to stand in relation to the extensional world as a *map* does to the *territory* it is supposed to represent. If a child grows to adulthood with a verbal world in his head which corresponds fairly closely to the extensional world that he finds around him in his widening experience, he is in relatively small danger of being shocked or hurt by what he finds, because his verbal world has told him what, more or less, to expect. He is prepared for life. If, however, he grows up with a false map in his head— that is, with a head crammed with error and superstition—he will constantly be running into trouble, wasting his efforts, and acting like a fool. He will not be adjusted to the world as it is; he may, if the lack of adjustment is serious, end up in a mental hospital.

5   Some of the follies we commit because of false maps in our heads are so commonplace that we do not even think of them as remarkable. There are those who protect themselves from accidents by carrying a rabbit's foot. Some refuse to sleep on the thirteenth floor of hotels—a situation so common that most big hotels, even in the capitals of our scientific culture, skip "13" in numbering their floors. Some plan their lives on the basis of *astrological* predictions. Some play fifty-to-one shots on the basis of dream books. Some hope to make their teeth whiter by changing their brand of tooth paste. All such people are living in verbal worlds that bear little, if any, resemblance to the extensional world.

6   Now, no matter how beautiful a map may be, it is useless to a traveler unless it accurately shows the relationship of places to each other, the structure of the territory. If we draw, for example, a big dent in the outline of a lake for, let us say, artistic reasons, the map is worthless. But if we are just drawing maps for fun without paying any attention to the structure of the region, there is nothing in the world to prevent us from putting in all the extra curlicues and twists we want in the lakes, rivers, and roads. No harm will be done *unless someone tries to plan a trip by such a map.*

7   Similarly, by means of imaginary or false reports, or by false inferences

from good reports, or by mere rhetorical exercises, we can manufacture at will, with language, "maps" which have no reference to the extensional world. Here again no harm will be done unless someone makes the mistake of regarding such "maps" as representing real territories.

8   We all inherit a great deal of useless knowledge, and a great deal of misinformation and error (maps that were formerly thought to be accurate), so that there is always a portion of what we have been told that must be discarded. But the cultural heritage of our civilization that is transmitted to us—our socially pooled knowledge, both scientific and humane—has been valued principally because we have believed that it gives us accurate maps of experience. The analogy of verbal worlds to maps is an important one and will be referred to frequently throughout this book. It should be noticed at this point, however, that there are two ways of getting false maps of the world into our heads: first, by having them given to us; second, by creating them ourselves when we misread the true maps given to us.

Apparatus for: Map and Territory

Discussion: *Theme*

1. Were you aware that you live in two worlds? Are there other worlds in which you also live?
2. Which is more valuable, the verbal world or the extensional world?
3. How prepared for life is the "average" college freshman in terms of having his mind filled with the verbal world? That is, how well does one generation prepare the following one for coping with the complexities of life?
4. How guilty are you of beliefs similar to those mentioned in paragraph 5? Should you be?
5. What harm can occur if someone follows an inaccurate "map"?

1. _____

   _____

2. _____

   _____

3. _____

   _____

4. _____

   _____

5. _____

   _____

Writing Suggestions

1. Just Follow the Signs—You Can't Miss
2. I Carry a Rabbit's Foot
3. From your own experience, discuss the concept of maps and territory.
4. Describe some false "maps."
5. In the light of Hayakawa's essay, analyze a letter to the editor of your local newspaper.

V. PARAGRAPH DEVELOPMENT: DEFINITION

Definition is a convenient and natural technique for developing your ideas in a theme. In your college writing you will frequently need to use words and phrases that have various meanings, or shades of meaning. If such terms are the key to the entire essay, define them in the opening paragraphs. If they introduce supporting ideas, define them at the beginning of the appropriate subdivisions of your theme. In either case, you can eliminate any possible misunderstanding of your meaning by the reader.

Definitions fall into two categories: *logical* and *extended.* The logical definition is similar to that frequently used in dictionaries, and can often be expressed in one sentence. It first places the term to be defined into its general class, and then shows how it differs from all other members of its class. Thus, the *human eye* might be defined as a *bodily organ* (general class) of *sight* (differentiation). Similarly, a *carpet* is a *floor covering* (general class) of *woven or felted fabric* (differentiation). A simpler kind of logical definition is the use of a synonym for the word to be defined. In this fashion, a *patella* is defined as "kneecap," and *melee* as "a fight." Since they are usually brief and concise, logical definitions often require further illustrations, example, or discussion; consequently, they function well as topic sentences.

Because some words and terms are too complex or abstract to be defined in a single sentence, or because they are used in a special or unusual way, you will want to extend their definitions for a paragraph or longer. Although extended definitions can be developed in a variety of ways, three methods work particularly well: giving the history or background of the term, supplying examples, and comparing and contrasting the word to be defined with other terms.

The historical background is often the best approach to defining a word

153

whose origin is closely related to its present meaning. *Platonism,* for example, cannot be discussed adequately without alluding to the contributions of Plato and succeeding generations of philosophers. Similarly, any discussion of words such as *puritanism* and *renaissance* requires historical references and background information.

Another method of defining a word is through the use of examples. By showing what the *term* means, you will help your reader know what *you* mean. In defining the terms *Gothic* and *Doric* as they relate to architecture, for instance, examples would be important. Obviously, the examples that you cite must be typical, if your reader is to understand your use of the term. The use of examples is particularly effective when defining abstract terms. Your meaning of the term *socialism,* for instance, would be clarified if you referred to examples of countries whose governments adhere to that philosophy.

Often a term can best be defined by showing what it is *not* like, and then what it *is* like. This method, comparison and contrast, is particularly helpful in distinguishing between words that are often used erroneously as synonyms, such as *wit* and *humor,* or *love* and *infatuation.* For a more detailed presentation of techniques used in comparison and contrast, see Chapter VII.

At times your extended definition will be confined to a paragraph, and thus subordinated to the main thesis of the theme. At other times your entire theme will be, in reality, an extended definition. But regardless of their length or the methods of development, extended definitions are useful only for words that are likely to be ambiguous or completely unknown to your reader. For this reason, in writing extended definitions, avoid words that are vague, figurative, or more difficult than the word you are defining.

By observing the techniques of definition used in the essays that follow in this section, you can improve your own skill in this valuable method of paragraph development.

13. THE NEW SOPHISTICATION: DEFINING THE TERMS *

STEPHEN WHITE

1   Misrepresentation is not to be lightly regarded, and it might be well to begin by establishing the general nature of the inquiry. It deals with sophistication, which is a slippery kind of notion. As a word, I am sure that it has a well-documented lineage, and that it is derived from two or more Greek words meaning something or other. This is all very well for those who are interested in knowing where a word was, but it has little to do with where it is or where it is going. (*Superstitious,* if I recall my Latin correctly, means "one flight up," but I have never yet employed it to describe a cheap hotel.)

2   Some mention should be made, however, that the word *sophistication* is currently used in two senses, the first being scholarly, and in particular scientific: we hear of a "sophisticated theory" or a "sophisticated experiment." A sophisticated theory, as the scientist understands it, is one that covers an extremely wide range of phenomena, that is characterized by great perception or insight, and that in its essentials is not exclusively derivative from the theories of others.

3   In the second sense of the term we are concerned largely with an attitude or state of mind. This is our sophistication in general—an attitude or point of view—and it commands the same virtues of breadth, judgment, and self-assurance of which we have been speaking in connection with the scientist. Thus we find that the two senses of sophistication are one and the same thing, which is a very orderly state of affairs, if unexpected.

* Reprinted by permission of *Esquire Magazine,* © 1961 by Esquire, Inc.

4   But this only in the way of a beginning, for any definition of sophistication applied to America and Americans must carry with it some identifiable characteristics. First of all, it is entirely an urban phenomenon. The Bad Lands of South Dakota, or North Dakota, or wherever the Bad Lands may be, simply do not provide the variety of experience that lies at the basis of sophistication. A sheepherder may be a very estimable fellow, wise in the lore of the uplands and capable of doing well by his sheep under all conceivable circumstances. But you can't very well call him sophisticated. You can't even narrow the word to a point adjacent to total disappearance and call him "sophisticated about sheep," since the only sheep he is likely to know are those under his direct tutelage, and these are hardly enough. The best you can say about him is that he is a damned good sheepherder. This is no small accomplishment, particularly so far as the sheep are concerned, and on the Day of Judgment may move the sheepherder well up toward the head of the line, but it is not what we are talking about.

5   Next, sophistication requires some kind of association with money. Once more we are confronted with the fact that sophistication calls for a wide variety of experience, and experience does not come cheap. One way or another, you have to gain access to it, and there is always someone at the door taking tickets. You can travel quite a way on the experience of others, but the benefits are limited unless you have a wealth of experience of your own against which to measure it, and the matter of cold cash enters once again.

6   I hope it will be noted that I did not stipulate that the Sophisticate must possess money—merely that he have an association with it. This is a real distinction. A journalist, for example, may have every opportunity to become excessively sophisticated, for his daily labors carry him frequently within the atmosphere of wealth and offer him all the variety of experiences that money can buy. It will, of course, always be someone else's money. (It must be admitted that very few journalists are indeed sophisticated, but it is not for want of opportunity; in most cases they are so tremendously impressed by the fact that they are journalists that no further experience ever impinges upon their awareness.) In a general way, however, it is quite possible for those who work for the rich to enjoy a measure of sophistication that their employers never achieve: Jeeves is a true Sophisticate, where Bertie Wooster, with all his charm, is not.

7   The last prerequisite, upon which in a sense we have already touched, is awareness. The person who is aware of nothing but his own narrow interest, or his own private cares, or his own circumscribed environment, is not likely to be much affected by what goes on in the great world around him. Awareness, in this context, is not to be confused with intelligence, for it is conceivable that great intelligence can lead a man to become totally unaware of anything but the narrow environment to which his brain, for one reason or another, has become pinned. He may thus make of himself a great mathematician, or a great

chess player, or a great philatelist, or even a great lover; and he will still remain among the ranks of the unsophisticated.

8   This kind of obtuseness may often be inherited, in a loose manner of speaking. Standards, more often than not, are first set for the child within the family circle, and obtuse parents are in a fair way to have obtuse offspring. There is no discrimination here between rich or poor, brainy or stupid. Narrow-mindedness runs in the very best families and the child born into such a one has much to accomplish during his adolescence if he is to emerge into the light.

9   In our search for the meaning of sophistication, I have set forth three prerequisites: urbanism, the association with money, and awareness; and I am struck by the fact that the society which houses us today possesses these prerequisites in greater supply than they have been at any other time, or in any other place, in history.

10   Certainly we are an urban country. I have no statistics at hand, and no great urge to seek them out, but no man in his right mind would call us rural. Adopt the most rigid definition of "city dweller" that you can defend, and you will find that two thirds or more of our citizens come under it. Be a little more realistic: take cognizance of the automobile, the superhighway, the feeder airline, and you find in all the senses that count we are almost one hundred per cent urban; the only people who escape the net are the deeply poverty-stricken, a few eccentrics, and the small remnant of the truly isolated.

11   Money, too, is more widely distributed than it has ever been. What we mean here by money—in fact, perhaps the only true meaning of the word—is what remains after food and clothing and shelter have been provided, and a few cents set aside for the burial plot. For almost all of us today, something does remain and we are free to spend it upon what we wish. It may well be that in general we spend it upon the wrong things, but that is quite another matter. The money is available, as it has never been before.

12   As for the opportunity to develop an awareness of the world around us, the development of communications and the growing attention that is paid to communications make it almost inescapable. Consider the enormous effect of television. What appears on the face of the cathode-ray tube is almost entirely trash—ninety-eight per cent trash if you like. But there is so much of it, so overwhelmingly much of it, that the remaining two per cent constitutes the greatest and most widespread dissemination of the worthwhile that our civilization has ever seen. And the very nature of the medium imposes it upon the attention. In the process of waiting placidly for *Gunsmoke,* the viewer is likely to be exposed willy-nilly to a sudden insight into worlds he never knew existed. It is true that the television networks are doing their utmost to eliminate this aspect of television and make it all *Gunsmoke*. But it is beyond them. Directors and writers, for the most part, are reasonably literate, reasonably knowing men; and try as they may, something of this insinuates itself now and then into

their most tawdry efforts. They work manfully at their tasks, and in time they may well be able to increase the ninety-eight per cent trash to ninety-nine per cent trash, but they are only human. Something is bound to slip through, and that something, reduce it as they may, is quantitatively more than the great mass of people has ever enjoyed.

13 If these are indeed the prerequisites for sophistication, we should be prepared to discover that there are more Sophisticates in this country, or a higher level of general sophistication, than we have ever enjoyed. And of course the straightforward fact is that such is exactly the case. Even before we have agreed upon what we really mean by sophistication, we can arrive at this sub-agreement. Whatever your personal choice in music, or food, or theatre, or wine, or clothing, or conversation, you will find that more of it is available, in more places, under more circumstances, than you could conceivably have envisaged a generation ago.

14 But all this should not lead us to assume that we have become a nation of prime Sophisticates, for we are not. By and large we are no doubt more nearly sophisticated than any nation has ever been, but we still have more than our share of Unsophisticates and their presence, in large numbers, serves as an indispensable reference point for the measuring of our progress.

15 The Unsophisticate is the man who has no access to the infinite world of experiences and activities, either because he is physically remote, or because he does not have the means, or because he is unaware. In the first two cases we can be sorry for him, and say little more about it. The unaware man warrants more consideration, if only for the light he throws upon the general subject.

16 He is a man trapped in his environment, who regards all alien environments with fear, or distrust, or ridicule. The customs of his narrow world are his customs, once and for all, and they are not to be questioned. Those who behave differently are either ludicrous or sinful. He is happy to point this out; indeed, he can become quite exercised about it, although his debating tactics are not quite fair, for if he finds himself driven toward obviously untenable positions he will call theology or the legislative assembly to his aid. Since most theologists and all legislators see eye to eye with him, he is very nearly in an unassailable position.

17 But he is not necessarily a bad fellow, nor even a dull one, provided that you make no attempt to thrust him across the borders of his world. Above all, there is nothing that requires he be stupid; on the contrary, he may very well be the best pediatrician, or real-estate man, or husband, in the neighborhood. But he is definitely not a Sophisticate. This causes him no pain. He has no wish to be a Sophisticate, nor to be taken for one; he has an overwhelming contempt for sophistication and is generally quite eager to make it known. He is likely to associate it with decadence: with femininity in men and depravity

in women. In all, he is quite happy as he is, outnumbers all the rest of us combined, makes our laws, runs our schools, and is the backbone of the Republic. God bless him, and let us proceed to less-cheerful cases.

18   Having disposed of the unsophisticated, we are left with those who are aware of the multiplicity of experiences and the plenitude of activities, among whom our Sophisticates will be found. Of these, the largest group comprises the undiscriminating. They are thoroughly aware that the world is quite full of a number of things, but they are totally incapable of distinguishing one thing from another. In their own terms they are the tolerant, the relativists, the liberals. Yet we should not permit them to call themselves liberals, for they bear no closer relationship to the true Liberal than they do to the true Sophisticate. A Liberal is a man who discriminates carefully and in a certain manner among possible political attitudes and pursues the course so indicated, whereas the men and women of whom I speak are characterized by their unwillingness to discriminate at all. I shall call them the Slobs.

19   The Slobs differ from the Unsophisticates in a critical respect: they consider themselves to be sophisticated. As a result they are nuisances. Because there are so many of them, they are able to infect whole areas of activity, as right now they are infecting literature and the arts in general. In a great many parts of the country they have affected food by hauling it outdoors and somehow confusing cuisine with duck-hunting, or by encouraging a veneer of French high style on what previously were perfectly respectable beaneries.

20   When the Slob breaks out of his immediate neighborhood, however, he is met with a new problem. Since there is indeed an infinity of experiences and activities, it now becomes necessary to choose from among them, to establish somehow a set of criteria against which all this wealth of possibilities may be judged and ordered.

21   The Slob refuses to do this. Others find it quite simple. Such criteria exist, thoroughly codified, in any number of forms: the criteria of the crowd at "21" or the Stork or the Harwyn or wherever the smart set accumulates today; the criteria of the faculty of Harvard University; the criteria of Elsa Maxwell and other dear friends of the Duke and Duchess of Windsor; the criteria of Lolly Parsons and Hedda Hopper. Each of these is self-perpetuating but committed to a process of irrational slow change; the men and women who are members of the various sets seem to move together under some unknown, even unimaginable stimulus, like lemmings.

22   This is the pathological aspect of sophistication, and it even has its pathologist. We must all be grateful to the pathologist, for it is only when he has identified the malignant cell or the diseased organism that we can be certain of the benign and the healthy. In this particular case, we owe our thanks to Stephen Potter, who has described, in a splendid series of books, the Gamesman, the Lifeman, the One-Upman. "What?" says the One-Upman after the

concert. "You stayed for the Debussy?" There is of course nothing wrong with leaving before the Debussy, provided you dislike Debussy. But with the One-Upman there is always the realization that a distaste for Debussy has nothing to do with it. He is looking nervously over his shoulder at the rest of his set, or the set he has chosen to emulate. Next year they will all be staying for the Debussy and leaving before the Bach. It is entirely a matter of motive. The criteria of the One-Upman may be, from time to time, thoroughly admirable— I meant no sneer at the faculty of Harvard University. But if they are held imitatively and uncritically, as they usually are, they relegate the holder to the ranks of the One-Upman.

23   The One-Upmen bear a unique relationship to the Sophisticates in that they are most commonly confused with the Sophisticates. This is not at all surprising, since it may be quite difficult to distinguish between them on brief acquaintance; the distinction, I repeat, is quite likely to be one of motive. I know a man, for example, who has been drinking Beefeater Gin for fifteen years, because he likes it. He still likes it, and he still drinks it, but at the moment he competes for gin with whole hordes of One-Upmen who this year all drink Beefeater Gin. By the time this appears in print, of course, they may be drinking something entirely different, or not drinking at all, or rubbing crème de menthe in their hair.

24   This phenomenon, viewed in reverse, illustrates the tightrope along which the One-Upman must make his way. His criteria, if they are to serve his purpose, must be in some degree exclusive and he must always guard against the possibility that something he is doing will become genuinely popular. John McNulty once quoted a statement he overheard concerning a well-known Third Avenue saloon: "Nobody goes there any more—it's too crowded." The One-Upman lives in constant dread of falling back to even, or of losing touch, however momentarily, with the set he has chosen to emulate.

25   It is interesting to notice the close similarity between the One-Upman and the Unsophisticate. They are both ineluctably trapped within a narrow environment. The environment of the Unsophisticate is imposed upon him, and changes very slowly from without; the environment of the One-Upman is freely chosen, and changes from within. But they are both trapped, and each invironment seems thoroughly absurd when viewed from outside it. Let us be sorry for the One-Upman, and leave him.

26   We must deal, finally and briefly, with one more subgroup. These are the men who have indeed broken through to the wide world, but who have chosen to make their cut into it vertically rather than horizontally; that is to say, they have become superbly knowing and superbly discriminating about some single experience or some single activity, and paid for it by developing a total ignorance of anything else. Their interest may lie, for example, in clothing, and on the subject of pants, vests, jackets, and even redingotes they are astute without limit. They are supremely well-dressed at all times, and decorative at any

gathering. They are delights to talk to when you wish any sort of information about pants, vests, jackets, or even redingotes. All the rest of the time they are miserable bores.

27   All the same, we must not be hard on them. They are often useful, and at worst they provide a kind of standard against which it is often good to compare our own. But, almost regretfully, we must deny them the title Sophisticate. They are the Exquisites, and perfectly content to be exactly that.

28   We have ruled out the Slob, the One-Upman, and the Exquisite. What have we left? There remains the man who has come into contact, directly and indirectly, with a wide range of experiences and who is anxious to come into contact with more, who is aware that these experiences are by no means of equal value, and who is man enough to take upon himself the task of deciding which are worth his while and which are not. This, at last, is the Sophisticate.

29   He is the man who possesses breadth, judgment, and self-assurance. His title is guaranteed by the fact that there are others, much like him, who recognize his breadth and respect his judgment.

30   "Respect his judgment," mind you, and not, "adhere to his judgment." It has an odd sound, but the family of Sophisticates is a community of individuals. It is by no means true that they all like the same things, or do the same things, or hunger after the same things. But their differences are not fundamental; in general they reflect nothing more than the fact that not all men of judgment have identical tastes, or identical weaknesses, or identical backgrounds. Even a wild idiosyncrasy is acceptable. I consider it highly unlikely that a Sophisticate will harbor a deep affection for the music of Lawrence Welk, but I do not rule it out. There is, of course, a limit, and if a man has a closetful of Lawrence Welks his general judgment is at once suspect.

31   This constitutes the Sophisticate: breadth, judgment, self-assurance. Strike out breadth and you have the Exquisite. Strike out judgment, and you have the Slob. Strike out self-assurance and you have the One-Upman.

32   We have distinguished, so far, in a sort of abstract fashion. Let us now see how these distinctions are represented in, for example, the spectrum of attitudes toward wine.

33   We may start with the Unsophisticate. His attitude toward wine is totally uncomplicated. He doesn't drink it. He never did drink it. He never will drink it. (I speak, of course, of the home-grown Unsophisticate.) He is thoroughly convinced that those who do drink wine are either fools or unbearably pretentious, since they can't possibly like the taste of it compared to good wholesome Coca-Cola. Well, as I said before, God bless him. There is nothing wrong with Coca-Cola, and he doesn't like wine. I wish he would stop passing laws making it difficult for the rest of us to drink wine, but it's his country.

34   The Slob is responsible for the statement, to be found regularly in all our

most glossy magazines, that wine is a good thing and it doesn't really matter what wine you drink. He is, therefore, to be found in the best restaurants, a plate of oysters before him and a bottle of Mogen David at his side. Or perhaps a nice heavy red Burgundy. I do not like the Slob.

35   The One-Upman, on the other hand, is not interested in wine at all, but he is a fervid admirer of labels. At any given moment there are the right wines to drink and the wrong wines to drink, and he concentrates on the right wines. Next year, perhaps, they will change places: nobody will be drinking Château Mouton Rothschild, everybody will be drinking Grands Echezeaux. And not 1946 or 1948, but 1947. Or perhaps wine will be passé altogether, and the right people will all be found swilling down Aalborg Aquavit with limewater and cucumber rind. It may taste like hell, but that's what Yul Brynner drinks. (Actually, Yul Brynner drinks nothing of the kind, but you know what I mean.)

36   With the Exquisite, we revert after a fashion to the Unsophisticate in that he, too, is not likely to drink wine. He may sip it, he may savor it, he may roll it around in his mouth and spit it out into a silver salver, he will certainly talk about it, but he isn't really drinking it. He is studying it. We may all benefit from his labors, but let us not emulate him. Good wine is worth drinking.

37   And the Sophisticate? He has drunk, in his time, a good many wines, and has taken the trouble to learn something about them, perhaps in conversation with the Exquisite. He knows a great many wines that he likes very much, and a great many wines that he likes, and a great many wines that do not suit him. He will drink a favorite wine when he can, and upon occasion he will drink a tenth-rate wine rather than be disagreeable, or perhaps simply because he feels like it. With hot dogs he drinks Coke.

38   An experience of my own comes handily to mind. Some years ago, when the Restaurant de la Pyramide in Vienne was without question one of the best half-dozen restaurants in the world, I visited it for the first time. After I had ordered my meal, the sommelier appeared to set before me a wine list of surpassing amplitude and excellence. But as I cast my eyes down this unbelievable offering of the world's most tantalizing wines, the sommelier bent over me and pointed out a wine of which I had never heard, ticketed at a price one-fifth that of its illustrious neighbors. "Monsieur," said the sommelier, "I would suggest this one. It is a local wine, a very good wine. It is not a great wine, but after all, monsieur, you are likely to pass this way only once. The great wines you will find everywhere; this wine you will find only in Vienne. I would like you to try it, while you have the opportunity." This, to my mind, was true sophistication—on the part of M. Point for having the wine and on the part of the waiter for offering it.

39   Breadth, judgment, and self-assurance—that seems to be all there is to it. Perhaps I have not stressed adequately the importance of self-assurance. The

Sophisticate is not a timid conformist, nor is he, for all of that, an equally timid nonconformist. I have known men who are afraid to telephone from their tables in a good supper club, and I have known men who are afraid not to telephone from their tables in a good supper club—in both cases because of what the waiter might think. In a year when fashion calls for hair to be worn in a sort of high, varnished billow, the truly sophisticated woman is the one who has poise and curls together. Next year, when curls come back, she will still be wearing curls if she chooses.

40   This means also that there is simply no such thing as sophistication divorced from real people, and no such thing as "the sophisticated thing to do." Sophistication, after all that has been said here about it, becomes in the end merely a word for the manner in which certain persons behave. This means in turn that there is no easy way to achieve it, which is all for the good.

41   At this point, some qualifications. People do not fall as neatly into groups as I may have suggested. We are all of us part Slob, part One-Upman, even part Exquisite. This is most important to realize in the person who has given himself, heart and soul, to some worthwhile activity and has been forced reluctantly to foreswear others. The poet, the surgeon, or the scientist simply does not have the time in one short life to do all the other things he would like to do. Consequently, he selects, and for the rest gives up a great deal that he would truly enjoy. He is therefore no Sophisticate, but he contributes a great deal more to his society than the most sophisticated person among us. Strike him from the list—and respect him all the more for it.

42   Finally, I may emerge from all this as a stuffy sort, who has attempted to take all the romance out of the notion of sophistication. I can best conclude by saying that this seems to me to be just right. I do not, myself, think of sophistication as being particularly romantic, but rather as something at the same time quite simple and quite desirable, like clean fingernails. Right or wrong, I like to think of myself as a Sophisticate, and I would like to feel that I have as many fellows as possible. What is more, considering this country today and this country as it was way back when I began worrying about these things, I would say we were moving pretty rapidly in the right direction. We will always have with us the Unsophisticate, the Slob, the One-Upman, and the Exquisite, but the Sophisticate gains ground steadily. What more can we ask?

Apparatus for: The New Sophistication:
Defining the Terms

Vocabulary: *Supply a synonym for each of the following words.*

1. sophisticated theory (¶ 2) — *hypothesis*

2. urban phenomenon (¶ 4) — *metropolis*

3. tutelage (¶ 4) — *guardianship*

4. impinges (¶ 6) — *clashes, collision*

5. obtuseness (¶ 8) — *bluntness*

6. cognizance (¶ 10) — *perception*

7. dissemination (¶ 12) — *diffusion*

8. insinuates (¶ 12) — *indirect hints*

9. ludicrous (¶ 16) — *comical*

10. unassailable (¶ 16) — *unattackable*

11. cuisine (¶ 19) — *kitchenette*

12. codified (¶ 21) — *hidden*

13. benign (¶ 22) — *favorable*

14. ineluctably (¶ 25) — *inevitably*

15. idiosyncrasy (¶ 30) — *a particular share*

16. sommelier (¶ 38) — *waiter*

Discussion: *Rhetoric*

1. Where does the first definition of the "New Sophistication" appear in this essay? Why does the author trace the word through other uses before he gets to the one he is actually writing about?
2. Notice that paragraphs 1 and 2 have internal organization which ties them together. What is this structural tie?
3. Most of us were warned against using *but* and *and* to begin sentences with, yet we find good writers doing it all the time. Count the times these two words are used in this essay to begin sentences.
4. Paragraphs 4 through 9 comprise a section within this essay. What is the central concern of these paragraphs? How does the author help us to remember the points he makes here?
5. The author's attitude toward his subject is very clear. What contributes to this clarity?
6. The selection makes good use of the examples and illustrations. Point out the effective use of two or three.

1. In the 3rd ¶ Words have gathered new meanings over the years
2. In ¶1 it describes the lineage, & ¶2 it defines it.
3. 15
4. Trying to show the meaning of sophistication. Gives examples
5. Examples
6. Diogenes, philatelist, association with money, urbanism, awareness

Apparatus for: The New Sophistication:
Defining the Terms

Discussion: *Theme*

1. Do you agree with the author's definition of sophistication? Must one who is sophisticated live in an urban area, be associated with money, and be aware? Is there more to sophistication than these would indicate?
2. How would you define sophistication? Would you consider this "taste" an especially revealing quality?
3. How many of your friends would qualify as a sophisticate using the author's definition? Would you?
4. Many feel that the word "awareness" best describes a truly sophisticated person. Would you agree? Others use "sensitive" to describe such a one. Do you agree?
5. Take each of the subgroups and discuss them. For example, do the "Slobs" actually run the world, as many suspect? See paragraph 17.

1. _____

_____

2. _____

_____

3. _____

_____

4. _____

_____

5. _____

_____

Writing Suggestions

1. Choose someone you know well and describe him in terms of the definition given for the sophisticate. Then make a judgment about the person as a true sophisticate.
2. Take one of the subgroups and describe in detail someone who fits that description. Place the person in situations where he will reveal by his actions that he is indeed a member of that subgroup.
3. Some of my favorite neighbors are bigots.
4. The Slob Outnumbers All the Rest of Us Combined.
5. Nobody Goes There Any More—It's too Crowded.

14. SLANG AND ITS RELATIVES *

PAUL ROBERTS

1   Slang is one of those things that everybody can recognize and nobody can define. Not only is it hard to wrap slang in a definition; it is also hard to distinguish it from such similar things as colloquialisms, provincialisms, jargon, trade talk. As we shall see, these areas blend into one another, and it is often a waste of time to look for the boundary.

2   One characteristic of a slang term is that it exists side by side with another, more general term for the same thing. Take for example the word *chick,* which has been used by some speakers in the meaning *girl* or *young woman.* The difference between *chick* and *girl* can be stated only in reference to the people who use the words: some say, "This chick is my sister"; others "This girl is my sister." *Chick* is slang and *girl* is not, because *chick* is used by a limited part of the population, mostly young people, whereas *girl* is used by everybody, including those who use *chick.*

3   It is often said that a slang term ceases to be slang when it is "accepted by the dictionary." This is not really the test. You will find many slang terms duly registered in dictionaries and still slang terms. The term ceases to be slang when it drives out of use its respectable synonym, or when it acquires a meaning that cannot be expressed otherwise. If, for instance, people ceased to use the word *girl* and all used *chick* instead, then *chick* could no longer be called a slang term.

4   Such things have happened. The term *hot dog* was once a slang term, but it

couldn't be considered so now. No one in America would go up to a counter and order a "sausage sandwich." Similarly *varsity,* originally a slang contraction of *university,* has acquired special meanings which only it expresses and is no longer slang. *Jazz,* when it means a particular kind of music, is scarcely a slang term, since there is no more respectable word meaning that kind of music.

5   Certainly respectability must enter into any discussion of slang. Slang is essentially not respectable. There is always a more elegant way of saying the thing, but one chooses the slang term for reasons. The reason may be a desire to be thought witty or clever or up to date. More often it is a desire to show, by a particular use of language, that one is a member in good standing of a particular group of people.

6   Criminals have always been prolific producers of slang because they are so obviously marked off from respectable society. They deliberately widen the gulf by multiplying language differences, and they often use the differences for practical purposes: to recognize one another, to shield their conversation from hostile ears. Criminal groups of the seventeenth and eighteenth centuries in England developed large vocabularies of slang—or *cant,* as it was then called—which rendered their talk almost meaningless to an outsider.

7   Much of the slang in common use today comes ultimately from characters on the other side of the law. This will be recognizable, for example, in words relating to American money. For "money" in general we have such terms as *dough, lettuce,* the *green* or the *big green, folding stuff,* and various others. The different denominations all have their slang terms: *singles* or *fish* for one dollar bills; *fin* for a five; *sawbuck* for a ten and *double sawbuck* for a twenty; *C-note* or *century* for a hundred; *grand* for a thousand. All of these are old, well-weathered terms and are familiar to many people who wouldn't dream of holding up a drugstore. But it is clear that they have their highest frequency in those districts where policemen would prefer to go in pairs.

8   In games, slang is common everywhere, but it is most prolific in those games which are more or less disreputable. Bridge and golf have their slang terms, but gambling games have more; and roulette, for which the participants may wear evening clothes, has fewer than craps or poker, for which they usually do not. Poker has a wide variety of slang terms—or at least had when the writer had the game explained to him by an obliging friend. Thus, in addition to the general names for the cards—*ace, deuce, king*—another set of slang terms are, or were, in use: *bull* or *bullet* for "ace," *cowboy* for "king," a *pair of ducks* for "a pair of deuces." Two aces and two eights are a *dead man's hand,* three tens are *thirty miles* or *thirty miles of railroad,* a flush of any sort is *all blue.*

9   Dice, even more disreputable than poker, has a correspondingly higher incidence of slang terms.

10   The connection between slang and the criminal element is seen again in the

dope racket, the terms of which have been made more or less generally familiar by the movies and television. The word *dope* itself is originally slang, but it is now in more general use than *narcotics*. Within the racket, terms abound. The words *marijuana* and *heroin* seem scarcely to occur among users or peddlers of the drugs, as is suggested by the fact that addicts speaking of heroin on a television program pronounced it to rhyme with *groin*. Usually, apparently, they say *H* or *big H* or *horse* or *caballito* (a Spanish word meaning "little horse" or "horsey"). Marijuana is referred to by several slang terms, of which *hay* seems to be most enduring. An injection of a narcotic is a *fix*. To inject it in the vein is to *mainline*. A salesman or peddler is a *pusher*. An addict is a *junkie*. To rid oneself of an addiction is to *kick the habit*. It will be seen that a narcotics addict can discuss his troubles at some length without being understood by anyone outside the circle.

11   Musicians are another fertile source of slang terms. Again the element of more or less respectability enters: symphony orchestras are less prolific of slang terms than are purveyors of more popular music—jazz, swing, bebop, rock 'n' roll bands. Many of the slang terms in this area, as in others, have only the briefest existence, but others linger. Even the youngest readers will be acquainted with *dig* (understand or appreciate), *cool* (excellent or moving), *crazy* (inspired), *cat* (talented musician or knowledgeable music lover), *real* (exceptionally moving).

12   High school and college slang probably derives as much from music language as from any other source. More than one college professor in the 1950's had to learn that the expression "dig that crazy course," coming from one of his earnest young disciples, was not a criticism but a high tribute. But colleges fill out their slang with terms that apply particularly to college activities. Many of these terms are simple abbreviations: *math, prof, exam, poly sci, econ, phys ed*. Others are names, varying from year to year and from campus to campus, for hard or easy courses, hard or easy teachers, passing and failing, studying, cheating, flattering the teacher (*apple-polishing* is an old term that persists). There are slang terms for those who raise class averages and for those who don't, for campus politicians, for campus reporters, for deans and college presidents, for football players, for serious students, for frivolous students, for fraternity and sorority men and women, for nonfraternity and nonsorority men and women, for pretty girls, for other girls, and for girls in general. Everyone and everything connected with college life can be referred to by a slang term as well as by a more general one.

13   Slang words are mostly nouns and verbs, but the adjective class has its slang too. Any college group at any given time uses one adjective to express general approval. This can be anything at all, even a newly coined noise. It is just something that slips into the pattern. "That's very _____," and means that the speaker likes whatever is referred to. When the writer was in college the word was *gruesome*. If, in those days, you said "She's a real gruesome

girl," you meant that she attracted you strongly and compelled your admiration.

14   Since then scores of words have successively taken the place of *gruesome.* The life expectancy of slang in this particular slot is not great. Middle-aged readers will perhaps remember *zorch* and *George,* both illustrations of the truth that all a word has to do to become an adjective is to occur in an adjective pattern. *George,* which until 1952 or so had been an unassuming proper noun, became an adjective as soon as people started saying "That's very George," or, more likely, "That's real George." This started the practice, short-lived, to be sure, of pushing other proper nouns into this position: "That's real Robert" (good), "That's real Tom" (bad), "That's strictly Alexander" (genuine).

15   Slang connects with grammatical structure at more points than one. For example, it could be stated almost as a law of language that an irregular word which picks up a slang meaning will be regularized. Thus the irregular verb *slay* at one time acquired, in addition to its older meaning of "kill," the slang meaning "interest, amuse": "You really slay me, kid." In this meaning it never occurs with the old past form *slew.* One would say not "He slew me" but always "He slayed me." Similarly *louse* has the plural *lice* when it refers to insects but *louses* when it refers to people.

16   It is sometimes said that the trouble with slang is that it is constantly changing, that a term becomes old-fashioned almost at birth. It is certainly true that some terms, particularly those that get quick and heavy use, wither faster than the rose. One has only to consider how obsolete terms like *zorch, George hot* (hot music), *skirt* (girl), *flame* (girl or boy friend), *squire* (escort) sound today.

17   However, a short but merry life is by no means the rule for slang terms. Some linger on decade after decade, century after century indeed, never becoming quite respectable and never dying out either. The word *dough* for money is just as hardy as it ever was, though no more reputable. Others which seem likely to outlive the century are *cop* (policeman), *nuts* (insane), *plastered* (drunk), *wino* (drunkard), *limey* (Englishman), *jalopy* (automobile), *cram* (study hard). There are thousands of such—well below the salt but also well established at the table.

18   Teachers of English are often libeled to the effect that they are dedicated to a relentless pursuit of slang and are never so happy as when they are stamping out a slang term. This is part of the larger charge that teachers of English aren't people. Everybody uses slang as a natural result of speaking a language, though it is presumably true that the young and effervescent like to play with language more than their elders do. It is also true that what sounds gay and cute and clever to the young may sound merely banal to older ears.

19   The effect of slang is closely bound with the personality of the user. It is not simply a question of whether the slang is new or not or clever or not or

incisive or not. It is a question of the total effect of the speaker. The writer can remember a friend who used a rather small selection of slang, none of it particularly witty, and used it rather constantly with no infusion of new terms; yet his conversation always seemed to have a pleasant sparkle to it, presumably because he himself sparkled pleasantly. On the other hand, there was another character who always—*always*—greeted one with the salutation, "Dig that crazy cat." He usually prefaced this with the expression "Hey, hey!" This grew tiresome.

20 Slang spreads fast sometimes, but it doesn't transfer very easily. A person who moves into a new group and brings with him an old group's slang *may* find his language admired and imitated. More likely people will consider him boring or affected or unpleasantly foreign. If he persists with his old talk and doesn't adopt that of the new group, he will find that people begin saying, "Here comes that type; let's get out of here."

21 The language that we call slang merges imperceptibly with other varieties. Every trade or profession, vocation or avocation has a set of terms more or less peculiar to it and often differing little or not at all from what we think of as slang. Trade talk often serves much the same purpose that slang does—to give coherence to the group and to exclude outsiders. If you think of peddling dope as a profession, then such terms as *fix, mainline, horse, junkie* are not slang but technical terms of the business.

22 A familiar example of terms of a trade are those employed on ships. Since sailors have for centuries led a life apart, a whole vocabulary has grown up, not only for those activities peculiar to the sea but also for many that go on under other names ashore. Thus a sailor speaks of a *ladder,* not a *staircase;* a *deck,* not a *floor;* a *bulkhead,* not a *wall;* a *head,* not a *toilet;* a *companionway,* not a *corridor;* a *galley,* not a *kitchen; fore* and *aft* and *port* and *starboard,* not *front* and *back* and *left* and *right.*

23 These terms, as in many other trades, are often jealously guarded. The landlubber inspecting the ship, the apprentice making his first trip, are likely to evoke the seaman's cheerful scorn as they use land words for sea things. On the other hand, the landsman isn't any better off if he comes aboard with the proper vocabulary. During the Second World War, when young men were trained ashore in their duties before being assigned to ships, they would often come onto the ships with the right words and lisp assuredly of going below and going aloft, of galley and messroom and fo'c'sle. This also would irritate the oldtimers, who sometimes revenged themselves by talking of going downstairs instead of below and out on the front porch instead of to the bow.

24 Ship talk is but an obvious example of the kind of special language that any trade or profession or occupation, indeed any coherent human activity cultivates. In printing, in wrestling, in dentistry, in the automobile trade, the participants tend to develop terms which they use and the outside world does

not. One difference between this trade talk and slang is that the trade term has a respectability that the slang term lacks. Thus one can say that *dope addict* is more dignified than *junkie, policeman* more dignified than *cop*. But one could hardly say that ship's *wall* is more dignified than ship's *bulkhead*.

25   Slang and much trade talk too merge imperceptibly with that broad area of language that we call *colloquialism. Colloquial* is a rather vague word, with different meanings for different people, but it would seem most generally to mean words and constructions that occur more commonly in speech than in writing. As such it would include slang but would not be limited to slang. It would include all the forms that people—educated as well as uneducated—use in conversation but tend to avoid in writing. A further distinction is that *slang* usually denotes words rather than phrases, whereas *colloquialism* can mean a word, a phrase, a sentence—indeed, can apply to the whole tone of the utterance.

26   Compare the sentences "He better take it easy" and "He should proceed carefully." Both might be uttered by people of impeccable breeding and both might occur in writing as well as in speech. The difference is simply one of frequency and likelihood. "He better take it easy" is what you are likely to say if you are chatting casually with someone about the activity of a mutual friend. "He should proceed carefully" is what you are likely to write in a letter to the newspaper.

27   Colloquialisms are not hard to find, since they make up the bulk of our daily conversation. At random we can compare such colloquial and literary expressions as "do your darndest" (strive), "put something over on someone" (fool), "lend a hand" (assist), "kept his mouth shut" (refused to divulge something), "hit the books pretty hard" (studied diligently), "an awfully cute kid" (a strikingly handsome young man), "who you trying to fool" (whom are you seeking to mislead).

28   At some periods of history people have had the idea that writing is better the farther it is from speech and that colloquialisms should therefore regularly be avoided. But this is scarcely the mood of the present day. Naturally, if you want to sound dignified—and one *does* want to sound dignified sometimes—you choose dignified language and eschew terms that smack of shirtsleeves and ginger ale. If you're seeking a position with a corporation, you might damage your chances by writing, "I sure hope you'll let me take a crack at the job. I got a notion I'd do real well at it. Sure would try anyhow." It would normally be better to say, "I am hoping that you will find it possible to try me in the position. I feel that I would be able to do the work successfully. Certainly I would try very hard."

29   However, it is undeniable that the trend of much modern writing is toward a more colloquial tone. Not only in advertising, which is ever pally, but also in more or less serious books, magazine articles, newspaper accounts, the tend-

ency is to reflect more and more the words and rhythms of ordinary speech. One finds, for example, a greater use than formerly of contracted forms: *don't, shouldn't, he'll,* in place of *do not, should not, he will.* Plain or folksy or even slang words are often preferred to elegant ones, and writers pay less attention than their predecessors did to the niceties of schoolbook grammar.

30   The explanation of this trend is no doubt to be sought in sociological developments. The educated class, formerly a pretty exclusive group, is now the great mass of the population. Reading and writing, even a hundred years ago, was the accomplishment of relatively few; now everybody does it. Today's writer is talking not to the country club set but to everybody in town, and he tries to talk everybody's language.

31   But he shouldn't try too hard. Writing should above all be consistent and natural and honest, and the writer who labors the "jus' us plain folks" approach is spotted as a phoney by the plain folks as well as the fancy ones. Here, from a cereal box, is an example of nobody's language:

> Often, when I'm out ridin' the range, I find myself thinkin' about all the daredevil deeds the Indian Chiefs did in days gone by, and of the unforgettable adventures of the gallant scouts and frontiersmen who met them in battle. I reckon all you young pardners of mine would like to hear all about them, too!

Even the youngest pardners may have an inkling that this cowboy rides the range on his portable typewriter.

32   One of the troubles of colorful language, slang or other, is that its color rubs off. The first time you hear and understand an expression like "Dig that crazy cat" you may find it exceptionally expressive, piquant, and moving. The second time you hear it, it isn't quite so exciting. The tenth time it has no effect at all. The fiftieth time it grates a little. The five hundredth time it may make you want to brain the speaker with a trombone.

33   If language isn't colorful to begin with, it doesn't pale. You can hear the sentence "Listen to that musician" five hundred times with no more pain the last time than the first. Clichés, or trite expressions, are simply dried-up metaphors, figures of speech. They are racy ways of saying things but they have slowed down.

34   The first person who said "It was like walking on eggs" thought up a pretty clever comparison. When you read this for the first time, you get not only the information that the situation was delicate but a picture that reinforces and impresses the message. But this happens the first time only. After that you get only the information that the situation was delicate plus the fact that the writer is not very inventive. So also with "He fought like a tiger," "He behaved like a lamb," "He ran like a deer," "He ate like a pig," "He took a powder," "He pulled the wool over my eyes," "He's all wool and a yard wide," "She's pretty

as a picture," "He spelled out the government's policy," "We'd better shake a leg," "An ocean of faces looked up at him," "A forest of masts filled the harbor," "She led him a merry chase," "It slid off him like water off a duck's back," "You can't fly on one wing," "He was as drunk as a lord, but his brother was as sober as a judge." All of these were more or less effective once.

35   Some groups of people seem to run more to clichés than others. Politicians are notorious, and some of their clichés, like "point with pride" and "view with alarm," have been laughed out of use. Sports writers and announcers also have difficulty avoiding trite phrases. One thinks of such expressions as "the fourth and final quarter" (one knows that the fourth quarter of a football game is the final one, but announcers seldom fail to point it out), "the bags are bulging," "circus catch," "smart little field general." All quarterbacks are smart little field generals, though some of them are also magicians. Line drives, proceeding toward the outfield, always scream, unless they go past something, like first, in which case they whistle. Pitchers are mostly big right-handers or little southpaws. Successful players come through in the clutch.

36   In fairness we should realize that sports writers and sports announcers deserve sympathy as much as criticism. They have to report, day after day and year after year, activities in which the same features are endlessly repeated. Moreover, they must always report these activities feverishly. The announcer is scarcely at liberty to say that today's football game is a pretty routine affair and the performers of no more than average competence. He must, every Saturday, bubble about how this is the most exciting grid spectacle that he and his colleagues have been privileged to see in a long time and how he wishes all us fans could be out there in the stadium with him to see these two great teams fighting their hearts out.

37   The cliché is every writer's enemy. Good writers fight clichés all the time, but few, even among the very best, win all the time. The triter the phrase, the more readily it comes to the mind, the more likely it is to slip into the sentence. You want to describe a mob, and you don't want to just say it was a big mob. You want to impress the reader with its size. "Sea of faces," you think, and you write it down. The trouble is that so many other writers have also written it down that it's lost all its blood. It no longer means anything more than "big mob," so you might as well have written "big mob" and been done with it.

38   The cliché is a difficulty for the young writer particularly, because he may not recognize the cliché when he sees it. "Sea of faces" may strike him as a bright new figure, not only expressive but original. One solution to this problem is experience. As we mature as readers, we become better equipped to recognize the stock phrases of the language as stock phrases. But the principal solution is to learn to distrust the pleasing phrase that comes too readily. It is only reasonable to suppose that the metaphor that jumps at you will have jumped at thousands of others before you.

39   It is very easy to write, to speak, to think in clichés. That's what most people do. They don't think for themselves but let the popular mind think for them. Their language is not personal but general, composed of public sentences with a few names changed to fit private conditions. There is nothing sinful about talking in clichés, and nobody can avoid it altogether. But those who don't avoid it at all betray laziness and mediocrity.

Apparatus for: Slang and Its Relatives

Vocabulary: *List any troublesome words you find in this essay. Look up each one in your dictionary and write out the full definitions.*

provincialisms - words particular to

jargon - a dialect

prolific - highly inventive

effervescent - show exhilaration

imperceptibly - gradually

pally - became dull

Discussion: *Rhetoric*

1. Although the author says it is difficult to define *slang,* he does so by writing an essay (actually a chapter from a book) on the word. Would you say that the author achieved a definition?
2. Many examples are used to give us specific ideas of the various areas of slang. Where are these examples used most effectively?
3. Beginning with paragraph 34, the author deals with a specific problem of language—the cliché. What is his attitude toward it?
4. Which is the strongest section of this essay—the beginning, middle, or end?

1. _Yes_

2. _Colloquialsms, clichés_

3. _He doesn't like it._

4. _Middle_

Apparatus for: Slang and Its Relatives

Discussion: *Theme*

1. How would you define slang? Especially important here is the difference you would make between (or within) slang and jargon, colloquialism, and provincialisms.
2. Sit for one hour in your student center and list the most colorful slang terms you hear.
3. Another project worthy of some time is to list all the slang terms being used around you to signify approval and disapproval.
4. What is the value of slang?

1. _____

_____

2. _____

_____

3. _____

_____

4. _____

_____

Writing Suggestions

1. Explain the trend in language usage toward more informal patterns. Is there, for example, a relationship between the informal dress we notice today and language usage?
2. Take one of the questions mentioned under "Discussion of Theme" above and develop it into an essay.
3. You will find that Webster's Third International Dictionary omits the usage label *colloq*. Write a paper on the reasons for this change from the Second International.
4. Write a satiric paper in which you use as many clichés as you possibly can.
5. The use of slang in conversation has been compared to the use of pepper and salt on food. Is this a valid analogy?

15. THE HARD KIND OF PATRIOTISM *

ADLAI E. STEVENSON

1   It is not easy to be a patriot these days—not because it is difficult to love one's country. The difficulty lies with loving one's country in the right way.

2   The love itself is profound and instinctive, rooted in our childhood discovery of all the infinite delights of being alive—for me, the vast skies, the spring green of the corn, the fall colors and winter snow of the Illinois prairie; for all of us, the shining Christmas trees, the colored mesas and bright flowers of the desert, the rocky shores and pounding seas "way down East," the aspens showering autumn gold on the slopes of the Rockies.

3   It doesn't matter what your picture is. For all of us, it is "home," the place where we spent the endless, dream-filled days of childhood, the place that still nourishes our secret, life-giving imagination, the place we love as we love bread, as we love the earliest image of maternal care, as we love life itself. In doing so, we love what has largely made us what we are. The difficulty is, as I have said, to love it in the right way.

4   I think the complexity of modern technological society makes the loving difficult for everybody, but here in America we have some quite special problems, which come not from our complex present but from our historical inheritance.

5   Some states emerge from some pre-existing tribal unity, some grow up within an already established culture, and some are forged by conquest, with victor and vanquished settling down to a new synthesis.

6   None of these routes was followed by America. Our people have come from

* Adlai E. Stevenson, "The Hard Kind of Patriotism," *Harper's Magazine,* July 1963.

every "tribal" group; they have largely had to create their own civilization as they went along to absorb a continent. They have never been conquered or had any sort of synthesis imposed upon them. Their community had, in fact, a unique beginning—it was from the moment of its birth a land "dedicated to a proposition" that men are born equal, that government is a government of laws, not men, and exists to serve them, that "life, liberty, and the pursuit of happiness" are man's inalienable right.

7   But consider the consequences of this astonishing start. We are Americans because we belong to a certain ideal, visionary type of political and social order. We can't point back to a long, shared civilization. It is true, most of us have Europe and the West behind us. But not all—and, anyway, it is a concept of the West that we create rather than inherit. And no one is standing on our necks keeping us down and together.

8   The result is a community, surely, whose instinctive, rooted, taken-for-granted unity has to be all the more dynamic. If we are not dedicated to our fundamental propositions, then the natural cement in our society may not be enough to take the strain.

9   I would agree that there are substitutes. When a President said that "the business of America is business," he told us something about the degree to which a standard of living can do stand-in duty for a way of life. But the question, "What manner of people are we?" cannot be everlastingly answered in terms of two-car families or split-level homes.

10   America is much more than an economic or geographical fact. It is a political and moral fact—the first community in which men set out in principle to institutionalize freedom, responsible government, and human equality. And we love it for this audacity! How easy it is, contemplating this vision, to see in it—as Jefferson or Lincoln saw in it—"The last, best hope of man." To be a nation founded on an ideal in one sense makes our love of country a more vital force than any instinctive pieties of blood and soil.

11   But it also demands a more complex and discriminating love. Will the fabric hold if the ideal fades? If the effort to realize our citizens' birthright of freedom and equality is not constantly renewed, on what can we fall back? As a going concern, we can no doubt survive many shocks and shames. It was Adam Smith who remarked that "There is a great deal of ruin in every state." But can we survive, as a confident and growing community, if the essentially liberal thrust of our origins is forgotten, if we equate liberty with passive non-interference, if we exclude large minorities from our standards of equality, if income becomes a substitute for idealism, consumption for dedication, privilege for neighborly good will?

12   Well, you may say, "Why be so concerned; after all, one of the most forceful elements of our free society is precisely our discontent with our own

shortcomings. Because we are free, because we are not the victims of censorship and manipulated news, because no dictatorial government imposes on us its version of the truth, we are at liberty to speak up against our shortcomings. We don't confuse silence with success. We know that 'between the idea and the reality . . . falls the shadow,' and we are determined to chase away that shadow in the uncompromising light of truth."

13   But *are we?* It is at this point that our patriotism, our love of country, has to be a discriminating, not a blind force. All too often, voices are raised, in the name of some superpatriotism, to still all criticism and to denounce honest divergencies as the next thing to treason. We have risen up from the pit of McCarthy's time, when honest men could lose their jobs for questioning whether there were 381 known Communists in the State Department. But the intolerant spirit which equates responsible criticisms with "selling the country short" or "being soft on communism" or "undermining the American way of life" is still abroad.

14   I can give you no comfort in suggesting there is an easy way around this type of criticism. Our position today *is* equivocal. We *are* in one sense a very conservative people—for no nation in history has had so much to conserve. Suggestions that everything is not perfect and that things must be changed *do* arouse the suspicion that something *I* cherish and *I* value may be modified. Even Aristotle complained that "everyone thinks chiefly of his own, hardly ever of the public interest." And our instinct is to preserve what we have, and then to give the instinct a colored wrapping of patriotism.

15   This is in part what the great Dr. Johnson meant when he said: "Patriotism is the last refuge of a scoundrel." To defend every abuse, every self-interest, every encrusted position of privilege in the name of love of country—when in fact it is only love of the status quo—that indeed is the lie in the soul to which any conservative society is prone.

16   We do not escape it—but with us, an extra edge of hypocrisy attaches to the confusion. For our basic reason for being a state is our attempt to build a dynamic and equal society of free men. Societies based on blood ties can perhaps safely confuse conservatism and patriotism. People with long backward-looking traditions can perhaps do so. Countries under the heel of dictators must do so. But if the world's first experiment in the open society uses patriotism as a cloak for inaction or reaction, then it will cease to be open—and then, as a social organism, it will lose its fundamental reason for existence.

17   Do not, therefore, regard the critics as questionable patriots. What were Washington and Jefferson and Adams but profound critics of the colonial status quo? Our society can stand a large dose of constructive criticism just because it is so solid and has so much to conserve. It is only if keen and lively minds constantly compare the ideal and the reality and see the shadow—the

shadow of self-righteousness, of suburban sprawl, of racial discrimination, of interminable strikes—it is only then that the shadow can be dispelled and the unique brightness of our national experiment can be seen and loved.

18 The patriots are those who love America enough to wish to see her as a model to mankind. This is not treachery. This—as every parent, every teacher, every friend must know—is the truest and noblest affection. No patriots so defaced America as those who, in the name of Americanism, launched a witch-hunt which became a byword around the world. We have survived it. We shall survive John Birchism and all the rest of the superpatriots—but only at the price of perpetual and truly patriotic vigilance.

19 This discriminating and vigilant patriotism is all the more necessary because the world at large is one in which a simple, direct, inward-looking nationalism is not enough.

20 We face in Communist hostility and expansionism a formidable force, whether Mr. Khrushchev and Mr. Mao Tse-tung pull together or apart. They disagree so far only on whether capitalism should be peacefully or violently buried. They are both for the funeral. So long as this fundamental objective remains, we must regard the Communist bloc as a whole with extreme wariness.

21 Even if the Communists are divided and confused everywhere—even if they have scored of late none of the victories in Africa, East Asia, and the Middle East our doomsayers predicted—still the Communist bloc is aggressive and powerful and determined to grow more so. Taken individually, the European states are all outnumbered. Even America has only a margin of superiority over the tough, austere Soviet Union. Even if the Russian forces in Cuba are not going to conquer the Americas, still their presence in this hemisphere endangers the peace.

22 So we have sensibly concluded in the NATO Alliance that our separate sovereignties and nationalisms must be transcended in a common, overwhelming union of deterrent strength. Together our weight keeps the balance of power firmly down on our side, and it removes from each state the temptation of playing off one state against another and weakening the overall power in order to strengthen its own. This is the first reason for transcending narrow nationalism.

23 The second follows from our economic interdependence. The Atlantic world has taken 70 per cent of world trade and absorbed 70 per cent of its own investments for the last seventy years. We are an interwoven international economy. Bank rates in Britain affect investments in New York. Restrictions here affect carpet makers in Belgium. French farmers affect everybody. We can only avoid the mismanagement of this community if we pursue joint policies. My friend Jean Monnet has outlined the essential list: expansion of demand, currency stability, investment overseas, trade with the developing nations,

reserves for world trade. Without joint policies here, we could easily slip back to the debacle of the period between the great civil wars of Europe of 1914 and 1939.

24   In this context, separate, divisive nationalism is not patriotism. It cannot be patriotism to enlarge a country's illusory sense of potency and influence, and reduce its security and economic viability. True patriotism demands that, in some essential categories, purely national solutions be left behind in the interest of the nation itself. It is this effort to transcend narrow nationalism that marked the supremely successful Marshall Plan. It marks the great enterprise of European unification—after so many tribal wars. It could mark the building of an Atlantic partnership as a secure nucleus of world order.

25   So our vision must be of the open society fulfilling itself in an open world. This we can love. This gives our country its universal validity. This is a patriotism which sets no limits to the capacity of our country to act as the organizing principle of wider and wider associations, until in some way not yet foreseen we can embrace the family of man.

26   And here our patriotism encounters its last ambiguity. There are misguided patriots who feel we pay too much attention to other nations, that we are somehow enfeebled by respecting world opinion. Well, "a decent respect for the opinions of mankind" was the very first order of business when the Republic was created; the Declaration of Independence was written, not to proclaim our separation, but to explain it and win other nations to our cause. The founding fathers did not think it was "soft" or "un-American" to respect the opinions of others, and today for a man to love his country truly, he must also know how to love mankind. The change springs from many causes. The two appalling wars of this century, culminating in the atom bomb, have taught all men the impossibility of war. Horace may have said: "It is sweet and fitting to die for one's country." But to be snuffed out in the one brief blast of an atomic explosion bears no relation to the courage and clarity of the old limited ideal.

27   Nor is this a simple shrinking from annihilation. It is something much deeper—a growing sense of our solidarity as a human species on a planet made one and vulnerable by our science and technology.

28   For, on this shrunken globe, men can no longer live as strangers. Men can war against each other as hostile neighbors, as we are determined not to do; or they can coexist in frigid isolation, as we are doing. But our prayer is that men everywhere will learn, finally, to live as brothers, to respect each other's differences, to heal each other's wounds, to promote each other's progress, and to benefit from each other's knowledge. If the evangelical virtue of charity can be translated into political terms, aren't these our goals?

29   Aristotle said that the end of politics must be the good of man. Man's greatest good and greatest present need is, then, to establish world peace. Without it, the democratic enterprise—one might even say the human enter-

prise—will be utterly, fatally doomed. War under modern conditions is bereft of even that dubious logic it may have had in the past. With the development of modern technology, "victory" in war has become a mockery. What victory —victory for what or for whom?

30   Perhaps younger people are especially sensitive to this growing conviction that nowadays all wars are civil wars and all killing is fratricide. The movement takes many forms—multilateral diplomacy through the United Nations, the search for world peace through world law, the universal desire for nuclear disarmament, the sense of sacrifice and service of the Peace Corps, the growing revulsion against Jim Crowism, the belief that dignity rests in man as such and that all must be treated as ends, not means.

31   But whatever its form, I believe that, far from being in any sense an enemy to patriotism, it is a new expression of the respect for life from which all true love springs. We can truly begin to perceive the meaning of our great propositions—of liberty and equality—if we see them as part of the patrimony of all men. We shall not love our corner of the planet less for loving the planet too, and resisting with all our skill and passion the dangers that would reduce it to smoldering ashes.

32   I can, therefore, wish no more for the profound patriotism of Americans than that they add to it a new dedication to the world-wide brotherhood of which they are a part and that, together with their love of America, there will grow a wider love which seeks to transform our earthly city, with all its races and peoples, all its creeds and aspirations, into Saint Augustine's "Heavenly city where truth reigns, love is the law, and whose extent is eternity."

Apparatus for: The Hard Kind of Patriotism

Vocabulary: *Supply a definition for each of the following words.*

1. synthesis (¶ 5)

    combination of part[s]
    that which cann[ot]
    should not be trans[ferred]
    to

2. inalienable (¶ 6)

3. audacity (¶ 10)

    presumptous

4. equivocal (¶ 14)

    open to suspicion o[f]

5. transcended (¶ 22)

    surpassed
    to be able to be ab[le]

6. viability (¶ 24)

    capabilities

7. ambiguity (¶ 26)

    vagueness

8. annihilation (¶ 27)

    destruction

9. bereft (¶ 29)

    sad

10. fratricide (¶ 30)

    killing a broth[er]

Discussion: *Rhetoric*

1. Defining highly charged abstract words like *patriotism* is usually difficult, but Stevenson has done an uncommonly good job here; he is clear in his own attitude toward our country; he does not hesitate to disagree with some; and he is sympathetic to the problem of loving this land in the right way. Point out the several steps Stevenson takes in developing his definition.
2. Where does the author actually give a definition? Where does he give the characteristics of a patriot?
3. In paragraph 12, Stevenson quotes a section of a poem by T. S. Eliot called "The Hollow Men." Where else does he make literary allusions?
4. Where does the end of this essay begin? How does the author strengthen his definition by the quote at the very end of the essay?

1. _He SAys whAt people think it is._
What it isn't WhAt it is.

2. _is PrisoN._

3. _15, 11, 29, 32_

4. _P 31_

Apparatus for: The Hard Kind of Patriotism

Discussion: *Theme. Explain the following statements taken from "The Hard Kind of Patriotism."*

1. "The difficulty lies with loving one's country in the right way."
2. "We *are* in one sense a very conservative people—for no nation in history has had so much to conserve."
3. "Do not, therefore, regard the critics as questionable patriots."
4. "We will survive John Birchism and all the rest of the superpatriots. . . ."
5. "They [Khrushchev and Mao Tse-tung] are both for the funeral."
6. "For, on this shrunken globe, men can no longer live as strangers."

1. _____

   _____

2. _____

   _____

3. _____

   _____

4. _____

   _____

5. _____

   _____

6. _____

   _____

Writing Suggestions

1. Choose any one of the quotes in the "Discussion of Theme" and develop it into a theme.
2. Analyze your own love for this country, showing what form and action this love takes.
3. What do you consider to be the strongest (or weakest) factor in America's concept of freedom?
4. Who or what is America's greatest enemy?
5. Choose one of the popular forms of dissent and show how it is (or is not) a demonstration of patriotism.
6. Should Communists be allowed to speak on college campuses? Give your views in a theme.

VI. PARAGRAPH DEVELOPMENT: EXAMPLE

Early in his history man began to communicate by sounds. But as he became more sophisticated, he began to draw pictures. Sometimes, of course, one picture—such as a wild animal with a spear in its side—was enough to tell a story. At other times a series of pictures was needed to tell the story. These early men would have had great difficulty, however, in drawing a picture or even a series of related pictures that said that "Happiness is peace of mind," or "Hate is the opposite of love." These statements are generalizations and personal opinions. Although early man could not deal with them in pictures, modern man constantly uses general or abstract statements. One of the best, yet simplest, ways to make them clear is with examples or illustrations.

A reader cannot be expected to accept a generalization or personal opinion without knowing *who* thinks this way, *why* the statement is made, or *how* this idea holds true. A clear, accurate example or illustration begins to answer such questions. It should be noted here that examples are rarely used in isolation, but are more often used with other forms of paragraph development, such as comparison and contrast, reason and evidence, or definition. In this chapter we will consider how examples can help a reader understand what a generalization means.

As used in this chapter, the word *example* covers all the illustrative and exemplifying methods of development: anecdote, quotation, and illustration, as well as example.

When a writer gives an illustration, the reader should be able to see in clear terms just what the writer means. And there is a further benefit: The reader does part of the work. That is, the reader is asked to apply the example to the generalization and conclude, with the writer, that the idea is valid. Reader involvement, then, is important and easily attainable through the use of effective examples.

Let's take an example ourselves. This paragraph (taken from "What Happened to 'America the Beautiful'?" by Robert Bendiner) deals with the problem of the gaudy distractions that surround Gettysburg.

> Where these commercial sideshows achieve their greatest degree of uglification is precisely in those areas where real sites of history or natural beauty exist. Of the millions of Americans who are moved to visit Gettysburg, for example, few can brood long over the meaning of the Civil War under the barrage of huckstering to which all comers are subjected—a broadside only a little less deadly than that faced by General Pickett. On one road to "this hallowed ground" is an irrelevant "Indian Village," and on the other an equally irrelevant "Horse 'n' Buggy Museum." Unless things have changed recently, a motel stands within a few hundred feet of the spot where Lincoln spoke his immortal lines; and something called "Fantasyland," featuring Mother Goose, faces General Meade's headquarters—all in addition, of course, to the exhibits, museums, and the Gettysburg Cyclorama, complete with sound track, which exploit the battle itself.

In this paragraph the author's intention is clear, and the mental picture of this cluttered historical area is sharp. But more important, you became momentarily involved because you pictured in your mind the cluttered landscape. And when you think with the writer, you are on his side. In your own writing, then, remember to illustrate your opinions.

Another advantage of using an example the reader can visualize is that the illustration has more significance—because it is specific. As readers, we tend to accept a concrete expression more quickly than an abstract one. Your task as a writer, of course, is to be certain that your examples are accurate and truly reflect the general statement you are supporting.

In addition to making a generalization specific, good examples make three other contributions to your writing: They add interest, they lend support, and they create involvement.

Good writing is vivid, and a good example helps to create a clear impression on the reader. As a result, the selection becomes more interesting. Notice how our interest increases in the following paragraphs when we come to the specific examples. (They are from "The Day JFK Died: What People Remember Now," by Alan Levy.)

> There were many different reactions to that day: poignant, grotesque, disgusted, disgusting, sentimental, violent, inspiring, patriotic. Virtually all were spontaneous and genuine.
>
> In a Warwick, Rhode Island, obstetrician's waiting room, the jarring bulletin from Dallas came over an all-music FM station. Without a word, a dozen expectant mothers stood up and went home. On Death Rows, murderers wept. In Denver, fighter Sonny Liston wept. In Brooklyn, a subway conductor started to announce the next station on his public address system—and broadcast his sobs instead. In Manhattan, an elderly news dealer tried to shout "Extra! Extra!,"

but what emerged from his heart was a wail of anguish: "Oh, my God, this is a young tree chopped down!"

At a medical convention in Dallas, a local hostess was about to award an honorary Texas citizenship to a distinguished physician when the news came about what had happened in her city. "I can no longer present this to you," she said with shame, slowly tearing up the elaborate document.

Writing, then, is more interesting when we can see exactly what the author has in his mind. In order to add that important ingredient of good writing—interest—use examples.

Supporting evidence is important whenever a personal opinion is given or a generalization made. Examples are one way of lending support to a general statement. The author of the following paragraph is supporting his assertion that the problem of billboards is getting worse. (The selection is from "What Happened to 'America the Beautiful'?")

In most of the remaining 34 states, and away from the expressways of those that have accepted the federal government's bonus, the billboard problem seems to be getting worse by the year. Cubbedge [author of *The Destroyers of America*] tells of trees chopped down along New York's scenic Route 17 through the Catskills, just to make sure the billboards can easily be seen. "In the historically romantic Suwanee River country of Florida," he reports, "there are today sixty billboards per mile." A spot survey by the American Automobile Association in Wisconsin found a 2.7-mile stretch of road through lovely rural country with 122 signs on the southbound side and 99 on the northbound. And along some of the most thrilling desert drives of the Southwest, billboards not only provide a jarring contrast to the scenery, they all but blot it out.

In the following paragraph (also taken from "The Day JFK Died: What People Remember Now") we see the use of a series of examples.

Scientists are studying now what happened to us that day. The University of Chicago's National Opinion Research Center surveyed 1,400 adults and found that half of them wept. A comparable number had trouble sleeping. At least two out of five experienced an upset stomach. At least two Ph.D. candidates at universities are analyzing the birth rate nine months later. Others are even investigating the dreams that people reported having. But no scientific paper can recall the dreamlike cloud through which we wandered on that day.

Even when evidence is given in concrete detail, the reader may not agree with your overall thesis; but he will probably acknowledge that your evidence is accurate.

As mentioned earlier in this chapter, involvement is a healthy by-product of a good example. One thing is certain: You want your reader to share your ideas and your judgments. When you relate a personal incident, you take your reader into your trust. Consider the following paragraph by Mark Twain (from "Advice to Youth").

Never handle firearms carelessly. The sorrow and suffering that have been caused through the innocent but heedless handling of firearms by the young!

Only four days ago, right in the next farmhouse to the one where I am spending the summer, a grandmother, old and gray and sweet, one of the loveliest spirits in the land, was sitting at her work, when her young grandson crept in and got down an old, battered, rusty gun which had not been touched for many years and was supposed not to be loaded, and pointed it at her, laughing and threatening to shoot. In her fright she ran screaming and pleading toward the door on the other side of the room; but as she passed him he placed the gun almost against her very breast and pulled the trigger! He had supposed it was not loaded. And he was right—it wasn't. So there wasn't any harm done. It is the only case of that kind that I ever heard of. Therefore, just the same, don't you meddle with old unloaded firearms; they are the most deadly and unerring things that have ever been created by man. You don't have to take any pains at all with them; you don't have to have a rest, you don't have to have any sights on the gun, you don't have to take aim, even. No, you just pick out a relative and bang away, and you are sure to get him. A youth who can't hit a cathedral at thirty yards with a Gatling gun in three-quarters of an hour, can take up an old empty musket and bag his grandmother every time, at a hundred. Think what Waterloo would have been if one of the armies had been boys armed with old muskets supposed not to be loaded, and the other army had been composed of their female relations. The very thought of it makes one shudder.

Through the use of examples, then, you will give a personal touch to your writing. We no longer draw pictures to communicate specific ideas, and we could never draw pictures of general statements; so we do the best we can: We create mental images with examples and illustrations. This is an easy, effective, and time-honored way of supporting abstract statements.

16. WHAT HAPPENED TO "AMERICA THE BEAUTIFUL"? *

ROBERT BENDINER

1 To most English-speaking people the very sound of the word *meadow* conjures up the freshness of long, soft grass spotted with clover. But if you happen to live in the vicinity of New York, the word will more likely call up a picture of the "Jersey Meadows," a vast and noxious swampland of industrial wastes that assails the eye and nose of the visitor approaching from the west just as he catches sight of the Manhattan skyline shimmering in the distance. As though to underline this triumph of ugliness over grandeur, half-buried in the same marsh and clearly visible from a train window are the broken Doric columns that were chopped out of Pennsylvania Station when that architectural gem was wrecked to make room for a thousand more offices and a sports arena.

2 The thought that America the Beautiful has allowed herself to get dowdy and down at the heel requires no visit to the Jersey Meadows, however—or, in fact, extensive travel of any sort. It is as apparent in California as it is in New York, in Florida and Massachusetts as it is in Arkansas and Indiana. All too often the great roads that are our national pride connect urban rot with suburban blight, while secondary roads lined with honky-tonk establishments stretch out into a countryside marred by auto graveyards, gravel pits, and billboards.

3 For more than a century Americans have taken in their stride this progressive assault upon one of the world's loveliest landscapes. In the pioneer past it was always possible to move on to fresh pastures and untouched beauty; and when the land filled up and the era of the ever-beckoning frontier ended, it was

* Robert Bendiner, "What Happened to 'America the Beautiful'?" *Redbook,* June 1965. Reprinted with permission.

not easy to drop the slipshod habits of an earlier period. But inevitably came the day when, looking about them at the slashed hillsides and dirty streams, at the despoiled forests and decaying cities, men began to take stock of what they had done to the land. As long ago as 1916 the philosopher Josiah Royce observed that "Local pride ought above all to center, so far as the material objects are concerned, about the determination to give the surroundings of the community nobility, dignity, beauty. . . . We Americans spend far too much of our strength and time upon injuring our landscapes, and far too little upon endeavoring to beautify our towns and cities."

4   Today such sentiments would be regarded as exceedingly mild. In books, articles, and speeches the ugly word *uglification* has come to the fore. Planners who a few years ago thought mostly in terms of superhighways are beginning to lose ground to others who have come to question whether much of what Americans travel at high speeds to see is worth seeing when they get there.

5   By all odds the most emotional of these inquiries is a book called *God's Own Junkyard,* and it is calculated to jolt the most complacent American right out of his armchair. "This book is not written in anger," says Peter Blake, its author. "It is written in fury—though not, I trust, in blind fury." But if Mr. Blake's prose is emotional, the photographs he displays—and 103 of his book's 144 pages consist of pictures—are not emotional at all. They are the camera's quiet but devastating testimony to the ways we have found for converting natural beauty into unnatural squalor. A few examples:

6   Nestled in the lap of a Colorado valley, an auto junkyard framed by majestic hills.

7   A giant sequoia, the trunk of which has been hollowed out to accommodate what a huge ugly sign proclaims as a "World-Famous Tree House. 'Believe It or Not.' "

8   The handsome New York Central Building, in New York, before and after its contours were blurred by, rising behind it, the drab and gigantic Pan Am Building now sitting astride Grand Central Station.

9   The long vista of motels on a Miami Beach road, each hawking in lurid neon its offerings in the way of air-conditioning, private pools and cocktail lounges.

10   A wooded grove alongside a Hawaiian road in which the trees bear huge-lettered pleas to vote for Jimmie Kealoha and "Peanuts" Kunihisa.

11   An airplane dragging across the sky a monstrous banner proclaiming the virtues of somebody's beer, the photo captioned with an ironic quotation from Thoreau: "Thank God, men cannot yet fly, and lay waste the sky as well as the earth."

12   Blake pictures more than a hundred such eyesores, and no doubt every

half-sensitive American can see in his mind's eye scores of others—historic shrines turned into cheap bazaars; woody glades littered with beer cans; the green waters of a mountain lake streaked with oil from powerboats; picnic-littered beaches; and perhaps most oppressive of all, vast stretches of what was once countryside now cluttered with cracker-box houses dropped planlessly on the land with no more regard for blending the works of man with the works of nature than one would have expected in a mining camp in the days of the Gold Rush.

13 Far from being a lone voice crying in the despoiled wilderness, Peter Blake's is one of a swelling chorus. From his outsized volume (in both hard and soft covers), the protests range downward in bulk to Robert E. Cubbedge's little paperback *The Destroyers of America* and upward again through Stewart Udall's *The Quiet Crisis* and Michael Frome's *Whose Woods These Are* to that comprehensive, magnificent and costly work, *Man-Made America, Chaos or Control?* by Christopher Tunnard and Boris Pushkarev.

14 In general, Blake's and Cubbedge's books are popular and indignant. Secretary of the Interior Udall's is inspirational; Frome's is specialized; and the volume by Tunnard and Pushkarev, although intended primarily for architects, planners and designers, is, according to the publisher, "also for the layman who wishes to understand what is happening to his environment and how he can help to improve it." It is even more lushly illustrated than Blake's, and in a class by itself for analyzing the relationship between man and his landscape.

15 Starting out on the open road, long a symbol of America's zest for high adventure, we find Blake denouncing today's highways for the most part as "scars that cut across mountains and plains, across cities and suburbs, poisoning the landscape and townscape with festering sores along their edges." And as they cut across our cities, "they form massive walls that mutilate our communities by chopping them up into disconnected bits and pieces."

16 The charge is sweeping, no doubt, but it accurately reflects the sober comment of many experts. Conrad L. Wirth, until recently head of the National Park Service, put it this way: "We have destroyed a lot of wonderful scenery by slapping our high-speed roads down the fastest routes, regardless of anything else. We build these superhighways so you can go one hundred and twenty miles an hour. But men and women can't drive a car more than sixty miles an hour for any length of time without fatigue setting in. . . . If our highways were designed to be scenic, as well as to get you from one place to another at reasonable speeds, we would see a tremendous lot of pretty country that we're missing."

17 His sentiment is echoed by the Secretary of the Interior himself, who has observed, "We need these new highways, they're fine, but let's wind them around a little bit so they go to different spots. Let's not destroy historic objects or fine scenery; let's make it available for people to enjoy."

18   It should be said at once that such roads do exist, although too few of them. There is, for instance, New York's Taconic State Parkway, a flowing ribbon in space which Tunnard and Pushkarev picture under the caption, "The ultimate harmony of art and nature."

19   Does it pay the traveler to leave the turnpikes and the throughways with all their general monotony and take to the major but less pretentious roads? Not, our critics suggest, if you have any measurable degree of sensitivity. For on these much-traveled routes are the great commercial strips. Here the road-houses compete with the diners; the filling stations flag you down with pennants; the motels scream out their neon-lighted endorsements—by Duncan Hines, the American Automobile Association or the Diner's Club—and the billboards all but run into each other, merging the merits of beer, autos, shaving cream, and candy in a running plea to spend your money fast and keep the whirligig going.

20   Where these arteries run through resort areas—whether in the Adirondacks or the Great Smokies, along the Florida coast or the shores of Lake Superior—their normal commercialism is intensified by scores of roadside attractions of doubtful merit, especially designed to trap tourists en route with restless children. These are the Zooramas, Indian Trading Posts, Storybook Towns, Reptile Gardens, North Poles and the like, where unwary parents are not only clipped on admission but forced to run a gantlet of gaudy gift stands loaded with mementos of the spot—usually fresh from Hong Kong.

21   The deserved success of such fine reconstructions as Colonial Williamsburg, in Virginia, Sturbridge Village, in Massachusetts, and the whaling town of Mystic Seaport, in Connecticut, has inevitably encouraged a spate of imitations of vastly lower caliber. And often enough, especially in North Carolina and parts of the West, caged and pathetically scrawny bears, deer and even wildcats appear along the roadside as lures for gift shops, service stations and diners. In *Whose Woods These Are,* Michael Frome indignantly describes one such scene: "Gracing the foreground of the historic gateway to Pisgah National Forest is a roadside souvenir and refreshment stand. Here you can buy a Coke, hand it to a bear through the bars of his cage and watch him drink it. The purpose of his presence is to attract your interest and trade."

22   Where these commercial sideshows achieve their greatest degree of uglification is precisely in those areas where real sites of history or natural beauty exist. Of the millions of Americans who are moved to visit Gettysburg, for example, few can brood long over the meaning of the Civil War under the barrage of huckstering to which all comers are subjected—a broadside only a little less deadly than that faced by General Pickett. On one road to "this hallowed ground" is an irrelevant "Indian Village," and on the other an equally irrelevant "Horse 'n' Buggy Museum." Unless things have changed recently, a motel stands within a few hundred feet of the spot where Lincoln spoke his immortal lines; and something called "Fantasyland," featuring Mother Goose,

faces General Meade's headquarters—all in addition, of course, to the exhibits, museums and the Gettysburg Cyclorama, complete with sound track, which exploit the battle itself.

23   Gettysburg is typical of scores of national shrines across the country, all forced to compete with money-making come-ons that crowd around them, each brassily heralding its presence for 20 miles on every side with billboards that tell you that you "must" stop and see them or presumably your children will be underprivileged.

24   The authors of *Man-Made America* point out in this connection that French law takes into account the entire surroundings of a building or site thought worthy of preservation, and no ugly structures are allowed to mar its setting or divert the visitor's attention. Two doors from the Lincoln house in Springfield, by way of contrast, is a gift shop with life-size statues of Grant and Lee in the window under Union and Confederate flags, presumably to encourage the patronage of tourists from the South as well as the North. And visible from the street is a six-foot figure of Lincoln, with a sign inviting tourists to take each other's pictures standing next to the Great Emancipator—*free*.

25   Of all the billboards that force themselves on the attention of motorists and pedestrians alike, those that advertise such roadside culture spots are of course proportionately few. That the others are an eyesore of major dimensions is the theme of a long-standing but so far none-too-successful campaign to bring them under tighter control before they block out what beauty may be left along the highway.

26   Several of our authors are so impressed with the way Ogden Nash once formulated the problem that they include his observation in their works, and I shall do likewise:

> I think that I shall never see
> A billboard lovely as a tree.
> Perhaps, unless the billboards fall,
> I'll never see a tree at all.†

At that, the poet's commentary is mild compared with that of Governor Pat Brown of California, whom Blake quotes as saying: "When a man throws an empty cigarette package from an automobile . . . he is liable to a fine of fifty dollars. When a man throws a billboard across a view, he is liable to be richly rewarded. I see little difference between the damage done by these two litterbugs."

27   There is federal legislation on the books now to encourage the states to adopt tighter regulation of billboards, but it is exceedingly mild. In addition to the tax rebates that the federal government makes to states for building

† Ogden Nash, "Song of the Open Road," *The New Yorker*, Oct. 15, 1932. Reprinted with permission.

limited-access expressways, it offers a bonus of one half of one per cent to those states that prohibit more than two signs per mile within 660 feet of these roads. But even with "these bounties to protect their own historic and scenic attractions," as Cubbedge describes them, only 16 states so far have been induced to go along.

28   In most of the remaining 34 states, and away from the expressways of those that have accepted the federal government's bonus, the billboard problem seems to be getting worse by the year. Cubbedge tells of trees chopped down along New York's scenic Route 17 through the Catskills, just to make sure the billboards can easily be seen. "In the historically romantic Suwanee River country of Florida," he reports, "there are today sixty billboards—count 'em— sixty billboards per mile." A spot survey by the American Automobile Association in Wisconsin found a 2.7-mile stretch of road through lovely rural country with 122 signs on the southbound side and 99 on the northbound. And along some of the most thrilling desert drives of the Southwest, billboards not only provide a jarring contrast to the scenery, they all but blot it out.

29   A regrettable effect of even such weak legislation as we have is that outdoor advertisers are taking to signs of spectacular size and character so that they can be seen beyond the requisite distance of 660 feet. Still worse, specially lighted and moving signs seem to be in the offing; and a recently invented gadget called the "Skyjector," with the power of 60 giant searchlights, threatens to project slides on the sides of mountains, on the Grand Canyon and on the very clouds!

30   A unique characteristic of Americans is that they not only are aware of their faults as well as their virtues, but sooner or later find scientific ways to measure them. This is true now on the "uglification" front. Keep America Beautiful, an organization dedicated to the purpose set forth in its name, has not only evolved a "litter index" for cities but also discovered that the average citizen of the United States produces exactly twice as much trash as his British counterpart (which, as it happens, squares perfectly with the ratio between the two countries' Gross National Product). So much of this waste, unfortunately, winds up on the streets and highways of the nation that if it were concentrated on a 3,000-mile route between New York and San Francisco, the entire road would be buried "a foot deep in discarded wrappers, cartons, paper cups, plates, tissues, cans, bottles, garbage and such assorted trash as old mattresses and automotive parts."

31   As trash disfiguring the landscape, these last-named products of an affluent society are in a class by themselves. There is a superstition that when elephants are about to die they retire to hidden burial grounds and decently settle down for the ages. About the automobile, which serves as our elephant, there is no possibility of such a legend. From New England to the Pacific Coast, the United States is pocked with rusting mounds of discarded autos and auto parts. Cubbedge tells of a junkyard in Southern California (where everything seems to

grow to excess), with old cars piled to the height of a four-story building.

32   An article in a recent issue of the *Wall Street Journal* estimated that there are some 8,000 of these strange and unattractive mounds in the country, which may baffle the archaeologists of a distant day as much as Stonehenge puzzles ours. Nor does this take into account the thousands of hulks of old cars which in poorer areas are abandoned individually, in empty lots or by the side of the road. Speaking to an Oregon audience a few months ago, President Johnson was moved to remark, "The skeletons of discarded cars, old junk cars, litter our countryside—and are driving my wife mad." It is one of the things that is now being looked into by a Presidential task force on the Preservation of Natural Beauty, the very existence of which is a remarkable acknowledgment of the need for aesthetic improvement. The task force might well take note that Sweden's discarded autos are simply dumped some 15 miles out in the Baltic.

33   The pollution of American rivers with industrial wastes is so enormous a problem in sanitary engineering and economics that its aesthetic aspects tend to be sloughed off as merely incidental. But anyone who has seen the Missouri River, aptly described as a "thousand-mile sewer," will appreciate the depressing impact this industrial vandalism can have. For those who have not seen it, the description by Public Health Service engineers, cited in *Lane, Wood and Water* by the late Senator Robert S. Kerr, should more than suffice:

34   "The mouth of the Floyd River, at its juncture with the Missouri, appeared almost clogged with untreated packing-plant wastes. Floating masses of grease solids lined the banks, extended well into the stream, and clung to every solid object on the surface of the water. Where the water was not red with bloody wastes, it was gray with decomposing organic wastes. Offensive odor filled the atmosphere." An Iowa state official reported seeing "patches of floating grease in the current solid enough for crows to ride on."

35   Less sensational only by comparison with the Missouri has been the fate of scores of American rivers—the Detroit, the Passaic, the Merrimack (once a fisherman's delight), stretches of the Hudson and even the Potomac, which threads its polluted way through the capital city.

36   "Uglification" is not merely the careless destruction of natural beauty. It may, and often does, reside in the planless and incompetent works of men, which brings us inevitably to the nature and deterioration of American cities. Here is a subject so vast and complex that libraries have been written about it, which obviously cannot be more than suggested in this brief review of our national inelegance. But even the suggestion should not leave the impression that all is bleak and hopeless. On the contrary, if the tide is turning anywhere, as we shall see, it is in many of our cities, where civic leaders are working to undo the neglect and anarchy of generations.

37   The great change that brought our cities low, robbing them of their true character, has been the flight of almost everything but office-transacted business from their central districts. For as Tunnard and Pushkarev put it, "The heart of the city has always been considered the center of our civilization." Now, without the old mixture of commerce, market, cultural life, service, and livability, the central city runs to physical and social monotony, to traffic-paralyzed canyons between walls of steel and glass. "Its convenience has disappeared," say Tunnard and Pushkarev. "The old easygoing days of city living in which a housewife could call up a store and have a package delivered by the streetcar conductor at the end of the street are gone forever, and such new 'convenience' devices as drive-in tellers and pigeonhole parking garages have not proved an adequate substitute. New attractions which might have brought more people to the central business district have seldom been forthcoming—the movie houses have been turned into television studios, the best restaurants are likely to be out on the highway with plenty of free parking. . . ." The result is "a series of not very skillfully related projects of a commercial-servicing nature, separated by surface parking lots and garages and containing a large population in daytime and almost none at night."

38   With this strong tendency toward crowding our business districts with more and more office buildings of a discouragingly monotonous style, it becomes harder by the year to tell whether one is in Providence, Toledo or Omaha. By contrast, Cubbedge quotes a traveler who vividly recalled 18 European cities he had visited three years before, because each one was built around a square or monument or fine boulevard or park "with public buildings usually prominent in the concept."

39   European cities were built for people, the criticism runs, and American cities for commerce. "Almost every civilized city of Western Europe has a waterfront dedicated to its inhabitants," Blake writes, citing Copenhagen, Stockholm, London, Paris, Zurich and Naples. "American cities have six- or twelve-lane highways instead. It is entirely possible that some of our cities fronting the Atlantic, the Pacific, or the Gulf have more water frontage than Venice; alas, there is no way of finding out, unless one is airborne." How many of New York's miles of harbor and river shore are accessible to pedestrians? Once one could sit on a bank overlooking the Narrows and watch the ships come in, and even walk a wooded path along the Hudson, but there is no longer room for such niceties of civilization. If you can afford the rent and your apartment is high enough, you can watch the river from your living-room window, but for most New Yorkers the water is situated on the other side of a great traffic barrier, because "highway experts rarely if ever talk to city planners."

40   In the same way, few of our cities have the pleasant little parks, the numerous benches, the pedestrian malls and open spaces, the deliberate blending of architectural styles and the abundance of flowers that brighten so many cities abroad. Interviewed on the subject of the American landscape a few years ago,

Conrad Wirth, then director of the National Park Service, reminisced about the public flower beds that used to decorate our cities—there were even flower boxes on the lampposts in his native Minneapolis. "I'd like to see us go back to planting flowers and getting some color into our towns—a breath of freshness across the whole country," he said.

41   The difficulty in which the large American city finds itself is circular. Having lost much of its middle-income citizenry to the suburbs, it grows poorer in revenues and shoddier in aspect. And the shoddier it grows, the less likely it is to win back those fugitives who require and support the very aspects of a city that make it livable—theaters, music, parks, good restaurants, attractive houses, trees, flowers and all those other amenities that make urban life rewarding.

42   To bring back these exiles, slum clearance alone offers no promise. Admittedly, the replacement of rotting tenements with decent low-income housing is vitally necessary, and as far as the worst slums go, surely this deserves priority. But it has little to do with restoring the character of the city as a generally desirable place to live. It is neither an inducement to suburbanites to return nor is it in its very nature likely to be an aesthetic feature. A growing number of cities have been registering an awareness that aesthetic renaissance is as necessary to urban renewal as slum clearance; it is impossible now to travel around the country without becoming impressed with what some of them are doing to restore the graces of urban living.

43   To cite a few examples: Hartford, Connecticut, has practically remade its central city area. San Francisco has acted just in time to save its colorful waterfront from being blocked off by a freeway. Pittsburgh has rebuilt its Golden Triangle, the business section at the point where the Allegheny and the Monongahela rivers meet to form the Ohio; and downtown Boston is getting a much-needed overhauling. But nowhere, I think, is the process of beautifying a city going forward so impressively as in Philadelphia, where a conscious effort of serious proportions is being made to lure back the city's solid burghers by the remodeling and restoration of blocks of 18th-century row houses on Society Hill.

44   This historic section, purchased from William Penn by the Free Society of Traders, and in Franklin's day, *the* residential area of the city, had been allowed to degenerate into a shabby stretch of boardinghouses along an ugly commercial waterfront. With city, federal and private money and a concentrated dose of intelligent planning, the old houses, stripped of a century's grime and newly trimmed, are emerging with all the beauty of their colonial lines intact. Old warehouses and other eyesores are being torn down, new houses designed to blend with the old are springing up, three apartment towers are rising and patches of green are being spotted throughout the area. A parkway is planned to run along the Delaware, which borders the district, and the shabby old piers are to be replaced with marinas. Altogether this section, including Independ-

ence Hall, which is now set off by a long mall, should be one of the most attractive residential areas in the country—all a ten-minute walk from Broad Street, in the very heart of the city.

45 In suburbs across the country, however, the picture is less encouraging, primarily because responsibility is so scattered. Surrounding all our cities are metropolitan areas far larger than the cities themselves, but there are no metro-politan-area governments to correspond. Hence the planlessness with which new, commercially conceived colonies sprout like weeds in what were once farm valleys and wooded hills, imposing strains on the surrounding communi-ties and adding nothing to the delights of the countryside. "Thus, about half of California's 15 million residents," Cubbedge reports, "now live in unincor-porated communities, sometimes called 'slurbs,' which started out with almost no ground rules whatever."

46 Growing into communities of a sort, these "slurbs" are totally lacking in the kind of center that gives character to a town. Shopping centers sometimes assume this function, but a collection of chain-store units is hardly a substitute for the "downtowns" that created the familiar and attractive regional patterns for American towns in the past. These too, in fact, are fading before an advanc-ing uniformity, as Tunnard and Pushkarev point out: "A white New England village center around an irregular green and a Texas courthouse town with its central building on the square are still very different habitation patterns; but now that both have been invaded by standardized subdivisions, identical gas stations, garages, restaurant chains, stainless steel 'diners,' auto courts and parking lots, their distinctive character has largely been dissipated."

47 In Blake's view, "the mess that is suburban America" stems chiefly from the tradition that every family should live in its own house on a small lot. The result in lower-income developments is a wholly uneconomic use of land whereby front yards are cultivated for show but not for use; back yards, too small for real use, are neglected; and any serious attempt to preserve the beauty and natural advantages of the land is impossible.

48 An alternative that in the past few years has been coming into its own is the concept of the cluster. Here the pattern of one lot, one house—all evenly spaced out and deadly monotonous—is abandoned in favor of a scheme in which a number of houses are grouped more closely, even attached, and the appreciable acreage left over is made available for the common enjoyment. This community land might wind up as an open green or be left as woods or be turned into a recreation area complete with swimming pool. A large develop-ment, with a number of such clusters irregularly placed, could obviously have a considerable variety of open spaces, with vastly greater prospects of giving visual pleasure than would a hundred "ranchettes" set out in a gridiron, each with a postage-stamp lawn that can be worked but not used.

49 From the cluster concept there has evolved an innovation of even greater promise—the "new town." This is the completely planned community—not

simply a housing development. In an area originally under the ownership of one man or company, provision is made not only for a variety of clustered houses to accommodate families of different size and income, but also for commercial zones, community centers, schools, churches and recreational facilities. A number of such skillfully planned towns are already in being or under construction, notably Don Mills, near Toronto; Park Forest, Illinois; Reston, Virginia, near Washington; Columbia, in Maryland's Howard County; and some 15 more in varying stages of development in California. Reston, the only one I have seen, is being planned for a population of 75,000 and promises from the start to offer every charm a community can enjoy except age and eccentricity.

50   Signs are not lacking, then, that as a nation we are slowly turning away from the concept that an attractive environment is only an incidental good, desirable as long as it doesn't cost any appreciable money or get in the way of more material progress. Besides making a start at refurbishing our cities, planning some fifty "new towns" and building at least some roads with an eye to scenic pleasure rather than efficiency alone, we are making serious long-range attempts to preserve the little that *is* left of the quiet wilderness for the contemplation of harried 20th-century man. Last year's 88th Congress is regarded by conservationists as the best on record, not only for the Wilderness Act, which safeguards many forests and other uncultivated areas throughout the country from exploitation, but also for the financial aid it voted to state and local governments committed to acquiring more land for outdoor recreation.

51   For all these encouraging signs, however, it is clear that the monumental work of restoring the beauties of America has scarcely been started. The renaissance of cities has only begun and "slurbs" are everywhere. The magnificent redwood forests of California are yet to be saved from extinction at the hands of highway builders and loggers. The wild Colorado River is scheduled to be tamed by federal dams, with the consequent loss of much of its primeval appeal. The Hudson River Valley at its loveliest part is threatened with disfigurement to provide industry with more electric power in the most expedient way. And our national parks, pocked by trailer camps and parking lots, are unable to accommodate the ever-swelling waves of tourists, vandals included, and still provide the serene pleasures that are the reason for their existence.

52   If America really sets out to beautify itself—not merely to pick up its litter but to clean its waters and rebuild its waterfronts, to restore the hearts of its cities and the charm of its countryside, there will have to be a formidable combination of private pressure and governmental response on all levels—local, state and national. Cubbedge points out the effectiveness of that combination in Maryland, where citizens successfully fought to save their highways from the "billboard desecraters"; in Chicago, where public protest prevented the razing of historic landmarks; and in California, where irate San Franciscans saved their waterfront. Cubbedge urges the formation of a Citizens Vigilance Committee to "stamp out the slobs." He suggests that the group work through legis-

lation, through education and by such direct action as vigorously taking to task or reporting to the police those public nuisances who spoil the landscape for others. In Germany or France a vandal seen littering a public road or tramping down the fresh grass of a public square will be brought up sharp by the nearest fellow citizen.

53   Actually there are many private groups working toward the beautifying of America, though they may not think of themselves as vigilantes. The citizen who wants to do something to preserve the charm of his country can join one or, if necessary, start a local one of his own. Keep America Beautiful, a national organization with headquarters in New York City, has been conducting a vigorous and effective war against litterbugs. State and regional garden clubs have been active in the fight to regulate billboards, and so has the American Automobile Association. The American Society of Landscape Architects and the American Planning and Civic Association, among others, have concerned themselves with improving the appearance of the public environment, and there are local groups throughout the country devoted to preserving the landmarks and natural attractions of their respective areas. It is not impossible that some of these organizations may band together—as the publication *Landscape Architect* urged not long ago—in a national alliance of citizens with these objectives: "To preserve, enhance and improve this nation's great bounty of natural and man-made beauty; to conserve irreplaceable natural and scenic resources; to encourage and publicize superior design in landscape architecture, architecture and urban development; to prevent blight, neglect, and uglification; and to develop an educated public vigorously supporting these goals."

54   To most critics in the field, however, the hope lies chiefly in laws and in leadership—far more stringent zoning laws, laws to reduce land speculation, laws to encourage good building and discourage bad, laws to prohibit open dumps and regulate earth removal, laws to require the refilling of gravel pits and the screening of junkyards, and laws to forbid billboards on arterial highways. But so massive a legal program is not realistic without a public that is eager for it and leadership that can inspire it. "With education," Tunnard and Pushkarev suggest, "most Americans would no longer tolerate big, flashy automobiles crowded on ugly highways seen against a background of fields littered with their just-discarded predecessors; they would prefer modest and durable vehicles on expansive freeways with views of well-landscaped surroundings."

55   If this is true, certainly education is urgent. For as Secretary Udall puts it, "We cannot afford an America where expedience tramples upon aesthetics and development decisions are made with an eye only on the present." Technology has its place but, after all, "a glimpse of grouse can be more inspiring than a Hollywood spectacular." And conjuring up the spirit of Thoreau, the Secretary goes so far as to suggest the very words that that eccentric philosopher might have used to advise those who are overwhelmed by the complexities of modern life: "If you want inner peace, find it in solitude, not speed, and if you would find yourself, look to the land from which you came and to which you go."

Apparatus for: What Happened to "America the Beautiful"?

Vocabulary: *Using your dictionary, substitute synonyms for the italicized words in the following sentences.*

1. . . . a vast and *noxious* swampland . . . (¶ 1)   *harmful*
2. As though to underline this triumph of ugliness over *grandeur* . . . (¶ 1)   *beauty*
3. The thought that America the Beautiful has allowed herself to get *dowdy* and down at the heel requires no . . .(¶ 2)   *graceless*
4. . . . and when the land filled up and the *era* of the ever-beckoning frontier ended, it was not easy to drop the *slipshod* habits of an earlier period. (¶ 3)
5. Today such *sentiments* would be regarded as exceedingly mild. (¶ 4)   *orderless*
6. . . . and it is calculated to jolt the most *complacent* American right out of his armchair. (¶ 5)   *feeling*
7. They are the camera's quiet but *devastating* testimony . . . (¶ 5)   *benevolent*
8. . . . books are popular and *indignant*. (¶ 14)   *resentment*
9. . . . we find Blake *denouncing* today's highways . . . (¶ 15)   *disappraise*
10. . . . they form massive walls that *mutilate* our communities by chopping them up . . . (¶ 15)   *deform*
11. . . . where *unwary* parents are not only clipped on admission but forced to run a *gantlet* of gaudy gift stands . . . (¶ 19)   *negligent*
12. . . . has inevitably encouraged a *spate* of imitations of vastly lower caliber. (¶ 21)   *plenty*
13. . . . they can be seen beyond the *requisite* distance of 660 feet. (¶ 29)

14. . . . these last-named products of an *affluent* society . . . (¶ 31)

15. . . . tend to be *sloughed* off as merely incidental. (¶ 33)

16. . . . *reminisced* about the public flower beds that used to decorate our cities . . . (¶ 40)

17. . . . all evenly spaced out and deadly *monotonous* . . . (¶ 48)

18. . . . laws to forbid billboards on *arterial* highways. (¶ 54)

approching

learning

remembering

equal

communicating

Discussion: *Rhetoric*

1. This essay begins with a series of contrasts. Point these out and comment on their usefulness.
2. What does the word *this* refer to in paragraph 3? Is the first sentence of that paragraph the thesis of the entire essay? Or is this the thesis merely implied?
3. Why does the author use the word *uglification*? Does he adequately define it? Where is the definition?
4. Notice that paragraph 12 asks for the reader's participation. Just how does the author get the reader personally involved here?
5. In his discussion of "uglification," the author begins with a description of the commercial attractions "of doubtful merit." Then comes his attack on billboards. What is next to come under attack? What is the effect of such an arrangement?
6. The first two sentences of paragraph 36 could be considered a restatement of the thesis. Why does the author bury this restatement of the thesis?
7. How effective are the author's references to the way Europeans do things?
8. If we say this essay has a beginning, middle, and end, where does the ending begin?

1. *Meadows, effective*

2. *the changing years. Yes*
    No.

3. *Opposite of beautification*
    No. Rest of article

210

Apparatus for: What Happened to "America the Beautiful"?

4. _Makes you think of places you've been_

5. _Litter. Billboards were as bad as litter_

6. _No resolution_

7. _Plan city for people instead of commerce._

8. _P.S.Q._

Discussion: *Theme*

1. What additional causes would you add to this selection to account for the "uglification" of our land?
2. Is the whole picture as bleak as this essay paints it? Explain.
3. Should we Americans pay more attention to the way other countries have handled their natural beauty? Explain.
4. Should commercial businesses be allowed to operate next to our great shrines? Would the limiting of *where* be contradictory to the free enterprise system?
5. In your travels around the country, what has impressed you as the worst example of "uglification"?
6. Point out some examples in your own town where bad judgment has been used in preserving or destroying the natural beauty.
7. What do you consider to be the best plan for making our country free of unsightly billboards, car heaps, junk yards, and other unpleasant scenes?

1. _____

2. _____

_____

3. _____

_____

4. _____

_____

5. _____

_____

6. _____

_____

7. _____

_____

Writing Suggestions

1. Using information you know personally, write a theme similar to "What Happened to 'America the Beautiful'?"
2. Outline a program for returning your campus or city to the "Land of the Beautiful."
3. Read paragraph 32 and imagine you are the archaeologist who discovers such a mound a few thousand years from now. Then write a theme about this "discovery."
4. Write a paper pointing out some of the ironies in modern industrial life; for example, in making our people almost completely mobile and free to go, we have poisoned the air with car fumes.
5. Imagine you are the president of the largest billboard agency in the state; then write a letter to Ogden Nash (see paragraph 26) pointing out the necessity of billboards.
6. Write a paper on the "industrial vandalism" of polluting our streams and rivers.

17. THE DAY JFK DIED: WHAT PEOPLE REMEMBER NOW *

ALAN LEVY

1 When a waiter brought the news, the historian of Presidential politics, Theodore H. White, was lunching atop the Time-Life Building at Rockefeller Center. White raced downstairs to a news ticker and, confirming that the President had been shot, caught a cab for the airport—destination: Dallas. But when the taxi radio said that John F. Kennedy was dead, White switched to the air shuttle for Washington. His emotion, he says, was "absolute terror."

2 Later, in his second *The Making of the President* chronicle, White wrote: "The news struck the East Coast at mid-lunch, the Pacific Coast in midmorning; it stopped all presses in their run; interrupted all TV screens; stabbed with its pain men and women in the streets, knotted them about TV sets and paralyzed them in postures, first unbelieving, then stricken. . . . It was, for Americans, an episode to be remembered, a clap of alarm as sharp and startling as the memory of Pearl Harbor, so that forever they would ask one another—*Where were you when you heard the news?*"

3 On Friday, November 22, 1963, the entire nation (and possibly the world) was convulsed by what a psychiatrist calls "a massive grief reaction." There were all the symptoms of extreme anxiety that followed the death of Franklin Delano Roosevelt. FDR, like most Presidents, had been a "father figure"—and when he died, on April 12, 1945, a nation at war felt as though it had lost a parent. When John Fitzgerald Kennedy died, the nation lost a son and a brother and a husband as well as a father—a young man who, through the intimacy of television, had become a tower of faith or anger or worry in our daily lives. We knew him, even if he didn't know all of us.

* Alan Levy, "The Day JFK Died: What People Remember Now," *Good Housekeeping,* November 1965. Reprinted with permission.

4 In Los Angeles that day, a widow named Mary Seres lamented: "I can't stop crying. I lost my husband three months ago, but I think this is a greater shock. It's terrible."

5 Shock . . . disbelief . . . the vacant look of someone awaiting the punch line of a joke (surely it must be a joke) . . . an empty, dizzy, frightening sensation—these were some immediate reactions. There were variations: women greeting friends in a flurry of smiles and chatter, only to subside into an audible hush as the news was relayed . . . the tight grasp of one man's hand upon another's arm as they discussed the assassination.

6 Scientists are studying now what happened to us that day. The University of Chicago's National Opinion Research Center surveyed 1,400 adults and found that half of them wept. A comparable number had trouble sleeping. At least two out of five suffered loss of appetite. One out of five experienced an upset stomach. At least two Ph.D. candidates at universities are analyzing the birth rate nine months later. Others are even investigating the dreams that people reported having. But no scientific paper can recall the dreamlike cloud through which we wandered on that day.

7 Paul Kresh, a New Yorker with an afternoon on his hands in Chicago, was paying his way into an afternoon movie when the doorman said, "Did you hear that President Kennedy was shot?" The woman selling tickets shook her head in irritation. "Isn't it awful to go around kidding like that?" she exclaimed. Kresh nodded and hurried inside. Emerging two hours later, he wandered over to Marshall Field's to buy a gift for a little girl whose parents had invited him to dinner. The store seemed hushed and deserted. So this is the famous Marshall Field's, Kresh thought to himself. It's the glummest place I've ever seen. He chose a toy horse, but had to ask three times before anyone would take his money. Then he boarded a subway train, squeezed into a seat, and, for the first time, took heed of the glaring black proclamation on every front page.

8 A huge Negro woman in the next seat watched Kresh's face drain. "Isn't it terrible?" she sobbed, burying her head in his lap. "Maybe it isn't so," was all Kresh could say, but there was no consolation, no escape. When the train reached his destination, Kresh stayed aboard, the woman still weeping in his lap, and rode to the end of the line.

9 There were many different reactions to that day: poignant, grotesque, disgusted, disgusting, sentimental, violent, inspiring, patriotic. Virtually all were spontaneous and genuine.

10 In a Warwick, Rhode Island, obstetrician's waiting room, the jarring bulletin from Dallas came over an all-music FM station. Without a word, a dozen expectant mothers stood up and went home. On Death Rows, murderers wept. In Denver, fighter Sonny Liston wept. In Brooklyn, a subway conductor started to announce the next station on his public address system—and broadcast his sobs instead. In Manhattan, an elderly news dealer tried to shout "Extra!

Extra!," but what emerged from his heart was a wail of anguish: "Oh, my God, this is a young tree chopped down!"

11   At a medical convention in Dallas, a local hostess was about to award an honorary Texas citizenship to a distinguished physician when the news came about what had happened in her city. "I can no longer present this to you," she said with shame, slowly tearing up the elaborate document.

12   On a busy corner in Newark, New Jersey, pedestrians scattered as an angry old man slashed the air with his cane and shouted, "How could they do it? I'll join the Army now!" In a Chicago saloon, a burly laborer swept his glass of whiskey from the bar and stalked out growling, "For God's sake!" In Champaign, Illinois, Pierre Salinger's brother, Richard, banged his fist on a glass countertop in a china store and exclaimed: "The dirty ————!" Under the elms of Harvard, where John F. Kennedy had often sauntered, students wept, and one of them slammed his fist into a tree as though it were a punching bag. Across the river, on Arch Street in Boston, a six-year-old boy asked a passer-by, "Hear about President Kennedy?"

13   "Yes," said the stranger.

14   "I loved him," the boy said matter-of-factly and walked away.

15   On the twenty-second floor of an apartment skyscraper in Manhattan, Mrs. Joe Hamilton was supervising four workmen who had come to hang draperies in her living room. Recognizing her as Carol Burnett, the four men had requested autographs. While they worked, she switched on the TV to watch *Password*—and instead saw Walter Cronkite fighting tears. The workmen came down from their ladders. There was a report that a Negro had been spotted running from the scene in Dallas. "Oh God, oh God, I hope not!" said one of the two Negro workmen in the foursome. (Later, it was learned that the Negro in Dallas had had a child with him and was running for safety.)

16   Carol Burnett poured five cans of beer. The comedienne and the four laborers sat solemnly all afternoon, watching television and consuming two six-packs. Then the men went home. When they returned the next week, nothing was said about the previous visit except, "Sorry to have left you in the lurch, Mrs. Hamilton." But Carol Burnett recalls, "We felt a kind of kinship, having been let in on the news together."

17   Barbra Streisand was shopping with her business manager for a bracelet on West 47th Street:

18   "All the radios were on and they were all saying the President was shot and I thought he must have gotten shot in the arm. I never thought it would be fatal. Then one of the clerks said it was the head. And I thought no, it couldn't be, it must be some Orson Welles trick—I mean, it was all so theatrical that it just couldn't be true.

19 "It turned my stomach and we had to get out of there. We went into the car, and we were driving and listening to the radio when the announcer said slowly, 'John—Fitzgerald—Kennedy—is—dead.'

20 "It was such a shock, so incredible, it didn't leave any time to tell him you liked him, that he was a great President. Had he been alive a few hours, he might have known people cared.

21 "I was going to go somewhere, but I decided to go home. But first we pulled the car over to the curb and just sat. I was depressed for a long time. I felt terribly guilty about the bracelet, about being in a jewelry store then."

22 Myrna Loy wept when Eddie Fisher told her the news. . . . Mary Martin implored her press agent to intercept a columnist who was scheduled to interview her. "How could anyone talk about themselves at a time like that?" The columnist never showed up anyway. Hearing the news on his way, he had repaired to the nearest bar.

23 When the first flash reached the Irwin Memorial Blood Bank in San Francisco, hardly anyone there comprehended it—until, seconds later, a sandy-haired man appeared at the registration desk and said in a rich Irish brogue, "I want to give my blood for President Kennedy." He was Nicholas V. Mc-Eneaney, forty-one, a native of County Monaghan. "I would give more than my blood," he told the workers who took his donation. He had left by the time the President's death was announced. Across the nation, hundreds of citizens deposited blood to the "account" of John F. Kennedy—and later received acknowledgments from Jacqueline Kennedy.

24 Another man who did something about it was Herschel Hadfield of Dearborn Heights, Michigan. He posted a $100 reward for information leading to the capture and conviction of the assassin. "Kennedy was my President and I want his murderer punished."

25 It was the Friday before Thanksgiving, but Christmas preparations were already under way. Within a short radius of Times Square, there were 76 Santa Clauses; the Volunteers of America major who had posted them that morning quickly dispersed them. The Christmas lights at Saks Fifth Avenue dimmed, and the main window display became a photograph of President Kennedy flanked by urns of red roses. At Best's, it was an American flag with black crepe on the staff. Department-store loudspeakers switched from *Rudolph the Red-Nosed Reindeer* to Verdi's *Requiem*.

26 "I'm awfully sorry little Caroline can't have Christmas with her father," Harriet Carroll, thirteen, of Miami, wrote in her diary. "How is Jacqueline going to tell her she has no father any more?" (Nearby, in Hialeah, a teenage boy phoned police to inquire: "Is it O.K. to go on with my birthday party?") "If they catch the man who did this," said a small boy outside Baltimore's

Public School 2, "I hope they put him in jail for a hundred years—until Christmas is over."

27 Postmasters pondered a dilemma. Should they lower their flags or wait for an official order? Children everywhere didn't hesitate. It was raining in Greenville, Mississippi, and in St. Louis, but youngsters lowered flags in school yards there. Elsewhere, farm lads who had neither flags nor flagpoles hung makeshift Old Glories at half mast from trees.

28 In Colorado's oldest town, San Luis, a third of the 1,300 inhabitants were in Most Precious Blood Catholic Church less than an hour after the President's death was affirmed. The bells of Atlanta's oldest Roman Catholic church, the Shrine of Immaculate Conception, tolled 46 times—once for each year of John Fitzgerald Kennedy's life.

29 In Manhattan, when Mrs. Mary McGrath, an elderly cleaning lady, heard the first bulletin she dropped everything and ran toward church. Darting through midtown Manhattan, she repeated to passers-by: "Jesus, Mary, Mother of God, the President was shot!"

30 "He's dead!" someone said.

31 Mary McGrath fell to her knees on the sidewalk of New York and wept. Then she prayed. Men in Brooks Brothers suits and a woman in furs knelt with her and prayed too, in the grimy, stony heart of Manhattan.

32 The bells of St. Patrick's Cathedral began tolling at 2:35 P.M. The carillon of St. Thomas Episcopal Church took up the lament, and soon churches all over New York were echoing the refrain. Many Americans hurried that day to the nearest house of worship, whether it was one of their own faith or not. Long before sundown Friday—when the Jewish sabbath begins—synagogues were filled with mourners for the nation's first Catholic President. Later, they said Kaddish—the mourner's prayer, usually spoken only by members of the be-reaved family, who stand during the recital. That night, however, entire con-gregations arose for Kaddish.

33 At his home in New Rochelle, New York, the tenor Jan Peerce was rehears-ing the 13th Psalm (*How Long O Lord Wilt Thou Forsake Me?*) and *Ma-cushla, I Hear You Calling Me* for a December charity banquet. Then the phone rang. There would be no feast that year. The guest of honor was dead.

34 In Austin, Texas, "CANCELED" went up on the marquee of the audito-rium where John F. Kennedy was to have attended a $100-a-plate dinner that night. In East Rome, Georgia, a high school play called *The New Frontier* was canceled too. At Aqueduct Race Track, on Long Island, where races were canceled after the seventh, a flashy redhead dabbed at tears with a winning ticket. A Baltimore barfly prophesied, accurately, into his booze, "Now they'll close everything." All of Times Square's ballrooms but one shut down. There,

a middle-aged woman marched up to the box office and said, "You're open? That's shocking!" Then she bought a ticket and went in.

35   Telephone calls that day were 150 percent above normal. In San Francisco, the lines were so jammed that the Superintendent of Schools couldn't reach his principals to tell them to cancel classes—he had to send police cars to notify them. Hearing the news in a Baltimore hotel, Mrs. Angier Biddle Duke, wife of the then U.S. Chief of Protocol, kept saying, "It can't be! Not the President! It can't be!" Her repeated phone calls failed to reach her husband, the White House, or any Washington officials; she had to verify the news by calling her maid. In Chicago, a woman shopper raced for a phone to call her husband at his office—but couldn't remember the number though she had known it for almost twenty years.

36   In Dallas, Myron Hauser, stockbroker, watched the Kennedy motorcade pass below his office on Main Street. The President was smiling and waving. After a few minutes, Hauser went back to his desk to talk over the direct line to Wall Street. One of Hauser's New York associates said, "I hear the President's been shot in Dallas."

37   "Quit making jokes," said Hauser. "I just saw him five minutes ago."

38   At the Trade Mart in Dallas, the organist was warming up with *Hail to the Chief* when a man stepped to the rostrum to say that the luncheon's guest of honor had been shot. District Attorney Henry Wade was there, and his first reaction was, "You're kidding—aren't you?" As the truth sank in, prosecutor Wade turned to Fred Bruner, a leading defense attorney. "Fred, would you defend a man who shot down the President of the United States?"

39   "Definitely not," said Bruner.

40   Elsewhere in Dallas, a Pepsi-Cola sales meeting was awaiting *its* guest of honor, Joan Crawford. But the actress heard the first unconfirmed bulletin on her hotel radio and phoned one of the officials at the luncheon: "Bob, the President's been shot!"

41   "Yup, yup," said Robert Windt facetiously, unbelievingly.

42   "Do you want to hear the sirens?" said Joan Crawford, guessing what the wailing outside was about. She took the phone over to the window and glanced down. That was how Joan Crawford happened to see the car bearing John F. Kennedy to Parkland Memorial Hospital.

43   Restaurant patrons left meals uneaten or checks unpaid or simply large sums of money to cover bills for which they couldn't wait. In a District of Columbia restaurant, Robert Auburn of Pasadena, California, guessed what had happened just from overhearing one word: "Assassinated!" He explained to his wife: "Ordinary people get *killed*. Important people get *assassinated*."

Many Americans did not come back from lunch that afternoon. Mrs. Herbert Rosenberg, an editor in New York City, forced herself to return to a book she was editing on deadline—*Ohio Scenes and Citizens,* by Grace Goulder. When Mrs. Rosenberg reached her desk, she discovered that she had reached the chapter about James Abram Garfield, the twentieth President of the United States, who himself died of an assassin's bullet. She went home.

44   (It was Garfield who, as a young Congressman hearing of Abraham Lincoln's assassination, said, "God reigns, and the government at Washington still lives!")

45   In Birmingham, Alabama, 450 members of Americans for Constitutional Action heard a keynote speech advocating "ballots, not bullets or bayonets." Then the state president stepped forward to make "a very sad announcement" and the convention ended abruptly. Near the boardwalk in Atlantic City, where President Kennedy had expected renomination in 1964, a waiter handed a napkin to an official at the New Jersey Bar Association's luncheon meeting. On the napkin was penciled: "PRESIDENT KENNEDY SHOT IN DAL-LAS." The official took it to the kitchen and asked if the message was a prank. A worker sadly shook his head. The official trudged back to the head table and told his fellow lawyers.

46   Stunned, the Houston Symphony Orchestra suspended rehearsal for a Monday concert. The conductor, Sir John Barbirolli, sent to Detroit for copies of Elgar's *Enigma Variations,* music traditionally played in Britain on the passing of a monarch. Nineteen hundred miles away, the Boston Symphony had already started its regular Friday afternoon concert. After a Handel concerto, men in shirtsleeves distributed sheet music to the musicians. A buzz in the audience about "unpreparedness" and "informality" was stilled, shockingly, when conductor Erich Leinsdorf announced, "Ladies and gentlemen, we have a press report over the wires . . . that the President of the United States has been the victim of an assassination." To a gasp that hit him "like a vast billow of horror," Leinsdorf continued, "In honor of the late President, we will now play the Funeral March from Beethoven's *Eroica* Symphony."

47   Turning, Leinsdorf raised his hands. The solemn, majestic strains of Beethoven flooded Symphony Hall in John F. Kennedy's home town. And all 2,600 concertgoers arose, many with heads bowed, to stand throughout the march. A cellist fought to control twitching face muscles. Another musician lay down his violin, dabbed at his eyes, and then rejoined the ensemble. At the end, Leinsdorf's hands dropped, the music ceased, and the conductor froze in an attitude of prayer.

48   William Colleran, the television producer who is married to Lee Remick, was on the verge of taping the next week's Judy Garland Show. He and Miss Garland decided to scrap the prepared script in favor of a cavalcade of American music, from *Yankee Doodle* to the present. At the very end, Miss Garland

would simply say that the show was dedicated to "John F. Kennedy and his memory." But the network vetoed the idea, according to Colleran, on the ground that "people will want to forget about it by next week."

49 "If people can forget this day," Colleran protested to an official, "then they ought to be annihilated." But the memorial show did not go on.

50 Vaughn Meader, who had made a career of impersonating President Kennedy, flew into Milwaukee to do just that at a Democratic rally. A taxi driver asked the comic if he'd heard. "I figured he recognized me," said Meader, "and I asked what the gag was." When it turned out not to be one, Meader left Milwaukee—but not before remarking that "It's like seeing a John Wayne movie go wrong. You just know that Wayne has been mistaken for dead and will come out alive."

51 (Meader had recorded a satire on *The Night Before Christmas,* as President Kennedy might have told it to Caroline: *C:* "Daddy, will there really be peace on earth?" *JFK:* "I hope so, Caroline, I sincerely hope so." It was never released.)

52 Eugene Burdick, professor of political science and co-author of *The Ugly American* and *Fail-Safe,* was at his beach house in Aptos, California, putting finishing touches on a novel. *The 480* was to have been the story of a computerized Republican candidate for President who licks everything in sight in 1964 —except the Kennedy magic.

53 Upon hearing the news, Burdick "wept a bit and drank about six ounces of booze." Not only did he assume that *The 480* was done for (it was later revised and published), but he also decided that he was having a heart attack. A veteran of a previous coronary, Burdick phoned his doctor. Burdick's doubly distraught wife, Carol, managed to drive him to the doctor's office, where the physician took one look at them and treated Carol Burdick first. Her pulse, he reported, was "enormously elevated." Then he took an electrocardiogram of her husband. Burdick had *not* suffered a second coronary. (It was only a 20-month reprieve. Burdick collapsed on a tennis court and died of a heart attack last summer.)

54 False heart attacks were just one of many symptoms of the "Kennedy grief reaction" reported by psychiatrists. "Why do I react so strongly to this man's dying when I never knew him?" asked one patient. The doctor assured him that—particularly in this age of scattered, mobile families—the First Family often plays a significant role in Americans' lives.

55 People who had talked against Kennedy suffered extreme reactions—such as temporary amnesia. And almost all of us at first blamed an object of our own wrath for his death: Birchers, segregationists, leftists, Negroes, Jews, Castro, Texas, police, psychiatrists ("The idea! Letting armed lunatics roam the

streets!"), and even Kennedy himself ("Why on earth did he go to Dallas?"
. . . "And in an open car!").

56   In Denver, Mrs. Fletch Swan, Republican National Committeewoman for
Colorado, sat in her office, weeping for President Kennedy, when the phone
rang. "Are you happy now?" a coarse male voice inquired.

57   When the late Adlai Stevenson, who had been spat upon in Dallas, heard
the news at the United Nations, he blamed himself. "I should have *insisted* that
he not go to Dallas." Richard Nixon had left Dallas that very morning, predict-
ing that Lyndon Johnson would be dropped from the Democratic ticket in
1964 as a "political liability in both the North and the South." He heard the
news in a cab taking him to Manhattan from Idlewild (which became Kennedy
Airport a few days later). Nelson Rockefeller was lunching with Thomas E.
Dewey in a private dining room when a maid entered, crying. Barry Goldwater
was already on a sad journey—accompanying the coffin of his mother-in-law
from Phoenix to Muncie, Indiana. A nephew met him with the news at a
Chicago airport.

58   Friday, November 22, 1963, was John Nance Garner's 95th birthday. In
Uvalde, Texas, the former vice-president had taken a congratulatory call from
Fort Worth that morning. "You're my President and I love you," said "Cactus
Jack" Garner to his well-wisher. "I hope you stay in there forever. God bless
you." When he arose from his midday nap, Garner learned that his morning
caller was dead. Garner went back to bed.

59   Three hundred miles away, at Parkland Memorial Hospital in Dallas,
Jacqueline Kennedy touched her dead husband's foot, kissed the instep, and
then clung to his hand. Lyndon Baines Johnson waited in another room at the
hospital. "I found it hard to believe that this had happened," he recalled later.
"The whole thing seemed unreal—unbelievable. A few hours earlier, I had
breakfast with John Kennedy; he was alive, strong, vigorous. I could not believe
now that he was dead. I was shocked and sickened. . . . I suppose, actually,
that the only outlet for the grief that shock had submerged was our sharp, painful, and bitter concern and solicitude for Mrs. Kennedy." Johnson had not yet
been sworn in as 36th President of the United States, but the transfer of power
had already begun. A computer in the Government Accounting Office in Washington stopped John Kennedy's pay for Friday at 14/24ths of a day's work.
At the National Cathedral School for Girls, two Secret Service men called for
Luci Baines Johnson.

60   In Washington, Congressman Robert G. Stephens, Jr., of Georgia, had just
left his office when the perky music on his car radio was interrupted by a grim
bulletin. Stephens recalls: "I couldn't believe it. When they repeated it, I turned
around and started back to the Capitol. The sun had been shining when I left,
but it was cloudy now."

61 It had been such a balmy day in Washington that Attorney General Robert Kennedy took two of his subordinates home to Hickory Hill in McLean Virginia, for a swim (which only he took) and an outdoor Friday lunch of clam chowder and tuna sandwiches. The meal ended when J. Edgar Hoover phoned from the White House. As Bobby Kennedy took the call, a workman appeared in the doorway to tell Ethel Kennedy, "It says on the radio that the President was shot."

62 The President's other brother, Edward Kennedy, was presiding over the U.S. Senate when a press aide rushed up and whispered, "Senator, your brother has been shot!" Teddy Kennedy could guess which brother. He gasped "No!" and left at once. The Chaplain of the Senate proclaimed, "We gaze at a vacant place against the sky, as the President of the Republic goes down like a giant cedar."

63 Teddy Kennedy's wife, Joan, was at Elizabeth Arden's having her blonde hair done. The news swirled through all five floors of the salon. But it was kept from Joan Kennedy. Nobody there had the heart to tell her.

64 Joan Kennedy stepped out, unknowing, onto Connecticut Avenue, where newsboys were shouting "Extra!" and a crowd had gathered before a TV set in a store window. Hearing that her husband's brother had been murdered, she drove to the White House to look in on Jacqueline Kennedy's children. Caroline, who would be six on Wednesday, was eating lunch. John, who would be three on Monday, was napping. Their aunt stayed with them, awaiting further word. Later that night, they were taken to the home of Jacqueline Kennedy's mother, Mrs. Hugh Auchincloss.

65 The White House had first heard the news when United Press International phoned Helen Gnass, a press aide, to request clearance for a reporter.

66 "Why does he want to come here?" Miss Gnass asked. "There's nothing happening."

67 "The President has just been shot," she was told. Minutes later, a car began circling the White House grounds. It bore a banner reading: "THE WRATH OF GOD IS UPON US."

68 Miss Gnass' boss, Press Secretary Pierre Salinger, was aboard a jet with six Cabinet members, en route to Tokyo for a meeting with their Japanese counterparts. One hour out of Honolulu, a teletype machine began clacking in the plane's radio room. A crewman tore off the message and handed it to Secretary of State Dean Rusk: "PRESIDENT JOHN F. KENNEDY WAS SHOT BY AN ASSASSIN IN DALLAS, TEXAS, TODAY. HE IS BELIEVED DEAD." As the plane turned around and conflicting reports poured in, Secretary of Agriculture Orville Freeman, a Marine veteran of Guadalcanal, said, "I was shot in the head and survived. He'll make it." But 12 minutes after the first flash, the high-level passengers learned he hadn't.

69 By the time Pierre Salinger was back in Washington, the White House switchboard had received the first of several calls like the one that follows. As luck would have it, this one was put through to Malcolm Kilduff, the red-eyed press aide whose unexpected task in Dallas had been to announce John F. Kennedy's death to the world.

70 "I want to complain about the television," a lady in Shreveport, Louisiana, told him. "There's nothing but things about the dead President and it's disturbing."

71 "Turn it off," Kilduff said.

72 "But the children like television."

73 "Well, turn it on," said Kilduff.

74 "But I don't want them to watch this sad thing."

75 "Well, turn it off then."

76 "Mr. Kilduff, we don't seem to be getting anywhere with this," she said. "I really called for advice. What should I do?"

77 The answer she received is unprintable.

78 That day was not without its macabre twists. In a Denver elevator, a businessman remarked, "It couldn't happen at a better time." As his fellow passengers glanced around in dismay, he added hastily, "On Friday I mean. With the market closed until Monday, people won't be so panicky. . . ." His voice trailed off as he realized that this was no time to talk money. The New York Stock Exchange suspended trading at 2:07 P.M., after twenty minutes of panic selling in which the market plummeted twenty-one points.

79 In Honolulu, a visitor from North Carolina made a $1,000 profit on Friday afternoon by selling $1 bills with small photos of John or Jacqueline Kennedy pasted over George Washington's face. Price: $3 each, or two for $5.

80 At 17th and Market in Philadelphia, a peddler sold leftover 1960 Democratic campaign buttons, draped in black, for $1 apiece until he suddenly became the target of mob anger. The police who rescued him from a snarl of pedestrians also charged him with vending without a license.

81 In bars, where the majority watched TV for further news, a minority insisted on playing the jukeboxes. "Hey, you got no sense or something?" said one proprietor, pulling the plug from its socket.

82 Death in Dallas seeped into the public awareness as if by osmosis. In Atlanta, a jury weighing a divorce case in a sealed-off room returned to ask for "instructions" from the judge. The jury's question was: "Is it true that President Kennedy has died?" The judge said yes—and recessed the case. In Norfolk, Virginia, a jury had been deliberating for eight hours on a $250,000 lawsuit.

But U.S. District Judge John A. Butzner summoned the jurors, told them the President was dead, and declared a mistrial. "It would be asking too much of an American citizen to remain in the custody of a U.S. Marshal at such a time."

83 From coast to coast, policemen, as uniformed oracles, were consulted by disbelievers. Sidewalk orators were struck dumb. At New York's City Hall Plaza, a young man with tears streaming down his face waved his fist at passers-by: "What's wrong with you people? Don't you know the President's been shot?" Someone asked him, innocently, "President of what?"

84 For two weeks church attendance tripled in the South, but in Greenville, Mississippi, three-fourths of the "men in the street" interviewed by a *Delta Democrat Times* reporter admitted that, in one way or another, they were glad "that rascal" Kennedy was gone. A Birmingham youth phoned an "Open Mike" program to say, "Mr. Kennedy got exactly what he deserved. I'm sorry for his family. But I want to say that any man, any white man, who did what he did for niggers should be shot." In Atlanta, students at an insurance class laughed and applauded. One of them even remarked that the assassination was "the best thing that could have happened for the country." Amidst all this elation, the instructor put his head down on his desk and wept.

85 In New York's Cuban colony, garbled early reports about the suspected assassin prompted a pro-Castro leader to proclaim, "If a Cuban did this, then I am no longer a Cuban." Ninety miles from Florida, Fidel Castro was lunching at Varadero Beach. A woman secretary, wearing guerrilla fatigues, told him Kennedy had been shot. Castro said three times in Spanish, "This is bad news."

86 At the Sheraton British Colonial Hotel in Nassau, six Negro porters were called to the lobby to sing hymns to the predominantly American guests.

87 Americans abroad heard the news in many ways. In Warsaw, Embassy staff members, along with hundreds of Poles, were attending a variety show. The star, Paul Anka, rushed onstage before his entrance was due. "Stop the show!" he commanded, his voice choked with tears. "My President has just been assassinated. I can't go on." Anka had been listening to Radio Free Europe in his hotel room.

88 Milt Moritz of Los Angeles was traveling on business in Europe. When an Italian associate met him in Rome with a distressful look and the halting words, "Meelt—I have bad news for you," he braced himself for tragic tidings about his wife or two sons back home. He confesses to a small momentary sigh of relief when he heard the bad news didn't involve his family. . . .

89 It was 6:55 A.M. in Saigon. An American, tuning in an English language station, heard a disc jockey say breezily, "Stick around. We really have some news for you this morning." Five minutes of jazz followed, then, "John F. Kennedy, the President of the United States, has been assassinated," followed by the latest football news.

90   Mr. and Mrs. Ronald Schiller of Larchmont, New York, were clearing customs at Mexico City Airport when a man accosted them with the news. "Don't pay any attention," Mr. Schiller told Mrs. Schiller. "He's probably talking about some banana republic." The Schillers, however, pricked up their ears when their cab driver suggested that they stay south of the border until the revolution in their homeland blew over. . . .

91   In many parts of the world, the natives looked at Americans with compassion and sometimes embraced them and no English needed to be spoken.

92   Xavier Cugat was in Madrid. "Everybody was crying—even those who had been saying to me, before, 'Yankee go home.' "

93   At *The New York Times,* an editor's son phoned in for confirmation of the bulletin he had heard on his transistor. Nobody in the newsroom could lay hands on a radio. One reporter gave up trying and raced two blocks to Stern's department store.

94   The death of President Kennedy was reported to the first floor of Stern's by a transistor radio inside an ornate whiskey bottle (an expensive novelty item that had just been placed on sale for the Christmas trade). A salesman turned the bottle cap, which flicked on the radio. As the news from Dallas blared out, his customer, a woman, drew back as if the bottle were a snake.

95   "It's a lie! It's a lie!" screamed a saleswoman across the aisle. Two middle-aged women shoppers began to cry softly.

96   As the reporter headed for the exit, a brittle-looking blonde importuned someone, anyone, to wait on her. "Please, I'm in a hurry. I'm on my lunch hour."

97   A saleswoman snapped at her, "The President's dead, for God's sake, the President's dead."

98   The blonde turned on her high heels and clicked out of Stern's.

99   On the second floor of the Dallas *Morning News,* an advertiser—a former Chicagoan who had lived in Dallas for 16 years—had been placing an ad. Now he remarked disgustedly, "I will have to leave Dallas."

100   But he didn't. His name was Jack Ruby.

Apparatus for: The Day JFK Died: What People Remember Now

Vocabulary: *Make a list of any troublesome words in this selection. Look up each one in your dictionary and write out the full definitions.*

convulsed

sauntered - walked

carillon -

Discussion: *Rhetoric*

1. Why does the author of this selection begin by telling where a famous man, Theodore H. White, was when President Kennedy was assassinated?
2. This essay is constructed from a long series of examples relating what people were doing and what their reactions were to the assassination. Can you find a further internal organization? In your answer, take note of paragraph 9.
3. Some of the author's phrases are cogent and memorable; for example, "the glaring black proclamation on every front page." (Par. 7). Cite other examples.
4. Why does the author cite the location of so many famous people when President Kennedy was assassinated?
5. What is the most impressive example of behavior that the author cites?
6. What is the strongest feature of this selection? The weakest? If you were describing the essay, what would you say about it rhetorically?

1. _____

_____

2. *Serious answers* _____

_____

3. _____

_____

4. *If a Cuban did this I am no longer a Cuban" People*

_____

5. _____

_____

6. _____

_____

Apparatus for: The Day JFK Died: What People Remember Now

Discussion: *Theme*

1. Where were you when President Kennedy was assassinated? What were you doing? What was your reaction?
2. How do you account for the unusually disgusting behavior of some when they heard of the death?
3. Can you recall details from your own life when you received news of a death in your family or of someone else close to you?
4. How do you account for the unparalleled grief that virtually everyone shared at the news of Kennedy's death? How much of the grief was for him and his family? How much was the result of the magnitude of the tragedy?

1. _____

_____

2. _____

_____

3. _____

_____

4. _____

_____

Writing Suggestions

1. Write a theme in which you try to capture some of the feelings you had when you heard of President Kennedy's assassination.
2. Write a report of one of the many books that treat the Presidency of Mr. Kennedy.
3. Account for the statement, "Ordinary people get *killed*. Important people get *assassinated*."
4. Give the reasons why you believe (or do not believe) that Kennedy's presidency was great.
5. For an extended library paper, compare the growth of the Kennedy legend with that of the Lincoln legend.

18. HYPNOSIS: WHAT IT CAN AND CAN'T DO *

ARTHUR J. SNIDER

1 When Pat Collins, the blonde stage hypnotist, goes into her night club act of suspending a member of the audience between two chairs, the patrons howl, but the professional therapists fume.

2 They are trying to reclaim hypnosis from theatrical trappings and restore it to the clinic as a treatment tool. Amusing stage antics impede their efforts, they believe. As it is, patients often think that submitting to hypnosis is akin to putting themselves in the power of a real-life Rasputin.

3 The fact is that hypnosis today is a legitimate, effective adjunct of therapy that is widely used in the medical profession.

4 For more than 170 years practitioners of medical hypnosis have sought to make the technique respectable and acceptable. They suffered a serious setback in the late eighteenth century when their patron saint, Franz Mesmer, a Viennese physician, was called a charlatan for practicing hypnosis. He died in obscurity, although his name lives in the term *mesmerize*.

5 In the nineteenth century, hypnosis enjoyed a revival, only to suffer rejection when Sigmund Freud, father of psychoanalysis, announced he was abandoning its use.

6 Once again, in World War I, a flash of interest occurred, only to fade. In World War II, when psychiatrists were faced with the need of a short-cut technique to deal with combat neurosis, they rediscovered hypnosis. This time, the interest appears to be sustained.

* Arthur J. Snider, "Hypnosis: What It Can and Can't Do," *Science Digest,* October 1965. Reprinted with permission by *Science Digest.* © The Hearst Corporation.

7 Support has come from the American Medical Association which, after years of skepticism, issued a report in 1958 endorsing the responsible use of hypnosis by those qualified through training.

8 Today, several thousand babies are delivered each year with the mother in a hypnotic trance. Surgeons can perform such major operations as removing a thyroid gland, opening an abdomen or amputating a cancerous breast without using anesthesia. Patients who never before have been able to enter a dentist's office for fear of the anesthetic needle and the drill are having their teeth fixed. So widespread is its use, many conservative practitioners are fearful hypnosis will become oversold and the public led to expect quick therapeutic triumphs every time.

9 How does hypnosis work?

10 In one respect, hypnosis is like the state of ordinary sleep when the conscious thoughts of the waking hours have been put aside, leaving the mental area clear for unconscious thoughts to come to the fore. There is an important difference, however. Whereas the mental shifting comes automatically in sleep, it is forced by the therapist in hypnosis. A further difference is that the patient holds on to the ability to hear, understand, feel and sense.

11 After reaching the unconscious mind, the therapist implants suggestions designed to influence the patient favorably when he returns to a waking state. The patient does not surrender his will. He retains the right to accept or reject the suggestions.

12 Dr. Milton Erickson, editor of *The American Journal of Clinical Hypnosis,* draws a similarity between a hypnotized person and an actor who is willing to take his cues from the director of a play while on stage but when off stage, in real life, re-establishes his own control of behavior.

13 Dr. Seymour Hershman, a founder of the American Society of Clinical Hypnosis, compares the hypnotic state to a music lover who closes his eyes at a concert to better pick out the different instrumentations. He narrows his field of awareness by removing visual distractions. His attention is completely taken up by what he wishes to focus on.

14 A movie patron so intent on the picture he pays no attention to the noisy munching of popcorn beside him is in a sense hypnotized. A fisherman sitting in a boat for several hours, oblivious to the world around him, has been subjected to a type of hypnotism by the shimmering and dancing water.

15 In spite of its misuse by cafe performers and its occasional failure in the hands of well-intentioned but incompetent therapists, hypnosis has established its validity in several medical and paramedical areas. Among them are:

16 *Childbirth:* Here hypnosis finds its most popular use. Since it does not depress uterine activity as do some commonly-used anesthetic drugs, a marked

shortening of the labor period is usually obtained. Dr. Milton Abramson and Psychologist William Heron, writing in the *American Journal of Obstetrics and Gynecology,* reported an average reduction of two hours in the first stage of labor.

17 Hypnosis is often used when a mother has a cardiac condition or tuberculosis and cannot tolerate drug anesthesia. It has no depressive effect on the infant's respiratory and nervous system and thus enhances the safety of birth, the most hazardous event in an individual's life.

18 The anesthesia degree is easily controlled. If it needs to be lightened or deepened, a simple suggestion will accomplish the goal. When chemical agents are used, they can be counteracted only by other drugs, by oxygen, or by time.

19 Some women cannot be deeply hypnotized. Therefore, a combination of hypnosis and a drug is used. "Some patients will require no chemical anesthesia, others will require 10, 20, 50, or even 90 per cent as much as they would have required if they had not learned hypnosis," Dr. Hershman points out. "But even when the amount of anesthesia is reduced only 10 per cent, the patient is benefitted."

20 In a report on 850 deliveries, Dr. Ralph V. August of Muskegon, Mich., said only five per cent needed drugs and hypnoanesthesia.

21 Some women become so skilled in undergoing hypnosis, they are able to enter a deep trance at their own volition. The advantage is the patient's ability to select the depth of the hypnotic state, according to Dr. Donald Coulton of Bangor, Maine.

22 Dr. William Kroger, Los Angeles obstetrician, has hypnotized several of his patients in labor by long-distance telephone when an engagement has taken him out of the city.

23 *Surgery:* Hysterectomies, thyroid removal, abdominal operations, and even heart operations have been performed with hypnosis as the anesthetic. At Cedars of Lebanon Hospital, a 14-year-old deaf girl underwent a five-hour operation during which her heart was opened and circulation maintained with a heart-lung machine. The child wore a hearing aid in order to respond to hypnotist's suggestions during the surgery.

24 A cataract extraction was done under hypnosis in a patient who had been unable to undergo the operation previously because of sensitivity to drugs.

25 A surgeon amputated both breasts in a cancer patient while she showed no sign of pain or distress. Many tonsillectomies and appendectomies have been done under hypnoanesthesia.

26 Two Indianapolis surgeons described in the *Journal of the American Medical Association* their operation on a 38-year-old man to relieve epileptic attacks caused by an accidental gunshot wound in the forehead. General chemical

PARAGRAPH DEVELOPMENT: EXAMPLE

anesthesia was ruled out because of the need to monitor electrical activity of the brain. Under local anesthesia, the patient's uncooperative disposition might have proved a problem.

27 In emergency rooms, hundreds of fractures and dislocations have been set, foreign bodies removed, lacerations sutured, and abscesses drained, particularly when it has been found the patient had just eaten a heavy meal and might aspirate food into the lungs under drug anesthesia.

28 An unusual use of hypnosis in plastic surgery was disclosed by a hospital in Salisbury, England. To repair a portion of the right foot lost in an accident, it was necessary to obtain tissue from the abdomen by way of the forearm. In the first of a two-stage operation, it was necessary to keep the left arm locked across the abdomen for three weeks. After that graft had taken, it was necessary to hold the drawn-up right foot in tight contact with the abdomen for four weeks. Hypnosis permitted the patient to maintain the rigid and unnatural positions without discomfort.

29 "Hypnoanesthesia is no longer an experiment," says Dr. Milton J. Marmer of Los Angeles. "With it, virtually every body cavity has been entered and almost every organ operated on."

30 *Dentistry:* Hypnosis has been the answer for the nervous patient who fears the anesthetic needle. It also is useful for patients who set up defense mechanisms to postpone the technical procedures. These include the head-bobber, tongue-explorer, conversationalist, and nose scratcher. It is helpful to those patients who do not submit to dental treatment easily and who repeatedly break appointments, says Dr. Irving Secter of Chicago.

31 There is also some evidence that better control of hemorrhage can be obtained in some patients but not all. Dr. Oscar N. Lucas of Philadelphia has performed more than 100 extractions on hemophiliacs without serious bleeding.

32 Hypnosis has been employed by dentists to control gagging and nausea and eliminating patient fatigue caused by long, drawn-out sessions in the dental chair. It has particular application to children, who have been hypnotized as young as age two.

33 *Pain relief:* Sick, suffering patients have been able to live their last months of life free of pain resulting from cancer. Through use of hypnosis, rather than narcotics, the patient is able to maintain a degree of cheerfulness and rational thinking. It also has been tried with varied degrees of success in painful conditions resulting from arthritis, bursitis, sprains, and fractures.

34 *Skin diseases:* When skin disease is a reflection of underlying emotions, such as anger, hate, and fear, Dr. Michael J. Scott, Seattle dermatologist, finds hypnosis a good tool. He has relieved itching due to psoriasis, urticaria, eczema, and neurodermatitis. Some success has been claimed in removal of warts.

35 *Obesity:* There is no good treatment for overeating except use of will-power, asserts Dr. Herbert Mann of San Jose, Calif., and hypnosis can strengthen the desire to reduce. He has used the technique on groups of over-weight women.

36 "Our goal is to convert the craving for large quantities of fattening food to an appreciation of the delight in learning to enjoy subtle flavors of small portions of nonfattening foods, to take delight in creating and serving attractive salads, fruits, and high-protein food," he says.

37 "We encourage the patient to eat slowly and to take pleasure in savoring each small bite of food, to indulge the palate rather than the appetite."

38 Of 27 patients who responded to hypnosis, Dr. Murray Elkins of Howard Beach, N. Y., said, only eight were successful in maintaining their weight loss. He concluded that the "time, energy and expense of trying to lose weight by this method are not justifiable."

39 *Habits:* Dr. Hershman describes a woman patient, 44, who smoked 44 to 50 cigarettes a day. She could not refrain from smoking more than 15 minutes at a time. When attending the theatre she would leave her seat to smoke at frequent intervals. After three hypnotic sessions, she was down to 10 to 12 cigarettes a day, her desired quota. A year later, she was still smoking no more than the self-imposed quota.

40 Others have reported lesser success in curbing smoking. The impact of hypnosis on this and other habits is open to question. Among the habits attacked are drug addiction, excessive drinking, thumb-sucking, nail-biting, uncontrollable blushing, tics, and bed-wetting.

41 *Psychiatry:* In Wisconsin, a 37-year-old man lay on his side, rolled in a ball with knees pressed against his chest and arms tightly gripping his legs. When no physical reason could be found for his unnatural position, doctors attributed it to a severe emotional shock at age 15. He adopted a prenatal posture as an unconscious desire to return to the security of the womb. Through hypnosis, it was possible to achieve some movement of arms and legs although surgery was necessary to sever some of the fibrotic tissue.

42 Hypnosis has been used by many psychiatrists as a short-cut in therapy but there is a constant warning to the non-psychiatrically-trained doctor to be wary lest in removing a neurotic symptom he precipitate something more drastic.

43 Dr. Harold Rosen of Johns Hopkins cites the case of a psychotic obese person who committed suicide after her compulsive eating habit was hyp-notized away.

44 A similar circumstance was reported by Dr. J. J. Harning of Chicago. A patient had developed functional blindness as an escape from an intolerable life

situation. When her symptoms were removed by hypnosis, she committed suicide.

45 "Great harm can be done when an untrained operator attempts to cure individuals with serious personality problems," Dr. Harning said.

46 In a recent evaluation of the dangers of hypnosis, Dr. Louis J. West, University of Oklahoma psychiatrist, said it can make an existing mental disorder worse, or it may revive symptoms of an illness that was improving.

47 He also warned that a patient might become excessively dependent on the hypnotist but conceded that this danger is disputed.

48 One normal subject underwent such a pathological dependency reaction that she often went into a trance upon hearing the operator, a psychology graduate student, speak even in an ordinary social situation, Dr. West said. "Hypnotized repeatedly as a subject in demonstrations, eventually she could not make the most trivial decisions without consulting the hypnotist, and when he moved to a city 1,500 miles away, she followed him, leaving family, friends and her job."

49 Dr. West's conclusion: Hypnosis is a valid tool but there are dangers in its misuse to the patient, to medicine and to hypnosis itself.

Apparatus for: Hypnosis: What It Can and Can't Do

Vocabulary: *Use your dictionary to trace the history of the following words from their original source and meaning to their present meaning.*

1. therapist (¶ 1)   *Greek - a servant or attendant.*

2. hypnotist (¶ 1)

3. professional (¶ 1)

4. legitimate (¶ 3)

5. psychoanalysis (¶ 5)

6. neurosis (¶ 6)

7. amputating (¶ 8)

8. hypnoanesthesia (¶ 20)

9. hemorrhage (¶ 31)

10. circumstance (¶ 44)

1. The introduction of this essay includes background information about hypnosis. The beginning is, of course, very important to an essay. How effective is this one? Note that it ends at paragraph 8.
2. The second section of this essay includes paragraphs 9 through 15. We could label this part "How Hypnosis Works; What It Is Like." How effective is the author's use of *example* in this section?
3. The next part of the essay deals with the actual uses of hypnosis. Once more, examples are used extensively; how informative is this technique?
4. Make a list of the four best examples cited by the author.
5. The conclusion of this selection is a short final paragraph. Can you account for such a brief ending? Is it effective?
6. In paragraph 10, the author compares hypnosis to ordinary sleep but, of course, with some differences. Cite other examples of this technique.
7. Of the four parts in this essay mentioned above, which is the strongest in terms of rhetoric?
8. Comment on the level of the language used in this selection. Is it appropriate for the subject under discussion?

1. _It shows how widespread Hypnosis is being used._

2. _He uses examples the reader has had._

3. _____

4. _____

5. _____

6. _____

_____

7. _____

_____

8. _____

_____

Discussion: *Theme*

1. Why do professional therapists fume when hypnosis is used in "theatrical trappings"?
2. If you have been hypnotized, describe the experience to your classmates.
3. Why does hypnotism have a rather dubious reputation?
4. Would you be willing to be hypnotized in order to avoid the pains associated with dentists?
5. This essay says that the person under hypnosis "retains the right to accept or reject" suggestions. If this is true, why does the general fear exist that one will do something he should not while under hypnosis?

1. _____

_____

2. _____

_____

3. _____

_____

4. _____

_____

5. _____

_____

Writing Suggestions

1. Contrast some of the popular fears associated with hypnosis with the comments about hypnosis found in this essay.
2. Write a report of someone who has had hypnosis administered in order to avoid anesthesia.
3. "Why I would like (or not like) to be hypnotized"
4. Do you think there should be more stringent laws regulating the use of hypnosis?
5. Write a report on the early experiments of Franz Mesmer.

VII. PARAGRAPH DEVELOPMENT: COMPARISON AND CONTRAST

When discussing girls, boys, cars, teachers, or television programs, you often point out similarities and differences. And when taking tests in college, you are frequently asked to show how two or more chemicals, authors, philosophical theories, or political parties are alike or different. In both instances, you are using one of the most effective means of organizing and presenting ideas: comparison and contrast.

When you *compare,* you tell what an object, a person, or an idea is like. Generally, the familiar is used to explain the less familiar. The game of cricket, for example, might best be explained by showing how it is similar to American baseball. The Federal budget could be explained, in part, by comparing it to the family budget. *Contrast,* on the other hand, points out the differences between two similar objects: It tells what a thing is *not* like. The language of Shakespeare's times could be studied by showing how it differs from modern English. Or the basic ideas of communism might be presented in terms of how they differ from those of capitalism.

Generally, you can develop paragraphs through the use of comparison and contrast when you wish to explain the unfamiliar, illustrate an idea, show the superiority of one thing or system to another, or argue a point of view. Obviously, then, comparisons and contrasts are often used to support expository and argumentative themes.

If organized carefully, a theme using comparison and contrast has a unity and logic enabling the reader to grasp your ideas with ease. But if your theme is merely a series of scrambled likenesses and differences that follow in no particular order, the result will inevitably be chaos. For this reason, your composition must have a plan. Two patterns of organization commonly used for developing a theme by means of comparison and contrast are: *point-by-point,* and *object-by-object.*

Most students will find the point-by-point or item-by-item pattern easier to use in their college writing. It is particularly valuable for showing the similarities or differences between two objects, ideas, or people. For example, in a theme attempting to demonstrate the superiority of one presidential candidate over another, you might begin by contrasting the foreign policy of Candidate A with that of Candidate B. Next, you could examine the views of each on needed domestic reforms, again considering first the statements of A, and then those of B. Likewise, the background and experience of A could be presented, followed by that of B. In a similar fashion, the rest of their platform could be contrasted through the alternate presentation of their views.

Because it helps the reader keep in mind the two things being compared or contrasted, the point-by-point approach is usually preferred for complex comparisons. It is particularly recommended for longer papers. Note how the point-by-point pattern gives unity and coherence to the following paragraph:

> Speech and writing are our two main channels of communication, yet they differ in several respects. The most obvious difference is in their respective method of expression. Speech is phonological; that is, it depends on sounds. Writing, on the other hand, is graphological: it uses written symbols. Another distinction is their relative ages. Linguists estimate that speech was invented about 500,000 years ago. Written language, however, is a recent development in man's history, having been invented only about 6000 years ago. As every student knows, speech is usually less formal than writing, employing contractions and slang. The word choice of writing is often relatively formal. Speech utterances characteristically use elliptical sentences, simple phrases, and even single words. Such verbal shorthand is avoided by most writers, unless they are striving for particular effects. Pronunciation and accent sometimes suggest the geographical origin of the speaker, and give rise to regional dialects. These variations are virtually ignored in writing, since a standard diction and spelling system prevail in the written language of most countries. Finally, speech relies heavily on expressive features such as gesture, loudness, and the rise and fall of the voice. Because writing lacks these features, it must be more carefully organized and controlled. Careful speakers and writers are aware of these differences.

You should note that the topic sentence of the preceding paragraph indicates the organizing pattern. Several distinctive features of speech and writing are then contrasted. Finally, a concluding sentence wraps up the paragraph. A single paragraph using the point-by-point pattern of organization can often be concluded effectively by a sentence summarizing the differences or similarities of the things compared. Similarly, an entire theme developed in this pattern often profits by a closing paragraph that presents a conclusion based on the comparison or contrast established.

A paragraph or theme using the object-by-object pattern of organization first presents all of the relevant details or aspects of one object, and then all of the corresponding qualities of the other. A concluding sentence or paragraph usually follows, summarizing the likenesses and differences or expressing an opinion. If, for instance, you wish to contrast city living with country living, you might first list all of the advantages of urban life, then present the advantages of life in the country. A concluding statement might argue for the superiority of one of them. Observe how the object-by-object pattern adds to the clarity of the following paragraph:

> Students of the piano often find that their dexterity at the keyboard aids them when learning to use the typewriter. Playing the piano requires the ability to coordinate the movements of the eyes and hands, as the pianist reads the musical score and places his fingers on the appropriate keys. And if the pianist hopes to play with any measure of success, he also needs a sense of rhythm. Typing requires these same skills. An accurate typist must read carefully the material he is typing, scarcely glancing at his hands on the keyboard. If he wishes to type rapidly, he must develop a rhythmic pattern in the movements of his fingers. It is not surprising, then, that many pianists are excellent typists.

As you can see, the first object is completely described or defined; then the second object is given equal time and space. Because your reader might have a short memory, you should use this organizational pattern only when there are few points of similarity or difference to be cited. Furthermore, you should be certain that you do not allow digressions to destroy the design of your paper—be sure that you give the same treatment to both items being compared or contrasted.

In the essays in the following section, observe how each author has skillfully used comparison and contrast as a means of developing his paragraphs and essay. In "The Battle of the Ants," Henry David Thoreau sustains two comparisons simultaneously. First, he compares the warring red ants with the larger black ants. Then he compares their battle with historical conflicts from the pages of man's history. And in "Sweden's New Battle Over Sex," J. Robert Moskin presents the contrasting arguments for and against compulsory sex education.

19. THE BATTLE OF THE ANTS

—from HENRY DAVID THOREAU, "Brute Neighbors," Walden

1   One day when I went out to my wood-pile, or rather my pile of stumps, I observed two large ants, the one red, the other much larger, nearly half an inch long, and black, fiercely contending with one another. Having once got hold they never let go, but struggled and wrestled and rolled on the chips incessantly. Looking farther, I was surprised to find that the chips were covered with such combatants, that it was not a *duellum,* but a *bellum,* a war between two races of ants, the red always pitted against the black, and frequently two red ones to one black. The legions of these Myrmidons covered all the hills and vales in my wood-yard, and the ground was already strewn with the dead and dying, both red and black. It was the only battle which I have ever witnessed, the only battle-field I ever trod while the battle was raging; internecine war; the red republicans on the one hand, and the black imperialists on the other. On every side they were engaged in deadly combat, yet without any noise that I could hear, and human soldiers never fought so resolutely. I watched a couple that were fast locked in each other's embraces, in a little sunny valley amid the chips, now at noon-day prepared to fight till the sun went down, or life went out. The smaller red champion had fastened himself like a vise to his adversary's front, and through all the tumblings on that field never for an instant ceased to gnaw at one of his feelers near the root, having already caused the other to go by the board; while the stronger black one dashed him from side to side, and, as I saw on looking nearer, had already divested him of several of his members. They fought with more pertinacity than bull-dogs. Neither manifested the least disposition to retreat. It was evident that their battle-cry was Conquer or die. In the meanwhile there came along a single red ant on the hill-side of this valley, evidently full of excitement, who either had dispatched his foe, or had not yet taken part in the battle; probably the

latter, for he had lost none of his limbs; whose mother had charged him to return with his shield or upon it. Or perchance he was some Achilles, who had nourished his wrath apart, and had now come to avenge or rescue his Patroclus. He saw this unequal combat from afar,—for the blacks were nearly twice the size of the red,—he drew near with rapid pace till he stood on his guard within half an inch of the combatants; then, watching his opportunity, he sprang upon the black warrior, and commenced his operations near the root of his right fore-leg, leaving the foe to select among his own members; and so there were three united for life, as if a new kind of attraction had been invented which put all other locks and cements to shame. I should not have wondered by this time to find that they had their respective musical bands stationed on some eminent chip, and playing their national airs the while, to excite the slow and cheer the dying combatants. I was myself excited somewhat even as if they had been men. The more you think of it, the less the difference. And certainly there is not the fight recorded in Concord history, at least, if in the history of America, that will bear a moment's comparison with this, whether for the numbers engaged in it, or for the patriotism and heroism displayed. For numbers and for carnage it was an Austerlitz of Dresden. Concord Fight! Two killed on the patriots' side, and Luther Blanchard wounded! Why here every ant was a Buttrick,—"Fire! for God's sake fire!"—and thousands shared the fate of Davis and Hosmer. There was not one hireling there. I have no doubt that it was a principle they fought for, as much as our ancestors, and not to avoid a three-penny tax on their tea; and the results of this battle will be as important and memorable to those whom it concerns as those of the battle of Bunker Hill, at least.

2   I took up the chip on which the three I have particularly described were struggling, carried it into my house, and placed it under a tumbler on my window-sill, in order to see the issue. Holding a microscope to the first-mentioned red ant, I saw that, though he was assiduously gnawing at the near fore-leg of his enemy, having severed his remaining feeler, his own breast was all torn away, exposing what vitals he had there to the jaws of the black warrior, whose breastplate was apparently too thick for him to pierce; and the dark carbuncles of the sufferer's eyes shone with ferocity such as war only could excite. They struggled half an hour longer under the tumbler, and when I looked again the black soldier had severed the heads of his foes from their bodies, and the still living heads were hanging on either side of him like ghastly trophies at his saddle-bow, still apparently as firmly fastened as ever, and he was endeavoring with feeble struggles, being without feelers and with only the remnant of a leg, and I know not how many other wounds, to divest himself of them; which at length, after half an hour more, he accomplished. I raised the glass, and he went off over the window-sill in that crippled state. Whether he finally survived that combat, and spent the remainder of his days in some Hôtel des Invalides, I do not know; but I thought that his industry would not be worth

much thereafter. I never learned which party was victorious, nor the cause of the war; but I felt for the rest of that day as if I had had my feelings excited and harrowed by witnessing the struggle, the ferocity and carnage, of a human battle before my door.

Apparatus for: The Battle of the Ants

Vocabulary: *Using your dictionary, define each of the following words as it appears in context.*

1. incessantly (¶ 1)   *unceasing*

2. internecine (¶ 1)   *mutually slave*

3. resolutely (¶ 1)   *steadily*

4. pertinacity (¶ 1)   *persistency*

5. assiduously (¶ 2)   *~~att~~ persisten*

Discussion: *Rhetoric*

1. Although this essay is about ants in battle, it makes some keen observations about men as well. Point out some of the major similarities between the ants and actual persons and places.
2. Why did Thoreau use so many classical references?
3. In the beginning of this selection, the author describes the battle in general; then, he narrows the view to a single chip and to three ants. Describe the effect of this focusing of viewpoint.
4. Did Thoreau's choice of words and emphasis make you *feel* that you had, in any way, witnessed an actual struggle? Do you think he achieved his desired effect?

1. _____

2. _To show the "conquer or_
die" idea.

3. _____

4. _Yes, Yes_

Apparatus for: The Battle of the Ants

Discussion: *Theme*

1. Who were the Myrmidons? Achilles and Patroclus?
2. What understanding of human behavior is gained by observing animal behavior?
3. What are some of the reasons why animals engage in death struggles like these ants?
4. Is there an actual *balance of nature?*

1. _____

_____

2. _____

_____

3. _____

_____

4. _____

_____

Writing Suggestions

1. In a theme patterned after "The Battle of the Ants," compare an object or animal from nature with man and his creations. You might consider, for example, a bee hive and a modern city or a fish and a submarine.
2. Write a theme describing the process by which one animal attracts another animal in courtship.
3. In a theme, answer the question, "Do animals talk?"
4. Describe an aviary or some other facility connected with animal life
5. "Even if they had been Men"
6. "Like ghastly trophies"

20. ALL COWS ARE MEAN*

J. O. HARVEY

1   I have before me a textbook on Animal Behavior. After reading the first few pages I decided that the author was no respecter of animals. As I labored on through the devious experiments, becoming more and more bewildered by the lack of rapport between the professor and his victims, I realized something I had long suspected—that our men of science have become so urbanized as to have lost all contact with intelligent animals.

2   Anthropologists allow myriad generations for Man to have perfected stone tools adequate to cope with large mammals, but Henry Ford devastated our continent of domestic animals in fifty years. He not only supplanted our animal kingdom with cars and tractors, leaving the general public in a vacuum of animal experience, but his Model T Ford seems to have inspired three generations of Deterministic Behaviorists.

3   After thirty years of raising and selling dairy cows, I have to report that the theories of the various behaviorists fail utterly with cows.

4   Cows band together in herds. Believers in Mechanistic Behavior explain the cow as "a creature of herd instinct." On the other hand the Blood-and-guts Behaviorists, who discredit instinct as motivation, maintain that "social" animals herd together simply for purposes of breeding, vigilance, and defense. Now, I doubt if cows indulge in instincts, and I *know* cows do not depend on their herd for breeding, vigilance, or protection.

5   Take breeding. When the heat is on, any heifer over ten months old will

* J. O. Harvey, "All Cows Are Mean." Copyright © 1966 by Harper's Magazine, Inc. Reprinted from the September 1966 issue of *Harper's Magazine* by permission of the author.

leave her herd, fly over electric fences, run several miles, and mate with the least desirable bull in the county. If her affections are unrequited, she will hide out in the bushes for twenty-four hours. I prevent under-age and undesirable mating by tying these sex obsessives with log chains in narrow stalls, and barricading the barn doors.

6   Cows need no help with their love affairs, and in combat they are rather more dangerous than their masculine counterpart, since the bull charges blindly with his head down, and the cow focuses on her victim with one eye, head up, body on a slight diagonal, ready to shoulder you down if you dodge one way, and catch you with her head if you dodge the other way. I had a Hereford who once tried to bite a chunk off a veterinary. Cows are mean.

7   If they have any instinct, it is to be mean. The behavior pattern of an expectant mother cow is revealing. Unless she is locked in the barn delivery room, she leaves the herd and hides her silly offspring in the bushes. After a couple of hours she rejoins the herd and tries to act as if nothing had happened. The other cows take a "so what of it" sniff of the new mother and proceed to ignore her. A cow can only stand a few hours of being ignored and, besides, her distended udder is making her uncomfortable, so she returns to her calf, gets it up, feeds it, polishes it, and begins its training. For the next day or two, the mother cow will try to keep her herd in sight but will not join it until she has her calf well-disciplined and obedient. She will move the calf half-a-dozen times a day by keeping it hungry and making it come to her by voice command. Finally she struts back into the herd accompanied by the obedient calf.

8   A calf does not nurse instinctively. If the mother does not teach it, the herdsman has to, but the mother will not bother to nurse her calf if the dairyman relieves the pressure in her udder before the calf has "caught on." Cows with long hairs on their udders will hold up their milk, wean the nursing calf, and dry right up rather than suffer the discomfort of having the long hair pulled.

THEIR SOCIAL AMBITIONS

9   What a cow seeks from the herd is status. And, let's face it, ladies, cows are not the only women who regard a promising offspring as definitely status. When beef became more profitable than milk, I decided to have certain dairy cows bred to Hereford semen. Consequently, in addition to my herd of purebred Guernseys I have several crossbred Herefords. Three weeks ago a Hereford heifer had a spunky little white-faced daughter which was the envy of the entire herd. Grandmother Guernsey had to be restrained from interfering with the calf's feeding, and was so jealous of the little darling she pushed out a barn door, stole the baby, and had it hid out all morning. The proud mother, no longer a nonentity, now stands off Grandma with the cow's traditional stare of supercilious hostility.

10   In the foreword of this textbook on Animal Behavior, the author says he has studiously avoided "anthropomorphic sentimentalism." (If he had not I would not be able to spell it.) But I have no such scruples. I would count myself an inaccurate observer, or an unconvincing liar, if I did not remark that my cows enjoying an afternoon's rumination on a sunny hillside duplicate in attitude, gesture, murmured admonition, and condescending sniffs what one would see at an alumnae reunion or a PTA picnic.

11   Actually, cows do not join a herd; they are forced into a social pattern by some bitchy old dowager and by their own social ambitions. The homely brutes nourish prima-donna temperaments and domineering social pretensions. The cow, vigorously chomping her cud, is not dreaming of green pastures; she is plotting to do somebody in, or polishing her one-upmanship technique. This makes her much more of a society dame than a social animal.

12   Sheep are true herd animals and individual identities are completely submerged in the herd. Sheep follow a leader in blind trust. The cow, on the contrary, preserves her individuality by continually striving to better her herd standing. Cows *seem* to trail their leader submissively but every adult cow in the herd is just waiting watchfully for a chance to rebel, while the leader is ready to maintain her position by dirty tricks and physical violence. It is a kind of game with them; the prize is authority, represented by the Number One herd position.

13   My maternity ward is a box stall and represents special privilege. My Number One cow, Bossy, preempts it as her due when it is not in use for calving. Ordinarily, when I want my cows, I call Bossy. If they happen to be lying down, Bossy will rise with ponderous dignity and glare at each member of her herd, one after another, until they are all standing. Bossy will then march to the barn, pausing once or twice to glare back and make sure her platoon is properly marshaled.

14   When Number Three cow, July, was due for the maternity ward, I knew I would have trouble with Bossy, so when the cows came to the pond near the barn for water, I called July to come in. With the smug air of responding to a well-deserved honor, she came at once without waiting to drink. Bossy, knee-deep in the pond, exploded out of there and scrambled to intercept July. I barely had the gate closed behind July when Bossy arrived, bellowing with rage, and tried to break down the gate. Bossy was a violent and embittered misogynist until the new calf was weaned and July returned to her old stall.

15   Proud of her first calf and her promotion to the box stall, July was inspired to rise above her Number Three position. On her return to pasture, she refused to fall in line, but tramped alongside looking for a chance to pass Bossy's tossing horns. Bossy's track for two days was as erratic as a sailboat tacking into the wind as she hurried to intercept July's advances. Number Two cow, Princessa, would then try to lead the remainder of the herd on down the path

before Bossy returned to it. In the end, Princessa, who is almost too charitable to be a cow, finally resigned Number Two position to July, and July was triumphantly following Bossy through the barnyard gate when Bossy turned on her with two days' accumulation of animosity. I had to build a new gate.

ENTERTAINED BY A TRACTOR

16 Such devotion to prestige and protocol may possibly be duplicated in diplomatic circles in the world's capitals. If the behavior pattern of a well-provided and luxuriously cushioned dairy cow is not the product of an active but idle mind struggling to entertain itself, the Blood-and-guts Behaviorists are wasting their time researching on animals. They should be out frisking high society for what they call "Endocrine Interrelations."

17 It is a pertinent fact that no human can be as excruciatingly idle and bored as an animal. Humans have words as counters for thoughts. We can pronounce a word with our lips and recall it with our minds; consequently we occupy our inactive moments mulling over family or business worries. An animal thinks with its nerves, senses, and muscles. A cow cannot pronounce the word "apples" in its mind, yet my cows have been so emphatically berated for breaching the fence under our apple trees that I can trigger their memories by saying, "Apples, girls," and send them off toward the orchard. I find this ploy useful for getting my animals out of the barnyard when I am trying to haul manure.

18 With all its physical needs provided, a domesticated animal is many times more idle than a wild animal, and cows are always bored to death anyway because they have to stay awake an extra six hours a day to chew their cuds. Since cows have to occupy these periods of fretful insomnia as best they can, any activity or change in their environs is of intense interest to them. Instead of being frightened by a tractor, for instance, cows are entertained by it. They will run along with the tractor, daring it to chase them, and, if allowed to investigate to their hearts' desire, will nudge and prod the machine out of kilter, and lick off the paint.

19 Cows are not only born busybodies and mischief-makers, they are quick to learn. Their suspicious and competitive disposition impels them to alert and analytical attention. No nuance of tone or gesture is lost on them, and their desire for praise, prestige, privilege, and leadership makes them apt pupils. Also, they have all the time there is to think about anything which affects them. They have nothing else to do.

20 A zoologist can accept the fact that cows control their calves and each other with audible commands since such utterances are classified by the authorities as "instinctive cries," permissible to lower animals. Abstract concepts such as

good and evil, discipline and authority, inferiority and superiority are the unique prerogatives of Homo Sapiens. So when Bossy deserts her half-eaten breakfast in order to lead her associates through the barnyard gate, she could not possibly be declaring with mind and muscle, "Social position means more to me than food and drink." Or could she?

21   All animals communicate in a universal language easily understood by other genera and by such humans as are not completely hypnotized by mere words. Recently my neighbor's four-year-old daughter ran to me in great excitement, screaming that our saddle horse had "looked at" her over the fence. The mother mistook the child's excitement for fright, but I was about the same age as the child when I toadled out to our barn and began talking to the animals there as naturally as other little girls talk to their dolls. A young child knows so few words that it depends for information on facial expressions, voice tones, gestures, and motions. The horse had looked down deep into that child, recognized her as a fellow being, and said, "Hello, there."

22   An understanding of this basic, universal language is of key importance when it comes to milking, for neither bells, bruises, nor moral suasion will induce a cow to let down her milk. She will part with just as much, or as little, as she pleases. I have a simple program for keeping milk production at phenomenal levels. The program begins the moment I decide a heifer calf is worth raising. Aside from her social aspirations a cow is a rational being. Unloved and unlovely, she is too cynical to hope for happiness, but she does like to be comfortable. An empty stomach and an overstrained udder make her physically uncomfortable, so I explain to my cows that a full milk pail earns a full feed bucket. Cows are particular to the point of being absolutely meticulous about anything which affects them; they know to within an ounce when their feed ration is slighted. For the benefit of Behaviorists, however, I will explain that in hand-raising my heifer calves, I am careful to show them that gaining my approval earns soft words and extra grain, but that misbehavior evokes, "Ouch, dammit!" and a whack. By the time a calf is a month old, it understands the words "good" and "bad" and what they portend. By milking age, my cow has the hearing vocabulary of a three-year-old child, but I can snatch away the feed bucket if it does not obey.

A TALKING DIGESTIVE TRACT

23   On a winter afternoon a warm barn fragrant with hay is a pleasant place, but it is not quiet. Cows are never quiet. They get up, they lie down, they bring up their cuds with the affected plop of an after-dinner speaker clearing his throat. They rattle their neck chains, bounce their salt blocks around in the manger, test every board in their stalls for weakness, and lean against the partitions, swaying rhythmically, delighted if the strained boards shriek and complain. Cows are always working on something.

24   They work on each other. If any other cow succeeds in making enough noise, Bossy comments with an irritated swish and thump of her tail, twists around in her stall and glares over at the offender. The offender, safely tied three stalls away, replies with a disdainful sniff. July, in the intervening stall, rattles her horns against her hayrack, nervously protesting, "Don't look at me— I'm not doing it." Princessa will sigh, "Oh, lay off, you two."

25   These cows are practically shouting at each other. They also shout at me. Princessa grits her teeth to signify she is dying of hunger, and Bossy will put in her claim for attention by asking with a strangled gasp for a bucket of water. I give each of them a negative stare, as Princessa is too fat already, and Bossy only wants the water to upset in her stall and make a mess for me to clean up.

26   For ordinary conversation a cow uses the entire length of her digestive tract. These murmurs, squeaks, and burbles are only audible to me as I sit milking with my ear close to the cow's abdominal wall, but when Bossy starts an argument the other cows pause to listen in unnatural quiet so I know their hearing is more sensitive than mine. When I am milking, the cow talks not only to me, but also discusses me with the rest of the herd. Bossy has to be milked first, and she can put every cow in the barn on the alert with, "Watch it, girls, she's feeling grouchy this morning." When Bossy is feeling smug and ready to be milked, she chomps, gurgles, and pops her cud at the north end as expressively as a gum-chewing adolescent, but if her sensitive ego feels frustrated, abused, or even slighted, her intestines twitch, rumble, squeak, and presently explode at the south end (a cow's vocabulary is not always fit for human ears). I abandon her immediately, taking her grain ration with me and exclaiming, "Bad, bad girl."

27   Bossy will yearn after her vanished meal, and the behavior of my milk cows will be excellent—for about two weeks. Then Bossy will try that trick again. Cows are always on the make.

28   About 1910 our agricultural colleges began promoting a dairy-management program which called for keeping cows fastened in narrow stalls, year in and year out. Secured thus for the convenience of the management, and lavishly stoked with a procession of scientific nutriments, cows were supposed to lapse into a cooperative and contented stupor. For fifty years, dairymen have been going broke at the progressively disastrous rate of an annual 30 per cent, and the only ones in business now either turn their herds into pastures or exercise lots, weather permitting, or leave their cows free in a "lounging area," and bring them separately into a "milking parlor" for operations. These diminished herds continue to oversupply demand because somebody also started the idea of feeding cows after they were milked, one pound of grain for three pounds of milk. The idea spread, and the cows must have caught on fast, for the intelligent cow gives now three times as much milk as her pampered ancestor, thirty years ago. Since my cows are breeding stock I do not feed a high-protein milk ration, yet my cows part with four pounds of milk for every pound of feed.

29 A few days of storm shows exactly how cows react to confinement. While the blizzard howls, the cows shudder delicately when I open the barn door. They are not exactly grateful for their warm barn, but express their appreciation by complaining of drafts. The second day they are more murmurous. They shift in their stalls to watch each other, and I get the impression they are as conversational as a group of society matrons planning a charity ball to further their own ambitions. The third day finds the cows shouting at each other—and me. The veiled innuendos and subtle cattiness of yesterday's chatter have germinated into thwarted ambitions and insulted egos. If I cannot let those girls loose to work each other over, I know there will be hell to pay.

30 On the fourth morning, I am not surprised if I find that Bossy has slued around in her stall and deposited manure (a cow's substitute for thumbing its nose) on July's backside. In retaliation, July has tried to climb over the partition and is half-hanged with a foreleg hooked over her neck chain. Excited by July's struggles, May has forced out the front of her stall and is caught on the shattered boards with her head in the feed alley. Both the yearling calves will be wrong way to, in their stalls, and Princessa will be bellowing with concern, Bossy with rage, July with frustration. Down in the steer barn the Herefords will be gloating, "Teehee, now you'll catch it." Cows have a genius for expressing their personalities.

31 When the moment for release comes, cows have to be sent out of the barn separately or they will linger in the passageway and try to swipe or ram each other in the doorway. Females are not necessarily ladies. Before I could buy fatherhood in a test tube, I had my own bulls; they either ignored their ladies' social activities, or attended them with mild disapproval, making no effort to suppress the riots. But the bulls, at least, were gentlemen.

32 I could appreciate their problems. My reverend father commonly had to negotiate with a wife, two organists, a choir leader, and a social director—all women, so when I found one of my bulls off in the woods all alone, down on his knees and either swearing or praying as he savaged a rotten tree stump, I just tiptoed away, leaving him to his private devotions.

THE BRAINS THEY NEED

33 People are wonderful; we are more fortunate than all other animals in being equipped with opposable thumbs, mouths capable of exquisite articulation, and limbs arranged so we can scratch wherever we itch. We are built for accomplishment. Yet, without our advantages, the other animals crossed the slippery glaciers, survived the hazards of the age of mammals, and got here. They survived, so they must have all the brains they need—which is more than can be said for a lot of humans in our Great Society.

34 Personally, I cannot understand how anyone working with animals can

fail to realize that humans are not as smart as they think they are, and animals are not as dumb as we think they are. The zoologist who virtuously refuses to interpret animal behavior as the result of rational processes, and discards embarrassing evidence as "anthropomorphic sentimentalism," is winning his game with loaded dice. When we know we have animal bodies, and that the animals have gray-matter brains, failure to establish anthropomorphic interpretation rather suggests that the researcher has not oiled his cogwheels recently.

35   From such a situation, I turn for contrast to the wisdom of a certain riding-stable instructor who roars at his advanced pupils, "You can't run a horse like it was a machine. That's flesh you got under you, not tin. It's got heart and feelings, so you've gotta have heart and feelings, too. And, by damn, you just better remember *the brute's only human!*"

Apparatus for: All Cows Are Mean

Vocabulary: *Find a word in the indicated paragraph that means:*

1. tricky (¶ 1)   *devious*

2. innumerable (¶ 2)   *myriad*

3. unreturned (¶ 5)   *unrequited*

4. swollen (¶ 7)   *distended*

5. proud (¶ 9)   *supercilious*

6. thought (¶ 10)   *scruples*

7. wealthy widow (¶ 11) *dowager*

8. woman-hater (¶ 14)   *misogyny*

9. social behavior (¶ 16) *protocol*

10. subtlety (¶ 19)   *nuances*

11. indicate (¶ 22)   *portend*

12. insinuation (¶ 29)   *innuendos*

Discussion: *Rhetoric*

1. What is the *real* attitude of the author toward cows? Is it stated, or merely implied throughout the essay?
2. How would you classify the level of the language in this essay?
3. At the end of paragraph 4 there is a kind of internal outline which serves for the next 3 or 4 paragraphs. Find other such aids to internal organization.
4. How effective is the humor in this selection?
5. Does the author seem to have genuine insight into animal behavior?
6. Comment on the sentence structure in this essay.
7. Notice paragraph 32; how effective is it?
8. Endings often give writers a great deal of trouble. Do you think this writer had trouble ending her essay? Why or why not?

1. *He likes them, Implied*

2. *High, level*

3. *sick!*

4. *No*

5.

6. *Yes*

Apparatus for: All Cows Are Mean

7. _____

_____

8. _____

_____

Discussion: *Theme*

1. What kinds of animal behavior have you observed that strike you as humorous?
2. Do you think animals ever are cunning in the sense that they plot against man? Explain.
3. How do you view "herd instinct"? Do animals have instincts? Do people follow "herd" instincts?
4. In paragraph 22, the author speaks of a "universal language." Is there such a language? What is the evidence, if any?

1. _____

_____

2. _____

_____

3. _____

_____

4. _____

_____

Writing Suggestions

1. In a theme similar in tone to "All Cows Are Mean," write an account of a pet you have had.
2. In an expository theme, analyze the current theories about animal language. Consider, for example, the language of porpoises.
3. Describe an experience in which your dog or cat has demonstrated "human" intelligence.
4. "The Brute's Only Human"
5. "Vivisection should (or should not) be allowed in medical schools."

21. SWEDEN'S NEW BATTLE OVER SEX*

J. ROBERT MOSKIN

1   The Swedes are making sex dangerous—by American standards. They are stripping away the old taboos. Their open attitude intrigues many Americans and stimulates visions of a land where magnificent blondes enjoy their sexuality, but it also generates worry here that our young may get some Swedish ideas in their heads.

2   If the Swedes are less frightened by sex than we are, this is because they are taking the prurience out of it, in the way man has always taken the fear out of mystery: by education. They have now had compulsory public-school sex education for ten years. Every child from the first grade on is supposed to be taught, in detail, the facts of life. The program is imperfect and controversial even among broad-minded Swedes, but it exists, while we are still tiptoeing nervously.

3   Sex education is having a significant effect on Sweden. High-school graduates, to a great degree, are now realistically informed about sex. And many who have gone through the program over the past decade are, as parents, less inhibited about informing their own youngsters of sex facts and attitudes.

4   There is a chicken-and-egg puzzle about Sweden's teen-agers and sex education. Most high-school-aged Swedes regard premarital sexual relations as natural and acceptable. This radical change in attitudes is engulfing young people in other Western cultures, including our own. Swedish conservatives may charge that sex education stimulated the new attitudes, but most experts

* J. Robert Moskin, "Sweden's New Battle Over Sex," *Look,* November 15, 1966. Reprinted by permission of the Editors of LOOK Magazine, copyright © 1966, Cowles Communications, Inc.

deny that the program came before the new mores. In fact, many insist that the program be broadened to deal with the problems created by the new teen-age ideas. So pressing has their demand become that a Royal Commission has been set up and is re-examining the program, especially the teaching of sexual morality.

5   Although Swedes are called libertine, they are troubled and disputatious about sex and sex education. What is unique is that most accept the fact of youthful sex activity; they want to educate the young to handle sex, much as we have driver education to prevent highway accidents. They are more truly conservative than Americans who deny youthful sexuality and leave youngsters to learn in the streets.

6   This is the heart of the battle over sex in Sweden today: Should schools treat the sex problems of young people realistically or continue simply to preach continence? The kind of issue being fought over is whether high-school students should be taught more about how contraceptives work and how to use them.

7   To Americans, the Swedish program seems daring. While many Swedes say it is not daring enough, it goes beyond anything immediately imaginable in the vast majority of American school districts. And it contains principles that could be imitated by Americans who want to give young people honest information and an awareness of the responsibilities created by their sexual urges.

8   One principle is that every child has as much right to learn this subject as arithmetic or history. Many parents are unqualified to do the job because they have too little information or because their inhibitions make them poor teach-ers. Often, parents avoid the subject entirely. Even among those who believe fervently that sex should be taught only in the home, there is widespread acknowledgment that home instruction can pass down to the young the older generation's squeamishness and repressions.

9   The Swedes are convinced that sex education should be a continuing proc-ess starting in the earliest grades. Dr. Maj-Briht Bergström-Walan, an interna-tionally known school psychologist, believes it should begin at home before school age. Children start school when they are seven, and first-grade teachers are supposed to bring the fundamental facts into the normal classroom discus-sion, perhaps when a new baby arrives in one of the pupils' homes. There is no birds-and-bees approach, but a direct dealing with the question: Where do babies come from? The instruction prescribed by the Royal Board of Educa-tion, which has published the national handbook for teachers, covers at this stage: sexual anatomy, how egg and sperm meet, how the fetus develops and receives nourishment, how the baby emerges from the mother's body. All this is presented in terms of the child's relationship to the family.

10   In the fourth through sixth grades, instruction includes facts about puberty, menstruation, masturbation and nocturnal emission. Most sex education takes

place in biology class from grade seven through nine. By the ninth grade, the last year of compulsory school, the teacher deals with ethical considerations, family relationships, abortion, contraception, sterilization, children born out of wedlock, and venereal disease. In some schools, ninth-grade classes visit birth-control centers to learn contraceptive techniques. On one ninth-grade test, students were required to define these terms: gynecologist, menopause, seminal emission, erection, prostate hypertrophy, defloration, exhibitionism, sodomy and pedophilia.

11   All instruction is given to boys and girls together. The reasoning is that every aspect of sexuality is important to both, and that if they are taken into separate rooms for this one subject, sex will seem secretive and abnormal. Although some parents are still troubled by common instruction when its treats menstruation and menstrual hygiene, Swedish educators feel it works. They believe it makes possible discussion between boys and girls and, hopefully, between man and wife later on. It is interesting for an American observer, talking with Swedish high-school students, to find that boys and girls in a mixed group feel entirely free to say that they want more information about what the other sex experiences during sex relations.

12   The battles over the Swedish program center on three issues: the qualifications of teachers, instruction about contraception and the moral aspects of sex, especially sex relations between young people.

13   Even after ten years, there are still Swedish children who get no sex education whatsoever, and at least half receive so little that it is totally inadequate. Many teachers are excellent, but an estimated 50 percent avoid the subject, much as parents do. Some teachers ignore it entirely, others hand out pamphlets and let it go at that. The official handbook advises teachers who feel embarrassed to pass the task on to others, but many are too embarrassed to confess their embarrassment.

14   There is pressure to start a compulsory teacher-education program. Since sex education is given by the regular classroom teachers and biology teachers, the absence of such training has made it impossible to give every child sex education. One school in Gothenburg has experimented with programmed sex instruction from a teaching machine, and the national students organization, which has a representative on the Royal Commission now reviewing the system, wants specialists who can travel among schools and provide skillful sex teaching.

15   The battle over instruction about contraception involves both the physical and moral aspects of sex relations. As recently as 1938, it was illegal to prescribe or even to discuss contraceptives in Sweden. Now, less than 30 years later, they can be purchased by anyone in about 40 special shops run by the private National Association for Sex Education (RFSU) and from automatic vending machines that make them available at all hours. Authorities see this

change as a victory in the struggle to give women equal rights and protection in a previously male-dominated society.

16 As in this country, some in Sweden think that the availability of contraceptives encourages young people to have intercourse because they fear pregnancy less. The writers of the Royal Board of Education handbook seem to have held this view. The book barely touches on contraception and emphasizes that no contraceptive is fail-safe.

17 Others insist that it is sensible to make contraceptives available and to teach their use. They argue that the present approach to contraceptives in the sex-education program, and particularly the admonition that contraceptives are unsafe, encourages young people not to use them to prevent unwanted pregnancies and venereal disease, both of which have been rising in Sweden. Educators are appalled by such statements in the official handbook as this one in a sample lesson for 14- to 16-year-olds: "Since you know that boys and girls who are still growing up should not have sexual relations, you will understand that contraceptives should not be used by them."

18 Of the handbook, Dr. Bergström-Walan says, "It's quite wrong. These things should be discussed in the school to give the right attitude and knowledge." The trend in Sweden seems to be running overwhelmingly toward this view, and certainly spokesmen for the students are demanding better contraception instruction.

19 The rising incidence of venereal disease in Sweden over the past eight years, despite the virtual absence of prostitution, the presence of sex education and the easy availability of contraceptives that would prevent most cases of gonorrhea, baffles the experts. "This is a very unpleasant situation," says Dr. Malcolm Tottie, senior medical officer of the National Health Board and a World Health Organization expert on venereal disease. "It's quite fantastic how some kids are not motivated to prevent pregnancy or VD." He is an advocate of sex education, but says, "Education does not influence the VD rate. To influence sex behavior is something we cannot do much about. We are trying to."

20 The Royal handbook on sex education lays stress on morality. It tells teachers to emphasize that sex "cannot be divorced from character and conscience," and that "sex only reaches its full development when conjoined with love." A sample lesson for 14- to 16-year-old students has the teacher saying, "At your age, and in general while you are still growing up, you should not engage in sexual relations . . . you ought to be led to live a life of continence during the years while you are growing up." Such statements, running through the entire book, contradict the popular American impression that Swedes are being led toward promiscuity and sexual reveling. The sex-education program seeks to control youthful sexual urges with the cold water of information and heated warnings against moral wrongdoing.

21   Those who demand reform say that the moralizing goes so far that it is irrelevant to young people's thinking about their sexuality. They insist that the moral content has no more impact than a modern Sunday morning sermon and, because it preaches total continence, is rejected by many youngsters.

22   The reformers do not advocate stimulating sex relations among the young. They say intercourse should be recognized as a reality for many, and that those who do have sex relations should be taught how to avoid pregnancy and venereal disease. They want young people to be guided toward responsible sex behavior.

23   Mrs. Birgitta Linnér, marriage counselor of the Stockholm Family Counseling Bureau, whose book *Sex and Society in Sweden* will be published here next year, says, "The bad thing about the sex-education program is they knew premarital sex existed but tried to make the people more moral and to wait with sex relations. Now, they must admit that sex exists among young people and try to teach them about contraception. They really have to know about contraceptives. Those who don't want to start sex relations don't have to use contraceptives."

24   She feels that as a result of the sex-education program, "Young people get more biological facts and more opportunities to discuss psychological attitudes. They are less afraid of their sex urges, especially the girls. They can handle sex relations. It helps them to know when to say Yes and when to say No." She adds, "Earlier, so many women couldn't give themselves to good sex relations because they were so afraid of getting pregnant."

25   Mrs. Linnér, who last year testified before a U.S. Senate subcommittee on birth control, writes in her forthcoming book: "To contend that promiscuity is any more widespread in Sweden than in the United States is nonsense. What we have in Sweden is permissiveness, that is, we accept sex as a reality for both men and women. It is a situation that prompted one of my colleagues to remark, 'This young generation does openly what our generation did stealthily and with guilt feelings. Surely, their behavior is more healthy.' "

26   Mrs. Lis Asklund, who broadcasts on sex for teen-agers over Sveriges Radio, the national system, says, "If two young people are in love and mature, we do not discourage that. Both must be willing and must be responsible if they bring a child into the world." She and Torsten Wickbom have written a controversial book for teen-agers that goes well beyond the official handbook in its frank discussion of masturbation, orgasm and the clitoris. She says, "Children have the right to truthful answers to their questions—even small children. So much individual happiness depends on it really." And she adds, "We have accepted premarital intercourse to a great degree. We are not saying live as you like. We are still talking morally—against promiscuity. The biggest problem is that girls are younger and younger when they enter puberty. What

are you going to do? Shut your eyes as most countries or help them? In Sweden, we want to help them."

27   There have been surprisingly few attempts to determine the sex activity and attitudes of Swedish youth. But recently, some beginnings have been made. One research project in the city of Örebro covered nearly 500 students whose ages averaged just under 18 years. Of the boys, 57 percent, and of the girls, 46 percent, had had intercourse, and of these, the great majority had repeated experiences. Average age of the boys at the time of their first experience was 16, of the girls, 17.

28   A team of specialists under a professor at the Caroline Institute has begun a major attitude study in Stockholm. They will analyze 1,500 youths between the ages of 16 and 25, and another 1,500 who have had gonorrhea. A preliminary study of 450 21-year-olds in the army found that 83 percent of them had had intercourse before they were 20. Seven percent said they had not, and ten percent would not answer. The median age of first intercourse was below 16.

29   The investigators compared these young men with groups studied earlier. They found that the incidence of intercourse has risen, and the age of first experience has dropped. The most dramatic change was among students: Of a group born in 1922, only 40 percent had had intercourse by the age of 21, while among those born in 1944, 75 percent had. Concludes Professor Joachim Israel of the University of Stockholm, "The real change seems to be in those social groups that had a more Puritan attitude." He says, "Today, most children in Sweden are brought up in the traditional ways. At the same time, you take away taboos. The result is some people use sexuality as an escape. The school has a tendency to be against heterosexual activity—in effect, to teach that it is better to masturbate than have intercourse. I want to teach children sex is pleasurable but also involves a responsibility toward the other person."

30   Figures in Sweden indicate that premarital intercourse is common and increasing. Studies in girls' schools found the incidence of intercourse has risen more than 20 percent in the past five years. Half of the boys and girls who have had intercourse began before their eighteenth birthday. A study of 1,325 urban women delivering their first child found 26 percent unmarried. And the experts report that one in three brides in Sweden today is pregnant on her wedding day.

31   The problem is, in great part, the widening time gap between sexual development and marriage. The age of first menstruation is going down and now occurs on the average at thirteen and a half years. The average marriage age for Swedish men is 26, and for women, 24. The reasons are chiefly economic, including a severe housing shortage that leaves young couples dangling on waiting lists for as long as seven years. Dr. Tottie also blames changes in society: "Now, we have this great urbanization. The ties of community feeling are broken up. How do you get contacts? Sleeping together gives you a feeling of contact. We have more or less accepted that young people are sleeping

together. In the United States, they stop before the bitter end." In Sweden, he says, petting more often leads to intercourse.

32 Dr. Tottie asks, "Which is better: for your daughter to sleep with an unknown boy in the forest under a fir tree or for your daughter to sleep with a boy known to you in your house? If you are a parent in this country, you have to answer this question."

33 Whatever the reasons, the situation has aroused an angry dispute within the official Evangelical Lutheran Church. Some critics even disagree with the religious idea that love should be a requirement for premarital sex—but not for sex in marriage. Several years ago, the editor of the church's magazine, *Our Church,* Carl Gustaf Boëthius, declared the Lutheran bishops were wrong when they said that intercourse belongs only inside marriage. In reply, 744 pastors wrote to the church's Central Board demanding that Boëthius be fired. The Board refused, saying that the editor was in error but the church should permit free discussion. Boëthius, who is a member of the Royal Commission, explains that he feels the bishops were mistaken "because in reality, there are many young couples not yet married who are living together and are not acting immorally." He would accept some forms of what might be called premarital monogamy, and says, "We must have respect for all opinions." He estimates that 80 percent of all those getting married in Sweden had sex relations with their partner before marriage.

34 The clashing conservative view of many pastors is voiced by the Rev. Claes Robach, co-minister of the Oscar Parish, which embraces four churches in Stockholm. With the bishops, he believes that the main aim of sexuality is to beget children and that intercourse outside marriage is always wrong. "If many people are stealing, the government wouldn't say stealing is right," declares Pastor Robach, who is 48 and the father of four. "We should have a good sexual education, which gives the facts needed about reproduction and pregnancy. But it should be done in the framework that monogamous marriage is the only normal situation for sex relations. And it should say abstinence is healthy and the only sure prevention from fertilization."

35 Pastor Robach wants sex instruction for boys and girls to be kept separate and fears what he calls "a kind of sexual dictatorship in the schools," when teachers shape young people's ideas. He worries that sex is being overemphasized today and warns, "Sex has the power to dominate your life to a great extent so you just forget about the world for it. . . . The strong stress on sex education just now is because there are some forces that want to leave Christian morality. They want to say you should not be prevented by any commandments from God or man from having sexual experience."

36 The Rev. Ingmar Ström, director of the church's Central Board, takes quite a different approach to the problems of youthful sexuality. He has written a confirmation book he entitled *Come and See* because, as he says, "I only

invite them to come and make up their own minds. I don't decide for them what they can believe." He opposes promiscuity, but speaking of young people's moments of sexual excitement, he says, "If they know how to behave in such moments, it is better than if they don't." He notes that girls who start sex relations do not first take contraceptive pills for 21 days: "You start first, and then you ask for these things."

37 Director Ström's teaching about sex has a strong moral content. "I tell them it's a fine thing to wait. Love is a great thing—not only something to play with." He believes that marriage is "for the whole life until death." His book makes five moral assertions: 1. It is necessary to give—not to take—in love. 2. "If you need your boy or girl friend's body as the instrument of your own pleasure, it is not right." 3. Young people should know that to break off an emotional relationship is always painful. 4. "There is no way back. You are not satisfied with holding hands when you have gone further." 5. "It's a good thing to learn to wait. It is a thing you can learn." Ström sums up: "I say these five things, and they have to make their own conclusions."

38 Traditionalist religious thinking troubles Ström: "I think in churches the world over we have to take a new view of these things. We had only one reason —the child—and when that is not there any more, I'm not sure it is necessary to find a new reason." Now, he says, "it is 100 percent sure to have intercourse without babies." A father of five, he concludes, "Many of my own children's friends have sex relations together, and I think it's all right because it is worse if they have to wait years until they can have a home of their own and marriage."

39 The leaders of the national Swedish Student Organization (SECO) feel the sex-education program fails to face up to these problems. Torbjörn Båth, who is 21 and SECO's executive secretary, says he received sex education only in the twelfth grade: "It was very bad. The teacher gave propaganda for pre-marital abstinence. We don't think the schools or the government should take a position on that." Hans Dahlgren, 18, SECO vice-president, agrees: "We believe in objective education. The schools should not make propaganda for the Christian church or the Communist party." He, too, feels the program is not being carried out: "Very few teachers actually give sex information. I've only had it in one grade in eleven years I've been in school." Neither student leader was taught about contraception. Says Båth, "The handbook should not stress that contraceptives are so unrelia...

40 Dr. Gösta Rodhe, the Royal Board of Education's chief medical officer, joins the critics of the teaching about contraception. He says thoughtfully, "We are trying to find a moral principle that is acceptable to everyone. And there is one: You don't hurt your neighbor."

41 Dr. Lars Engström, medical director of the independent RFSU, says, "I'm quite convinced that sex education is something we will keep and improve. My

children know what is right and wrong. Sex is not a secret they cannot talk about. They have discussed it and come to their own ideas. If sex education has any effect, it has a good effect. Telling people they can go to bed together or what to do in bed together is not sex education. If they get sex education, they know what is happening not only physically but psychologically and socially."

42   In the problem of youthful sexuality, Dr. Rodhe sees a common dilemma: "Many people in America believe there is no activity there. This is not true. The situation in Sweden is the same as other countries, only we talk about it." He affirms the purpose of Sweden's sex-education program: "to make people more free—to not be so terribly inhibited. Even married people are terribly inhibited. They can't talk about sexual feelings. Society is not only young people. It is important even for married people to get less inhibited in their sexuality."

Apparatus for: Sweden's New Battle Over Sex

Vocabulary: *Make a list of any troublesome words in this selection. Look up each one in your dictionary and write out the full definitions.*

_____

_____

_____

_____

_____

_____

_____

_____

_____

Discussion: *Rhetoric*

1. The title of this essay, "Sweden's New Battle Over Sex," suggests at least two opposing views. In general, what are these contrasts in the two views? Notice, for example, that even the conservative view does not suggest giving up sex education.
2. The first sentence ("The Swedes are making sex dangerous") is meant, obviously, to get our attention. Does the essay fulfill the "promise" of this opening statement? Explain.
3. The last sentence of the second paragraph suggests a "pro and con" argument about sex education in Sweden. How does this help to organize the essay?
4. What evidence does the author give for his assertion in the fourth paragraph that a radical change is engulfing young people in the United States?
5. Moskin says that Swedes are regarded as libertines. Again, what evidence does he cite?
6. In paragraph 12, there appears a kind of internal organization device. What is it? Where does the author develop the ideas announced in this paragraph?
7. Why does the essay end essentially with a series of quotations?

1. _____

   _____

2. _____

   _____

3. _____

   _____

4. _____

   _____

5. _____

   _____

Apparatus for: Sweden's New Battle Over Sex

6. _____

_____

7. _____

_____

Discussion: *Theme*

1. In your judgment, is there enough formal sex education in the United States? Explain.
2. Does education always take the fear out of mystery? (See paragraph 2.) Explain.
3. Would you like to see more attitudes similar to those of Sweden prevail in this country? Why or why not?
4. What is the prevalent attitude in this country among high school and college students concerning premarital sexual relations? Is it markedly different from that of students in Sweden?
5. Re-read paragraph 11 and decide whether or not you agree with the views of the Swedish educators. Explain.
6. Should women have exactly equal rights? Explain.
7. Paragraph 31 quotes Dr. Tottie, "Sleeping together gives you a feeling of contact." In this statement he suggests that man is alienated and has little contact with his fellows in an urbanized society. Do you agree with his thesis? With his solution?

1. _____

_____

2. _____

_____

3. _____

_____

4. _____

_____

5. _____

_____

6. _____

_____

7. _____

_____

Writing Suggestions

1. "Education Takes the Fear Out of Mystery"
2. Choose a statement from this essay and, on the basis of your own knowledge or experience, defend or attack it.
3. Develop your views about some of the major areas of difficulty in sex education.
4. Define *sexuality, femininity,* or *masculinity.*
5. Man Is (*or* Is Not) Naturally Monogamous
6. The Sexes Are (*or* Are Not) Equal
7. Planned Parenthood Is Moral (*or* Immoral)

VIII. PARAGRAPH DEVELOPMENT: REASON AND EVIDENCE

When you wish to persuade, inform, or influence your reader, you will need evidence to support your position or argument. Most argumentative papers have three divisions. The *beginning* states, as objectively as possible, the problem or issue that you are going to consider, as well as the solution or position you intend to defend. The *middle* develops your argument through the use of evidence, and refutes, calmly and fairly, that of the other side. The *end* of your paper offers a restatement of your position, reinforcing the arguments you have set forth in previous paragraphs.

But if your reader is to accept your argument, your evidence will have to be based on established facts. Opinions, guesses, speculations, or gossip are not enough. The simplest kind of evidence is that based on *observation* or *personal experience*. If, for example, you want to make a generalization about the quality of education offered by high schools today, you might describe your own experiences as a student, as well as those of your friends. The use of *authority* as evidence is often valuable, particularly when the experience, reputation, and ability of the authority are beyond dispute. Your authority might be an individual or a book; in either case, you must be certain that it is qualified and unbiased. Evidence based on a *universal truth* (such as, "The sun rises in the east") is also sometimes helpful. Regardless of the type of evidence used, you should avoid an overly emotional tone to your writing, as well as evidence that is insufficient or atypical and therefore inadequate for the support of your argument.

To be effective, your argument must be developed in a pattern that is clear to the reader. Most argumentative papers are arranged according to either the *inductive* or the *deductive* method. A paper following the inductive pattern goes from the particular to the general; that is, it builds from specific statements to a general conclusion. When using the inductive method, then, you begin with your evidence—examples, statistics, instances, or facts—and arrive at a generalization or conclusion. Such a pattern discourages sounding off until all of the evidence is weighed and evaluated. Naturally, a generalization is only as valid as the evidence that supports it. For this reason, you should be certain that you have enough evidence. In "The Bunk about Health Foods," Ralph Lee Smith enumerates several "myths"; among the evidence he uses to disprove each myth are statistics, authorities, facts, and examples. At the end of his essay he offers his hypothesis, based on an evaluation of his evidence: Food faddism represents one of the biggest health-education problems in the United States today.

A paragraph developed inductively usually contains the topic sentence at its conclusion. The evidence is first presented, and the reader is led to the conclusion by the author. (Incidentally, *inductive* comes from a Latin word meaning "to lead into.") This method is particularly effective when the conclusion or hypothesis is one that might irritate or frighten away the reader if presented without evidence at the beginning of the paragraph or theme. Because of the controversial nature of their hypothesis, Donald H. Menzel and Lyle G. Boyd use the inductive method in several paragraphs in "The Saucer Worlds." Note the generalization at the end of the following paragraph:

> The published reports comprise a heterogeneous collection of facts, fiction, and guesses. The investigator must first separate and discard accounts that are obvious hoaxes or delusions. There are many of these. The remaining material he divides into two classes. The first includes statements made by competent, careful witnesses, describing what they have seen and heard—for example, "I saw a brilliant light moving swiftly without sound." The second class includes statements of opinion or belief about the thing seen—for example, "The strange light obviously was controlled by intelligence." Putting aside this second class of material for the time being, he looks at the information in the first and immediately faces an awkward conclusion: apparently no "typical" flying saucer exists.

The other pattern of argument, the *deductive,* is the opposite of inductive reasoning. A theme organized deductively goes from the general to the particular; that is, it begins with a generalization or proposition which is then applied to specific instances.

Paragraphs using the deductive method usually begin with the topic sentence, which contains the proposition or generalization. The generalization is then applied to a particular instance. A concluding or clincher sentence often re-states the original argument. Notice the arrangement of the following paragraph:

> The English language is always sticking a foot out to trip a man. Every week we get thrown, writing merrily along. Even Dr. Canby, a careful and experienced craftsman, got thrown in his own editorial. He spoke of "the makers of text-

books who are nearly always reactionary, and often unscholarly in denying the right to change to a language that has always been changing. . . ." In this case the word "change" quietly sandwiched in between a couple of "to's," unexpectedly exploded the whole sentence. Even inverting the phrases wouldn't have helped. If he had started out "In denying to a language . . . the right to change," it would have come out this way: "In denying to a language that has always been changing the right to change. . . ." English usage is sometimes more than mere taste, judgment, and education—sometimes it's sheer luck, like getting across a street.*

Other patterns, in addition to the inductive and deductive, can be used in argumentative writing to present reason and evidence. The cause-to-effect and the effect-to-cause are often effective, as is the question-to-answer pattern. In writing essays you will have occasion to use all of these methods, sometimes in combination. As a matter of fact, each of the three essays in this section contains paragraphs developed in a variety of patterns. The important fact to remember is that you must organize your argument according to a logical plan which helps your reader, and you must provide him with convincing evidence. Only in this way will you persuade, inform, or influence your reader.

* E. B. White, "English Usage," from *The Second Tree from the Corner* (New York: Harper & Brothers, 1952), p. 151.

22. THE SAUCER WORLDS*

DONALD H. MENZEL AND LYLE G. BOYD

1   Thousands of reports of "flying saucers," "unidentified flying objects," or "UFOs" have appeared in print during the last fifteen years. Although most of the things seen have later been explained as unusual but normal phenomena, some enthusiasts continue to regard them as mysterious, and thus help perpetuate the myth that the "saucers" are actually spaceships from other planets, busily carrying out a patrol of the earth.

2   This saucer myth owes an unacknowledged debt to Charles Fort, a talented reporter, writer, and self-appointed gadfly of science. With a strong curiosity about the world of nature but without training in the disciplines of research, Fort liked to challenge scientists in general and astronomers in particular with tales of "impossible" happenings culled from books of folklore, old journals, and newspapers. He mistrusted orthodox knowledge because, he believed, it smugly damned to oblivion all reports of marvels that it could not explain: pyrogenic persons; rains of fish, frogs, and stones; accounts of telepathy, teleportation, the vanishing of human beings, luminous objects in the sky. Although he never claimed that he believed the stories himself, Fort enjoyed collecting them and before his death in 1932 had completed four volumes of these anecdotes.

3   Science-fiction writers have found an inexhaustible mine of ideas in *The Book of the Damned, New Lands, Lo!,* and *Wild Talents,* which also provide the chief elements of the saucer myth:

4   "Unknown, luminous things, or beings, have often been seen, sometimes

* From THE WORLD OF FLYING SAUCERS by Donald H. Menzel and Lyle G. Boyd. Copyright © 1963 by Donald H. Menzel and Lyle G. Boyd. Reprinted by permission of Doubleday & Company, Inc.

close to this earth, and sometimes high in the sky. It may be that some of them
were living things that occasionally come from somewhere else in our existence,
but that others were lights on the vessels of explorers, or voyagers, from somewhere else."¹ These extraterrestrials may have been in communication with
earthmen for many years, Fort suggested, and they may sometimes kidnap and
carry away human beings.

UFO REPORTS AND THE AIR FORCE

5   Most flying-saucer reports have come from reliable citizens who have seen
something extraordinary, something they do not understand. Genuinely puz-
zled, they often report the incident to the nearest Air Force base. The evaluation of such cases is the responsibility of the United States Air Force. Since the
beginning of the saucer scare in 1947, the chief investigating agency has been
that at Wright-Patterson Air Force Base, Dayton, Ohio, and has borne a succession of names—Project Sign, Project Grudge, Project Blue Book, and the
Aerial Phenomena Group of the Aerospace Technical Intelligence Center,
usually known as ATIC. Until recently this group operated under the jurisdiction of the Assistant Chief of Staff, Intelligence. On July 1, 1961, it was transferred to the jurisdiction of the Air Force Systems Command. To simplify
discussion in this book, however, the group that investigates unidentified aerial
phenomena is generally referred to as ATIC.

6   In military parlance the phrase "unidentified flying object," abbreviated as
UFO, is used to indicate any air-borne phenomenon that fails to identify itself
to, or to be identified by, trained witnesses on the ground or in the air who are
using visual or radar methods of observation. Created in the early days of the
saucer era, the term UFO is unfortunately misleading because it seems to imply
that the unknown is a solid material object. Many of them are not. The more
dramatic phrase "flying saucer" is similarly misleading because not all the un-
knowns are shaped like a saucer, and not all of them are flying. Since no one
has been able to devise a more accurate brief term that will apply to all reports
in this category, both "UFO" and "flying saucer" have remained in common
use.

7   Air Force investigators and scientists have been able to account for almost
every reported "spaceship" as the result of failure to identify some natural
phenomenon. Some were the product of delusion or deliberate hoaxes. A few
remain technically "Unknown" because, although the probable explanation is
obvious, too few facts are available to permit a positive identification. No such
report suggests the possibility that interplanetary craft are cruising in our
skies.

¹ Charles Fort, *Lo!* (New York: Claude H. Kendall, 1931).

THE SCIENTIST'S VIEW

8   If a spaceship from another planet should ever visit the earth, no one would be more eager to acknowledge it than our government officials and our scientists. All governments would feel their responsibility to protect the human race if necessary, and to establish diplomatic relations with the alien race if possible. The scientists would want to study, analyze, and try to understand the nature of both the ship and its occupants.

9   Many persons, sincerely believing that flying saucers do exist, berate the investigator who denies their reality and characterize him as stupid, willfully obtuse, or intellectually dishonest because he does not accept the saucer reports at face value but weighs them by the same methods most of us use in weighing evidence in everyday life. When told there's a horse in the bathtub, for example, the sensible man realizes that the alleged visitation, while not impossible, is extremely improbable. Therefore he does not immediately begin speculating on the color of the horse, where it might have come from, what its purpose may be, and whether it will wreck the bathroom. Instead he adopts the scientific method and first goes to find out whether the horse is really there.

10   Like Fort, some flying-saucer believers are consciously or unconsciously antagonistic to the scientific method and resent its restrictions as a child objects to discipline. Suggesting that a strictly logical approach deprives us of valuable truths about the nature of the universe, and bluntly asserting that present-day physicists and astronomers have closed their minds to the possibility of new knowledge, these enthusiasts imply that we should require less rigorous proof for the reality of saucers than for other types of physical phenomena.

11   Because so many amateur investigators have misunderstood, misrepresented, and condemned the scientists' attitude, the authors of this book (asking the indulgence of their colleagues) will briefly outline the principles a researcher ordinarily applies to the study of any new problem—the nature of radioactivity, the cause of a disease, or the origin of flying saucers.

THE QUESTION OF "EVIDENCE"

12   Most physicists, chemists, biologists, and astronomers will agree that life in some form probably exists in other parts of the galaxy. These other life forms, if they exist, may or may not have a kind of intelligence similar to our own; if they have, we might or might not be able to recognize it. Such speculations, while fascinating, lie entirely in the realm of theory. They are not facts and do not provide the slightest support to the often-stated corollary that intelligent creatures do live on other planets and frequently visit the earth.

13   In approaching the spacecraft hypothesis, the scientist asks first: What facts are we trying to account for? And second: Does the spacecraft theory account for these facts better than the normal explanations that are already available? After studying hundreds of UFO reports, however, he concludes that much of the startling "proof" that saucers are spacecraft is merely inference. Of the established facts, none requires a new theory to account for it; and no evidence exists that even faintly suggests, to the expert, that interplanetary visitors are involved.

14   In the study of UFO phenomena this question of "evidence" is crucial. The careful investigator tries always to distinguish sharply between an observed fact, which is evidence, and an interpretation of the fact, which is not evidence no matter how reasonable it may seem.

15   As a simple analogy, consider this situation: A man is sitting in his living room late at night; the rest of the family has gone to bed. Suddenly he is startled by a loud noise somewhere upstairs. Trying to account for the noise, he thinks of various possible causes—a burglar, the "settling" of the house, a mouse in the wall, someone dropping a shoe, the wind rattling a door, the sonic boom from a distant plane. If, without having further information, he decides that any one of these is the true cause, he is accepting a guess as though it were a fact. The real cause of the noise may be one of these or it may be something else that he hasn't even thought of.

16   Amateur investigators of UFOs publish many reports which they characterize as absolute proof that spaceships exist. The expert, analyzing the same reports, finds no proof at all because the actual facts and the interpretations of the witnesses are hopelessly confused. An early UFO case provides a typical example.

17   According to Air Force records,[2] on the morning of December 6, 1952, a B-29 bomber was over the Gulf of Mexico returning from a training mission. At 5:25 A.M. the student radar operator, using an uncalibrated set, observed four bright blips (radar jargon for bright spots on a radarscope; such a spot indicates the presence of an object reflecting the radar pulses, but does not reveal the nature or shape of the object). The blips were apparently returns from objects about twenty miles away, in no specific group, which rapidly moved off the scope. Similar groups of fast-moving blips appeared at intervals during a period of about five minutes, and appeared also on two auxiliary radarscopes. After the first set was calibrated, the blips reappeared; none was observed after 5:35 A.M. From the radar data estimates of size and distance were made; calculations based on these estimates indicated a probable speed of 5000 to 9000 miles an hour. During the ten-minute period two visual observations were made, lasting about three seconds, which bore no obvious relation to the radar observations: at the right of the plane one crewman saw

[2] Air Force Files.

a single blue-white streak going from front to rear under the wing, and another crewman saw two flashes of blue-white light.

18   An explanation of the incident was not found immediately, and ATIC at first classified it as an Unknown. Some saucer enthusiasts interpreted the facts to mean that several groups of saucers had been in the area, machines flying so fast that they were visible only as blue-white streaks, whose presence was confirmed by radar. These conclusions were merely deductions from fact, not observed facts. The radarscope is not a camera and does not, at least at present, picture the shape or physical structure of the phenomenon it reports; it shows only spots of light that change position and size. Similarly, the blue-white streaks were mere flashes of light without size or shape.

19   In a later study of the evidence, the Air Force experts recognized this incident as one of false targets on radar. . . . The radar phantoms *may* have been caused by beacon returns triggered by another radar; by variations in the atmosphere; or, if "ducting" conditions existed, by reflections from objects that were far beyond the normal range of the radar set. The blue-white flashes had no relation to the radar returns and were probably meteors; the date corresponded with the beginning of the annual Geminid shower. . . .

20   This Gulf of Mexico incident is neither complicated nor puzzling. We mention it chiefly to illustrate why the saucer enthusiasts so often disagree with the conclusions reached by the Air Force experts. The amateur assumes that the instrument operated faultlessly and detected a solid object; he uses these assumptions to interpret the data, uses the interpretation as fact, and by this "bootstrap" process deludes himself into thinking he has proved what he assumed in the first place.

VARIOUS TYPES OF UFO

21   A biologist trying to identify a group of unusual animals which are said to represent a new species begins by collecting all possible information about their appearance and behavior. After he has determined their typical size, shape, color, mode of reproduction, manner of locomotion, etc., he compares these characteristics with those of animals of known species and eventually classifies the strange specimens. In a similar way the professional investigator of UFO phenomena begins by asking the question: What is a typical unidentified flying object?

22   The published reports comprise a heterogeneous collection of facts, fiction, and guesses. The investigator must first separate and discard accounts that are obvious hoaxes or delusions. There are many of these. The remaining material he divides into two classes. The first includes statements made by competent, careful witnesses, describing what they have seen and heard—for example, "I saw a brilliant light moving swiftly without sound." The second class includes

statements of opinion or belief about the thing seen—for example, "The strange light obviously was controlled by intelligence." Putting aside this second class of material for the time being, he looks at the information in the first and immediately faces an awkward conclusion: apparently no "typical" flying saucer exists.

DESCRIPTIONS OF UFOs

23   No two reports describe exactly the same kind of UFO. There are dozens of types of saucers, resembling each other as little as turnips do comets. Hoping to find some consistent pattern, the investigator opens his notebook and starts listing the data.

24   *Shape*—The flying saucer varies greatly in shape. At different times and places it may be a circular disk like a saucer, often with a small protrusion in the center like the knob on a teakettle lid; elliptical or bean-shaped like a flattened sphere; a circular base supporting a dome-like superstructure; a sphere surrounded by a central platform, like Saturn in its rings; long and thin like a cigar; a tapered sphere like a tear-drop; spindle-shaped, with or without knobs on the ends; or a double- or triple-decked form like a stack of plates.

25   *Size*—The saucer varies greatly in size. Estimated diameters range from 20 or 30 feet to several thousand. While under observation it may instantaneously increase or decrease in size.

26   *Color*—The saucer varies greatly in color. It may be white, black, gray, red, blue, green, pink, yellow, silver; may be luminous or dull; may be a solid color; may be circled by a central band of different color; may display flashing lights of various colors. It may change color or luminosity while being observed.

27   *Motion*—The saucer displays a wide variety of motions. It may travel very slowly; very fast, approaching the speed of light; at jet speed; at meteoric speed; may hover motionless over one place. At any speed it can instantaneously change velocity and direction of motion—can move horizontally, vertically, toward the observer, away from the observer, in a straight path, a zigzag, a spiral. Like the Cheshire cat, it can vanish instantly or slowly fade away.

28   *Means of propulsion*—Unknown. Some saucers move in complete silence; others produce noises: a hiss, a whistle, a roar, a thunderclap, or a detonation like a sonic boom.

29   *Incidence*—Saucers may appear at any hour of the day or night, but they appear most frequently in the hours before and after sunset, and before and after sunrise. Their numbers may suddenly increase at certain places and certain times. The objects can appear singly, in random groups, in groups showing a geometrical pattern. A single object may split and multiply into a

group, or a group may merge into one. Saucers almost always appear in the air, rarely on the earth's surface or in bodies of water. They almost never come within touching distance of the observer. The length of their stay varies greatly, from about two seconds to two or three hours.

30   *Structure*—Unknown. A saucer may be visible or invisible to the observer; visible to the human eye but not to the camera or radar; visible to the camera or radar but not to the eye. Some obey the laws of gravity and inertia, others do not.

31   *Purpose*—Unknown. No officials in the government, the press, the churches, or the universities have received any attempt at communication. No saucer has produced intelligible visible, audible, or radio signals.

32   Long before finishing this tabulation the investigator realizes that he is not dealing with one thing but with many. No single phenomenon could possibly display such infinite variety. However, before he starts trying to classify the descriptions and to explain them, he takes a look at the second class of material—the conclusions offered by saucer enthusiasts. Leaving the realm of observation for that of interpretation, he is suddenly catapulted into a world of fantasy.

Apparatus for: The Saucer Worlds

Vocabulary: *Using your dictionary, define the following italicized words as they are used in context.*

1. (¶ 1) Although most of the things seen have later been explained as unusual but normal (*a*) *phenomena,* some (*b*) *enthusiasts* continue to regard them as mysterious, and thus help (*c*) *perpetuate* the myth . . .

   a. A fact of scientific inter...

   b. FANANTIC

   c. To give enduring existence to.

2. (¶ 2) . . . self-appointed (*d*) *gadfly* of science. . . . happenings (*e*) *culled* from books of folklore . . . He mistrusted (*f*) *orthodox* knowledge because, he believed, it smugly damned to (*g*) *oblivion* all reports of marvels that it could not explain: (*h*) *pyrogenic* persons . . .

   d. PEST

   e. removed from

   f. SOUND in OPIN

   g. forget

   h. severed

3. (¶ 4) These (*i*) *extraterrestrials* may have been in communication with earthmen for many years . . .

   i. EXTRA EARTHLY

4. (¶ 6) In military (*j*) *parlance* the phrase "unidentified flying object" . . . is used.

   j. CONVERSATION

5. (¶ 7) Some were the product of (*k*) *delusion* or deliberate (*l*) *hoaxes.*

   k. False beliefs

   l. A PRATICAL JOKE

6. (¶ 9) Many persons . . . (*m*) *berate* the investigator who denies their reality and characterize him as stupid, willfully (*n*) *obtuse,* or intellectually dishonest . . .

   m. Chide

   n. ~~STUPID~~ DULL

7. (¶ 10) Like Fort, some flying-saucer believers are consciously or unconsciously (*o*) *antagonistic* to the scientific method . . .

o. *hostile*

8. (¶ 12) They are not facts and do not provide the slightest support to the often stated (*p*) *corollary* that intelligent creatures do live on other planets and frequently visit the earth.

p. *deduction*

9. (¶ 13) . . . he concludes that much of the startling "proof" that saucers are spacecraft is merely (*q*) *inference*.

q. *an logical conclusion*

10. (¶ 17) . . . using an (*r*) *uncalibrated* set . . .

r. *an uncertain*

11. (¶ 19) . . . the beginning of the annual (*s*) *Geminid* shower

s. _____

12. (¶ 22) The published reports comprise a (*t*) *heterogeneous* collection . . .

t. *dissimilar*

13. (¶ 24) . . . with a small (*u*) *protrusion* in the center like a knob on a teakettle lid . . .

u. *a protruding*

14. (¶ 25) While under observation it may (*v*) *instantaneously* increase or decrease in size.

v. *suddenly*

15. (¶ 28) . . . or a (*w*) *detonation* like a sonic boom.

w. *to explode with sudden violence*

16. (¶ 30) Some obey the laws of gravity and (*x*) *inertia*, others do not.

x. *the property which will remain at rest*

17. (¶ 32) . . . he is suddenly (*y*) *catapulted* into a world of fantasy.

y. *thrown*

Apparatus for: The Saucer Worlds

Discussion: *Rhetoric*

1. This selection is actually the beginning of a book, yet it reads like a complete essay for several reasons: It introduces a topic (flying saucers); it treats the major ideas surrounding UFO's; and then it summarizes the evidence concerning these phenomena. See if you can find the paragraphs that correspond to these divisions.
2. The authors begin their selection with a discussion of the "saucer" myth. How does this make for an interesting essay? Consider the fact that everyone has an opinion about this "myth."
3. The scientist's view of research in general and flying saucers in particular is discussed beginning in paragraph 8. How does this section add to the discussion? Consider the authors' attitude here.
4. This entire selection uses "reason and evidence," which is discussed in the inter-chapter preceding this selection. Notice how the authors of "The Saucer Worlds" bring the question of *actual evidence* to bear on the question of flying saucers. Comment on the effectiveness of paragraphs 12 through 20.
5. How do the authors relate persons who write about UFO's to Charles Fort; pyrogenic persons; rains of fish, frogs, and stones?
6. Find several uses in this selection of analogy; for example, in paragraph 28 the sound of saucers is "a detonation like a sonic boom."
7. In paragraph 17, the authors cite a UFO sighting. Do you think the explanation the authors offer is convincing? Explain.

1. ¶1-¶7   ¶8-3¶   ¶2¶-32

2. Most people enjoy myths although not all believe in them.

3. Shows how scientists feel is improbable but still look into u

4. Shows facts

5. people w ___ ___ ___ ___ ___

6. _____

7. _____

Discussion: *Theme*

1. Do you consider the evidence for UFO's convincing enough to commit yourself to belief or nonbelief? What kind of evidence would it take to change your mind?

2. Has the Air Force told us everything they know about UFO's? Should they?

3. Do you agree with the authors of this selection that there is a relation between Charles Fort and UFO's? Explain.

4. Is there any significance to the year 1947 when UFO's began to be reported in great numbers? Explain.

5. Is there any reason to disagree with the first statement of paragraph 8? Explain.

6. Flying saucer sightings have been explained as a kind of hysteria. Could you accept that idea as having any validity? Explain.

7. Will there be, in your judgment, any "proof" for or against UFO's in this century? Explain.

1. _____

2. _____

Apparatus for: The Saucer Worlds

3. _____

_____

4. _____

_____

5. _____

_____

6. _____

_____

7. _____

_____

Writing Suggestions

1. The Saucer Myth
2. The Reality of Flying Saucers
3. Use the following statement as the basis for a 800 word theme: "These extraterrestrials may have been in communication with earthmen for many years."
4. Write a paper in which you define unidentified flying objects. Note the authors' definition in paragraph 6.
5. Popular Fallacies and Misconceptions

23. GIVE THE GAMES BACK TO THE STUDENTS*

HENRY STEELE COMMAGER

1   Almost every year the public is startled by revelations of some new scandal in college athletics—the bribery of basketball players, the open purchase of football players, the flagrant violation of rules by the college authorities themselves.

2   It is regrettable that these scandals should excite so much attention, for, by dramatizing the ostentatious immoralities of college athletics, they tend to distract attention from the more permanent and pervasive immoralities.

3   Indignation at the more overt manifestations of corruption is thus a kind of moral catharsis; having expressed it, we then can contemplate with apathy the conditions which almost inevitably produce the corruption.

4   Thirty years ago a report of the Carnegie Foundation on College Athletics concluded as follows:

5   "The paid coach, the special training tables, the costly sweaters and extensive journeys in special Pullman cars, the recruiting from the high schools, the demoralizing publicity showered on players, the devotion of an undue proportion of time to training, the devices for putting a desirable athlete, but a weak scholar, across the hurdles of the examinations, these ought to stop and the intramural sports be brought back to a stage in which they can be enjoyed by a large number of students and where they do not involve an expenditure of time and money wholly at variance with any ideal of honest study."

6   "These ought to stop!" Instead, they have become all but universally ac-

---

* Henry Steele Commager, "Give the Games Back to the Students." © 1961 by The New York Times Company. Reprinted by permission.

cepted and legalized—nay, the malpractices themselves have become respect-able, and we can look back upon our old view of them with a certain nostalgia.

7 For today's malpractices are more extreme and more widespread. Worse yet, they have percolated down to the high school and they have corrupted large segments of our society.

8 For almost half a century now, educators have talked hopefully about de-emphasizing college athletics. And every year the emphasis has grown greater, not weaker.

9 The problem is not one of overemphasis. It is not even one of emphasis. The problem is the enterprise itself—intercollegiate athletics.

10 If we are going to solve that problem, we must begin by restating principles so elementary and so obvious that they should not have to be stated at all:

11 The function of colleges and universities is to advance education.

12 Whatever contributes to education is legitimate. Whatever does not con-tribute to education is illegitimate.

13 The only justification, therefore, for games, sports, athletics, is that these do in some way contribute to education.

14 By education we mean nothing narrow. Clearly, it involves physical and moral as well as intellectual well-being. But these are by-products of education. There are a number of institutions that have responsibility for the physical and moral well-being of the young, but the schools and colleges are the only institu-tions that have primary responsibility for their intellectual well-being.

15 Does our current system of intercollegiate or interschool athletics con-tribute either to the central function of education, or to its by-products?

16 Clearly, it does not. As now organized and directed in most colleges and in a good many, if not most, high schools as well, athletics contribute nothing whatsoever to education. They simply distract the time, the energy and the attention of the whole community from the main business of education—and from its legitimate by-products.

17 Our system of athletics does not contribute to the physical fitness of the young. On the contrary, it concentrates on physical training for a mere handful of students—whom it often harms by overtraining—and reduces the great majority of students to the role of passive spectators, or television viewers. Even the facilities provided for physical training are often monopolized by the "teams," to the detriment of most of the student body.

18 It does not contribute to sportsmanship—which was one of its original purposes. On the contrary, the tremendous emphasis on winning the game has largely destroyed sportsmanship and has corrupted both players and spec-tators.

19   It does not contribute to initiative, independence, alertness, and other desirable qualities. Instead, by centering authority in paid coaches whose primary interest is winning games, it has gone far to destroy initiative and independence on the part of players.

20   No impartial student of college and high-school athletics today can doubt that, on balance, these sports—far from making any contribution—actually do immense and irreparable harm. It is not only physical training and sports that are corrupted by the current malpractices; it is the whole educational enterprise. And since the whole community is involved in the educational enterprise, it is the whole community.

21   Educational institutions themselves are corrupted. They publicly confess that their athletic functions are more important than their academic, and acquiesce in malpractices that they would not tolerate in any other branch of their activities.

22   Colleges that spend more money on athletics than on the library, that excite more interest in basketball than in music, that cater to the demand for "winning teams" rather than for sportsmanship are faithless to their moral and intellectual obligations.

23   The community itself is corrupted by being bribed with athletic spectacles to support educational programs which should be supported on their merits.

24   Perhaps worst of all, the boys and girls of the country are corrupted: here is the real corruption of the innocent. Almost every newspaper, every weekly magazine, every television network makes clear to them that what is most important in education is athletics, and what is most important in athletics is winning.

25   No newspaper ever celebrates the scholarly achievements of local students in its biggest headlines. Why, then, should we expect the young to believe us when we tell them, on ceremonial occasions, that it is the scholarly achievements that are important? Alumni demand a winning team, and so does the community. Not long ago, a North Carolina coach was quoted as asking, "How can I be proud of a losing team?" Can we, then, expect young people to take us seriously when we tell them that it is the game that counts—not the victory?

26   What is the explanation of this deep and pervasive corruption of games and sports? What has happened to us?

27   What has happened is that we have taken games away from the students, to whom they belong, and given them to adults, to whom they do not belong.

28   We now require of high school and college boys—and, sometimes, girls—that they provide entertainment for the community and bring money to local shopkeepers and restaurants and other businessmen. (Recently a New York official said of an Army-Syracuse game that "the restaurants reported business

to be fabulous . . . the Transit Authority reported 28,000 extra riders that day . . . immensely increased hotel business.") They are expected to provide copy for the local newspapers, for magazines, and for TV and radio.

29   We do not permit children to work in shops or factories for our profit. Why should they be expected to make money for business interests in the community?

30   We do not permit our daughters to put on performances in burlesque shows or night clubs for our entertainment. Why should we require our sons to put on gladiatorial spectacles in stadia for our entertainment?

31   We do not expect the young to pay school taxes, or to support the chemistry department of a university. Why should we expect them to earn money for the athletic programs of the local high school, or to support the athletic departments of our colleges and universities?

32   The problem is deep and pervasive, but fortunately not complex. The solution is drastic, but fortunately not difficult; all that is needed is the will to apply it. The solution is threefold:
First, give games back to the students.
Second, eliminate all outside pressures to win games.
Third, take the dollar sign entirely out of school and college athletics.

33   First: Let students manage their own games, as they do at English universities. Let them play their games for the fun of it, not to entertain adults, or make money for the community or win glory for old Pugwash.

34   An end to games as spectacles. An end to bands in uniforms and drum majorettes and well-trained cheering sections, all of them artificial and all giving a fantastically exaggerated importance to the games. An end to the recruiting of players by coaches or alumni, to coaches who play games from the side lines and, for that matter, to formal coaching. If there must be coaches, let them depart on the day of the game and permit the players to play their own games. After all, professors do not help the students pass examinations!

35   Second: Eliminate all outside pressures. Alumni letters about the football team should go into the waste basket, where they belong. An end to pressure from coaches; their jobs should not depend on victories. An end to pressure from newspapers; let them report professional games, and leave students alone to play as well or as badly as they please. An end to pressure from public-relations offices of colleges; let them report academic activities or go out of business. An end to pressure from townspeople; they can get their entertainment, find emotional safety valves, and get rid of their vicarious sadism elsewhere.

36   Third: Eliminate money—all the way. No more paid coaches. Let students do their own coaching, or let school teams draw on "old boys," or get such aid as they need from members of the teaching staff who are primarily and legiti-

mately teachers. After all, paid coaches are both new and singular in history: They did not exist until this century, and they do not now exist in England or Europe. An end to all athletic subsidies, direct and indirect; to athletic "scholarships," a contradiction in terms. No student should be encouraged, in high school, to subordinate studies to athletic prowess. No student should be admitted to college on any grounds but those of academic competence; no student should be allowed to stay in college unless he is intellectually competent.

37 An end to separate athletic budgets; to admission charges for games; to the expectation that football or basketball will somehow "pay for" other parts of physical training. Games should be as much a normal part of school or college as music or drama or the college newspaper, and should no more expect to be self-sustaining.

38 An end to the building or maintenance of costly stadia. Let us make drastic reductions in expenditures for athletic equipment, for uniforms, for other superfluities. No more travel expenditures for spring training camps, for fall training camps, for airplane junkets to the other end of the country. Let schools play their neighbors in the same town or—at an extreme—in the same state.

39 Adopt these policies and nine-tenths of the evils that plague intercollegiate athletics would evaporate overnight.

40 Of course, if they *were* adopted, the games would deteriorate—as spectacles. Those who want to see brilliant performances in football or basketball can then go to professional games, as even now they go to professional rather than to college baseball games.

41 Let the fans—the subway alumni of Notre Dame or the vicarious old grads of Michigan—organize city or state football and basketball teams, just as the English have city or county soccer teams.

42 Naturally, student interest in organized athletics will decline; it should. Sensible students already know that if they are going to get on with their education—if they are going to get into a law school or a medical school—they have no time for organized athletics.

43 European universities have managed to survive for centuries without the benefit of "teams," and doubtless American colleges and universities can learn to do so.

44 Of course, there will be a falling-off in enthusiasm for old Siwash among certain kinds of alumni. Perhaps, in time, colleges can produce alumni whose interest is in intellectual rather than in athletic programs. In any event, there seems to be a pretty close correlation between high-powered athletics and low-powered finances. It is a sardonic commentary on the current scene that public pressure for winning teams rarely finds expression in lavish gifts or in generous appropriations. Institutions such as M. I. T. and Amherst, at any rate, seem to manage pretty well without the exploitation of athletics, and

institutions such as Ohio State, which has yielded to pressure for winning teams, are treated with niggardliness by an ungrateful Legislature.

45   These are negative consequences which we may anticipate from the elimination of money and of pressures from college athletics and the return of games to the students. The positive consequences which we may confidently anticipate are exhilarating.

46   This simple program will restore integrity to athletics, making clear once more the blurred distinction between the amateur and the professional. And it will enormously improve programs for physical education for the young people in schools and colleges, an improvement desperately needed.

47   It will release the energies of educators and students for the primary job of education. The colleges will be freed from improper pressures and influences and permitted to do what they are best equipped to do and what they have a moral responsibility to do: Educate the young.

48   But is all this a counsel of perfection? Can this program of cleansing and restoration be achieved? Well, it has been achieved at Johns Hopkins, at the University of Chicago, and at M. I. T. It has been achieved at Swarthmore and Oberlin and Reed. Somehow, all continue to flourish.

49   No halfway measures will do. As long as nonacademic organizations have an interest in athletics, as long as games belong to coaches or alumni or townspeople or the business community instead of to the young people who play them, all the evils which have afflicted school and college athletics in the past will continue.

50   Radical surgery is needed. But it is radical surgery from which the patient is sure to recover and which guarantees good health and good spirits.

Apparatus for: Give the Games Back to the Students

Vocabulary: *Using your dictionary, write a personally usable definition of the words as used in this selection.*

1. flagrant (¶ 1) — *conspicuously bad*

2. ostentatious (¶ 2) — *pretentious*

3. pervasive (¶ 2) — *passive*

4. indignation (¶ 3) — *anger excited an unworthy*

5. overt (¶ 3) — *open to public*

6. catharsis (¶ 3) — *eliminating of complex by bring it to conciences*

7. contemplate (¶ 3) — *to meditate on*

8. apathy (¶ 3) — *want of feeling*

9. inevitably (¶ 3) — *unavoidable*

10. variance (¶ 5) — *disagreement*

11. nostalgia (¶ 6) — *homesickness*

12. percolated (¶ 7) — *oozed through*

13. segments (¶ 7) — *sections*

14. illegitimate (¶ 12) — *not good*

15. passive (¶ 17) — *not active but active upon*

16. monopolized (¶ 17) — *taken over*

17. detriment (¶ 17) — *disadvantage*

18. initiative (¶ 19) — *drive*

19. irreparable (¶ 20) — *not reparable*

20. acquiesce (¶ 21)   *to accept as inevitable*

21. pervasive (¶ 26)   *passive*

22. gladiatorial (¶ 30)   *pertaining to gladiators*

23. stadia (¶ 30)   *a temporary station*

24. prowess (¶ 39)   *courage*

25. competent (¶ 39)   *able*

26. superfluities (¶ 41)   *insufficiencies*

27. deteriorate (¶ 43)   *fall apart*

28. vicarious (¶ 44)   *acting on behalf of another*

29. sardonic (¶ 47)   *bitterly scornful*

30. niggardliness (¶ 47)   *in the manner of a niggard*

31. exhilarating (¶ 48)   *to enliven*

Apparatus for: Give the Games Back to the Students

Discussion: *Rhetoric*

1. This essay makes use of a clear organizational pattern: First, the author states the problem; second, he states his thesis and shows how former efforts have failed; third, he admits his solution has "negative consequences," but claims they are outweighed by the positive results; and fourth, he concludes with an affirmative conclusion. Find these divisions and discuss their effectiveness.
2. Where does Commager define education? Is his definition crucial to his argument?
3. The author is impressive in his use of comparisons or analogies; for example, he suggests a relationship between burlesque and football. Find other examples.
4. Where does Commager place his strongest argument against athletics as presently practiced in our colleges?
5. What is the effect of the author's outlining his solution before he actually discusses the threefold prescription?
6. What do you consider the strongest feature of this essay?
7. Do you get the feeling of completeness in this selection? What contributes to your judgment?
8. Is the title a good one? Explain.

1. ¶ 1+8/5   ¶ 9 16-24 4   ¶ 96 -31
   ¶ 32 - 8   ¶ 40 -46   47-48
2. ¶12   yes

3. ¶ 2-3   ¶ 8

4. ¶ 8

5. INSIGHT

6. $P 27-31$

7. YES

8. YES

Discussion: *Theme*

1. What do you consider to be the strongest argument in favor of intercollegiate athletics? Against?
2. Is the expense of college football justified? Does it in fact pay for itself?
3. Do you think all pressures to win games should be eliminated? Explain.
4. Should money be eliminated from sports in college—all the way? Explain.
5. Should athletic "scholarships" be completely eliminated? Explain.
6. How do you explain the fact that nonparticipating schools like MIT and University of Chicago get huge amounts of money?
7. How serious is the problem of college athletics?
8. Is it true that sportsmanship is learned on the playing field? Explain.

1.

2.

3.

Apparatus for: Give the Games Back to the Students

4. _____

_____

5. _____

_____

6. _____

_____

7. _____

_____

8. _____

_____

Writing Suggestions

1. Choose some other area of your college—automobile regulations, dress code, or class attendance—and write a paper discussing and defending your views.
2. Find out the amount spent on football in your school and compare that amount to the expenditures in other areas, such as the school paper; then come to some judgment about the way monies should be spent.
3. Defend the integrity of athletics in colleges.
4. Take the Games Away from the Coaches and Alumni.
5. Compare American emphasis on sports in colleges and the emphasis on athletics in European colleges.
6. Basketball Is for the Birds.
7. Like Commager, take an unpopular view of some phase of college life and defend it.

24. THE BUNK ABOUT HEALTH FOODS*

RALPH LEE SMITH

1 Food faddism—the belief in the desirability or necessity of eating certain "miraculous" foods—is as old as civilization itself. The Egyptians believed that garlic was a "wonder food," and they fed it to the laborers who built the pyramids. The Romans thought that if a citizen were confused, he could clear his mind by eating lettuce.

2 Tomatoes have been the subject of much food-fad lore. When first introduced into Europe they were thought to be an aphrodisiac. Later they were seen as a sure-fire cancer cure. Americans took a dimmer view; for a long time, they regarded tomatoes as poisonous.

3 But never before in history have absurd notions regarding nutrition enjoyed such widespread popularity as in our present modern 20th century. Based on misstatements of the facts on nutritional disease, food faddism has emerged as a whopping multimillion dollar business, observes Dr. Kenneth L. Milstead, of the Food and Drug Administration (FDA), adding that "it has become the most widespread kind of quackery in the United States." An estimated 10 million duped Americans—more than one out of every 17 persons—contribute handsomely to the perpetuity and prosperity of swindlers and crackpots, estimates Philip L. White, Sc.D., director of the Department of Foods and Nutrition, American Medical Association. The faddists have mounted an immense effort to undermine public confidence in the nutritional value of the food supply of the best-fed and best-nourished nation on earth.

4 Small wonder that food-faddist leaders proclaim that you must eat so-called

* Ralph Lee Smith, "The Bunk About Health Foods," *Today's Health*, October 1965. Reprinted by permission of author and publisher.

"health foods" or "natural foods" and that you should take vitamin-mineral dietary supplements "to avert the danger of improper nutrition." It is from the sale of these products that many of them have amassed their fortunes. Throughout best-selling books, radio scripts, in lectures, and in the tons of literature which faddists compile can be found ridiculous statements on nutrition, such as was made recently by a Dr. Joe D. Nichols, president of Natural Food Associates (NFA), that "the average American today cannot go into a store and come out with a food supply that will give him proper nutrition."

5   Organizations spreading the natural food gospel are numerous. They include the American Nutrition Society, the American Academy of Applied Nutrition, the Boston Nutrition Society, and Natural Food Associates, a recent FDA report reveals, making special note of the fact that "they have as their principal objective the promotion of so-called natural or unprocessed foods. They carry on a continuous propaganda war against other foods which they refer to as processed or refined." Having as their primary tenet that the major cause of disease and poor health is "devitalized" foods, they spread the four myths of nutrition:
   Myth I: Most, if not all, diseases are caused by faulty diet.   Fad foods and dietary supplements are offered for the treatment of prevention of everything from "tired blood" to cancer.

6   *The Truth:*   Very few conditions or diseases are caused by dietary deficiency. "Tired blood," a feeling of being "run down," or experiencing fatigue, is rarely, if ever, due to faulty diet in this country. In fact, so rare are diseases such as beriberi and scurvy, which are due to dietary insufficiency, in the United States, that doctors have difficulty locating cases for study.
   Myth II: American soils are impoverished, and they produce foods which are inferior in nutritional value.

7   *The Truth:*   Both parts of this proposition are false. Commercial U.S. agriculture treats soil as a precious commodity and keeps it rich through crop rotation and fertilization. Even if our soils *were* widely impoverished, this would *not* mean that foods grown on them would be nutritionally inferior.

8   "Infertile soil means limited yield per acre but no inferiority in make-up per plant," emphasizes the Greater Los Angeles Nutrition Council. From the American Dietetic Association we learn that "the nutritive value of a given crop, such as wheat, is influenced more by the kind of seed planted than by the fertility of the soil." Thus, corn can be bred to contain more niacin or starch and tomatoes can be bred to contain more vitamin A or vitamin C, but this is achieved by the development of new seeds and strains and bears little or no relation to soil fertility.

9   *Myth III: The American food supply is devitalized by overprocessing.* This is the great selling pitch for "health food stores" and "natural food stores" which offer a wide range of "unprocessed" or "organic" foods in addition to a

fantastic variety of vitamin-mineral supplements containing many substances that almost nobody really needs.

10   The faddists reserve their choicest vocabulary for processed foods—such as the perfectly good canned goods you find in your neighborhood grocery— calling them "counterfeit," "prefabricated," "worthless," and "carbohydrate paste."

11   *The Truth:*   Americans have to go out of their way, nutritionally speaking, to avoid being well-nourished, the FDA points out. Conducting regular market-basket samples studies in five cities to determine the nutritive value and safety of foods offered for sale in representative American cities, the FDA found that "foods readily available at ordinary groceries and supermarkets contain ample quantities of vitamins." Analyses were made after normal kitchen preparation and cooking.

12   As for the faddist condemnation of processed foods, an article by the late Martha F. Trulson, Mary B. McCann, and Frederick J. Stare, M.D., chairman of the Department of Nutrition, Harvard University School of Public Health, reveals that "fresh fruits and vegetables are not in practical nutrition superior in food value to commercially canned and frozen foods. Good nutrition depends upon securing sufficient amounts of the specific nutrients and it makes little difference if the amino acids come from beef or grasshoppers, or the ascorbic acid from oranges or potatoes. Food faddists fail to grasp this concept of nutrition—that health can be achieved by a variety of foods. Thus, they preach the merits of a particular food and the demerits of others."

13   The foods sold by health-food stores often cost more than the foods available at regular food stores and supermarkets. For the most part, they may be good and nutritious foods. But why pay a premium price when you can procure all the nutritious foods you need from your regular food market at a fraction of the cost?

14   *Myth IV: Most Americans suffer from "subclinical deficiencies" of needed vitamins and minerals, and should therefore take vitamin-mineral supplements and eat "health foods" to insure health.*   This is the *scare myth.* You may be undernourished, say the faddists, even if there is no evidence of it that modern science and medicine can detect. This myth is often used to hawk vitamins and dietary supplements to healthy people. For those who cash in on nutrition nonsense, it is the gimmick that has brought in a golden harvest.

15   *The Truth:*   "According to the subclinical deficiency myth," reports FDA, "anyone who has 'that tired feeling,' or an ache or pain in almost any part of the body, is probably suffering from a 'subclinical deficiency' and needs to supplement his diet with some concoction . . . Of course, no normal person can go through even a small part of his life without experiencing some of these symptoms. There is no basis for believing that they are usually due to subclinical deficiencies."

16   "When a tally is made of all the cases of clinically ascertainable incidences of vitamin deficiency in the United States in a single year, it adds up to less than 20,000—or less than one percent of our total population," says Dr. Victor Daniel Herbert, an associate in medicine in Harvard Medical School.

17   Genuine deficiencies, as opposed to mythical "subclinical deficiencies," should of course be diagnosed by a physician, instead of being treated by the dubious and dangerous method of self-medication which is so energetically promoted by food-fad groups.

18   Who are some of these people who find themselves at variance continuously with the recognized national authorities in the science of nutrition? Three illuminates had articles published in a recent single issue of the NHF *Bulletin*— Fred J. Hart, "Farmer, Scholar, Gentleman," V. Earl Irons—"An American with American Ideals," and Dr. Royal Lee, "Humanitarian."

19   Founder and president of the NHF, Fred J. Hart was for many years a principal officer of Electronic Medical Foundation, a leading distributor of fraudulent medical devices (see "The Strange World of Mechanical Quackery," TODAY'S HEALTH, November 1964). In 1954, he and Electronic Medical Foundation were enjoined from distributing 13 different devices which the FDA charged were misbranded with false claims for the diagnosis and treatment of hundreds of diseases. In 1961, he was again hauled into court by the government for violating the injunction. Entering a plea of "no contest," he was fined $500 in July, 1962 by the U.S. District Court in San Francisco.

20   V. Earl Irons was the distributor of Vit-Ra-Tox, a food supplement hawked by door-to-door vendors. He served a year in jail after the U.S. Court of Appeals upheld a lower court's 1957 conviction that he misbranded Vit-Ra-Tox.

21   Royal Lee, an NHF director and board member, is a nonpracticing dentist who issues reams of food-fad literature under the name of Lee Foundation for Nutritional Research in Milwaukee, Wisconsin, which he superintends. In addition, Lee is the proprietor of Vitamin Products Company, a commercial firm selling vitamins, dietary supplements, and fad foods. Twice convicted of violating the Federal Food and Drug Law, he received a one-year suspended prison sentence on April 23, 1962, and was put on probation for three years. Vitamin Products Company was fined $7000 in a case in which Lee and the company were prohibited by the court from shipping in interstate commerce 115 different dietary products and fad foods which were offered for the treatment of more than 500 diseases and conditions.

22   Roy F. Paxton, a recent NHF director, is a twice-convicted promoter of "Millrue," a worthless cancer remedy. Fined $2500, he received a three-year prison sentence from the Federal District Court at Springfield, Illinois, on his second conviction. The corporation, Millpax, Incorporated, was fined $1000.

23 Another NHF leader is Andrew G. Rosenberger, listed as the group's "nutrition chairman." Rosenberger and his brother Henry are the principals of Nature Food Centres, a thriving chain of health-food stores based in Cambridge, Massachusetts. On June 19, 1962, the Rosenbergers were each fined $5000 and Nature Food Centres was fined $10,000 for misbranding dietary products carried in their stores. Each received a six-month suspended prison sentence and was put on probation for two years. These sentences were upheld by a Court of Appeals.

24 NHF's Washington representative, Clinton R. Miller, is the proprietor of the Clinton Wheat Shop in Bountiful, Utah. One of his products, "Dried Swiss Whey," has been seized by federal marshals on charges that it was misbranded by false claims representing it to be a treatment for intestinal disorders. Action on the seizure is pending.

25 Last but not least, Don C. Matchem, editor of the monthly magazine *Herald of Health,* has been active for years as a writer advocating the worthless Millrue and Hoxsey cancer remedies as well as other equally worthless medications.

26 Steadily growing in members and in financial backing since it was launched in 1954, NHF is the same organization which in 1963 sponsored a "Congress on Medical Monopoly" for the express purpose of blasting the AMA and the FDA, during AMA-FDA Second Congress on Medical Quackery.

27 Organized food faddism does not withstand the test in a court of law, as is illustrated by the suit that the Boston Nutrition Society brought against Harvard's Doctor Stare.

28 At issue was a favorite theme of the faddists—that enriched white flour and white bread are at best nutritionally worthless and at worst poisonous.

29 This Boston organization had worried the wrong mother when it issued the statement:

30 "The enriched bread fed to the American public is a national scandal. First of all, the wheat grown on poor soil and fertilized with water-soluble commercial fertilizer is of low protein content. . . . The modern flour mill removes the precious vitamins and minerals. This is then bleached with a powerful oxidizing agent, chlorine dioxide (which is a poison); and to this lifeless mass, a few dead synthetic chemicals (improperly called vitamins) and inorganic iron are added. We not only think these foodstuffs are worthless; we believe that many of them are positively harmful . . . We know that we are a nation of sick people. Our hospitals are crowded to capacity. All the metabolic diseases are increasing by leaps and bounds. Coronary thrombosis is attacking young men in their 20's. Cancer is the leading cause of death in children under 14. Diabetes and mental disease are on the increase even in children. And dental caries are rampant!"

31 Sending this statement to a leading magazine, the worried mother wrote: "Since two of my boys refuse to eat any but white bread, I am naturally terribly concerned. Is there any connection between white bread and all these diseases?" The magazine referred the query to Doctor Stare, whose reply was later published:

32 "These scare tactics are typical of the food faddist organizations," Doctor Stare answered in part. "The name 'Boston Nutrition Society' sounds good, but if you were to telephone them you would discover, as we did, that the phone number is the same as for the Copley Square Diet Shop, purveyors of so-called 'health foods.' . . . From a practical viewpoint in most American diets, *dark flour and enriched white flour are the same in food value* and both make important contributions to our diet. To imply or suggest that enriched white flour can cause or contribute to the diseases listed in the clipping is a cruel and reckless fraud."

33 Bringing suit against Doctor Stare for his statement, the Boston organization lined up Natural Food Associates' president, Doctor Joe D. Nichols of Atlanta, Texas, as an expert witness. He acknowledged authorship of an article reprinted by both Natural Foods Associates (NFA) and the Lee Foundation for Nutritional Research, excoriating white flour as "unfit for human consumption" and decrying enriched bread, for containing synthetic vitamins and for the bleaching of the flour with chlorine. He said coronary thrombosis and "metabolic disease" are related to the use of enriched, devitalized foods.

34 On cross-examination, it was revealed that Doctor Nichols had never done any research, and knew of none, on the alleged toxicity of the chlorine bleaching process for white flour. Neither did he know anything about the chemical composition and vitamins in bread.

35 Doctor Stare's attorney asked Doctor Nichols what he thought about the addition of vitamin D to white bread. He replied that the vitamin D added to white bread was poisonous and that there is considerable evidence of this vitamin's toxicity. Doctor Nichols is wrong on both counts, but small matter at this point.

36 "Do you happen to know," the attorney asked, "that vitamin D isn't one of the enriching articles in enriched white bread?" Nichols finally had to admit that he didn't know this.

37 After deliberating about 15 minutes, the jury acquitted Doctor Stare.

38 Perhaps best known of the several lecturers, radio commentators, and book authors who augment the work of food-fad organizations are Lelord Kordel, Gaylord Hauser, and Bob Cummings, the movie star. They have reached many people by expounding on nutrition, many of which run counter to the prevailing opinions of science, and they have made large sums of money from the commercial aspects of their activity.

39   The author of such best-sellers as *Eat and Grow Younger* and *Eat Your Way to Happiness,* Lelord Kordel has also been president of Detroit Vital Foods, a "health food" store. In 1946, he was fined $4000 for misbranding vitamin-mineral supplements and "health foods." Later, in 1957, while running an operation called Nutrition Enterprises, Kordel signed a consent order with the Federal Trade Commission (FTC) agreeing to discontinue certain claims for a dietary supplement called "Super-Nutri-Way." The FTC charged that no need had been established for 16 of the "35 garden fresh nutritional elements," the product contained, "that protect your health."

40   In 1961 the FDA caused seizure of a quantity of "Michigan Brand Korleen Tablets," along with several of Kordel's best-selling books and other accompanying labeling, charging that the books and other literature made false and misleading claims for the product. Kordel fought the seizure but it was upheld in federal court. Also in November, 1961, federal marshals empounded on court order nearly a ton and a half of honey being offered in Kordel's retail store, Detroit Vital Foods, under claims that it was a cure for "premature death," and helpful in preventing or treating waning virility, rheumatism, arthritis, and weak heart. The claims, said FDA, caused the honey to be misbranded.

41   Gaylord Hauser (also known as Bengamin Gayelord Hauser) is another best-selling author. As early as 1937, a firm called Modern Health Products was billing Hauser as "the famous Viennese scientist." "He is not a doctor of medicine, not a Viennese, and certainly not a scientist," said an article in the April 7, 1937, issue of the *Journal of the American Medical Association.* "Hauser endorses the concoctions of the Modern Health Products, and the Modern Health Products—of which Carl S. Hauser is vice president and treasurer—endorses Bengamin Gayelord Hauser."

42   In 1934, the FDA acted against Modern Health Products for selling two products, "Santay-Swiss Anti-Diabetic Tea" and "Nutro-Links," under fraudulent claims. In 1936, the FTC entered into a stipulation with the company in which the firm agreed to discontinue a number of claims for the Hauser-plugged product "Swiss Kriss." In 1937, three more concoctions of Modern Health Products—"Slim," "Correcol," and "Hauser Potassium Broth," all of which had been endorsed and recommended by Hauser—were seized and destroyed by court order after the FDA made charges that they were misbranded and sold under fraudulent claims.

43   In 1951, the FDA obtained seizure of copies of Hauser's book *Look Younger, Live Longer* along with a quantity of Plantation Blackstrap Molasses. Claims for molasses in the book, such as "add five youthful years to your life," and "regrowth of hair on bald spots," were false, said FDA, and caused the molasses to be misbranded.

44   Among Hauser's recent books is the best-seller *Mirror, Mirror on the Wall,*

published in hardcover in 1960 and in paperback in 1963. The basic thesis is that women can achieve beauty by following his "cosmetic diet," involving an intake of basic nutrients substantially surpassing the standard amounts required for good nutrition. "The cells can get along on a subsistence diet," Hauser postulates. "But for vitality and beauty they need that something extra, an abundance of the health-giving, beauty-giving foods. That is why my 'cosmetic diet' is fortified with extra amounts, not a minimum but a maximum, of complete proteins, vitamins, and minerals."

45   The book also includes a section on "special diet shops . . . formerly known as Health Foods Shops," for such items of the Hauser "beauty-full diet" as "unprocessed foods," brewers yeast, rose hips, "iodine-rich" tablets made from "sea greens," sunflower seeds, and sesame seeds. It appears Hauser has provided a new "wrap" for an old theme.

46   Author of *Stay Young and Vital,* a book on nutrition, movie star Bob Cummings also served as "vice-president in charge of research" for Nutri-Bio, a vitamin-mineral supplement distributed by door-to-door salesmen. His 1961 salary with the firm was $76,641, plus $7453 set aside under the company's profit-sharing plan. Apparently the company's opinion of Mrs. Cummings was equally high; she received a salary of $76,141 during the same period. Each of the Cummings' five children—several under 10 years of age, judging from the family pictures in his book—received salaries of $166 a month.

47   A 1962 release from the Food, Drug, and Cosmetic Division of the National Better Business Bureau says, "Of the 37 ingredients in the Nutri-Bio formula, there are 21 for which no need in human nutrition has been established." AMA's Doctor White agreed, saying, "The need in human nutrition has not been established for over half of the ingredients on the label." (Philip L. White, "Something to Think About: A Close Look at NUTRI-BIO," Today's Health, January 1962).

48   The FDA has made a number of seizures of shipments of Nutri-Bio and accompanying literature, on misbranding charges. Seizures have included 50 tons of literature designed for use by 75,000 distributors, and copies of Cummings' book. Late in 1962 Cummings resigned as a director of the firm and disposed of his stock.

49   In all forms, nutrition nonsense and food faddism represent one of the biggest health education problems in the United States today. The American people are eager for information on health and nutrition, and food faddists have thus found receptive ears for their misleading ideas.

50   Contrary to the harbingers of nutritional doom, the basic American food supply is more than adequate to sustain topnotch health in normal persons, says Doctor White.

51   Food faddism can cause harm in two ways. It can substantially increase the

family food bill for costly "nature foods," "organic foods," and misleadingly-named "health foods," vitamin-mineral preparations, and dietary supplements for which there is absolutely no need in the American diet. Worse still, it can cause a person to attempt do-it-yourself dietary treatment for diseases and abnormal conditions that, contrary to the food faddists, have nothing whatever to do with dietary deficiency. Needless to say, persons with some abnormality should not resort to self-medication; bad guessing can even cost one's life.

Apparatus for: The Bunk About Health Foods

Vocabulary: *Match the definition in the right column with the appropriate word in the left column.*

_D_	1.	lore (¶ 2)
_a_	2.	aphrodisiac (¶ 2)
_k_	3.	nutritional (¶ 3)
_h_	4.	perpetuity (¶ 3)
_f_	5.	tenet (¶ 5)
_e_	6.	fatigue (¶ 6)
_b_	7.	hawk (¶ 14)
_G_	8.	ascertainable (¶ 16)
_J_	9.	dubious (¶ 17)
_i_	10.	excoriating (¶ 33)
_c_	11.	harbingers (¶ 50)

a. A food or drug that is said to arouse one sexually
b. heralds
c. to peddle
d. popular knowledge about a subject
e. weariness; exhaustion
f. an opinion; principle; dogma
g. finding out for certain
h. unending; perpetual
i. tearing; chafing; denouncing
j. doubtful; uncertain; questionable
k. that which deals with food and nourishment

Discussion: *Rhetoric*

1. Why does the author begin his essay with a discussion of the background of food faddism? Is this beginning an effective one?
2. What is the basic organizational pattern of the entire essay? In your answer note how the author uses the idea of "myths of nutrition."
3. In your own words describe the *evidence* which the author uses to answer the myths mentioned in paragraphs 6, 8, 11, and 16. Does the author's use of the word *truth* in paragraphs 7, 9, 13, and 17 influence your thinking? Or is the answer itself persuasive?
4. Is the essay convincing in its attack on food faddists? Consider the author's use of quotations, statistics, and examples, and explain your opinion.
5. How does the author bring doubt to our minds concerning Lelord Kordel, Gaylord Hauser, and Bob Cummings? Note paragraphs 40 through 50.
6. What is the effect of paragraphs 37, 38, and 39? That is, are they more than merely interesting? Do they contribute to the overall emphasis of doubt about food faddism?
7. Describe the effectiveness of the paragraphs in this essay. Are they too long or too short?
8. Is the ending of the essay more, or less, effective than the beginning? Explain.

1. _____

_____

2. _____

_____

3. _____

_____

4. _____

_____

5. _____

_____

Apparatus for: The Bunk About Health Foods

6. _____

_____

7. _____

_____

8. _____

_____

Discussion: *Theme*

1. Do you think there is a great deal of bunk about health foods? Explain.
2. If you believe differently from the author, how would you answer his assertions?
3. What foods do you consider to be especially healthful?
4. Why do you (or do you *not*) take vitamins?
5. Has the author been convincing (enough so that you will change your habits), or has he given you his own brand of "bunk"?
6. This is a subject about which honest men have differed, and it might not be a bad choice for a research paper. Where would you go for specific information, other than the library?
7. Is our nation as healthy as the author of this essay suggests?
8. Which contribute more to illnesses: poor eating habits or poor food? Explain.

1. _____

_____

2. _____

_____

3. _____

_____

4. _____

_____

5. _____

_____

6. _____

_____

7. _____

_____

8. _____

_____

Writing Suggestions

1. The Bunk About White Flour
2. Write a paper in which you further substantiate the author's position.
3. Write a paper supporting the health foods.
4. Trace some of the ideas concerning the power of "miraculous" foods back to the Egyptians or some other ancient civilization.
5. Choose a specific food, such as the tomato, and show how the American view has changed toward it.
6. Write a paper on the history of aphrodisiacs.
7. Use the following statement as the basis of a theme: "Most, if not all, diseases are caused by faulty diet."
8. Food Faddism

IX. BEGINNING AND ENDING A THEME

Beginning a theme is like meeting a girl or boy for the first time. If the date is to be worthwhile, then you must get his or her interest in an absorbing way—one that is not offensive or insincere. Clearly you would want the person to be interested in you not for phony reasons, but because you are yourself. So it is with theme openings—they must signal sincerity and depth.

Too many students labor over an opening sentence, finally get one written, and then sigh and hope for a second thought to appear magically—and so on, until about two inches of the top of the paper is covered with words; then the student rests from his task and calls *that* his beginning.

This may or may not be an exact picture of you and your methods, but it describes the problem of using a beginning paragraph merely to get started with, rather than using it to lead the reader into the subject. This is your task: Use the beginning of your writing to get the reader's attention and to introduce him to the subject matter of the paper.

Two brief warnings are in order: 1) don't refer to the title in your opening—let the title stand alone; and 2) don't try to mystify your reader—try to help him understand clearly your idea, your attitude, your belief, your feeling.

Just as there is no one best way for boy to meet girl, there is no one best way to begin a theme. But we can make specific suggestions:

1. *Provoke the reader.* Provoking a reader to question his own views is almost a guarantee to securing his interest. Perhaps the most often-used provocation is the formulation of a viewpoint opposite to the one held: "Cats are really man's best friend," or "Dating should not be allowed until the age of 25." Consider the following introductory paragraph, from Tom Mayer's "So You Want to be a Dropout":

You are in the middle of a pre-exam-period dead week frantically studying rocks for the imminent five-hour identification final in elementary geology, when suddenly you decide you don't give a damn anymore. It simply isn't worth the effort; you're going to fail no matter what you do. You haven't studied all term because the course was dull and the professor a fraud, and now it's too late.

2. *Relate an anecdote.* The technique of opening with an interesting little story serves to interest the reader in what he might otherwise think is a dull subject. The anecdote can be real or contrived, about someone else or about yourself. Consider the following example of an opening paragraph that uses an anecdote:

Although we had seen men walking barefoot on burning embers twice before, we were not prepared for the mass fire walk at Kataragama. The first time, on a pleasant summer afternoon, surrounded by playing children and laughing family groups, we watched four men walk quickly through a twelve-foot fire pit. The occasion was a Hindu festival, and the atmosphere was similar to that of a state fair in the United States. The second time, we had been among the guests of a Ceylonese planter who included in the evening's entertainment a fire-walking exhibition by six men. (From "Fire Walking in Ceylon" by Leonard Feinberg.)

Another effective opening, also employing a personal story, is utilized by E. B. White in his essay, "Once More to the Lake":

One summer, along about 1904, my father rented a camp on a lake in Maine and took us all there for the month of August. We all got ringworm from some kittens and had to rub Pond's Extract on our arms and legs night and morning, and my father rolled over in a canoe with all his clothes on; but outside of that the vacation was a success and from then on none of us ever thought there was any place in the world like that lake in Maine. We returned summer after summer—always on August 1st for one month. . . .

3. *Dramatize a problem or situation.* Problems of race relations, unfair advertising, student unrest or apathy are already interesting to the typical reader; but perhaps he needs information that differs from what he already knows, or he may feel he has no reason to continue reading. One of the best ways to involve the reader in a new way in an old subject is to play it up, or dramatize it. One does not have to be phony, however, to be startling. Consider the following opening paragraph from "We're Drowning in Phony Statistics," by Daniel Seligman:

In an otherwise admirable speech in Athens, Georgia, last spring, Attorney General Robert F. Kennedy declared at one point: "Ninety per cent of the major racketeers would be out of business by the end of the year if the ordinary citizen, the businessman, the union official, and the public authority stood up to be counted and refused to be corrupted." The underlying thought here was plausible enough, and certainly praiseworthy, but the statistic used to dress it up—the "90 per cent"—was, to put it bluntly, phony. There is no general agreement on what a "major racketeer" is or agreement on what constitutes standing up to be counted; and since these matters are necessarily ambiguous, it is phony to cast out a precise figure in discussing them.

Now, what do these openings have in common? First, they are *direct*. They get to the point, and they tell or show the reader something specific. Second, they evoke interest right away—no rambling here. Third, they are challenging in some way; either they ask us to re-think our convictions, or they contribute to our knowledge. Fourth, they try to bring the thoughts of the reader and writer together in an interesting, provocative, and informative manner. And finally, they state or imply an idea that serves as the main idea for the *entire* essay—thus giving direction to everything that follows. Make an effort, then, to provoke, to relate, or to dramatize in your opening paragraph.

ENDING PARAGRAPHS

A very real difference exists between abruptly leaving a blind date and parting gracefully in a friendly manner which leaves neither of you irritated. Similarly, the ending of your essay must be sensible, purposeful, and yet not abrupt or antagonistic. Three reminders:

1. *Be direct.* The ending of a paper should, like the beginning, be to the point. Don't drift off on new ideas or irrelevant details. Notice how the following example directly restates the main idea:

> If intercollegiate athletics are to be saved from extinction, it is high time that college and university presidents, deans, and faculties exert strong and courageous leadership, assert greater control over athletic coaches, eliminate practices not in accord with sound educational principles, and restore intercollegiate athletics to an amateur basis.[1]

2. *Be conclusive.* In many of your writing assignments, including the answers to essay questions, you will need to show that you have mastered the evidence, and that your conclusion is accurate and based on adequate information. Notice this concluding paragraph:

> Food faddism can cause harm in two ways. It can substantially increase the family food bill for costly "nature foods," "organic foods," and misleadingly-named "health foods," vitamin-mineral preparations, and dietary supplements for which there is absolutely no need in the American diet. Worse still, it can cause a person to attempt do-it-yourself dietary treatment for diseases and abnormal conditions that, contrary to the food faddists, have nothing whatever to do with dietary deficiency. Needless to say, persons with some abnormality should not resort to self-medication; bad guessing can even cost one's life.[2]

3. *Be emphatic.* You don't need a bizarre ending in order to state clearly

[1] From "The Scramble for College Athletes," by Paul Giddens, *Atlantic Monthly,* December 1965, p. 51.

[2] From "The Bunk About Health Foods," by Ralph Smith.

and forcefully that your conclusion is reasonable. In a paper in which you are trying to persuade the reader to accept a certain viewpoint, emphasize the course you want him to follow. Here is a good example:

> Dr. West's conclusion: Hypnosis is a valid tool but there are dangers in its misuse to the patient, to medicine, and to hypnosis itself.[3]

A good ending gives a piece of writing a feeling of completeness. The beginning tells us where we are going, and why we are taking a certain route; the middle of the paper is, of course, the trip itself; and the ending points out where we have been and shows us how our horizons should have been widened as a result of the journey.

[3] From "Hypnosis: What It Can and Can't Do," by Arthur J. Snider.

25. FIRE WALKING IN CEYLON*

LEONARD FEINBERG

1   Although we had seen men walking barefoot on burning embers twice before, we were not prepared for the mass fire walk at Kataragama. The first time, on a pleasant summer afternoon, surrounded by playing children and laughing family groups, we watched four men walk quickly through a twelve-foot fire pit. The occasion was a Hindu festival, and the atmosphere was similar to that of a state fair in the United States. The second time we had been among the guests of a Ceylonese planter who included in the evening's entertainment a fire-walking exhibition by six men.

2   But at the temple of Kataragama everything was different. There, on the night of the full moon in August, fire walking climaxes a week's ceremonies in honor of the Hindu god Kataragama. From all over the island, worshipers and spectators (Buddhist as well as Hindu, although theoretically Buddhists do not believe in gods) had been converging on the little settlement in the jungle of southeastern Ceylon. During the early part of the week, devotees had paid tribute to Kataragama by hanging colored papers on trees near the temple or by breaking sacrificial coconuts on a rock provided for that purpose. Toward the week's end, the nature of the sacrifices was intensified, and zealous worshipers perforated their cheeks with pins, or walked on nails, or imbedded into their naked shoulders meathooks with which they pulled heavy carts along a pitted dirt road.

3   By midnight the crowd was feverishly tense. Since the logs in the twenty-by-six-foot pit had been burning for four hours, the fire walking would presumably

take place about 4 A.M. But the tradition against making any sort of prediction about the immediate future is so strong at Kataragama that the local priest, asked by an American tourist when the fire walking would begin, replied that there probably would not be any walking at all. The crowd surged away from the pit slowly and steadily—slowly because every inch of the temple grounds had been packed for hours, and steadily because the heat from the pit was becoming unbearable. The men and women nearest the pit had held their places for days, eating and sleeping in one spot. The Ceylonese are ordinarily very clean, but the activity at Kataragama is more important than sanitation, and as the hours passed everything intensified: the heat, the tension, the odors of sweat and urine and incense. A wave of malevolent expectation permeated the air, a powerful undercurrent of suppressed sadism that made intruders like ourselves feel dilettantish, uncomfortable, and slightly ashamed. Fire walking is far more than just a spectacle to most of these people; it is a concrete symbol of intimate identification with a supernatural power. From time to time men would shout "Hora Hora," an Oriental form of "Amen" in honor of the god whose power transcends the science of the West.

4 About 2 A.M. people near us suddenly scurried to make room for a young woman carrying in her bare hands a clay pot full of burning coconut husks. She did not seem to be feeling any pain, but she was abnormally excited as she staggered to the outer sanctum of the temple. There she threw the pot down, exultantly showed the crowd her hands—they were gray, but not burned—and began knocking on the temple door. She apparently wanted to demonstrate to the priest, or the god, what she had accomplished, but no one was being admitted that night, and she was still pounding frantically at the massive door when the attention of the crowd shifted to another woman. This one too had a red-hot pot full of burning husks, but she carried it in the conventional Ceylonese fashion—on top of her head. And when she removed the pot, neither her hair nor her hands showed any sign of scorching.

5 Shortly before four o'clock an ominous grumbling swept through the crowd. Then angry shouts, threatening arms, protests. By climbing a stone wall I was able to see what the trouble was. A row of chairs had been reserved for several wealthy Ceylonese from Colombo and their European guests. But when they arrived they found that a group of Buddhist monks had occupied the seats and refused to move. (For more than a year, as a calculated technique of growing nationalism, monks had been usurping reserved seats at public gatherings.) The police officer tried to persuade the monks to give up the seats, but the yellow-robed figures leaned placidly on their umbrellas and pretended that he did not exist. There was no question where the sympathy of the mob lay, and when their protests became loud the police officer shrugged his shoulders and motioned to the legal holders of the seats. They dispersed to the edges of the standing mob, far away from the pit.

6 At four in the morning wailing flutes and pounding drums announced the

arrival of the walkers. The long procession was led by whiterobed priests, their faces streaked with red and yellow and white ash. By this time the flames had stopped spurting and the pit consisted of a red-hot mass of burning wood, which attendants were leveling with long branches. The heat of the fire was still intense; within ten feet of the pit it was difficult to breathe. Then the priests muttered incantations, the drums built up to a crescendo, and the fire walking began.

7   Among the eighty persons who walked the fire that night there were ten women. But in the mad excitement of the crowd's cheers, the drumbeats, the odors, the tension, it was difficult to identify individuals. Some men skipped lightly through the fire, as if doing a restrained version of the hop, skip, and jump in three or four steps. Some raced through, determined, somber. Some ran through exultantly, waving spears. One man danced gaily into the center of the pit, turned, did a kind of wild jig for a few moments, then turned again and danced on through. Another man stumbled suddenly and the crowd gasped; he fell forward, hung for a ghastly moment on the coals, then straightened and stumbled on. The crowd sighed. Two women ran through, close together, holding hands, taking five or six steps. In the phantasmagoric blur of roars, screams, and incantations, the fire walkers looked less like human beings than grotesque puppets in a macabre shadow play. For a long moment one person stood out in the hectic cavalcade of charging, gyrating figures: a short, siim man in a white sarong strolled slowly and serenely through the fire, stepping on the solid earth at the end of the pit as gently as he had stepped on the embers.

8   After going through the fire, the walkers, some shuffling, some running, a few helped or led by attendants, proceeded to a spot beside the temple where the head priest placed a smear of saffron ash on the forehead of each participant. The ash had been taken from the pit and blessed, and the fire walkers strode off proudly.

9   There are two types of fire walking, on stones (usually of volcanic origin) in Polynesia, and on embers in Asia and Africa. Theories which try to explain the secret of fire walking fall into three categories: physical, psychological, and religious. The most publicized attempts of scientists to find the solution took place in 1935 and 1936, when the London Council for Psychical Investigation arranged two series of fire walks at Surrey, England. The council took charge of building the pit and burning the logs, it provided a number of physicians, chemists, physicists, and Oxford professors to examine every stage of the proceedings, and it published an official report of its conclusions. Some of the scientists published individual reports, in general agreeing that fire walking can be explained in terms of certain physical facts, but they did not agree on precisely what those physical facts were.

10   At the first series of Surrey tests, an Indian named Kuda Bux walked uninjured through a fire pit the surface temperature of which was 430° C., the interior temperature 1400° C. In the 1936 test, for Ahmed Hussain, the surface

temperature was over 500° C. Both Bux and Hussain insisted that the secret was "faith," and Hussain claimed that he could convey immunity to anyone who would walk the fire with him. A half-dozen English amateurs, who had answered the council's advertisement for volunteers, did walk the fire behind Hussain and were "slightly burned." One of these amateurs managed, a few days later, to walk through the fire pit alone, in three steps, without suffering the slightest injury.

11   In brief, the official report of the council stated that fire walking is a gymnastic feat operating on this principle: a limited number of quick and even steps on a poor conductor of heat does not result in burning of the flesh. "The secret of fire-walking," the report said, "lies in the low thermal conductivity of the burning wood. . . . The quantity of heat transferred may remain small if . . . the time of contact is very short. . . . The time of contact is not above half a second in normal quick walking." To put it another way, it is safe to take three even steps, limiting each contact to half a second, on wood embers ("The thermal conductivity of copper . . . is about 1,000 times greater than that of wood"). The report conceded that "successive contacts . . . cause an accumulation of heat sufficient to cause injury, and . . . with fires whose temperature is 500° Centigrade or more, only two contacts can be made with each foot without erythema or blistering."

12   The weight of the walker makes a difference, the report suggested, each of the Indians weighing less than 126 pounds and sinking into the embers to a lesser degree, and for a shorter time, than the heavier English amateurs. An expert also has the advantage of walking steadily and distributing his weight evenly, whereas the inexperience and undue haste of the beginner make it difficult for him to avoid resting a part of his foot more heavily than he should. When the amateur walker took an uneven number of steps, the foot which had taken more steps suffered more burns.

13   Other observers of fire walking have offered various explanations, the most popular being that Orientals have very tough soles. They walk barefoot all their lives, often on hot surfaces. Sometimes they put out cigarette butts with their toes and, when marching in parades, step on burning husks which have fallen out of torchbearers' fires. This is true. But the English physicians who examined Bux and Hussain described their feet as very soft, not at all callused.

14   Another familiar conjecture is that fire walkers use chemical preparations to protect their feet. An American magician believes that a paste of alum and salt is applied, and other experts have speculated that soda, or soap, or juice of mysterious plants, or an anesthetic of some sort is used. But the physician and the chemist who examined Bux and Hussain at Surrey were positive that nothing had been applied to the feet; for control purposes, they washed one of Bux's feet and dried it carefully before he walked.

15   The "water-vapor protection" theory has a number of supporters. An

American chemist recently wrote, in a popular magazine, that he could walk comfortably on burning coals and apply his tongue painlessly to a red-hot iron bar by utilizing this principle: at a certain range of high temperature, a thin film of water acts as absolute protection against heat. The trouble with this theory, as the Surrey tests showed, is 1) the fire walkers' feet were dry, 2) it would be difficult, under any conditions, to supply a uniform amount of water to the soles during a fire walk, and 3) moisture is not advisable, because embers are likely to stick to wet soles and cause blisters.

16 Still another explanation was offered by Joseph Dunninger. He asserts that the trick used by fire-walking Shinto priests in Japan consisted of making the fuel in the trench shallow in the center and deep on the sides, and starting the fire in the center. By the time the walking begins, the fire has burned out in the center, is still blazing at the edges, and the priests step on the cool ashes of the center. That may be the secret of the Shinto priests, but the pit at Surrey was filled evenly under the supervision of scientists. And an English planter in the Marquesas Islands, who was once teased by a local chief into fire walking, reported that the fire was hottest in the center.

17 These are the physical explanations. The psychological theories are more difficult to test. Having watched fire walking in Japan some years ago, Percival Lowell of Harvard concluded that the feat was made possible by the less sensitive nervous organism of the Oriental and the ecstasy of the walker (as well as the extremely tough calluses on his soles). A variation on the "ecstasy" theory is the suggestion of one psychologist that hypnosis is the secret. The fire walker, he says, has been hypnotized and provided with the same immunity to pain that can be observed even in a classroom demonstration of hypnosis. The fire walker may not know that he is hypnotized, but hypnosis is what the priest is actually practicing when he gives the walker his last-minute instructions. After the performance, while ostensibly putting a mark of holy ash on the fire walker's forehead, the priest breaks the hypnosis. Most psychologists, however, reject this explanation on the grounds that hypnosis may lessen the subjective feeling of pain but cannot prevent skin from burning.

18 It is well known in the East that yogi and fakirs can attain so profound a state of concentration on a single object that nothing else distracts them. In this state, the practitioner may lie on a bed of nails, keep a hand outstretched for days, remain motionless for a week, or perform other feats whose practical value is limited but which do demonstrate a control over the body that most human beings are unable to achieve. According to some yogi, he who masters concentration can separate the soul from the body, so that the vacant shell does not feel pain. But since even a dead body will burn, this explanation is not satisfactory.

19 As far as the devout Ceylonese believer is concerned, the secret is simple: complete faith in Kataragama. Kataragama is a very powerful god. If, in desperation—at a time of serious illness, near-bankruptcy, dangerous competition

from a hated rival—a man or woman vows to walk the fire in exchange for Kataragama's help, Kataragama may give that help. The amateur walker, then, is either a petitioner for supernatural assistance or a grateful recipient of it. His preparation may begin as early as May, when he arrives at Kataragama and puts himself under the direction of the chief priest. For three months he lives ascetically, abstaining from all sensual pleasures, eating only vegetables, drinking only water, bathing in the holy river near the temple, and going through religious rituals conducted by the priest. If he does all this, and if he has *absolute, unquestioning, complete* faith in Kataragama's power, he walks the fire unafraid and unharmed.

20 On the night we watched the fire walking at Kataragama, twelve people were burned badly enough to go to the hospital, and one of them died. These people, the devout believer will tell you, lacked either faith or preparation. Another man who lacked at least one of these ingredients was a young English clergyman who visited Ceylon a few years ago. This Protestant minister reasoned that the faith of a Christian was at least as strong as that of a Hindu, and he volunteered to walk the fire with the others. He did, and spent the next six months in a hospital, where doctors barely managed to save his life.

21 It is believed by the Ceylonese that Kataragama exercises absolute and somewhat whimsical control of the area within a fourteen-mile radius of his temple. His portrait, presumably life-size, shows a handsome, seven-foot-tall, six-headed and twelve-armed god, with two women and a blue peacock for companionship and transportation. Although he is technically a Hindu god, many Buddhists also worship him, or at least ask for his help when they are in trouble. Officially the god of war and revenge, he is probably more fervently worshiped and more genuinely feared than any other god in Ceylon. He has an A-1 reputation for protecting his congregation and, according to numerous legends, exhibits a genial playfulness in devising disconcerting mishaps for those who violate his minor taboos.

22 Most Ceylonese try to make at least one visit a year to his temple, not necessarily during the August ceremonies, but at some other time of the year when the settlement in the jungle is sparse, quiet, and suitable for meditation. Everyone manages to get to Kataragama sooner or later, it seems. My Hindu friend in the police department went one week, my wife's Muslim jeweler another, my Buddhist tailor a third. It is considered especially commendable to walk all the way to Kataragama, and many Ceylonese do walk there, sometimes carrying a large, colorful, paper-and-wood contraption in the form of an arch, which indicates that they are fulfilling a vow.

23 Our driver on the trip to Kataragama was a young Singhalese who told us that his name was Elvis. (He told Englishmen that his name was Winston.) His driving got a little erratic as the day wore on, and he finally admitted that, though a Buddhist, he was taking no chances with Kataragama and had been fasting all day. While we were eating, he warned our friends and us about

certain taboos that visitors to the Kataragama territory were supposed to observe. One local rule forbade announcing an expected arrival time; that, said Elvis, was an infallible way of being delayed. Another dangerous thing to do was to speak disrespectfully of Kataragama. A Buddhist in a Renault immediately remarked that, the weather being ideal, we ought to arrive at Kataragama by six o'clock. And a Christian woman in a Vauxhall said that all this fear of Kataragama was nonsense; she had been there the previous year and had ridiculed the entire procedure, but nothing had happened.

24   When we finished eating we got into our Volkswagen and followed the other two cars. Suddenly it began to rain. It rained only for five minutes and, we learned later, only within a few hundred yards. As we carefully rounded a curve on the slick road we saw that the two other cars were now facing us. The Renault's hood was stuck halfway into a rock fence, and the Vauxhall was resting its side on the same fence. It turned out that the Renault had skidded and started turning in the road, and to avoid hitting it the driver of the Vauxhall put on her brakes. By the time the cars stopped skidding they had smashed into the fence. No one was injured except the scoffing woman, who had a painful but not serious bruise on the spot where an irritated parent might have been expected to spank his child. It took a long time to improvise pulling cables, disengage the cars, and tow them to a garage. We eventually reached the temple, just before midnight, and although all of these coincidences and superstitions can be logically accounted for, no one in our party made any more jeering remarks about Kataragama.

Apparatus for: Fire Walking in Ceylon

Vocabulary: *Using your dictionary, define each of the following words as it appears in context.*

1. devotees (¶ 2)

2. perforated (¶ 2)

3. malevolent (¶ 3)

4. permeated (¶ 3)

5. dilettantish (¶ 3)

6. ominous (¶ 5)

7. placidly (¶ 5)

8. phantasmagoric (¶ 7)

9. macabre (¶ 7)

10. conjecture (¶ 14)

11. ostensibly (¶ 17)

12. ascetically (¶ 19)

Discussion: *Rhetoric*

1. This selection is more than the mere personal account of a tourist; it analyzes the various reasons that have been advanced to explain fire-walking. What is the central organizational pattern of the essay?
2. Note the internal organization beginning with paragraph 9. What are the aids the author offers?
3. What is the attitude of the author toward fire-walking? Cite evidence from the essay.
4. At the end of the essay, why does the author tell us about the wreck?

1. _____

    _____

2. _____

    _____

3. _____

    _____

4. _____

    _____

Apparatus for: Fire Walking in Ceylon

Discussion: *Theme*

1. Do you think people can walk on fire without being burned? What kind of evidence would persuade you otherwise?
2. Was the incident mentioned at the end of the essay merely a coincidence, or was it a fulfillment of the prediction? Explain.
3. How much control does the mind have over matter?
4. Have you ever witnessed any feats that you thought were beyond your understanding or beyond reason and evidence? Explain.

1. _____

_____

2. _____

_____

3. _____

_____

4. _____

_____

Writing Suggestions

1. Write a theme in which you examine the evidence offered for (or against) an unusual happening, such as rain-making, ESP, or fire-walking.
2. Why I Am (or Am Not) a Believer in Miracles.
3. Write a theme in which you describe a séance or a levitation.
4. Review an article from a quality magazine, like *Scientific American,* dealing with a superstition or unexplainable phenomenon.

26. ONCE MORE TO THE LAKE *

E. B. WHITE

1 One summer, along about 1904, my father rented a camp on a lake in Maine and took us all there for the month of August. We all got ringworm from some kittens and had to rub Pond's Extract on our arms and legs night and morning, and my father rolled over in a canoe with all his clothes on; but outside of that the vacation was a success and from then on none of us ever thought there was any place in the world like that lake in Maine. We returned summer after summer—always on August 1st for one month. I have since become a salt-water man, but sometimes in summer there are days when the restlessness of the tides and the fearful cold of the sea water and the incessant wind which blows across the afternoon and into the evening make me wish for the placidity of a lake in the woods. A few weeks ago this feeling got so strong I bought myself a couple of bass hooks and a spinner and returned to the lake where we used to go, for a week's fishing and to revisit old haunts.

2 I took along my son, who had never had any fresh water up his nose and who had seen lily pads only from train windows. On the journey over to the lake I began to wonder what it would be like. I wondered how time would have marred this unique, this holy spot—the coves and streams, the hills that the sun set behind, the camps and the paths behind the camps. I was sure that the tarred road would have found it out and I wondered in what other ways it would be desolated. It is strange how much you can remember about places like that once you allow your mind to return into the grooves which lead back. You remember one thing, and that suddenly reminds you of another thing. I guess I remembered clearest of all the early mornings, when the lake was cool

and motionless, remembered how the bedroom smelled of the lumber it was made of and of the wet woods whose scent entered through the screen. The partitions in the camp were thin and did not extend clear to the top of the rooms, and as I was always the first up I would dress softly so as not to wake the others, and sneak out into the sweet outdoors and start out in the canoe, keeping close along the shore in the long shadows of the pines. I remembered being very careful never to rub my paddle against the gunwale for fear of disturbing the stillness of the cathedral.

3 The lake had never been what you would call a wild lake. There were cottages sprinkled around the shores, and it was in farming country although the shores of the lake were quite heavily wooded. Some of the cottages were owned by nearby farmers, and you would live at the shore and eat your meals at the farmhouse. That's what our family did. But although it wasn't wild, it was a fairly large and undisturbed lake and there were places in it which, to a child at least, seemed infinitely remote and primeval.

4 I was right about the tar: it led to within half a mile of the shore. But when I got back there, with my boy, and we settled into a camp near a farmhouse and into the kind of summertime I had known, I could tell that it was going to be pretty much the same as it had been before—I knew it, lying in bed the first morning, smelling the bedroom, and hearing the boy sneak quietly out and go off along the shore in a boat. I began to sustain the illusion that he was I, and therefore, by simple transposition, that I was my father. This sensation persisted, kept cropping up all the time we were there. It was not an entirely new feeling, but in this setting it grew much stronger. I seemed to be living a dual existence. I would be in the middle of some simple act, I would be picking up a bait box or laying down a table fork, or I would be saying something, and suddenly it would be not I but my father who was saying the words or making the gesture. It gave me a creepy sensation.

5 We went fishing the first morning. I felt the same damp moss covering the worms in the bait can, and saw the dragonfly alight on the tip of my rod as it hovered a few inches from the surface of the water. It was the arrival of this fly that convinced me beyond any doubt that everything was as it always had been, that the years were a mirage and there had been no years. The small waves were the same, chucking the rowboat under the chin as we fished at anchor, and the boat was the same boat, the same color green and the ribs broken in the same places, and under the floor-boards the same fresh-water leavings and débris—the dead helgramite, the wisps of moss, the rusty discarded fishhook, the dried blood from yesterday's catch. We stared silently at the tips of our rods, at the dragonflies that came and went. I lowered the tip of mine into the water, tentatively, pensively dislodging the fly, which darted two feet away, poised, darted two feet back, and came to rest again a little farther up the rod. There had been no years between the ducking of this dragonfly and the other one—the one that was part of memory. I looked at the boy, who was silently

watching his fly, and it was my hands that held his rod, my eyes watching. I felt dizzy and didn't know which rod I was at the end of.

6　We caught two bass, hauling them in briskly as though they were mackerel, pulling them over the side of the boat in a businesslike manner without any landing net, and stunning them with a blow on the back of the head. When we got back for a swim before lunch, the lake was exactly where we had left it, the same number of inches from the dock, and there was only the merest suggestion of a breeze. This seemed an utterly enchanted sea, this lake you could leave to its own devices for a few hours and come back to, and find that it had not stirred, this constant and trustworthy body of water. In the shallows, the dark, water-soaked sticks and twigs, smooth and old, were undulating in clusters on the bottom against the clean ribbed sand, and the track of the mussel was plain. A school of minnows swam by, each minnow with its small individual shadow, doubling the attendance, so clear and sharp in the sunlight. Some of the other campers were in swimming, along the shore, one of them with a cake of soap, and the water felt thin and clear and unsubstantial. Over the years there had been this person with the cake of soap, this cultist, and here he was. There had been no years.

7　Up to the farmhouse to dinner through the teeming, dusty field, the road under our sneakers was only a two-track road. The middle track was missing, the one with the marks of the hooves and the splotches of dried, flaky manure. There had always been three tracks to choose from in choosing which track to walk in; now the choice was narrowed down to two. For a moment I missed terribly the middle alternative. But the way led past the tennis court, and something about the way it lay there in the sun reassured me; the tape had loosened along the backline, the alleys were green with plantains and other weeds, and the net (installed in June and removed in September) sagged in the dry noon, and the whole place steamed with midday heat and hunger and emptiness. There was a choice of pie for dessert, and one was blueberry and one was apple, and the waitresses were the same country girls, there having been no passage of time, only the illusion of it as in a dropped curtain—the waitresses were still fifteen; their hair had been washed, that was the only difference— they had been to the movies and seen the pretty girls with the clean hair.

8　Summertime, oh summertime, pattern of life indelible, the fade-proof lake, the woods unshatterable, the pasture with the sweetfern and the juniper forever and ever, summer without end; this was the background, and the life along the shore was the design, the cottages with their innocent and tranquil design, their tiny docks with the flagpole and the American flag floating against the white clouds in the blue sky, the little paths over the roots of the trees leading from camp to camp and the paths leading back to the outhouses and the can of lime for sprinkling, and at the souvenir counters at the store the miniature birch-bark canoes and the post cards that showed things looking a little better than they looked. This was the American family at play, escaping the city heat, wondering whether the newcomers in the camp at the head of the cove were "common," or "nice," wondering whether it was true that the people who drove up for Sunday dinner at the farmhouse were turned away because there wasn't enough chicken.

9 It seemed to me, as I kept remembering all this, that those times and those summers had been infinitely precious and worth saving. There had been jollity and peace and goodness. The arriving (at the beginning of August) had been so big a business in itself, at the railway station the farm wagon drawn up, the first smell of the pine-laden air, the first glimpse of the smiling farmer, and the great importance of the trunks and your father's enormous authority in such matters, and the feel of the wagon under you for the long ten-mile haul, and at the top of the last long hill catching the first view of the lake after eleven months of not seeing this cherished body of water. The shouts and cries of the other campers when they saw you, and the trunks to be unpacked, to give up their rich burden. (Arriving was less exciting nowadays, when you sneaked up in your car and parked it under a tree near the camp and took out the bags and in five minutes it was all over, no fuss, no loud wonderful fuss about trunks.)

10 Peace and goodness and jollity. The only thing that was wrong now, really, was the sound of the place, an unfamiliar nervous sound of the outboard motors. This was the note that jarred, the one thing that would sometimes break the illusion and set the years moving. In those other summertimes all motors were inboard; and when they were at a little distance, the noise they made was a sedative, an ingredient of summer sleep. They were one-cylinder and two-cylinder engines, and some were make-and-break and some were jump-spark, but they all made a sleepy sound across the lake. The one-lungers throbbed and fluttered, and the twin-cylinder ones purred and purred, and that was a quiet sound too. But now the campers all had outboards. In the daytime, in the hot mornings, these motors made a petulant, irritable sound; at night, in the still evening when the afterglow lit the water, they whined about one's ears like mosquitoes. My boy loved our rented outboard, and his great desire was to achieve singlehanded mastery over it, and authority, and he soon learned the trick of choking it a little (but not too much), and the adjustment of the needle valve. Watching him I would remember the things you could do with the old one-cylinder engine with the heavy flywheel, how you could have it eating out of your hand if you got really close to it spiritually. Motor boats in those days didn't have clutches, and you would make a landing by shutting off the motor at the proper time and coasting in with a dead rudder. But there was a way of reversing them, if you learned the trick, by cutting the switch and putting it on again exactly on the final dying revolution of the flywheel, so that it would kick back against compression and begin reversing. Approaching a dock in a strong following breeze, it was difficult to slow up sufficiently by the ordinary coasting method, and if a boy felt he had complete mastery over his motor, he was tempted to keep it running beyond its time and then reverse it a few feet from the dock. It took a cool nerve, because if you threw the switch a twentieth of

a second too soon you would catch the flywheel when it still had speed enough to go up past center, and the boat would leap ahead, charging bull-fashion at the dock.

11   We had a good week at the camp. The bass were biting well and the sun shone endlessly, day after day. We would be tired at night and lie down in the accumulated heat of the little bedrooms after the long hot day and the breeze would stir almost imperceptibly outside and the smell of the swamp drift in through the rusty screens. Sleep would come easily and in the morning the red squirrel would be on the roof, tapping out his gay routine. I kept remembering everything, lying in bed in the mornings—the small steamboat that had a long rounded stern like the lip of a Ubangi, and how quietly she ran on the moon-light sails, when the older boys played their mandolins and the girls sang and we ate doughnuts dipped in sugar, and how sweet the music was on the water in the shining night, and what it had felt like to think about girls then. After breakfast we would go up to the store and the things were in the same place— the minnows in a bottle, the plugs and spinners disarranged and pawed over by the youngsters from the boys' camp, the fig newtons and the Beeman's gum. Outside, the road was tarred and cars stood in front of the store. Inside, all was just as it had always been, except there was more Coca-Cola and not so much Moxie and root beer and birch beer and sarsaparilla. We would walk out with a bottle of pop apiece and sometimes the pop would backfire up our noses and hurt. We explored the streams, quietly, where the turtles slid off the sunny logs and dug their way into the soft bottom; and we lay on the town wharf and fed worms to the tame bass. Everywhere we went I had trouble making out which was I, the one walking at my side, the one walking in my pants.

12   One afternoon while we were there at that lake a thunderstorm came up. It was like the revival of an old melodrama that I had seen long ago with child-ish awe. The second-act climax of the drama of the electrical disturbance over a lake in America had not changed in any important respect. This was the big scene, still the big scene. The whole thing was so familiar, the first feeling of oppression and heat and a general air around camp of not wanting to go very far away. In midafternoon (it was all the same) a curious darkening of the sky, and a lull in everything that had made life tick; and then the way the boats suddenly swung the other way at their moorings with the coming of a breeze out of the new quarter, and the premonitory rumble. Then the kettledrum, then the snare, then the bass drum and cymbals, then crackling light against the dark, and the gods grinning and licking their chops in the hills. Afterward the calm, the rain steadily rustling in the calm lake, the return of light and hope and spirits, and the campers running out in joy and relief to go swimming in the rain, their bright cries perpetuating the deathless joke about how they were getting simply drenched, and the children screaming with delight at the new sensation of bathing in the rain, and the joke about getting drenched link-ing the generations in a strong indestructible chain. And the comedian who waded in carrying an umbrella.

13 When the others went swimming my son said he was going in too. He pulled his dripping trunks from the line where they had hung all through the shower, and wrung them out. Languidly, and with no thought of going in, I watched him, his hard little body, skinny and bare, saw him wince slightly as he pulled up around his vitals the small, soggy, icy garment. As he buckled the swollen belt, suddenly my groin felt the chill of death.

Apparatus for: Once More to the Lake

Vocabulary: *Using your dictionary, indicate how the following words are pronounced.*

1. placidity (¶ 1)

2. primeval (¶ 3)

3. helgramite (¶ 5)

4. undulating (¶ 6)

5. infinitely (¶ 9)

6. petulant (¶ 10)

7. premonitory (¶ 12)

Discussion: *Rhetoric*

1. This essay revolves about a contrast between two trips to the lake. Who took each trip? When do we learn that it is about more than a fishing trip?
2. Comment on the diction of this essay. For example, is it vivid and appropriate?
3. Cite several descriptive phrases like "bedroom smelled of lumber."
4. There are two levels to the description in this essay: the physical and the psychological. Show where the evidence for these levels is apparent. Consider the last sentence of paragraph 4.
5. What is the attitude of the author toward his son?
6. How effective is the comparison in paragraph 12?
7. From your knowledge about fishing, do you think White knows much about it?
8. The last section of the essay begins with paragraph 11. Is it an effective ending?

1. _Father & Grandfather + Family_
   Son + Father
2. _Yest vivid_

3. _____

4. _____

5. _looked at him as he felt his_
   father looked at him
6. _____

Apparatus for: Once More to the Lake

7. _Yes_ _____

_____

8. _Yes_ _____

_____

Discussion: *Theme*

1. Are the "old days" ever better than the present ones? Explain.
2. What is the meaning of the last sentence in White's essay?
3. Have you ever recalled an experience of reminiscence like the one described by White?
4. What does the lake stand for in this selection?

1. _____

_____

2. _____

_____

3. _____

_____

4. _____

_____

Writing Suggestions

1. In a theme similar in content to "Once More to the Lake," describe a revisit of your own to a childhood scene.
2. "Fathers and Sons"
3. In a theme, analyze the value of reminiscing.
4. "To Revisit Old Haunts"
5. "It was a creepy sensation."

27. THE CASE AGAINST FRATERNITIES *

SLOAN WILSON

1 Not long ago a student at the Massachusetts Institute of Technology was killed while being initiated into a fraternity. He had been left out in the woods alone on a cold night by his "brothers" and was trying to find his way back to his campus. While crossing a frozen pond, which he may have mistaken for a snow-covered meadow in the darkness, he fell through the ice and was drowned.

2 Fraternities are allowed a good deal of latitude in the name of good clean horseplay, but they aren't supposed to kill people. All sorts of reforms were undertaken on the M.I.T. campus, and the paid executive secretaries of fraternities all around the country were kept busy writing statements about the good deeds their members have substituted for old-fashioned hazing.

3 In spite of this, the incident of the boy falling through the ice in the darkness dealt a hard blow to fraternities. A lot of people began to wonder what all these Greek letters really mean and whether fraternities aren't fundamentally vicious. I think this is too bad, because there is nothing vicious about fraternities. They can be called stupid, witless, juvenile and purposeless associations much like the "clubs" small boys organize in back-yard shacks, but they can't be called vicious. Most of them have a kind of Boy Scout code of honor which makes their members burst with pride.

4 It bothers me to see fraternities criticized for the wrong reasons. Fraternities

* Sloan Wilson, "The Case Against Fraternities," *American Weekly,* October 14, 1956. Reprinted by permission of Collins-Knowlton-Wing, Inc. Copyright © 1956 by The Hearst Publishing Co., Inc.

can easily prove they're not vicious, and they can easily change their initiation procedures to avoid unfortunate fatal accidents. In doing this, they may seem to have undertaken important reforms, and to have justified their existence. That, of course, would be nonsense. The existence of fraternities can't be justified any more than can many other manifestations of adolescence.

5   Very few people seem to understand what fraternities (and sororities and other secret clubs) are. They are organizations of students which ask some people to be members and exclude others. The standards of acceptance are vague and are established by the fraternity members themselves.

6   The goal of each fraternity usually is to get as its members the "best" students enrolled in an institution of learning. By "best" I don't mean the most brilliant or the most moral; I mean "best" as construed by the adolescents themselves. To some this means rich, handsome and white Protestants, a definition which in its guileless witlessness almost achieves innocence. To others, "best" means those possessed of the prevailing code of social behavior, or the best available after "better" fraternities have taken their pick.

7   Fraternities like to boast about getting "a good cross-section" of students as members, but on almost any campus an old hand will be able to tell which fraternities specialize in attracting the local version of socialites, which ones pride themselves on varsity athletes, and which ones are havens for the boy intellectuals. There are fraternities especially known for heavy drinking, for wild parties and luxurious living.

8   On almost any campus it is easy to find which fraternities are for white Protestants only, which ones are largely Catholic and which ones are largely Jewish. In the past, many fraternities oafishly placed written articles of racial or religious restriction in their constitutions. Recently there have been many hasty and red-faced attempts to bring the constitutions of fraternities into line with the constitution of the United States, but no one can seriously doubt that intolerance and bigotry is still practiced by many fraternities.

9   From campus to campus and from year to year the chapters of fraternities change, but each tends to seek students of like nature. On each campus there will be the "best" fraternity—the one which has attracted the most prosperous Protestant students of athletic, academic or social distinction.

10   The "best" fraternity sometimes can make the superficially believable claim that it gets a cross-section of the "best" students. But there can be only one "best" fraternity. Many others are established to assuage the feelings of those who fail to get in the "best" fraternity. If the "ins" organize, so do the "outs." If students, for one of many reasons, are excluded from one fraternity, the thin-skinned ones frequently organize a fraternity of their own.

11   Thus every student is neatly compartmented on many an American cam-

pus, and the main purpose of a college education is, in a sense, defeated. That is the irony of fraternities: They do the most harm to their own members.

12   In the past, many tears have been shed over the plight of students who aren't asked to join a fraternity. In my opinion these students are lucky. They may have momentarily hurt feelings, and they may even spend most of their college days feeling themselves to be outcasts, but they do not suffer the invisible injuries inflicted upon those who do become fraternity members. They do not have the stultifying experience of associating only with people of their own kind for their entire college career.

13   They are not blinded by false pride in having "made" an institution which was not worth making in the first place. They can, once their wounded pride is healed, become one with those very best college students of all: those who wouldn't think of joining a fraternity.

14   Today more and more students feel that their intelligence is insulted when they are invited to participate in the trick handclasps, juvenile insignia, the paddling of posteriors, the abandonment of young boys in the woods at night, and all the rest of it. For decades many American college students were notorious for their immaturity, but since the war they have shown signs of growing up.

15   The really brilliant students nowadays are taking a hard look at the "advantages" fraternities pretend to offer and are recognizing them as childish frauds. One of these "advantages" is "brotherhood," which is achieved by denying the fundamental brotherhood of all men, by excluding people of different mien or manner.

16   Mature students are realizing that they do not need Greek letters to have friendship. The veterans of World War II who returned to college found that they could drink beer without being "initiated," and they weren't enthusiastic about being paddled or taken on "scary" expeditions by beardless youths. Most of these ex-servicemen ignored fraternities. They have set a sensible example for their younger brothers and their sons.

17   Another so-called advantage of fraternities is the development of social ease, or "savoir-faire." Apparently a lot of clods who blushed at the thought of asking a woman to dance and who didn't know a salad fork from a pitch fork have, over the years, joined fraternities and found enlightenment in the field of modes and manners. Special classes for such poor souls could be provided—if fraternities should die of their own clownishness.

18   What other advantages do fraternities pretend to offer? A "sense of belonging" is one. Undoubtedly there are a few students on every campus who are afraid to stand up as individuals. For such people it is not enough to be a member of a family, a church, a college, a nation, and the human race. They like to believe they're something special, because they have achieved member-

ship in an organization which keeps others out. Fortunately, most colleges now have psychiatric clinics for such students.

19 There is one other "advantage" which fraternities dangle before the eyes of prospective members, but even the fraternity members themselves are sometimes ashamed to boast of it. That is the "advantage" of "contacts" made at college who will later be useful in helping a fraternity member to get a job. It would seem that many of the "brothers" lack confidence in themselves and are afraid they will be unable to get a job as good as they deserve without outside aid. Whatever the reason, fraternity members often show pathetic hope in, and dependence on, one another for help in earning a living. On what frail straws these poor souls lean!

20 I have been in the hiring business on several occasions, and I have been amazed at the eagerness of many fraternity "brothers" to blackball one another. On many occasions people have said to me something like this: "Jim Jones? He was a member of my fraternity in college, and I knew him real well. He's a bum—a real bum!"

21 In the business world, the accuracy of the recommendations a man gives others greatly affects his own reputation, and no old-school-tie sentiment affects the judgment given by capable and ambitious men. I suppose some jobs are reserved for down-and-outers by their fraternity brothers but, fortunately, government relief programs are relieving fraternities of these responsibilities. In any case, really capable students don't spend their days on the campus worrying about "contacts" for jobs after graduation.

22 No really brilliant student who is mature and psychologically whole could possibly become a member of a fraternity nowadays, any more than he could join the Ku Klux Klan, or one of those clubs whose only requirement for membership is the mailing of a cereal box top. It probably would be wise for teachers and parents to point this out to boys and girls of college age who are not bright enough to perceive it for themselves.

23 But let's not exaggerate the evils of fraternities. There is nothing vicious about the boys and girls who join such organizations. Even those initiation stunts which result in fatal accidents, like the one that happened at M.I.T., are not the product of evil thinking. They are the result of not thinking at all.

Apparatus for: The Case Against Fraternities

Vocabulary: *Using your dictionary, define each of the following words as it appears in context.*

1. latitude (¶ 2)   *liberal*

2. assuage (¶ 10)   *ease or less*

3. stultifying (¶ 12)   *to make one look stupid*

4. mien (¶ 15)   *air*

Discussion: *Rhetoric*

1. Note that the beginning of this essay tells of an incident which is then referred to at the end of the essay. This, of course, makes for a tightly knit piece of writing. What other device is used to give this essay "tightness"?
2. The last sentence of paragraph 4 states the thesis of the essay. Why has the writer waited until the fourth paragraph to state his purpose?
3. Does the title reveal too much? That is, if we knew before we read what the author's position is, how can he build suspense or interest?
4. Where does the author give a definition for fraternities?

1. _____

_____

2. _To get the reader_
   interested first

3. _No what is his stand?_

_____

4. _R 3_

_____

Apparatus for: The Case Against Fraternities

Discussion: *Theme*

1. Can you cite other examples of unfortunate accidents which have occurred at fraternity initiations?
2. Where does the author cite evidence for his accusations?
3. Do you agree that fraternities are juvenile? Should they be changed? Abolished?
4. Do fraternities do more harm than good to their members? Explain.

1. _____

   _____

2. _____

   _____

3. _____

   _____

4. _____

   _____

Writing Suggestions

1. The Case for Fraternities
2. Write a theme on "the irony of fraternities: they do the most harm to their own members."
3. Defend the right of students to regulate their groups—that is, write the rules and discipline their members.
4. Find an essay that defends fraternities and compare the evidence it cites with the attack against fraternities in this essay.
5. Do fraternities have the right to bar from membership people of various racial or religious groups?

X. TRANSITIONS

Driving on the highway, you must have noticed the many signs, signals, and warnings that help the driver. They tell you to slow down, to turn, or even to detour. If such signs and markers were not supplied, you might lose your way on an unfamiliar route. Transitions serve a similar function in your writing. They notify the reader of turns in the thought, of digressions or detours, and of divisions or sections in the development of your theme. Without transitions, the reader would find it more difficult to follow your thoughts from sentence to sentence, and from paragraph to paragraph. By helping the line of thought to move smoothly and clearly from beginning to end, transitions help to provide coherence.

Four techniques of transition make clear the relationships between sentences. 1) The repetition of an important word from a preceding sentence shows the reader that the thought is being extended or continued. 2) Pronouns that refer to an antecedent in a preceding sentence help the reader follow the direction of ideas. 3) Expressing ideas of similar importance or significance in parallel structure also provides continuity. 4) Finally, you can use connectives in one of the following ways: to show a contrast (*yet, but, on the other hand, however, on the contrary*); to designate supplementary or added material (*moreover, and, likewise, in addition, furthermore, next*); or to lead to the conclusion (*therefore, consequently, as a result, in summary, in conclusion, finally*).

An examination of the first paragraph of "Language Is Like a River," by J. N. Hook and E. G. Mathews (page 359) will demonstrate the skillful use of transitions to link sentences. The key words of the paragraph are announced in the first sentence: "language changes." Through repetition they are reinforced in the second sentence ("changes in language"). The third sentence begins with *but,* introducing a contrasting idea. The word *people* in this sentence serves as an antecedent to *they* and *their* in the next sentence. The fifth sentence begins with another contrasting connective (*Although*), followed by a reminder of a key idea: *changes*. This notion of change is again reinforced in the sixth sentence by the phrase, *alter a language*. Finally, the last sentence of the paragraph begins with a qualifying connective, *Even,* followed by a restatement of the key idea: *linguistic change*. By using transitions to show the relationship between sentences, and thus between ideas, the authors have given their paragraph coherence. As a result, the reader follows the thought with no difficulty.

Transitions between paragraphs are even more important than those between sentences. We expect all of the sentences in a paragraph to hang together, to be unified in their subject. Paragraphs, on the other hand, represent divisions of thought, and hence we must make a special effort to clarify their relationship for the reader. Transitional devices linking paragraphs usually appear at either the beginning or the end of the paragraph.

Three transitional devices are commonly used to show the relationship between paragraphs. By placing a transitional word (*also, next, finally, another,* etc.) at the beginning of the second paragraph, you show the direction of your thought. Using a pronoun near the beginning of a paragraph to refer to a noun in the preceding paragraph is another useful linking device. Finally, repeating in the opening sentence of your second paragraph an important word or topic mentioned in the preceding paragraph helps the reader to follow the flow of your ideas. Check Hook and Mathews' essay (page 359) again to see how they have indicated the continuity of ideas from paragraph to paragraph.

The fifth paragraph of "Language Is Like a River" (page 360) concludes with a reference to the Danish occupancy of England. This allusion serves as a bridge to the next paragraph, which contains a discussion of the linguistic contributions of the Danes. The seventh paragraph begins with a signal word ("The *next* big tributary . . .") indicating an extension of the thought. Paragraph 8 begins with a transitional word *now* that shows a time relationship; the next paragraph is also introduced by a signal word (*before*) that indicates a time relationship existing among the events described in the paragraphs. The first sentence of the tenth paragraph begins with a noun ("The two *groups*") that refers to key ideas mentioned in the preceding paragraph ("Normans" and "English"). Thus, by carefully linking the paragraphs of their essay, Hook and Mathews make clear the flow of their ideas, and enable the reader to read the essay without faltering.

As you read the essays in this section, notice each author's skillful use of transitional devices. Remember, also, that your own writing must show a design and sequence of ideas that is clear to your reader. A careful arrangement of your ideas will assist greatly in achieving this clarity; but without transitions that show the turns, curves, and divisions of your thought, your reader will be hopelessly lost.

28. LANGUAGE IS LIKE A RIVER *

J. N. HOOK AND E. G. MATHEWS

1   A language changes because things happen to people. If we could imagine
the impossible—a society in which nothing happened—there would be no
changes in language. But except possibly in a cemetery, things are constantly
happening to people: they eat, drink, sleep, talk, make love, meet strangers,
struggle against natural perils, and fight against one another. They slowly adapt
their language to meet the changing conditions of their lives. Although the
changes made in one generation may be small, those made in a dozen generations may enormously affect the language. The big and little phases of history
—fashions, fads, inventions, the influence of a leader, a war or two, an invasion
or two, travel to a foreign land, the demands of business intercourse—may alter
a language so much that a Rip Van Winkle who slept two or three hundred
years might have trouble in making himself understood when he awoke. Even
in a relatively quiet society, linguistic change proceeds inexorably.

2   Think, if you will, of the English language as a river. Its headwaters are the
closely interrelated Teutonic languages of the Angles, Saxons, and Jutes, who
lived mainly in the northern part of what is now Germany. They provided the
basic grammatical structure of the language that we call English; they provided
most of its linguistic heritage; they provided its basic words, the common
everyday words that still are the most important in our simple communications.
But to the basic elements brought in by these Teutonic peoples many additions
have been made.

3   When the Teutons began invading and settling in the British Isles in 449

* J. N. Hood and E. G. Mathews, "Language Is Like a River" (original title: "Why the
Language Has Changed"), from *Modern American Grammar and Usage*. Copyright ©
1956 The Ronald Press Company, New York. Reprinted with permission.

A.D., they found in possession the Celts, who previously had been pushed about by Roman soldiers for several centuries. The Teutons pushed the Celts about some more, finally tending to localize them in what we now call Ireland, Wales, and parts of Scotland. But the Teutonic language was influenced somewhat by the Celtic and indirectly by the Latin which the Celts had fragmentarily learned. So in English we have words of Celtic ancestry such as *brat, cairn,* and *crag,* and the place names *Aberdeen* (*Aber* = river mouth), *Avon* (river), *Caerleon, Cardiff, Carlyle* (*caer* or *car* = fortress), *Dundee, Dunbarton, Dunbar* (*dun* = hill), *Inchcape* (*inch* = island), *Kildare, Kilpatrick* (*kill* = church). And as a result of the early and indirect Latin tributary (which existed on the Continent even before the invasions of Britain), we have *wall* and *street* and *port,* words that give promise of enduring even longer than the Roman constructions that they name; and we have place names: Roman *Londinium* (originally Celtic) is now *London,* Eboracum (also once Celtic) has undergone considerable transformation to appear as *York,* and Latin *castra,* a military camp, appears both in England and the United States in *Lancaster, Worcester, Leicester, Gloucester, Chester, Dorchester, Rochester.* Thus Latin and Celtic are early tributaries of English.

4 By the end of the sixth century, Latin was to renew its influence upon English. In 597 Roman missionaries began coming to the British Isles in an attempt to Christianize the inhabitants. They introduced such church words as *altar, creed, mass,* and *nun* and some homely words such as *beet, pine, cheese,* and *cup.* Some of the words that the priests brought over had been borrowed by Latin from Greek: *bishop, deacon, martyr, church, devil, priest, monk, pope, psalm, dish,* and *plum.* So once more a double tributary entered the river of the English language.

5 In the seventh and most of the eighth centuries the Anglo-Saxon inhabitants of the British Isles lived a relatively peaceful existence—simple by modern standards, but maybe happier than a more complex society can be. But starting in about 790, "Northmen" or Danes began to invade the islands. They were rough and vigorous; in 793, "the heathen men miserably destroyed God's church at Lindisfarne with rapine and slaughter," a contemporary account says. The forays grew into expeditions; the Danes began to colonize; Alfred the Great for a while paid them tribute but then organized military forces and compelled the invaders to sign a peace treaty. One of the terms of the treaty was that the Danes accept Christianity. Since the chief difference between the Danes and the Anglo-Saxons had been in religion, this concession meant that the two groups, already speaking kindred and often mutually intelligible languages, would merge. However, attacks by new groups of Danes, not covered by the treaty, continued, and early in the eleventh century a Danish king, Cnut, ruled in England.

6 It is often difficult to separate the linguistic contributions of the Danes from the closely related Anglo-Saxon, but apparently we owe to Danish such words

as *fellow, husband, law, wrong,* and a number of words with an *sk* sound, as *skill, scale, scare, skirt* (*shirt*, a cognate form, is from Anglo-Saxon), *skin, sky, score,* and *bask*. Numerous English place names are Danish in origin. Danish *thwaite* (piece of ground) appears in many names such as *Stonethwaite, Hall-thwaite; thorp* (village) is in names like *Lowthorpe* and *Northorpe; by* (town) is in *Derby, Kirby, Selby, Whitby,* etc.; *toft* (a clearing) is in *Lowestoft*.

7   The next big tributary came from north via east. Northmen, later called Normans, had begun moving into France at about the time that the Danes invaded England. They were flexible people who adopted French as their language, changing it somewhat in the process. They made of Normandy one of the most vigorous and ambitious states of Europe. In 1066, after the death of England's Edward the Confessor, the Duke of Normandy decided that he would attempt to gain the crown of his late cousin, and at Hastings he earned the more glorious title of William the Conqueror. His people moved into the British Isles, relegated natives to the rank of second-class citizens, and eventually concentrated their grip upon England as they lost their continental footholds.

8   Now began the period of greatest linguistic turmoil that English has known. England was a country of two languages: the Norman French of the ruling classes and the English of the conquered. The Bishop of Worcester was deposed in 1095 because he was "an idiot who did not know French." French was used in the churches, in the courts, in important business transactions, and in the schools. But inevitably the two groups had to meet. A French landowner had to give instructions to his tenants; an English farmer or smith had to try to sell his goods or his skills; intermarriage became frequent. Each group picked up words from the other. However, just as American occupation troops learned only the rudiments of German, Italian, and Japanese after World War II, the Normans did not learn the intricacies of English nor did the English learn the intricacies of Norman French. Each group learned only the fundamentals.

9   Before the Norman conquest there had been signs that grammatical inflections were being reduced—the dative and accusative cases, for instance, were blending their forms. But the coming of the Normans seems to have expedited such change. At any rate, after the Normans had been in England for about three centuries, English inflections were not nearly so numerous.

10   The two groups gradually blended. So did their vocabularies, and to a much smaller extent their grammar, although the impact of Norman French upon English was less than one might think. But partly as a result of that impact, and more largely as a result of other, less tangible causes, grammatical gender was replaced by natural gender, word order became less free as inflections were reduced, pronunciations changed, and many words from Norman French, French, and Latin entered the language.

11   Chaucer's contemporary, John Gower, in the fourteenth century wrote three major works—one in English, one in French, and one in Latin. He chose

three languages because he was not sure which language would become standard in England, and he wanted one of his works to be in the language that
endured. Had he lived fifty years later, he would have had no difficulty in
seeing that English was going to be the winner.

12   During the Renaissance two more large tributaries entered English. These,
of course, were in the form of additional Latin and Greek contributions. Thousands of words came into the English vocabulary during this period, including
huge numbers of relatively useless terms that lived briefly and were then buried
in soon-to-be-forgotten graves. English spellings were also influenced by the
new interest in the Classical languages. Learned men perhaps foolishly proclaimed that the orthography of English words should reveal their Latin backgrounds. They therefore recommended the spellings *debt* and *doubt*, even
though the *b's* in these words were not pronounced, and even though the
French, from whom the English had borrowed both words, had already dropped
the *b's* that existed in Latin. A number of words with *tio*, like nation, had also
been taken from the French, which often used a phonetically accurate *c* instead
of *t;* in English the sound in question was pronounced as *s* or *sh,* but Renaissance scholars insisted that the Latin *t* be retained. Many other of our present
illogical spellings may be attributed to the scholars of the Renaissance.

13   During the Renaissance period and later, the feeling grew that English
grammar should be described in the terminology of Latin grammar. Sometimes
that procedure was not objectionable, for many elements of the two languages
were similar. But when the grammarians insisted upon finding in English everything that existed in Latin, when they made of Latin a procrustean bed into
which English must be in some way fitted, and when they ignored the fact that
English was basically a Teutonic and not an Italic language, they did irreparable harm to many generations of persons who wanted to acquire a clear
understanding of the structure and peculiarities of the language.

14   Since the Renaissance, many small tributaries have enlarged the stream
of English. These cannot be listed in chronological order. Latin has kept ap-
pearing, as have French and Greek. Italian has contributed many of the technical terms of music. Dutch has given sailing terms like *ahoy, boom, deck, hoist,
skipper, sloop,* and *yacht.* Spanish has given, directly or indirectly, miscellaneous
words like *matador, vanilla, armada, alligator,* and *mosquito.* North American
Indian has contributed such words as *hominy, Mississippi* (an Algonquin word
meaning "big river," not "Father of Waters"), *moccasin, moose, opossum,
papoose, pemmican, raccoon, skunk, squaw, toboggan, tomahawk, wampum,*
and *wigwam.* Among other contributing languages, with one or two representative words from each, have been Bengali (*bungalow*); Persian (*azure*); Slavic
(*polka, vampire, mammoth*); Hebrew (*amen, hallelujah, behemoth*); Hun-
garian (*goulash*); Tartar (*khan*); Malay (*amuck, gong, cockatoo*); Indian
(*rajah, nabob, khaki, yogi*); Australian (*boomerang, kangaroo*); South American Indian (*alpaca, condor, jaguar, quinine*); Polynesian (*taboo, tattoo*);

African (*gumbo, mumbo jumbo, okra*). Even Chinese has given us some words (*tea, typhoon, chop suey,* and *chow mein*); Chinese Pidgin English has contributed the familiar *chopstick;* Japanese has given us *tycoon, kimono, judo,* and *ju-jitsu.*

15 The borrowing has of course gone the other way, also, although the details need not concern us here. English and American gastronomic and athletic terms, for instance, have been incorporated in many European languages. An American can use the terms *cocktail* and *beefsteak* with satisfactory results in almost any European restaurant.

16 Why did English change? Simply because many things happened to many people in many countries. Had the Angles, Saxons, and Jutes moved southeast instead of southwest, the language of the British Isles might never have been Teutonic. Had Harold defeated William the Conqueror at Hastings in 1066, the language of today might have been considerably different, perhaps more complicated in morphology, more simple in syntax. Had the English been stay-at-homes, their language might have lacked some of the versatility, the expressiveness, and the color that we believe it now has.

Apparatus for: Language Is Like a River

Vocabulary: *Select a synonym from the lower list and substitute it appropriately for the italicized word.*

1. ". . . linguistic change proceeds *inexorably*." (¶ 1)   _____
2. ". . . linguistic *heritage*." (¶ 2)   _____
3. "The *forays* grew into expeditions . . ." (¶ 5)   _____
4. ". . . learn the *intricacies* of English . . ." (¶ 8)   _____
5. ". . . the *orthography* of English words." (¶ 12)   _____

a. raids
b. background
c. unyieldingly
d. spelling
e. complications

Discussion: *Rhetoric*

1. The basic organizational device of this selection is an image—a river. Point out in detail how the authors structure their selection around this image.
2. What transitional devices do the authors use?
3. How is this selection tied together at the beginning and end?
4. How helpful were the examples the authors used?

1. _____

_____

2. _____

_____

3. _____

_____

4. _____

_____

Apparatus for: Language Is Like a River

Discussion: *Theme*

1. What other image could we say language is like? Consider, for example, a tree.
2. What changes in languages have you observed in the last 10 years?
3. Choose one of the tributaries, such as the Danes, and comment on the words they gave us. Why, for example, do we get *fellow, husband,* and *law* from them?

1. _____

_____

2. _____

_____

3. _____

_____

Writing Suggestions

1. In an extended library paper, examine one of the languages that contributed to English as we know it and write a theme on the reasons for these contributions.
2. Make an evaluation of one page in a good dictionary in terms of the languages represented in the etymologies of the words.
3. Language Is Like a Tree.
4. Write a theme in which you make use of some famous quotes about the English language. Consider, for example, Churchill and Shakespeare.
5. Using the Oxford English Dictionary or an etymological dictionary, write a brief history of one of the following words: *tantalize, shibboleth, bedlam, sandwich.*

29. TEEN-AGE HEROES: MIRRORS OF MUDDLED YOUTH *

Thomas B. Morgan

1 Eighteen million American teen-agers growing older in a world they didn't make—a world overpopulated and underfed, overorganized and yet disorganized, impersonal and self-indulgent, machine-tooled, purposeless, yet filled with unrealized possibility and in danger of coming to an apocalyptic end—have settled a new world of their own. They have established a colony Out There in Teen-Land, a kind of pseudo-adult world. It is not a young world, if youth means daring and imagination, idealism and individualism, skepticism and iconoclasm. But it does have such a definite identity and appearance that one can visit it as a tourist, with camera, dictionary, and sick pills. (A nice place to visit, yes; but no place to live.) Because they have to live at home, go to school, belong to clubs, shop for supplies, and appear in court, the teen-agers' colony is attached to the American mainland and carries on foreign relations with it. The hearts and minds of teen-agers, though, are usually in Teen-Land; they are totally aware of themselves as Teen-Agers, something their parents never were when they were younger. They feel and are made to feel (no doubt by articles such as this) that they are a race apart, a minority in an alien land. Thus, they cling with fierce pride to a private set of folkways that seem mysterious and confounding in the extreme to outsiders. These folkways create pressures to conform and inhibit the individual as insistently as those in the adult world, but they give the teen-ager an illusion of choice. Paralleling the adult world, Teen-Land is built on insecurity and its greatest concern is for safety. The cost of safety is uniqueness of personality and the measure of it is membership in the herd.

* Thomas B. Morgan, "Teen-Age Heroes." Copyright © by Thomas B. Morgan, and reprinted with his permission. Material first published in *Esquire Magazine*.

2 To understand this complex, young world, one should get to know the heroes of teen-agers. Here is what prompted this inquiry: the assumption that heroes directly and indirectly reveal much about the hero-worshipers' values and that the heroes of teen-agers would contribute some understanding of those who idolize them in an era in which communication between generations has all but broken down.

3 This assumption isn't made because all teen-age heroes have special knowledge. Today, a young man is elected to heroship by teen-age girls who buy phonograph records without regard for his insights. The hero, after a short wait, is then accepted by teen-age boys, who buy him uncritically, perhaps to please the girls. The boys don't have feminine heroines of their own. There are girl singers who are popular with teen-agers, but none receive the adulation that the girls lavish on the males. It seems that teen-age girls, maturing faster than boys, have no interest in worshiping a member of their own sex. They are prepared to accept a male symbol long before the boys have extricated themselves from Mother. It has even been suggested that boys do not care for girl singers because the female voice reminds them of Mom and, worse, Discipline. As it works out, then, both sexes accept the choice of heroes made by one sex, and the weaker sex at that.

4 What makes the heroes themselves, in the flesh, a potential source of information about teen-agers is that they are, of course, more than mere show-business characters. Most of them are teen-agers and only one is out of his twenties. They not only perform; they also reflect those whom they are performing for and are approved by. They are part of Teen-Land as well as symbols of it. Some are virtually overnight sensations and none are so far from a time when they were nobodies that they cannot remember their own experiences as members of the teen world on the far side of the footlights.

5 Recently, some of these heroes were tarnished by the payola scandals. But in the outcry over payola, the essential nature of the idols themselves was ignored. The superficial crookedness of individuals in the record business was excoriated, leaving untouched something deeper—the irresponsibility of many who profoundly affect teen-age life.

6 One recent night, a nineteen-year-old boy named Frankie Avalon, a rock-and-roll ballad singer physically reminiscent of Frank Sinatra, was seen doing his turn at the Steel Pier Music Hall on the boardwalk at Atlantic City. When he stepped on the stage, about two hundred well-fed, well-enough-dressed girls in the first six rows and in the side balconies shrieked in the typically violent and mechanical way we have all come to know and love. The sound was a cross between an explosive high-school cheer and the mating call of the red squirrel. A number of the screamers were not looking at their hero, but at each other, to make sure that they were being seen screaming—that is, belonging. In general, the Frankie Avalon fans were seated screamers, not the old dance-in-the-aisle kind of naïve Sinatra days, which had merely been a kind of pre-

monition of things to come. A few, however, left their seats to run up the aisle and take flashbulb pictures of Avalon, screaming a little as they went. Back of the forward wall of noise, row upon row of teen-agers applauded conventionally. This may have been because they were less enthusiastic, but more than likely they did not scream because they were outside the bright glow of the footlights. If the management had turned up the house lights, they might have achieved a more perfect pandemonium.

7   But perfect or not, by enabling postpubescent girls to express themselves within the damp warmth and safety of the crowd, a modern teen-age hero, such as Avalon, fulfills his function and collects his money. The expression takes many forms. In New Haven, Connecticut, girls in summer frocks pulled the shoes off Avalon's feet in an attempt to drag him from the stage, into the audience. In Buffalo, New York, a wild herd of little women trampled him and sprained his back, while in Milwaukee twenty-one girls fainted during one show. When Avalon sang *Boy Without a Girl* on a television show, the camera panned on girls sobbing in the audience. After that, wherever he appeared in person, girls who had seen him on TV sobbed while he sang this song. Avalon's merchandising business keeps the idolatry percolating at long distance: Among his wares for young women are Avalon shirts, sweaters, bracelets, buttons and authentic locks of hair. The latter are collected when Avalon goes to the barbershop—which reminds one of that old boast of the hog business: "We use everything but the squeal."

8   Now the stimulus for all this is 5 feet 7 inches tall and weighs less than 135 pounds. On stage at the Steel Pier Music Hall, his hair was wavy, his face sweet-to-babyish, eyes sad, skin sallow under make-up, and mouth uncertain. His clothes were a careful combination of show-biz elegance and Pat Boone purity: silk suits and white buck shoes. By nature or design, his manner was gentle, a little frightened, and awesomely humble.

9   This humility, which is characteristic of many teen-age heroes (Fabian, Ricky Nelson, and the like), was a response to the felt need of the audience to identify with one who was celestial and yet not far out of reach. Since the aspirations of many teen-agers seem to be at the lowest level in the history of America, too much self was taboo and anyone too far away (or out) would be ignored. The cardinal principle of the successful hero would be that humbleness creates an indispensable aura of accessibility.

10   Avalon first sang *Pretty-eyed Baby,* the words of which were totally unintelligible, followed by *De De Dinah,* his first recorded hit song, which was also unintelligible. He sang with a microphone, but his voice was almost inaudible. He did a little soft shoe, which must have been intended to tell those who couldn't hear that the music was playing. Avalon was drowned out not only by the repeated squealings of the audience down front, but also by the orchestra itself, which played loud and hard, driving the backbeat. The trumpet was loud, in part deliberately and in part due to the fact that the trumpet player had

cotton stuffed in his ears against the waves of sound from the teen-agers. The drummer accented every second and fourth beat, which is the standard rock-and-roll accent. He kicked the bass drum like the pit man in a burlesque house. Indeed, Avalon's performance contained echoes of burlesque. His least suggestive movements produced ear-splitting cries for more, such as when he merely kicked the toe of a shoe out toward the audience. While this may not seem erotic in cold type, the girls who saw it sighed mightily.

11   The sum of his performance was very young, very immature, and even tender (all said at the risk of sounding old), because Avalon had so little audible singing ability and his audience needed to believe otherwise. Moreover, though they screamed like baby banshees, the girls were making believe they were adults. They struck poses which seemed to represent their idea of *adult* poses: in a moment of sudden restraint, some would sit back, place an index finger along a cheek, tighten their eyes, and listen critically. Like opera-goers, they whispered knowingly between numbers. When Avalon's half-hour was over, they wore expressions of adultlike sophistication on their faces: cool, satisfied, almost blasé.

12   At the stage door, still another crowd of girls gathered to wait for Avalon, held back by a chain. They might have been the same two hundred girls who had had the choice seats in the Music Hall. They milled about the door impatiently. A uniformed guard taunted them ("He ain't never coming out, girls!") while stealing looks through a small window into the hall that led to Avalon's backstage dressing room. When Avalon appeared in the hall, the guard unhooked the chain and demanded that the girls form two lines so that the star and his entourage could pass through to a waiting auto. Instead, the girls surged forward, breathlessly. Nonchalant at first, the guard swung the chain at them, rippling it softly. Then he cracked it hard across the front rank at chest level. The girls, who had been about to crush Avalon, fell back. Avalon walked behind a phalanx made up of his guitar player, the Steel Pier press agent, and three other men. "Touch me, Frankie!" girls shouted. "Over here, man. Just look at me!" Looking neither right nor left, Avalon escaped into the back seat of the waiting car. The entourage piled in after him. Female hands, heads, and torsos surged in at the windows and jammed open the front door. Two well-aimed, shoving blows from the driver cleared the front door, the windows were rolled up, and the car drove off with its precious cargo. The girls waved, disappointed but not angry. They had enjoyed the melee, the mob violence of which was the other side of the group sex rites that had taken place inside.

13   Ten minutes later, safe in a restaurant, Frankie Avalon said: "I think it's great to be a teen-ager."

14   Avalon had no more to say, really, than this one line. Yet even that underlined the modern, crowd-cultured teen-ager's deep and novel sense of belonging to a special group. Avalon was as unaware of his function as a hero of that special group as he had once been of his own potentialities. (He had started

in show business as a trumpet player.) He was their outlet for vicarious sex and real violence, those primitive means of self-expression to which one turns when prouder means—ambition, creativity, ability, the sheer desire to change the world—have been denied, devalued, or have failed. Avalon did not know it and, not knowing, felt no sense of responsibility for it.

15   While Avalon was in New Jersey, six teen-age heroes were in Hollywood pursuing their various commitments to television, movies, and night clubs. Ricky Nelson was taping "The Adventures of Ozzie and Harriet" with his mother and father. Edd "Kookie" Byrnes was acting in "77 Sunset Strip," a filmed weekly TV show. Pat Boone and Dick Clark (the non-singer of the group) were making movies and, simultaneously, Clark was producing some of his TV programs for tape. Fabian was working in a movie called *Hound Dog Man* and Bobby Darin had an adult-world night-club date. One could see them individually in the surroundings of their trade.

16   Ricky Nelson was rather well protected by his father and the family press agent in a barren office across from the "Ozzie and Harriet" TV-show sound stage. When they let him in edgewise, it was apparent that he was at least partly conscious of the nuances of his appeal to teen-agers. His commodity is sincere sex. He was most aware of the need for sincerity. It seemed crucial to him that no one should get the idea that he was different—"I'm just another teen-ager," he said—or that he was anything but sincere. Like most teen-agers, his sentences were larded with the phrase "you know," partially from habit, but also, it seemed, to impress one with his complete frankness and desire to be understood.

17   In 1957, when he was sixteen, Ricky studied guitar for a while, then walked on the stage of Hamilton High School in Los Angeles for his first public appearance as a prospective solo performer. He did not swing his hips or otherwise attempt to excite the audience. Yet, the screaming began before he sang a note, the girls got out of hand, and the members of the football team had to help him escape. Thus the hero was born, as all teen-age heroes are born, in the presence and at the pleasure of screaming young women. Six of his records have since sold over one million copies each, representing a cool net of $40,000 each. His personal appearances have been smashing, thanks in some degree to the careful organization of 10,000 fan clubs all over the country. His income last year was estimated to be $400,000. To earn it, Rickey selected each hit song by himself from hundreds of demonstration records submitted by publishers and song writers. He knew exactly what he wanted:

18   "The record should not be too complicated," Ricky said. "If it's not, you know, sincere, it's not too good. In a song, I hate to hear lingo, you know, about hop and bop. I like a song that tells a story without meaningless words, you know, like 'dig that crazy chick.' Now you listen to *Lonesome Town*. It should be a simple song like that, you know? *Lonesome Town* is about this fictitious town called Lonesome Town, you know, where you can forget this

girl. I mean lots of times you get jilted and feel like the end of the world's come. So, it's from what I feel sincerely, I decide to do a song. Now, you asked me about teen-age values. I feel my values are pretty good. I mean, I like anything I feel is sincere."

19   Edd "Kookie" Byrnes touches a different chord out of necessity. He is perhaps the only teen-age hero who achieved his exalted position by playing a role—that of "Kookie," the jive-talking parking-lot attendant of "77 Sunset Strip"—and maintains it by continuing to be what he isn't. In public, his speech sounds like a tape-recording made at the bar in Birdland. The rest of the time he talks like a conventional twenty-six-year-old. Seen at lunch and between scenes at Warner's, there was nothing about him that suggested the character of "Kookie" except the long brown hair and routine good looks. To teen-agers, however, he is "Kookie" whose long suit is a devilish narcissism. His trademark is a comb which he is endlessly passing through his locks. Teen-agers might be expected to frown on such self-conceit, but "Kookie" manages to convey the impression that he is just kidding. If teen-agers were really in revolt against the adult world instead of merely huddled together in their own adultified colony, Byrnes's "Kookie" probably would not be a strong-enough character to appeal to them. As it is, he is a symbol of a small rebellion. He says that the "77 Sunset Strip" adventure that won the teen-agers for "Kookie" involved an incident in which he was falsely blamed for an auto accident. "They think I did it," "Kookie" said, "because I'm young." The line could have been the title of a rock-and-roll golden record. Inevitably, as his fame grew, Byrnes turned to the teen-age record market. After a dozen or more attempts to record his first tune on key, the A & R man sent him home and pasted together a master out of pieces from each of the tapes. The result was *Kookie, Lend Me Your Comb,* which sold 2,000,000 single records, a monument to the taste and perception of our teens.

20   Fabian, like "Kookie," became a teen-age hero in spite of the fact that he was no bundle of singing talent. "Maybe I would have never made it if I could sing," Fabian has said. His appeal is similar to Ricky Nelson's, but also he elicits motherly sympathy from the girls because he is so obviously awkward and inept. It is now one of the hoary legends of Teen-Land that Fabian was discovered sitting on a doorstep in South Philadelphia by Bob Marcucci, a former waiter who is himself not yet thirty. With his partner, Peter De Angelis, Marcucci had discovered and then promoted Frankie Avalon to stardom. Having developed the magic touch, he searched for and found Fabian two years ago. Fabian was fourteen, had never sung a note in anger, and thought that the $6 a week he was earning in a drugstore was fair money. When last seen, he was getting $35,000 for acting (not badly, by Hollywood standards) in Fox's *Hound Dog Man.*

21   Sitting just behind the camera in one of those canvas chairs, Marcucci was watching every move his gold mine made. Marcucci is a short, swarthy man

who reminds one of a nervous assistant director at a boys' camp. He has the ability to analyze precisely the demands of the teen-age public and to know what to do about it. He has found a career in exporting talent to Teen-Land. First, he selects promising raw material. Then he molds it. He indoctrinates it for three months. Then he takes it to live TV shows so that it can see what the business is like. Then he lets it make a few test records. Since it cannot sing too well without an orchestra and the electronic facilities (echo chambers, bass and treble modulators, tape splicers and the works) of a recording studio, he teaches it to pantomime while its records play over the loud-speaker during its first public appearance before an audience of two hundred. He dresses it, first in sweaters and white bucks, then in open-Belafonte shirts and big belt buckles. He coifs it by modifying the duck-tail and getting more of the Ricky Nelson bob. He postures it, taking advantage of good shoulders, which should bunch forward, and narrow hips, which should always be off-keel. He takes it on the road, shows it to disc jockeys, and advertises it in trade papers. He decides (brilliantly) to use only its first name instead of its last. He interests Dick Clark in it, and after one shot on TV, it breaks up an audience of 24,000 in Albany, New York. It sells 300,000 copies of a record called *I'm a Man,* then 750,000 of *Turn Me Loose.*

22   In Fabian, Marcucci consciously or unconsciously produced a caricature that combined the sure-fire qualities of Ricky with those of his own Frankie Avalon. The mood in Teen-Land permits even such an obvious construction to become a hero. What Marcucci could not have planned, however, was the fact that Fabian's inability to sing would really be an asset. Marcucci tried to teach him; he went through four singing teachers trying. Fortunately, all efforts failed. Here was the ultimate in humbleness and teen-audience identification. Nobody in the audience could sing either, so that made the inept sex-pot, Fabian, seem all the more accessible. Mediocrity fell in love with its own image.

23   Bobby Darin has what Fabian doesn't have and vice versa. Instead of half-closed eyes, a build and a hairdresser, Darin has the most low-down, mature, masculine voice of all the teen-age heroes. During the past year, his records have sold more than 5,000,000 copies (*Splish Splash, Mack the Knife,* which got the Grammy award, etc.). Found at a Sunset Strip night club, Darin (without teen-agers) demonstrated that the humbleness required by them does not become him; he fairly bursts with self-confidence before an adult audience. He is about twenty-four, short, average-looking, and honest with himself. "I know I'm not a pretty boy," he said. "I feel a little out of place in front of teen-agers because even though they buy my records they don't have that fervor for me when they see me. It's a physical thing with them. I don't put them down for it, but I don't think I'm one of them." He said he would sing anything teen-agers wanted to hear—à la Avalon, the sense of responsibility was missing. "It's bad the way the papers have screwed them up. The kids have got the idea now that they all have to band together and act like teen-agers. They have phony heroes and no individuality. They don't know who's leading them. I feel

for them, but I'm *not* going to lead them, Charlie. You call the roll of commercial guys, put me first."

24 Pat Boone would save the teen-ager from himself if he could. His book, *'Twixt Twelve and Twenty,* was a tender try in that direction and he has said, "I hope that fellows like me and Ricky and Elvis aren't distracting kids from the real things in life and from becoming people instead of just fans." Boone has been around longer as a teen-age hero than anyone except Elvis Presley. He was a married man with a baby and a second (with two more in the future) on the way before he became a popular idol. He was deeply religious. Thus, he was absolutely safe and pure, too. This combination was immensely appealing to many teen-age girls. His records sold 20,000,000 at last count, second only to Elvis. On the movie set, *Journey to the Center of the Earth,* a wholesome Jules Verne tale, Boone seemed made for Victorian costumery. He does not have conventional good looks, but rather a strong, open boy's face which suggests ball games and picnics. He does not simmer like the members of the Presley-Nelson-Fabian-Byrnes syndrome. In his time, though, he has had his share of screaming and fainting and clothes-grabbing by teen fans. "I can't believe it's bad or abnormal," he said. "It's fun and a form of recreation and a release of tension."

25 Dick Clark has defended the teen-agers' *status quo* even more stoutly than Pat Boone. He has virtually become a go-between in the two worlds. To the teen-ager, he is an adult who likes them, a big brother who watches out for them, and an authority who sanctions both their idols and their folkways. For the adult world, he is an emissary from Teen-Land not many years out of the age group himself (he's thirty, looks twenty), a young man whose taste and judgment are respected (after all, indecent lyrics are banned from his programs); and a celebrity who approves of their children. With all this going for him, it's no wonder that Clark is one of the hot properties in show business. He has six TV shows a week on ABC, many magazine-writing assignments, and a fat contract with Columbia Pictures. (Until recently, when he was advised to withdraw, he had a music-publishing and record-pressing business.)

26 Television is Clark's first love. Both *American Bandstand* and the Saturday *Dick Clark Show* are major outlets for teen-age heroes and their music. The shows are so popular that Clark is probably the most powerful personality-and-song plugger in the teen field. Such power implies responsibility, so Clark is due his share of credit for conditions that prevail in Teen-Land. Last summer, after watching two Saturday shows from the wings (Clark tapes his summer Saturday shows mid-week), one could be sure Clark would never have one of those "There, that'll hold the little bastards!" episodes in his career. He is a careful man and, besides, he believes in teen-agers "the way they are." All of his TV programs devote many minutes to camera views of teen-agers.

27 Clark's magazine-writing career is based on a column in *This Week Magazine,* but his "talks to teen-agers" have also appeared in *Seventeen, Look,* and

others. He is the teen-agers' Norman Vincent Peale. His position is reassuring: the way teens live is pretty much okay. Nothing downs his optimism. Typically, he sums up his advice with, "Keep at it and I know you'll be successful"; or, "I think you will be surprised at how soon there will be nothing to worry about." Once, however, in a conversation, he said:

28 "I don't think teen-agers are doing anything today that adults don't do also. They have all the same problems that adults have nowadays—money problems, success problems, appearance problems. They are appreciated as a group as never before and they want to be looked on as adults. They're worldly, so much more worldly than we were. They're practically adults. They're sophisticated at a very early age. Take the day Sal Mineo was leaving my studio. He got in his car and a teen-age girl threw herself under the front wheels. 'Run over me, Sal!' she cried. That was dreadful, yes; but a week later in Atlantic City, a forty-year-old woman in a mink coat threw herself in front of Frank Sinatra's car and cried, 'Run over me, Frankie!' That's what I mean. There's no difference between teen-agers and adults."

29 Clark apparently meant this as a justification for himself as well as the teen-agers who idolize him. In any case, it was an accurate description of juvenile adults and adultified teen-agers.

30 What Clark and the others suggest in symbol and sentiment is that millions of teen-agers have taken refuge in a pseudo-world that is spoiled and banal and hypererotic and in headlong flight from reality and easily fooled and commercialized and exploited and fatuous. Such a world may be satisfactory for adults, but somehow one has greater expectations from youth.

31 Every world has means of expressing itself—a culture. Our 18,000,000 teen-agers (exceptions duly noted) spend $10,000,000,000 to support theirs. They have publications written in their own language (Teen-glish?) which keep them abreast of their times. *Dig, Ingenue, Seventeen, 16, Teen,* etc., instruct them in custom, ritual, propriety, sex mores, and proper-think; their goal is to inculcate group values. One magazine not long ago defined "What is a Square?" for its readers, who were told, among other things, that a square is one who refuses to go with a group to a movie he has already seen. Then there are motion pictures, television shows, and radio programs, which provide a kind of cultural game of ring-around-the-rosie. The teens influence the adults who provide the entertainments which in turn influence the teens and so on, and on. After sex and violence, the main theme of these entertainments is a kind of dead-pan morality which would be funny if it did not border on madness. Thus, the producer of *I Was a Teenage Frankenstein* defended himself against an attack on his very popular picture by pointing out that none of the young villains and monsters in the movie drank or smoked. And in the basic boy-meets-girl film, scripts are adjusted to make sure that a curious kind of justice, appealing to teen-agers, triumphs. In a teen picture, after the boy gets the girl pregnant, he's got to get stabbed. Watching rock-and-roll programs,

citizens of Teen-Land may learn the newest folk dances while they follow the fashions of the times. Hearing the disc jockeys on radio, too, teen-agers can absorb their culture. They are infused with meaningful backbeat rhythms and simultaneously absorb the philosophies of the modern jocks, which are a mixture of Beat, Babbitt, and Payola. Beyond these visual and aural items of acculturation, there is the automobile. What the frontier was to our pioneers, what Miami is to our modern adult culture, the auto is to the teen—the means of getting away.

32 Finally, away out on the fringe of Teen-Land, heroin takes some teen-agers where they cannot get by car.

33 The primary focus of the teen culture, however, is the teen-age hero who, like heroes of all cultures, represents the final expression of those values by which it lives. The seven aforementioned heroes are the Apollos and Zeuses of Teen-Land. A few years ago, the movies supplied most of the heroes for adolescent Americans. Marlon Brando and James Dean were two, but the former's receding hairline and the latter's death disconnected them from the young. Chances are they would have faded anyway, because rock-and-roll was bigger than both of them. Now, except for Dick Clark, every first-class teen-age hero is a recording star. No athlete, politician, businessman, or intellectual is accorded comparable esteem, nor could he be, given the teen-agers' demand for safety. The ideal athlete is admired for courage, the politician for principles, the businessman for enterprise, and the intellectual for devotion to hard truths —all represent values that tend to separate the individual from the crowd, that expose him, and that lead him into an uncertain and dangerous future. Teen-agers make virtues of conformity, mediocrity, and sincerity. It is a simple matter of survival; there's safety in the crowd. They can express themselves through their safe-sex heroes, each one of whom represents his own brand of sex—rebellious sex, sincere sex, clean sex, low-down sex, motherly sex, cool sex—at no risk. It's perfect: It's sex, but it's safe. Without leaving the warmth and security of the crowd, you can say what you want to say to the world.

34 You can have your cake without being eaten.

35 It is not easy to know precisely what the teen-agers want to say through their heroes. The means of expression is primordial; the words are often indistinguishable from straight static. In that they are designed (often willfully) to hold a mirror up to the nature of teen life, they offer perhaps our most significant clue.

36 Two of the most successful people in the teen-age song business are Jerry Leiber and Mike Stoller, a words-and-music team which seems to know precisely what it is that teen-agers want to say. Their rock-and-roll songs have sold over 30,000,000 records: *Hound Dog* sold more than 5,000,000 records; *Black Denim Trousers,* a supposed spoof of motorcycle bums which was taken seriously by them, sold more than 2,000,000 records; *Love Me, Loving You,*

Searching, Don't and *Jailhouse Rock* also sold more than 2,000,000; *King Creole, Charley Brown, Yakety Yak, Along Came Jones* and *Poison Ivy* sold more than 1,000,000. After eight years of song-writing (each is now but twenty-six years old) Leiber and Stoller have sold four times as many records as Jerome Kern sold in his lifetime.

37   It did them no harm that Elvis Presley (still in the Army as this is written) performed several of their songs. Along Tin Pan Alley, it is still generally assumed that Presley, the king of the teen-age heroes, could sell one million records of himself singing Clementine Paddleford's recipe for boiled beef to the tune of *Juanita.* He is expected to resume the throne upon his discharge this spring.

38   Leiber and Stoller had the good fortune to begin writing songs for teen-age heroes in the early Fifties when Negro music known as "rhythm and blues" was being discovered by white teen-agers. About 1953, this music was taken over for the commercial teen market although it had been played for years on Negro radio stations and had been sung down South as a form of the blues since the Civil War. At the same time, "country music" with its strong influence from both the Baptist church and white folk music was discovered. The two themes, one earthy, the other moralistic, both plaintive, came together and were revised downward to the teen-age level; they became "rock-and-roll." The rock-and-roll fad spread like a pox, carried first by independent record companies with singing groups, and then by Elvis Presley, with his country guitar and Gypsy Rose Lee hips. In Presley's larynx, songs that had arisen out of realistic needs for a job, a woman, or a drink were replaced by teen-age needs and expressions that were only dimly related to the sources of the new music. "Cold pouring down rain blues" became "They don't understand us because we're teen-agers rock."

39   Presley was followed by a horde of imitators. The surprise was that they were almost as successful as he was. Always before, a segment of youth had zeroed in on a single personality—a Vallee or a Sinatra—and had disdained copies of the real thing. Elvis, however, was more than a personality; he was the leader of a movement which provided a hero for every boy and girl, and finally resulted in the identification of teen-agers as a race apart. Leiber and Stoller wrote on the head of a drum.

"Anger and protest, self-pity and adulation, these are the things the teen-age heroes sing about," Jerry Leiber says.

40   Repeating the same salty, nasty phrase again and again, such a song as *Hound Dog* is a pure expression of hostility while *Don't* is equally pure self-pity. What teen-agers seem to want to say is, "I'm mad at the world, at authority, at the way things are," and "I can't do anything about it, so pity poor me." Both would be perfectly legitimate statements, loaded with potentialities, if that was what teen-agers actually meant.

41 "Basically," Leiber says, "these songs are a means of escape from reality. We write the lyrics deliberately vague. The songs aren't addressed to anybody real, but to dream characters. The songs are egocentric and dreamy. Lots of basic blues ideas wouldn't work as rock-and-roll ideas because the blues are too real, too earthy. You have to make them dream-like and very moral. That's why you're rarely going to hear even a plain *happy* rock-and-roll song, because happiness is a real emotion."

42 We have, therefore, not only rebels without causes, we have a generation with nothing to say. All that seems real about teen-age self-expression through the safe-sex heroes is their dedication to unreality, to songs of watered-down, self-pitying blues-that-aren't-blues, and to aimless hostility.

43 One can hope that in some area of life, teen-agers are giving as much passionate attention to the real business of youth—which is growing up as well as older—as they are giving to their heroes. But if Dick Clark is right, that there is no difference between the generations as he sees them, growing up may be as outmoded as the 78 r.p.m. phonograph record. There may be nothing to grow up to. Yet a comparison must be made. The adult world has an existence apart from its obvious responsibility for what has happened in Teen-Land. There are adults and there are teen-agers. Even on the teen-agers' terms, if a choice had to be made, one would a hell of a lot rather have his woman run over by Frank Sinatra.

Apparatus for: Teen-Age Heroes: Mirrors of Muddled Youth

Vocabulary: *Using your dictionary, note the etymology of each of the words below.*

1. apocalyptic (¶ 1) _____

2. iconoclasm (¶ 1) _____

3. alien (¶ 1) _____

4. extricated (¶ 3) _____

5. potential (¶ 4) _____

6. excoriated (¶ 5) _____

7. reminiscent (¶ 6) _____

8. pandemonium (¶ 6) _____

9. entourage (¶ 12) _____

10. nuances (¶ 16) _____

11. narcissism (¶ 19) _____

12. hoary (¶ 20) _____

13. syndrome (¶ 25) _____

14. banal (¶ 31) _____

Discussion: *Rhetoric*

1. Comment on the use the author makes of transitions. Consider, for example, paragraph 3, which begins by referring to an idea introduced in the preceding paragraph.
2. Has the author chosen his examples because they illustrate his own purposes, or because they genuinely reflect teen-age heroes? Explain.
3. Why does the writer follow Avalon more than any of the other heroes?
4. In paragraph 21, the author uses *it* to refer to a person. Why?
5. What is the level of language in this essay? Was it written for teen-agers?

1. _____

_____

2. _____

_____

3. _____

_____

4. _____

_____

5. _____

_____

Apparatus for: Teen-Age Heroes: Mirrors of Muddled Youth

Discussion: *Theme*

1. Compare the attitude of the author of "Teen-Age Heroes . . ." toward teen-agers with that of the author of "What's Happening, Baby?"
2. Is Morgan fair in his analysis of teen-agers? Is this selection about heroes or the persons who have heroes?
3. Why does the author skirt the serious, dedicated, and searching side of teen-agers?
4. About how many records have you bought of songs like those the author describes?
5. Is the writer correct in proclaiming that teen-agers have no heroes other than singers? (What about Robert Kennedy?)
6. What is the author's weakest judgment concerning teen-agers?
7. Do you agree with the ideas expressed in the final paragraph? Explain.

1. _____

_____

2. _____

_____

3. _____

_____

4. _____

_____

5. _____

_____

6. _____

   _____

7. _____

   _____

Writing Suggestions

1. In a theme, answer the charges against teen-agers by pointing out their positive qualities.
2. Analyze this essay in a theme. Study the author's examples and statistics, then reach a conclusion as to their validity.
3. The Real Teen-Age Heroes.
4. There's Safety in the Crowd.
5. _____ Run Over Me.

30. HOW THE INDIAN HUNTED BUFFALO *

Remi Nadeau

1 In the days when the American bison roamed the Great Plains, herds grazed peacefully in an open space, relying on an excellent sense of smell to warn of enemies. The wary bulls might notice what appeared to be two or three wolves moving near them on the downwind side. These were common companions whose presence excited little alarm. They generally attacked only old and infirm animals left behind by a migrating herd. The wolves would come up to within a few feet of the nearest buffalo, take aim with bow and arrow, and silently drop their quarry to the ground with a shaft through the heart. Still unaware that the intruders were Indians wearing wolfskins, the animals allowed themselves to be picked off until the hunters had all the meat they needed.

2 Such was the method used by American Indians to hunt the buffalo well into the nineteenth century. Taking advantage of the buffalo's weaknesses (particularly its poor eyesight), the stalker could get so close that he could hardly miss killing his prey on the first shot. Selecting a fat cow, he would take aim just back of the shoulder blades and loose an arrow with such force that it was often buried up to the feather. More than one early observer wrote of arrows going entirely through the animal and lodging in the ground beyond. One chronicler reported that the arrow usually protruded out of the other side, and before the wounded animal could fall the Indian would scurry around and pull the arrow through in order to save it for his next victim.

3 The Blackfeet, who prided themselves on hunting afoot long after they had acquired horses, attacked the buffalo in the thaws of springtime, when the earth

* Remi Nadeau, "How the Indian Hunted Buffalo," *Westways,* August 1966. Copyright 1966 Automobile Club of Southern California. Reprinted with permission.

was boggy and the heavy animals sank so deep in the soil they were nearly helpless. Other tribes, including the Sioux, stalked the buffalo on snowshoes in winter, when the animals sank to their bellies in the snow.

4   But the method was dangerous, since the hunter was afoot in the midst of powerful animals which, on good ground, were as fleet as horses. The bulls were ill-tempered and unpredictable; they might run away on the first panic, or they might turn on the hunters in defense of the cows.

5   By the late eighteenth century, horses brought to the New World by the Spanish had been acquired through barter and theft by most of the plains tribes. The horse enabled a village of warriors to slaughter an entire herd.

6   The buffalo was, of course, the essential factor in the life of the Plains Indian. Providing food, clothing, and shelter, it enabled him to maintain a reasonable existence without having to resort to agriculture.

7   It was therefore not surprising that the buffalo hunt became adorned with ceremony and custom affecting every member of a village. On the way to the herd the hunters exercised strict restraint; no one was allowed to get ahead of the others and spoil the hunt by a premature attack; any impetuous youths who did so were whipped with the quirts of the older warriors. If it was a long ride before the attack, the braves often jumped off their horses from time to time and ran alongside to keep their mounts fresh for the chase. The ponies themselves, thoroughly trained to run buffalo, pranced and snorted in anticipation.

8   After riding as close as possible under cover of hills without disturbing the buffalo, the hunters stopped to strip themselves of shields and all other unnecessary encumbrances; even quivers were discarded and half-a-dozen arrows were carried loose in the hand.

9   Then, if the land lay right, parties were sent behind hills and up dry washes to cover all sides of the herd before the attack. The final approach was made, and at a signal, the charge began at a full gallop, accompanied by savage yells and much whipping with the short Indian quirt. The stricken animals would stampede in one direction, only to be turned by a new attack. Finally, with dust filling the air, they would become a writhing mass surrounded and tormented by their enemy.

10   A good buffalo horse was so trained that, once it was clear which quarry his rider had selected, he would run up on the right side, the reins hanging loose upon his neck. At this point the Indian crouched forward on the left side of his horse, taking aim with his bow. As they thundered over the plain the horse followed the buffalo's every dodge and turn. When the pony was almost abreast of the buffalo, and sometimes as close as a bow's length away, the Indian shot his arrow into the animal's side. Then the horse would veer away to avoid further chance of collision.

11   The moment of shooting the buffalo was the most hazardous of all. Besides the chance of the horse stepping in a prairie dog hole and upsetting his rider under the feet of the stampeding herd, there was the real danger that the buffalo would suddenly stop, and with a quick movement to the right, attempt to hook his antagonist. If this occurred before the horse was fully abreast, he was trained to shift quickly to the left of the buffalo and thus avoid the horns. But sometimes it was too late to turn; the horse would rise on the horn of the buffalo and the rider would be thrown to earth, where he would scramble to his feet to avoid other trampling hooves. Generally a rope from the pony's neck was allowed to drag along the ground during the hunt, so that an unhorsed rider could grab it and retrieve his mount.

12   Sometimes spears were used, though they had nowhere near the force of the fully drawn arrow. The white man's gun was also used, but in the early decades of the nineteenth century the long, single-shot muzzle-loader was too awkward to aim at full gallop, took too long to reload, and the ball had less immediate effect on the buffalo than the arrow.

13   After the hunters returned to the village, the squaws and children went out to butcher the game. After skinning, the robe was laid on the ground with the hair down, and upon it was piled the meat. Then the robe was tied up to serve as a bag, and either slung upon a horse or carried on the squaw's back. Butchering each animal, according to one observer, did not require fifteen minutes. What was left on the ground the hordes of Indian dogs would pounce upon and devour.

14   Until the early nineteenth century, the Plains Indian killed only what buffalo he needed for his own use. But after the War of 1812, permanent white trading posts were established in the Upper Missouri River. A market for robes —skins with the hair remaining—had developed in the East (for such purposes as sleigh blankets). The frontier traders used every inducement, including whiskey, to get the Indians' business. The tribes began slaughtering far more buffalo than they themselves needed, taking only the robes and perhaps the tongues to trade at the river posts. By the mid-1830s the Oglala and Brulé Sioux had thinned out the buffalo at their hunting grounds in what is now central South Dakota, and moved down to the North Platte River to hunt and trade at Fort Laramie.

15   It is commonly believed, even by many Western history buffs, that the buffalo were plentiful until the professional white hunters began slaughtering them for the hide market in the early 1870s. This was, of course, the final coup that brought the buffalo almost to extinction. But the Indian himself, responding to the white man's demands, had greatly reduced the buffalo herds by the 1840s. By 1845 the covered wagon emigrants on the Oregon Trail were shooting buffalo for the sport of it. In 1846 the Indian Bureau superintendent for the plains tribes wrote:

16   "The buffalo is already greatly diminished in number, and . . . must, in process of time, be entirely destroyed."

17   Beginning in 1851 the United States gave the Plains Indians supplemental food rations to compensate for the loss of buffalo caused by the wagon train traffic. By the late 1860s a number of the Sioux bands were dependent on government beef rations to tide them through the winters.

18   The buffalo chase was already a dying institution when the hide hunters gathered for the final harvest.

Apparatus for: How the Indian Hunted Buffalo

Vocabulary: *Substitute a synonym for each italicized word.*

1. The *wary* bulls . . . (¶ 1)   _____

2. One *chronicler* reported . . . (¶ 2)   _____

3. . . . whipped with the *quirts* of the older
   warriors. (¶ 7)   _____

4. . . . attempt to hook his *antagonist*. (¶ 11)   _____

5. . . . the final *coup* . . . (¶ 15)   _____

Discussion: *Rhetoric*

1. This essay begins with a clear example of how the Indian hunted buffalo. How is the second paragraph related to the first?
2. Two excellent uses of transition occur at the beginning of paragraph 2 ("Such was the method . . .") and paragraph 4 ("But the method . . ."). Find other uses of good transition.
3. This selection first describes the simple methods of hunting buffalo; then it treats a more complex kill. Where does each section begin and end?
4. Paragraph 14 begins the final section. How does it differ in content from the rest of the essay?

1. _____

_____

2. _____

_____

3. _____

_____

4. _____

_____

Apparatus for: How the Indian Hunted Buffalo

Discussion: *Theme*

1. Can you find and add additional information about hunting buffalo?
2. Is there disagreement about who actually depleted the great herds of bison —the white hunters or the Indians? (See paragraph 15)
3. Why did the government wait until the bison was virtually extinct before taking drastic action?

1. _____

   _____

2. _____

   _____

3. _____

   _____

Writing Suggestions

1. In a theme similar to "How the Indian Hunted Buffalo," describe some other activity of the Indian, such as fishing or trapping.
2. Report on the defense mechanisms of several animals. Mentioned in this essay (paragraph 1) was the sense of smell of the buffalo.
3. In an essay describing a personal experience, relate a hunting or fishing trip.
4. *For the women.* "Why I Do (or Do Not) Like Outdoor Camping and Hunting."

XI. THE WHOLE THEME

I. *Suggestions Before Writing*

1. Be honest with yourself: Write only about what you know, believe, and regard as significant.
2. Be aware of the differences between spoken and written language.
3. Understand the need for convention in writing, especially mechanics.
4. Give attention to the "how" of good writing, as well as the "what."
5. Be critical of your own writing and thinking processes.

II. *Evaluating the Topic*

1. Is the topic important to you, and will it be to the reader?
2. Will the topic be interesting to the reader?
3. Does the topic come from your experience or an area you can learn about in the time allowed?
4. Does the topic represent resourcefulness: reading, listening, research?
5. Is the topic sufficiently limited in scope?

III. *The Central Idea*

1. Is the purpose of the paper clear?
2. Is the central idea sufficiently narrowed to be stated in one sentence?
3. Is the central idea concrete enough to be dealt with in one paper?
4. To the best of your knowledge, is the central idea accurate and true?
5. Will the central idea engage, rather than alienate, the reader?

IV. *Evaluation of Evidence*

1. Is there sufficient supporting evidence?
2. Is the evidence valid, or is it atypical?
3. Is the supporting evidence relevant and accurate?

4. Does your evidence consist of examples, comparisons or contrasts, authority, or personal experience?
5. Is your evidence placed in the most emphatic position?

V. *Arrangement of Material*
1. Does the paper have a clear beginning, middle, and end?
2. Is the material so arranged that the reader maintains his interest throughout the paper?

VI. *Word Choice*
1. Is the diction appropriate to the theme, purpose, and audience of the paper?
2. Are your words precise, clear, vivid, and concrete?
3. Have you used enough variety in your word choice?

VII. *Sentence Construction*
1. Does each sentence contribute to the central idea of the theme?
2. Have you varied the construction pattern of your sentences?
3. Have you used powerful rather than weak verbs?

VIII. *Beginning Paragraphs*
1. Is the beginning direct and accurate?
2. Does the beginning of the theme provoke the reader's interest?
3. Does the beginning set a tone consistent with the rest of the paper?

IX. *Middle Paragraphs*
1. Have you used effective topic sentences to guide the construction of the paragraphs?
2. Are the middle paragraphs used to support the central idea?
3. Are the paragraphs arranged in the strongest order?
4. Have you made use of transitions?

X. *Ending Paragraphs*
1. Are the ending paragraphs direct, emphatic, and conclusive?
2. Is the ending of the paper consistent in tone and emphasis with the rest of the paper?

XI. *Title*
1. Is the title clear, and does it reveal your subject?
2. Is it separated from the first paragraph?

XII. *First Draft, Second Draft, Final Copy*
1. Do you have enough information in order to write?
2. Have you allotted enough time to write the first draft at one sitting?
3. Have you corrected all errors of mechanics and of logic and organization when preparing the second draft?
Is your final copy typed or legibly written, and ready to hand in on time?

3!. THE CASE FOR NOT GOING TO COLLEGE *

JANE GRIFFIN WITH DANIEL CHAPMAN

1   America's latest panic mania is "higher education." Coaching begins in the
cradle. Billy must be groomed for membership in the proper nursery school,
to make the right private school, to land in the college of his parents' choice,
to be accepted in a good graduate school, so he can cinch a safe mate, a safe
job, and a safe material success. He must have a costly college degree at any
cost—monetary, emotional, or mental. He's *got* to make it.

2   Pressures and psychiatric facilities multiply at the better colleges. Mediocrity
swells at lower levels.

3   Mediocrity first. With the birth of 400 nakedly insufficient colleges in less
than ten years, the college degree faces drastic devaluation. A huge New Hamp-
shire resort hotel now clatters with a staff of comparatively inexperienced
teachers, calls itself a college and showers slick brochures on hopeful high-
school seniors. Iowa's Parsons College sets a brisk, businesslike standard for
educators who would run a new college in the black. The secret: motel-unit
buildings, open-door admissions, and guaranteed diplomas. Every man will
come packaged in sheepskin. His intellectual qualifications: time served, heroic
resistance to boredom, and cash.

4   But today's diploma is tomorrow's wallpaper. The college degree, far from
indicating anything special about the owner, is fast becoming the union member's badge of orthodoxy. Personnel men in large companies now clutch for this

* Jane Griffin with Daniel Chapman, "The Case for *Not* Going to College," *Look,*
November 29, 1966. Copyright © 1966 by Cowles Communications, Inc. All rights reserved. Reprinted with permission.

union card, a handy means of closing their shop to half the gray masses who assault their doors.

5   What the art of mass production did for America, Americans will do for their young. We will have not only disposable cups, but cave-in people; dumps for the cups, couches and asylums for the people. Pressures grow at the better schools. As a student service, Yale's "mental-hygiene" clinic is staffed by 20 hard-pressed headshrinkers. The University of Wisconsin has 28. Harvard does mental overhauling in a building so large that it goes by the name of "The Farnsworth Hilton," after the doctor who runs it.

6   A study by *Moderator* magazine foretells that one in 70 college students will threaten suicide during this academic year. Nine thousand will try. One thousand will succeed. True, our Vietnam death toll has averaged 2,500 a year since the beginning of 1965 and may go higher. But far from all recruits in our three-million-strong armed services are Vietnam bound, as bulging Coast Guard rosters show.

7   When the boys come marching home, should they go marching into college with the rest of their generation? Does college make sense? *The Case for* Not *Going to College* is not a brief against education nor a windy endorsement of free-speech movements in which the young halt lead the young blind. It is rather a warning against the national acceptance of higher education as a slogan that equates college with cash and brands FAILURE on the backs of the 60 percent who flunk, drop out, or even commit suicide.

8   It has grown fashionable recently to make a right case against college—for the wrong reasons. Of course many youngsters do drag their way through college for a diploma and the choice job it promises—not for an education. But if sheepskins were synonymous with job satisfaction, then Dad's $8,000 to $16,000 would be a properly paltry four-year investment. Sadly, the big-city mailrooms, switchboards, and reception desks are teeming with grads who thought their diploma-badge meant power. We hear tales of damage wrought by useless "cramming." But cramming—the fleet mastery of a sea of facts— may well be college's most valuable lesson.

9   We hear that too many girls go to college for the man of their choice, that boys waste too much time burning off youthful high spirits. If college performed these services well, it would be a parent's last golden gift to childhood.

10   But in the best universities and colleges, the scared seriousness of today's student is spoiling the fun and spoiling the seriousness. College heaps systematic corruption on all but the sallow book grub. There simply isn't time to do all the work for all five courses. Solution: Work hard on two favorites; feed back class notes on the rest and season with palatable bull. The book grubs go berserk in banks and clock towers a little bit later. More human types have problems now.

11   John X, 15, lives comfortably in a wealthy New York City suburb. His solicitous parents hauled him out of public school. They pay his way at a private pre-prep school so he will get into a respectable prep school, so he will get into a good college. John X is bright, but has no mind for abstract academics. He likes to feel a project take shape under his hand and sits in the rear of the classroom drawing intricately precise pictures of cars, boats, trucks, and buildings. One of his teachers is convinced John X might have made a great mechanic, a great carpenter, a great production foreman—a great architect.

12   But John X is a poor reader; his retention is bad. He has been laughed at so many times by his academically facile friends that he now supplies calculatedly clownish answers to the simplest queries from his teacher. Five years of college-oriented pressure have changed John X remarkably. He used to be a charming class leader, a natural athlete. Now, the class leader has become the court jester who causes laughter on purpose to prevent laughter by accident. When the teacher congratulated John X on making a low-pressure prep school nearby, the changed student was quick to say what others thought: "Thanks—they take all sorts of dumb people there."

13   Why should the John X's go to college? College deans of admission usually agree that students in the bottom half of their high-school class should approach ivied walls with caution, particularly if they lack verbal skill, seem ill at ease in a written world. And if they are science-minded but not comfortably at home with math as an abstract tapestry connecting all scientific matters, perhaps they should become a first-class mechanic instead of a bad systems engineer.

14   Not even the college deans really believe that the names, dates, facts, and formulas crammed into your skull will remain with you much beyond graduation. But most college courses have value apart from their specific subject matter. So it might be argued that history shows us the inflexible chain of cause and effect that binds us. English makes us analytical; art, observant; music, precise. Math proves the value of all abstraction. Science teaches a method of observation, deduction, and clairvoyance that can straighten out our harebrained lives.

15   Beyond this, it may help to know that if your stomach says "pizza," but your mind says "save for the weekend with Lulubelle," you are beset with a classic dilemma: determinism vs. free will; that if your roommate shoots a shotgun through the chaplain's window for the hell of it, he has succumbed to a modern vulgarization of existentialism.

16   But even the best college experience leaves the student alternately uncertain whether he is lodged on Parnassus or lost in limbo. Teaching is the dull villain. The simple fact is that teachers are promoted according to the quantity of research they publish. Good teaching may actually hold them back. It steals

time from their occupational rat race. Chances are your freshman and sophomore years will offer a mixture of pallid young instructors engrossed in the rari-
fied pedantry of their Ph.D. theses and nice old other-worldly profs on tenure,
who never die but just fade into the colorless pageant of passing days.

17   For others, the experience will record itself as a crazy quilt of recollected
vanities. William X, brighter than some, and sensitive, flayed his way through
a small Ivy League college without distinction. He remembers his sapient,
white-haired philosophy teacher, full of literary instances and phrases like
mes amis, holding forth in a large hall filled with frowning young faces. No one
could understand him. He remembers partying late and breaking doors; playing
badly in classical piano recitals; choking down plot outlines and incomplete
class notes to score well on tests that well-read students failed; losing three
friends to "sophomore slump." One flunked out; another was booted for
urinating on a hockey rink in a long camel's hair coat at half time on a $500
bet. The third simply flipped: He burned his mattress on the ground outside his
dormitory, then slipped out of William X's droning English class and climbed
the high, slippery roof in his socks before being caught and sent away.

18   William X's most informative experiences had little to do with formal education. He regrets the thousand small hypocrisies he practiced to make teachers think he gave a damn. He regrets that he still associates reading with duty
and guilt, teaching with ineffectual mystics and satisfied bores—because there
were three or four great teachers who changed his life.

19   For the William X's and many more, college, with its rigid division of
learning into narrow sectarian slots—physics, French, political science—tends
to wipe out alternative ways of thinking. Nowhere in academe's dusty grove is
there any systematic training in applied relativism, creative innovation, ambiguity, breaking set, simultaneous use of contradictory notions—in short, courses
suited to a mercurial world in which the sum of human knowledge (whatever
that means) doubles every ten years and the truly important thing is "not how
to remember but how to forget."

20   What alternative is there? The modern degreeless include: Ernest Hemingway, George Romney, John Glenn, Scott Carpenter, Sandy Koufax, Bobby
Fischer, David Sarnoff, Walt Disney, Mike Nichols, Barbra Streisand, William
Faulkner, Robert Frost, and John Lennon, BEATLE. Perhaps superb athletes
and chess players, aeronautical whizzes, born politicians and writers, green-
thumbed businessmen and gifted entertainers would rather mold the present
than bow to the past. . . .

21   America is still a land of opportunity for the degreeless millions, but mainly
west of the Hudson River. Get a job in St. Louis or Wichita, and then, if you
must, transfer to the nation's toughest city. Once you have worked, personnel
directors may be satisfied just to check with your old boss instead of a college
registrar.

22   For first-time job seekers in New York City, the picture is grimmer—but mixed. Here's what some New York firms think:

23   Half said they would hire talented high-school graduates, that performance weighed more than paper. But a third said no. Several said—all things being the same—they would hire Joe College over Harry High School. Two voiced the national maxim that a college degree, if nothing else, is a sign of initiative and stick-to-itiveness. Two would hire, but later insist the worker get his degree, aided by the company's tuition refund (100 percent for an A, 90 percent for a B, etc.).

24   Specifically: Ogilvy & Mather, McCann-Erickson, Young & Rubicam (advertising) say talented high-schoolers can work into "creative" jobs like copy writing and layout—not accounts, media.

25   First National City Bank says the high-schooler could start a four-year training program in commercial and trust banking, on the condition that he push for a college education with company help.

26   Union Carbide (chemicals) thinks the Army might qualify a man as well as college, cites cases where high-schoolers with technical training have been hired over liberal-arts college grads.

27   Equitable Life Assurance just hired 1,500 degreeless workers in a six-week period to fill clerical slots. Others work as contract and claims analysts. And two-thirds of Equitable's newly trained business-machine programmers are without degrees. However, Equitable (like Bell) favors college grads by writing for transcripts of marks and weighting salary scales appropriately.

28   Darker side of the news:

29   Esso said "no," without precise technical training.

30   Olin Mathieson (drugs, chemicals, metals) said the degreeless worker could barely clamber to a supervisory slot.

31   Of the three major television networks, only ABC felt a high-school grad could start in the mailroom (as messenger, page, clerk) and get ahead on television's technical side.

32   The verdict: Same as always, job hunting is a sustained humiliation, but the important thing is to get started now. Once inside the company, you are judged more on performance than on past credentials. It is hard to get fired. Dress Ivy League (i.e., well), speak good English, be frank, don't mumble, gulp down all extra responsibility, don't threaten to leave until they can't afford to let you go, then press for new responsibility, not a raise.

33   Beyond this, remember that the average blue-collar worker makes more than the average white; that diploma-toting teachers, librarians, economists, reporters, anthropologists, meteorologists, and social workers average between

$5,000 and $6,650, whereas degreeless *miserables*—commercial artists, electricians, truck drivers, asbestos workers, and plumbers—pull down between $6,500 and $13,500 a year.

34   Slews of state-supervised apprenticeships—from butcher–meat cutter to musical-instrument mechanic—pay you while you learn to earn. State-approved technical schools offer training in interior design, photography, electronics, travel-agency management, computer programming, and radio and TV announcing for sums between $210 and $800.

35   Mail-order courses, from missile electronics to landscape gardening or calculus, camera repair, criminal investigation, and cartooning can be learned from endless accredited schools listed by Washington, D.C.'s National Home Study Council.

36   On the theory that Mozart knew he would be a musician at the age of five but half of us choose our life work accidentally, the New York University Testing and Advisement Center, one of many university-linked counseling centers, charges $110 to put every client through some 15 hours of tests and talks to find the trade he's suited for.

37   But the race against time to make room for our young may already be lost: Alex Rode, who runs Washington, D.C.'s small (21 students) Walden School for verbally gifted high-school dropouts, nurtures their talents while teaching them clear writing, analytical reading, and necessary math. He counsels them earnestly to go on to college, but foresees 20 percent of young America working at noncompetitive subsistence jobs with regular hours. They will have copped out on today's rat race, the better to live, learn, and love life. A sort of "flop-out" wave is breaking over the Midwest, where college youngsters, pushed for 14 years to the limit of their capacity for study, are now physically unable to stay awake in class.

38   For those who cop, flop or want out, the word is: Wake up. Ask. Jump for the job, and get at it. For example, with a little initiative, you could make your first sale five weeks from today as a licensed insurance broker. Local insurance agencies are glad to supply study materials for taking the state test locally or at the commissioner of insurance's office. Cram. Take it. Learn, a month later, whether you've passed. If yes, cull names of newlyweds from society pages of local papers. Phone to set up an evening interview. Sell them a $10,000 policy. Make $82.50 (55 percent of their first $150 premium).

39   Take a cut on new-car sales—most dealers don't care who steers customers their way. Ask the nearby electronics plant to let you start a catering service; charge 20¢ for coffee that costs 5¢ a cup to make.

40   A San Francisco student refurnished the inside of his car and jumbled the outside parts, turned it into a mobile nightmare and called it the "First Psyche-

delic Taxi Service." All slack-jawed tourists are now fare game; he takes them where the happening's happening.

41 Life without college orthodoxy is what you make it, nothing more. Anywhere from $2,000 (a state university) to $4,000 (Ivy League with all the trimmings) can be saved each year by not going to college. If you worked at home instead of Harvard for four years, you would save your Dad $16,000 and maybe make $8,000 in that time—$24,000 in four-year installments to tool around with, buy a grocery store, play the stock market or blow on the black in Las Vegas.

42 But the breakaway life should be planned with all the nervous energy of a college senior cramming for comps. Here are some suggestions:

43 Start your own college. Jim Nixon is student president of the school he started, the Experimental College (of San Francisco State College), run by students for students. Enrollment has leaped in a year from 30 to 1,200. Fossilized syllabi in standard courses have been rewritten with the help of faculty from the parent college. Awakened by student offerings like "Styles of Thought," "Kinesthetics," "New Forms in Film" and "Music Since 1945," the older school has ended its six-year moratorium on experiment.

44 On the theory that you might want a conventional job someday, and that most personnel men grudgingly admit "a suitable ambitious substitute for college will do," start your own free-lance research outfit. Charge for custom studies on problems from community theft to college suicides. Use any nearby university for leads and follow Jim Nixon's reportorial technique: Ask, talk, think; "engage in a dialogue between your talking and your thoughts"; knock on any door for help; depend on no one but yourself.

45 Take a slow boat to Europe and go to school there. Average tuition in Great Britain: $200. Take what courses you want. Or learn to speak French in three weeks on the spot.

46 Talk mainly with people who know more than you. Talk is still one of the best educators available.

47 Master English. Young Winston Churchill, proudly at the bottom of his class at Harrow, waved aside the dead languages and worked alone in one current art—English. He choked down enough math to get into a military trade school, lapped up classic battles, lived and wrote his own version of history.

48 Read constantly, then read some more. Good books beat good college lectures. Proceed at your own speed—without the lecturer's delays and mumbling. Analyze your reading and argue it often with friends. Read *The Prince, 1984, Brave New World* for a unit in timeless chicanery; read Carl Sandburg's *Lincoln* for enduring word on the last best hope. Pick other great writers of

English—Conrad, Faulkner, or Joyce. Read everything by and about them, the substance of a graduate thesis; then, thank heaven that you don't have to demean yourself—and Conrad, Faulkner, or Joyce—by actually writing one.

49   Read John Fowles's *The Magus,* for a mystifying look at life's mysteries; S. I. Hayakawa's *Language in Thought and Action,* and never be fooled by language again; *Makers of the Modern World,* by Louis Untermeyer, for 91 short, startling biographies from Stalin to Schweitzer. Read all magazines and *The New York Times.* Don't read articles about America's education problems.

50   But by all means read Alfred North Whitehead's *The Aims of Education.* In it, you will find this: "Culture is activity of thought, and receptiveness to beauty and humane feeling. Scraps of information have nothing to do with it. A merely well-informed man is the most useless bore on God's earth."

Apparatus for: The Case for *Not* Going to College

Vocabulary: *Define the following phrases taken from the selection.*

1. panic mania (¶ 1)

    _____

    _____

2. nakedly insufficient colleges (¶ 2)

    _____

    _____

3. badge of orthodoxy (¶ 4)

    _____

    _____

4. hard-pressed headshrinkers (¶ 5)

    _____

    _____

5. the fleet mastery of a sea of facts (¶ 8)

    _____

    _____

6. season with palatable bull (¶ 9)

    _____

    _____

7. facile friends (¶ 12)

    _____

    _____

8. lodged on Parnassus (¶ 16)

    _____

    _____

9. lost in limbo (¶ 16)

    _____

    _____

10. For those who cop, flop, or want out (¶ 38)

    _____

    _____

Discussion: *Rhetoric*

1. The authors make one thing very clear—they feel that there is a cause for not going to college. They provoke thought by going on the attack. Where is their thesis?
2. Describe the beginning and ending paragraphs of this essay. Are they effective in terms of giving the essay a feeling of a well-rounded and complete piece of writing?
3. In the vocabulary exercises, several phrases are mentioned. Cite other uses of unusual phrases.
4. Find several instances of cryptic word groups like those in paragraph 5.
5. In paragraph 6, the authors cite a statistic about college suicides. Do they point out national averages or averages of those not in college? Would these change the emphasis?
6. Rhetorically, what is the level of usage in this essay? Explain.
7. To whom are the authors referring in paragraph 10 when they mention the clock tower?

1. _____

   _____

2. _____

   _____

3. _____

   _____

4. _____

   _____

5. _____

   _____

Apparatus for: The Case for *Not* Going to College

6. _____

_____

7. _____

_____

Discussion: *Theme*

1. Do you agree with the overall idea presented in this essay? If so, why are *you* in college?
2. Does the average college graduate actually make less money than the average non-college worker, as the authors claim?
3. Should success in life be measured in terms of annual income? Explain.
4. How do you account for the authors' leaving out such information as the fact that almost all basic research which gives us our standard of living is done by college professors and graduates?
5. Are you impressed enough with the list in paragraph 20 that you would want to drop out of college and be like one of these persons?
6. Why, do you suppose, in mentioning John Glenn, that the authors fail to point out that all the engineers and scientists who put Glenn into space were college graduates?
7. Is it reasonable to point to successful non-college persons without pondering what they might have been had they graduated? Explain.
8. Is there a case for not going to college? Should *everyone* attend?

1. _____

_____

2. _____

_____

3. _____

_____

4. _____

_____

5. _____

_____

6. _____

_____

7. _____

_____

8. _____

_____

Writing Suggestions

1. The Case for Everybody Attending College.
2. Analyze the evidence used to support the thesis of this essay.
3. Discuss some of the values of going to college which would be apparent only to someone who has attended.
4. Practicality Is Not the Only Measure.
5. Should grades alone be the determining factor for college admittance? Consider, for example, the student who discovers his own potentiality late in his high school career. Should he be admitted?

32. SO YOU WANT TO BE A DROPOUT *

Tom Mayer

1   You are in the middle of a pre-exam-period dead week frantically studying rocks for the imminent five-hour identification final in elementary geology, when suddenly you decide you don't give a damn anymore. It simply isn't worth the effort; you're going to fail no matter what you do. You haven't studied all term because the course was dull and the professor a fraud, and now it's too late.

2   But geology isn't your only problem. Recently you've decided that your friends are shallow, juvenile, and phony; your roommate snores, steals your razor blades, and leaves his dirty underwear on the armchair; and to cap it all, your girlfriend, Cynthia, has been seen repeatedly necking in a red Mustang with a lacrosse player from a rival fraternity. You feel hemmed in, harried, harassed; you haven't shaved for a month, bathed for ten days, eaten anything but Dexamil since day before yesterday, or slept in a week. You need peace and quiet and lots of it. If you look at five more rocks, you'll snap. They'll put you in the nut house, but you'll be so far gone they'll never be able to put you back together. You've got to get out. Out, out, OUT.

3   But how? Your mind churns wildly. Then, in a moment of revelation, you remember that the mechanics of dropping out are simple. Nothing to it. Most colleges are glad to be rid of you. Overcrowded classes, lack of dormitory space, not enough laboratory equipment. At the big state universities you're nothing but a number anyway. All you have to do is tell your adviser you want to take some time off to think it over. But tell him you're going to be gone only a year,

* Tom Mayer, "So You Want to Be a Dropout," *Atlantic Monthly*, November 1965. Copyright © 1965, by The Atlantic Monthly Company, Boston, Mass. Reprinted with permission.

or a semester, even though at the moment you're planning to emigrate to Zululand. Never burn bridges.

4   If your grades are in shape, there shouldn't be any problem. The worst that could happen is that you'd have to talk to a junior dean, explain to him that classwork has lost its kinetic excitement, that you feel under intense pressure and want your life to be inner-directed. You don't feel that you're doing the college experience justice, so you want to take some time out to re-examine your values.

5   The dean brushes a graying but boyish shock of hair off his forehead, taps his mahogany desk top with his fingernails, fills his pipe, sucks on it a few times, lights it, and tells you that your problem is fairly common. Many students suffer from your brand of malaise; it's become an integral aspect of higher education; the university understands and sympathizes. You're welcome to take off as much time as you want; the only things you should do are tell your draft board and let the university know when you want to come back. You thank the dean, shake his hand, and leave his office dwelling happily on your forthcoming year in Europe, African safari, beach shack at Malibu, or muscle-building job among the colorful he-men on a pulling unit in the West Texas oil fields.

6   The real problems of dropping out are not, you reflect, connected with university rules or administration attitudes. As a matter of fact, the university has been surprisingly understanding. Perhaps you've been doing it an injustice all along. But your parents are going to be quite something else. If they're liberal, urban, well educated, psychiatry-oriented, reasonably hip, relatively modern types—people who read the *New Republic,* have a family psychoanalyst, and worked as volunteers for Adlai Stevenson—the chances are you won't have much trouble when you break the news. A sigh from Mother, a suppressed grunt from Dad. They want you to be sure you know what you're doing, in much the same way that they wanted you to be sure you knew what you were doing last summer when you went to Mississippi, but once you convince them your head's screwed on right, that you merely want some time to find yourself, Dad says he's with you all the way and Mother nods agreement.

7   But God help you if Dad's a dirt farmer, insurance salesman, bean picker, truck driver, Republican, corporation executive, or mechanical engineer. He'll probably hit the ceiling. He's been spending a lot of money, maybe as much as three thousand dollars a year, to keep you in school; he's given you every opportunity, and you turn around and throw it in his face. You try to reason with him by saying that you only want some time to think. That, he replies, is what you go to college for. But, you say, I couldn't do any constructive thinking at college because there were too many pressures. I want to be inner-directed. Pressures, says your father. You think a corporation executive doesn't have pressures? Hell, yes, he has pressures. You gotta *live* with pressures.

8   Or Dad and Mother may be deeply hurt. They genuinely don't understand. They both came from poor families; they never went to college themselves: it's been a financial handicap all their lives. They've worked so desperately to put you in a position where you'll have some choice in life. They can't understand what went wrong. They drink nothing stronger than beer; they took you to church when you were young; Dad spent all his spare time with you—remember that fishing trip to Lake Chicahoocha when you were eight?—they've loved you more than anything else in the world: Where did they make their mistake? But, you say, I'm only planning to take a year off, not turn Communist or something. But why?, cries your mother. Yes, says your father, why? Don't we have a right to know?

9   So you try to explain that at college you were spinning your wheels. College ought to be a place where you do creative things with your abilities, not just dreary routines. There wasn't time to think or pursue your own interests.

10   Your father says he doesn't know anything about dreary routines, only that when he was a kid growing up back in the thirties, when things were really tough, a kid was lucky to be in college at all. A college kid had a job, a good job, waiting for him when he got out. Aha, you say. But not anymore. Now you've got to go on to graduate school, to business school, or medical school, or law school, or veterinary school. You've got to have an M.A. or a Ph.D. to teach even. You have to be sure before you get in so deeply. Your father says he hadn't thought of it that way, and you think maybe you're getting somewhere; however, your mother begins to cry hysterically, and that ends the conversation.

11   As always, arguing with your parents leaves you in a state of fist-clenched frustration. You are never able to express yourself fully to them. How do you explain motivations that are so subtle and deeply rooted that often you are not clearly aware of them yourself?

12   Dropping out probably reflects a good deal more than mere distaste for routines, slovenly roommates, and elementary geology; in reality, it may be a manifestation of some such psychological problem as a lifelong struggle to break out of a family pattern—perhaps you were forced to go to Dad's prep school, and Dad's college, and the prospect of graduation and living at home and going into the family investment firm or dry-goods business or grocery-store chain or optical company is more than you can stand. Possibly you went to an inadequate public high school, and in your freshman year at an Ivy League college you found yourself so ill prepared, overworked, socially inept, and plain scared that you developed a serious sense of inferiority. Everyone seemed wittier and more intelligent and better adjusted than you, so that life at college devolved into an infinite series of real and imagined humiliations. Or perhaps you came to college after four or more years at prep school and found that nothing stimulated you, that on the whole your college teachers were inferior to

prep-school masters, and that since college courses tended to be dull and super-ficial, the excitement and purpose had gone out of learning. Or you might be in love and get married, but either because you are poor or because your parents refuse to support you, you have to leave school and begin to earn a living. Or, sadly, you may have gotten a girl pregnant. Or perhaps you are dead earnest about pursuing a career in which a college education is of no substantial value. Professional athletes, entertainers, actors, musicians might fall into this category.

13   The point is that beneath your irritation with the surfaces of college life, you suspect some flaw in your own personality or background, or else you feel that attending college is essentially a frivolous and time-wasting undertaking. For you, even if you don't plan to depart college permanently, dropping out is a serious business; it seems a sharp and fateful departure from the norm of your generation, and it involves a major decision, arrived at by you, and by you alone, after a great deal of self-examination.

14   Finally, however, no matter why you left, or say you left, you get settled into your new job or apartment or marriage and begin life on the outside. Your parents have been reconciled to the inevitable or have disowned you; the draft board is breathing down your neck, but you're stalling them; in short, you ought to be happier than ever before. No papers, no classes, no pressures. Time to think. Time to set your life in order, decide what you really think about Zen, what ought to be done in Vietnam, how to handle De Gaulle, how to stop police brutality in New York.

15   You sink into a pattern of sleep and independent study, or travel, or begin an exciting relevant job, and everything ought to be fine; but, predictably enough, it isn't. Roughnecking turns out to be much harder than studying rocks, your African safari didn't pan out, or your year in Europe is off because your father won't finance it. He says he'll be glad to teach you the glue business from the bottom up, but he'll be damned if he'll ante up good dollars for you to waste playing around with a bunch of screwballs and perverts in a lousy city like Paris. He's only been to Europe once, as a guest of the goddamn govern-ment, but you can take it from him, there's nothing there but a bunch of per-verts and bedbugs.

16   Even your social life is awful. You've been away from home for a while; you've lost contact with most of your old friends from high school, and those you still know seem changed. Or maybe you've changed, but anyway, there's nobody to talk to, you never have interesting discussions, and the girls are strictly bad news. They wear too much makeup, and most of the good-looking ones are married or have moved away or are in college. You remember faith-less Cynthia longingly.

17   Time drags. You are not so innocent as to think that college will be a bed of roses when you get back, but at least things happened there. Or perhaps

you've become intrigued with the glue business but realize you need more chemistry before you can come up with any significant innovations. Several nights you've stayed late down in the vat room fooling around with a new formula for heat-resistant, cold-resistant, spit-resistant, sweet-and-sour-tasting, water-repellent stamp stickum, but after several explosions and one fire, you're modest enough and sufficiently objective to admit that you simply haven't got the background.

18   Of course there's always the possibility that you'll be one of the dropouts who stays out, in which case you may become a plumber or electrician or mechanic or brush salesman, or you might join the Army, or start a window-washing service. You might even make good. Perhaps you'll be like Dr. Edwin Land, who left Harvard, invented the Polaroid camera, and made about forty million dollars in the process. Or Sandy Koufax, who left the University of Cincinnati, went into the major leagues, and improved the curve ball. Or perhaps you'll be a writer or a painter. You always thought you were deeper, more talented, more given to reflection and philosophy than your contemporaries, and when you write your first short story—a delicate and melancholy tale about the time your great-aunt Gertrude had hepatitis—and sell it to the *New Yorker* for $462.15, you feel that truly you have a future in the arts. The social stigma attached to spending your life without a degree is something you are sure you can overcome; in fact, if you are at all successful, being a dropout has considerable reverse snob appeal.

19   But the chances are that out of boredom or fresh enthusiasm or new interests or the blunt realization that degrees mean more money, you'll return to college willingly. You'll go back with reservations and misgivings; you'll know that college hasn't changed, and perhaps in your heart of hearts you'll still believe that you could and should be doing something better, something less nebulous and more important—but you will go back. Your friends will be pleased, your parents will be ecstatic. Soon you'll be settled back in the old groove: classes, labs, fraternity parties, exams, rushing, football games, quizzes, papers, and Cynthia, or someone like her. It will be almost as if you'd never been away, except that late in those all-night bull sessions, when the jocks have gone to bed and you're tired of talking girls and the conversation turns to serious topics like values and meaning and significance, you'll be a man of experience, an intellect to be reckoned with.

Apparatus for: So You Want to Be a Dropout

Vocabulary: *Using your dictionary, define each of the following words as it appears in context.*

1. imminent (¶ 1) _____

2. lacrosse (¶ 2) _____

3. kinetic (¶ 4) _____

4. malaise (¶ 5) _____

5. inept (¶ 12) _____

6. reconciled (¶ 14) _____

7. innovations (¶ 16) _____

8. nebulous (¶ 18) _____

Discussion: *Rhetoric*

1. Tone is very important in this essay. How would you describe the opening section? Is the total impact of the essay one of sympathy?
2. How does the author support his views of dropouts by writing about only one hypothetical case?
3. In this article, the author suggests that a dropout rarely does so for the reasons that are on the surface. Where does he show the real reasons?

1. _____

_____

2. _____

_____

3. _____

_____

Apparatus for: So You Want to Be a Dropout

Discussion: *Theme*

1. Have you ever wanted to drop out of college? Why? Do you think you would be more ready for college later in life?
2. Describe someone whom you know who has dropped out. For what reasons did he give up?
3. Should everyone with at least normal intelligence go to college? Explain.
4. Do you agree with the author's categories of persons who would either accept or reject a son or daughter dropping out of college? Check paragraphs 6 and 7.

1. _____

_____

2. _____

_____

3. _____

_____

4. _____

_____

Writing Suggestions

1. I've Got to Get Out (*or* Stay In).
2. Analyze the reasons given for dropping college by someone you know.
3. Discuss some of the salient reasons you are in college.
4. How would you improve the attractiveness of the college environment?
5. Is American education getting better or worse? Give your personal views in a theme, citing evidence from your own experience.
6. Should college men be deferred from the draft?

33. ROAD OF PRINCES*

MORTON CATHRO

1   Provincial Highway 16 across the wilds of north-central British Columbia is a road of princes and pioneers.

2   It starts at booming Prince George, the only town in Canada where you're likely to see helmet-clad construction workers driving Cadillacs, and ends 478 fascinating miles to the west at booming Prince Rupert, where the commercial fisherman is the richest man in town and takes his annual vacation in Europe.

3   In between are soaring mountains, dense forests, fish-clogged lakes and streams, rolling farmland—and a hardy batch of twentieth-century pioneers, some of whom still use kerosene lamps, eat moose steak, shoot grizzly bears on their doorsteps, drive ninety-two miles to a movie on Saturday night, and listen to circuit-riding preachers on Sunday.

4   The tourist with a pioneering spirit to match will be well-rewarded on this road. Some seventy-five miles of it still are to be paved, but all 478 miles are hard to beat for raw scenic grandeur.

5   He'll drive for stretches of fifty miles or more without seeing a sign of human habitation.

6   He'll drive through winding valleys of the snow-tipped Coast Range Mountains, where stratus clouds grip the sides of the peaks in kid-glove softness.

7   He'll drive past golden shocks of oats on small, neat farms, and see butter-yellow daubs of aspen and poplar splattering the salad-green forests of hemlock, spruce, and fir.

* Morton Cathro, "Road of Princes," *Westways,* August 1966. Copyright 1966 Automobile Club of Southern California. Reprinted with permission.

8   He'll photograph ancient totem poles—the grandest stand of totems in all British Columbia—in desolate Indian villages and marvel at a modern paradox: television antennae atop the Indian's shacks.

9   He'll drive alongside rivers where the world's largest salmon and steelhead are caught. He'll hear about the small-town merchant who closes his shop at noon, drives a couple of blocks to the Skeena, hauls out his rod and reel, hauls in a fifty-pound salmon, and drives back to mind the store.

10   And he literally won't be able to see the forest for the trees.

11   This is sportsman's country, this Highway 16, this Totem Trail, this road of princes and pioneers. Up on the Kispiox north of Hazelton, the river bank is so choked in summer with camper trucks from the Golden State that the locals call the place "Little California."

12   It's right in the middle of the grandest trout fishing anywhere. For the last ten years, straight, the biggest and fightingest steelhead in the world have been caught in the Kispiox—the champ ocean-going rainbow trout weighing in, after a furious battle, at thirty-six pounds. Within the city limits of Terrace, a booming town (lumber) with $500 million in construction on the drawing boards and a TV station that covers the broadest area in North America, the fisherman-motorist can drive right up to the spot on the Skeena where a fourteen-year-old schoolboy pulled in the world's record ninety-two-pound salmon.

13   There are equal rewards to be found in short sidetrips from Highway 16, and that is why the motorist should budget at least three days for the drive— more, if he's a hunter or fisherman.

14   Forty miles north of Vanderhoof, for instance, is Fort St. James, oldest community in British Columbia, established in 1806 as a trading post of the Northwest Fur Company by Simon Fraser, Canada's Kit Carson. It's worth the drive over the unpaved, pot-holed road just to see the original buildings of the post, including the only fish cache on stilts remaining in all Canada.

15   But there is more.

16   The new Fort Hotel across the street from the ancient fort boasts comfortable rooms overlooking Stuart Lake, the favorite fishing haunt of a handful of knowledgeable southern Californians. Downstairs in the cocktail lounge, your companions are apt to be wrinkled Carrier Indian guides and their squaws. (Fort St. James is one of several communities on Indian reservations near or on Highway 16 whose white population is vastly outnumbered by native.)

17   The Fort also is the location of famed Douglas Lodge, a haven for well-heeled outdoorsmen for three generations. The late President Hoover once stayed there.

18   There are other lodges on Stuart Lake, and on the plane returning to Los Angeles, I sat next to a southern Californian who lodged at one.

19 "I intended to stay two weeks," he said, "but I got all the trout and moose I wanted in four days."

20 Farther west, Burns Lake on Highway 16 is the jumping-off place for numerous big fishing lakes—many accessible only by chartered bush aircraft—including Babine, some 110 miles long and the largest in the province.

21 Still farther west—through the gentle farmlands of the rich Bulkley Valley, past Smithers where they're drilling through 400 feet of glacial ice atop Hudson Bay Mountain into the world's largest deposit of molybdenite, past Hazelton's totem poles—Highway 16 suddenly becomes rough and unpaved. But the scenery, sightseeing, and salmon beckon irresistibly.

22 After sixty miles of difficult driving, pavement resumes at Terrace, and here again a sidetrip proves doubly rewarding. Just south of this bustling, progressive town laid out on benchland overlooking the Skeena is picture-postcard Lakelse Lake. At the adjacent Lakelse Hot Springs they tell of the old man, crippled with rheumatism, who was carried in to take the lithium-rich waters and later walked out, unaided, on snowshoes.

23 Thirty-six miles south of Terrace on an excellent road is Kitimat, one of the urban wonders of the world. Eleven years ago this Canadian Brasilia was carved out of the wilds from scratch by the Aluminum Company of Canada as an ideal site for its $440 million smelter: ample hydroelectric power from the surging rivers nearby, and a deep-sea port on Douglas Channel, a fifty-mile arm of the Pacific Ocean, from which to ship its product.

24 Designed for an eventual population of 50,000 Kitimat today is a city of 9,000, laid out like Suburbia U.S.A. but with one major difference—aluminum roofs. It is a city of young people, many of whom are recent immigrants to Canada and most of whom work at the smelter.

25 Over on the coast at Prince Rupert, a fishball's throw from the Alaska peninsula, the misty rain falls on the nasturtiums and marigolds, on prosperous fish canneries and freezing plants along the docks, and on the attractive homes along the hillsides facing Tuck Inlet, one of the world's finest natural harbors.

26 "It's such a lovely place when the sun shines," says a little old lady shopkeeper a bit wistfully, while a member of the younger generation confides that it's a swinging town, rain or shine. Rupert was the port of embarkation for Alaska and the North Pacific in World War II, and many U.S. servicemen were stationed there. In fact, much of Highway 16 into Rupert was built by the U.S. Army as an alternate supply line to the railroad.

27 Rupert is occupied now with fish, and preoccupied with totem poles. More than 1,100 commercial vessels dock here annually and pour millions of pounds of halibut, king salmon, and Dungeness crab into the processing plants. The visitor can tour these plants, but he should be bundled up; the temperature inside the freezing rooms into which he can peek is 75 degrees below zero.

₂₈   Besides the fine wooden totem poles standing in front of the visitors' center, there are in the adjoining museum perhaps the finest examples of rare argillite totems in existence. Carved from heavy black slate whose source on the Queen Charlotte Islands is a well-kept Indian secret, argillite poles sell for an average of $25 an inch. There's a magnificent twenty-six-inch specimen in the museum valued at $2,000.

₂₉   And then there are the Totem Theater, the Totem Gift Shop, the Totem Coffee Shop, ad infinitum, right down to the city's trash cans designed and painted like open-mouthed totems.

₃₀   Cruise ships on the Inside Passage route to Alaska call at Rupert regularly, and the port also is the beginning of the Alaska Marine Highway, or ferry, system. In 1963, their first year of operation, the ferries did more business in six months than was projected for the first four years. Forty-seven percent of the vehicles on board, incidentally, were camper trucks, and most of these were driven by Californians anxious to cut 624 driving miles off the round trip to Alaska that normally would begin at Dawson Creek north of Prince George.

₃₁   Meanwhile, over at the other end of 16 at George, the fastest growing city in western Canada is building the world's largest paper and pulp mill to match its boast of being the white spruce capital of the world.

₃₂   And it looks northward to the Peace River country where a huge dam is creating the largest hydroelectric development in North America. It also looks eastward across the Rockies to Jasper National Park, with which it hopes one day to be linked by road.

₃₃   But for the tourist, Prince George faces west, as the logical start of the Highway 16 trek and gateway to the wildlife and scenic riches beyond. At the other end he can board the auto ferry for Vancouver or Kelsey Bay to the south, or Alaska to the north.

₃₄   As indicated, the motorist should be of a pioneering spirit to negotiate the highway of princes and pioneers, but the hardships are bearable. The restaurant food, for instance, is undistinguished, two notable exceptions being, appropriately, at Prince George (the McDonald Hotel) and at Prince Rupert (the Crest Motel).

₃₅   And with the exception of the Crest, a first-rate establishment, most motels and hotels along the way seem constructed of green lumber. The floors squeak noisily and the walls are paper-thin, and sometimes you're lucky to find a washcloth in the bath.

₃₆   And soon after you fall asleep following a long day's drive, you're lucky to be awakened by early-rising hunters and fishermen clumping past your room en route to the great outdoors.

₃₇   But you shouldn't complain, really. You should join 'em.

Apparatus for: Road of Princes

Vocabulary: *Make a list of any troublesome words in this selection. Look up each one in your dictionary and write out the full definitions.*

_____

_____

_____

_____

_____

_____

_____

_____

_____

Discussion: *Rhetoric*

1. This short selection reads like a Chamber of Commerce appeal. But it is more; it attempts to describe a beautiful countryside without being banal. How does the conversational tone add to the author's obvious enthusiasm?
2. Do the short paragraphs add to the jaunty movement of this essay? For example, why is paragraph 15 so short?
3. Why has the author hit so hard on sporting activities?

1. _____

_____

2. _____

_____

3. _____

_____

Apparatus for: Road of Princes

Discussion: *Theme*

1. Would you like to travel this "Road of Princes"? Explain.
2. Do rough and unexplored areas intrigue something basic in man? Explain.
3. Why do size of fish and distance between human habitation seem always to be the criteria for beauty in the outdoors?

1. _____

_____

2. _____

_____

3. _____

_____

Writing Suggestions

1. Describe a beautiful area you have visited. Try to avoid clichés and banal statistics.
2. Write a theme of persuasion dealing with the need for more national parks.
3. What facilities should be added to your campus to make leisure time more enjoyable?
4. Do you think that superhighways are being built at the expense of more important natural resources?

XII. PRACTICAL POINTERS: SOME REMINDERS FOR THE STUDENT

The type of job you want will no doubt require a college education; and being successful in college will depend on your ability to write clear, effective prose. But many students encounter these areas of difficulty: lack of motivation, inability to concentrate, and inadequate organization.

Good writers are not born, nor are they created by attaining some magical insight into grammar. College writers must forget their negative attitudes about English, and concentrate on getting from the course whatever will help get them through college. Lack of motivation often stems from thinking, "I have no talent for writing; besides, why should I have to learn a bunch of rules?" But writing is more than "a bunch of rules"; it is also the awareness of organization patterns, word choice, sentence variety, and paragraph development. No one types 60 words per minute without practice; no one performs in the theater without rehearsing; and no one writes well without constant writing. Good writing is a goal, and you can achieve it with reasonable intelligence and a reasonable amount of effort.

Concentration, like motivation, is attainable only if you really want to do well. You can best achieve the ability to concentrate by finding areas of interest within the framework of any class. An English class, for example, lends itself to writing about any subject you want to know more about. Further, your English class is a perfect place to explore in an organized fashion your attitudes toward a myriad of subjects that surely are of interest—from theories on the origin of language to surfboard designs, from sex to the problem of nuclear disarmament. Concentration will cease to be a problem when you involve yourself with subject matter that is interesting to you.

Hardly anyone is adequately organized all the time in all ways. But the student who can assimilate materials for a theme and get them on paper is almost always the student who does well in college. Outlining, note-taking, and gathering sufficient material are three ways of assuring adequate organization. Broadly speaking, organization has to do with how one arranges his total life; but obviously the purpose here is not to solve all life's problems—but rather, to suggest simple ways of getting you pointed toward success in college writing. Several specific suggestions are in order. (They obviously are not restricted to your English classes.)

1. Attend class *every* time and *on* time.
2. Take notes, revise notes, and review notes regularly.
3. Read widely, especially good magazines, newspapers, and books.
4. Attend worthwhile films, public discussions, lectures.
5. Know and use your library.
6. Purchase and use a good college dictionary.
7. Work constantly on your vocabulary—make lists of new and useful words.
8. Get better use from your texts by making meaningful notations in the margins.
9. Be critical of your own writing.
10. Read each paper you write carefully to catch errors in spelling and mechanics.
11. Do not be afraid to ask help from your instructor; that's what he's there for.

Assessing your own strengths and weaknesses will contribute to the probability of your success in college.

34. THE LANGUAGE OF COLORS, MYTHS, AND SYMBOLS*

ROGER BASTIDE

1   What's in a color? The answer is, sometimes a great deal. Down through the centuries, particular colors have been used to signify certain qualities or conditions. Crimson was the imperial color of the ancients, just as today yellow is the imperial color in the Far East. Among English-speaking people, blue often stands for wisdom and spiritual truth, and red for courage. Colors are often given spiritual or religious significance.

2   Although this symbolic significance is generally recognized, the symbolism itself gives rise to some controversy. Some people—among them Frederic Portal, author of a well-known book, *Les Couleurs Symboliques,* published in Paris in 1938—maintain that colors have the same meaning for all peoples in all periods of history; that white, for instance, is always the symbol of divine wisdom, and red of love. Yet a study of Portal's book shows that all the examples he gives are taken, with very few exceptions, from the same cultural region. If the inquiry was extended to other parts of the world, would we come across the same tradition or find different symbolic meanings?

3   Furthermore, are such systems based, in the final analysis, on actual observation? In other words, is there any real basis for the symbolism of color, and, if so, should it be sought in outward, visible things or in man himself? Should we attribute the significance of red, for example, to the fact that this is the color of blood or, instead, to the stimulating effect red-colored objects are known to produce on the human nervous system?

4   Psychoanalysts have recently taken a hand in the solution of this problem,

* Roger Bastide, "The Language of Colors, Myths, and Symbols." Reprinted from *UNESCO Courier,* June 1958, with permission.

and they have tried to combine the individual symbolism of colors with their traditional symbolism by a theory of the collective libido—the energy or motive force, either so far as derived from the sex instinct (according to Freud) or as derived from the primal and all-inclusive instinct to live (according to Jung).

5   Certain aspects of nature, such as the blue of the sky or the green of grass and trees, obviously tend to arouse in all human beings, whatever their racial origin or culture, identical feelings which may produce the same kinds of symbolism. It has also been shown that the various wave lengths of light have similar effects on all nervous systems, and, applying this knowledge, doctors sometimes use red in the treatment of smallpox, or blue bandages for patients who have just had an operation. Psychiatry has confirmed these facts. Studies of paintings done by mental patients reveal that the colors used correspond to changes in the patient's emotional behavior and that, in cases of periodic psychosis, dark and light periods alternate.

6   However, neither nature nor emotions can do more than suggest things to the mind; they do not offer a basis for a coherent system of symbols. Psychoanalysis may attribute a certain variation in the significance attached to colors to the fact that human feelings are ambivalent; thus, red can express both love and hate; yellow, the mystic impulse and deceit; and green, hope and perversity. While these extremes may explain certain traditional systems of symbols, where yellow, for instance, can stand equally for God the Omnipotent, for strikebreakers, and for a cuckold, they cannot account for a whole series of facts emerging both from the paintings of great artists and from those of mental patients. Here, the symbolism is an individual one and not that of a group, and this becomes clear when either painters or patients are questioned—when they are asked, for example, why they have painted their fathers blue, or cypresses red. And when individual and group symbolism tally, it is not that psychological factors explain sociological features, but that, on the contrary, outward civilization imposes its standards and traditions on the individual, even though he may be mentally ill.

7   Color as the expression of certain emotional reactions must therefore be dissociated from the problem of color as a symbol. The physiological impressions of our sense organs, which cause us to talk of stimulating or depressing, cheerful or gloomy colors, may well, like the underlying impulses of the libido, converge with the cultural symbolism of color; they may also oppose it or even ignore it completely. The cultural symbolism of color must, therefore, be considered independently of physiology or psychoanalysis.

8   Every civilization has its system of symbols. Historians of medieval art come across many examples. In the Middle Ages, the Church specified the colors that artists were to use for the figures in religious paintings; the Virgin Mary had to have a blue robe, and Christ, who is also attired in blue during his period of preparation, is clad in black during the temptation in the wilderness, and in

white or red after his resurrection. The reason for the blue garments is that the Virgin Mary and the Messiah come from heaven; black represents the encounter with the Prince of Darkness; and white and red stand for the two aspects of God's nature, his wisdom and his love.

9 The real question, however, is whether or not the same system of symbols recurs in all civilizations. So far, it has been the practice to compare the use of the same color in a number of entirely different countries or during periods of history as distant as possible from one another. We might take as an example, Bacchus' red cloak, the crimson robe of the priest of Eleusis, the red mantle donned by Mohammed on Fridays, the garments of the Roman Emperors, the robes of Roman Catholic cardinals, and so on, and seek the same significance in things which may have a variety of meanings. (To find the real meaning, one really needs to study color in every historical or cultural context and, above all, to consider all the uses made of red: for example, the practice of the Amerindians who smeared their bodies with annatto before going off to hunt or to do battle.)

10 Research on the symbolism of color is within the sphere of ethnography and, before using the comparative method, one must first make a study of each of the various systems of myths, proceeding slowly from one cultural area to the next, or following the routes of the great protohistoric or historic invasions. If we take two African systems as examples, we shall see that colors have a given significance only within certain contexts.

11 For the Dogons, the Blacksmith who fashions men and their society comes down to earth on the rainbow and takes its various hues to color the stones from which the limbs of men are to be wrought, the various human organs, the seeds of plants, and the compartments of the celestial granary. Although this system is coherent, it would be very difficult to establish a link between the black of the left leg, the red of the left arm, or the white of the right arm and the Western tradition of black for the devil, red for love (or for hate), and white for innocence. The significance of the colors depends upon the myth as a whole; in another myth, they would have a different meaning.

12 The Dogon system is very familiar to Africanists, but the Yoruba system is less well-known, at least in this particular connection, so I shall describe it in rather more detail. Every god has his own special color: Oshala (the sky god), white; Shango (the thunder god), red; Oshossi (the god of hunting), green and yellow; Oshoum (the goddess of fresh water and love), yellow, and so on. It is easy to understand how this classification of colors originated; white is reminiscent of the dazzling brightness of the sky; red, of the fiery thunderbolt; green and yellow, of the forest; and Oshoum's yellow of the muddy water of the rivers.

13 After that, however, the system runs on by itself, that is to say, any god, even if his powers or sphere of action do not suggest any color, has one attrib-

uted to him in order that there may be no gap in the series. The history of the gods also connects further colors with them; for instance, because Shango carried his father, Oshala, who could no longer walk, in his arms, white is henceforth added to his red, although white has nothing to connect it in the first instance with the thunder god. It is the myth which creates the symbols and not the existence of symbols with constant and previously fixed meanings which explains the myths. Moreover, as Oshala is white and it is he who created the first man and woman, white becomes the symbol of birth, and young women who enter a "convent" for initiation ceremonies—that is, to be reborn —wear white, even if they are subsequently to dedicate themselves to some other god, whose symbolic color they will then wear.

14   Another example is provided by the chief wife of Shango, Yansan, who, as she steals the "magic" of lightning from her husband, also takes on his two colors, red and white, while his two other wives or concubines keep their original colors. Here once more the color owes its significance to the myth, or, in other words, it is the god who transforms it into a symbol.

15   The example of the Yoruba is interesting from another point of view: The Negroes of that nation, borne off to the American continent as slaves, took with them their own symbolic classification of colors, which there clashed with another classification, that of Christianity. This is proof that each civilization attributes different meanings to colors. Oshoum, for example, whose daughters wear yellow, was assimilated with one of the forms of the Virgin Mary, whose children are dressed in blue.

16   As time passed, however, in Rio de Janeiro the African system began to show the influence of the Christian system, and certain gods, like Ogoun, the god of war, changed their colors. Ogoun took on the red of Shango, while Shango's sons wore white and Oshala added yellow to his white. The reason why Ogoun became red is that, for Western people, red is one of the symbols of war (when angry, we "see red"), and Oshala added yellow to his original color because golden-yellow is the symbol of the Supreme Being. However, as one realizes on reading the books published by the leaders of Umbanda Spiritism (this being the form which the African religion takes in Rio), the symbolism and the myth are so closely linked that, in changing color, the gods also change their personalities.

17   An interpretation of color systems should be undertaken with reference to an interpretation of cultures, and it would then become obvious that certain patterns can, in fact, be distinguished. There is, for instance, the dualistic pattern, which need not necessarily be white and black; in China, it is red and green; and among the Etruscans, it was red and black. There is also the cosmic pattern where the colors may be linked with the cardinal points or with celestial bodies used in finding directions (which of course differ in passing from one hemisphere to the other) or with the seasons, winds, forms of vegetation, and natural elements, as among the Mexican Indians.

18   The problem of symbolism is not only of theoretical interest; it also has practical implications. Although we may not believe that the system of accepted symbols depends wholly or mainly on feelings, we do believe, on the other hand, that the opposite is true and that symbols may influence feelings in certain ways. There is not only color symbolism; there is also color prejudice, which is affected by the symbolism. Examples might be taken from ancient Egypt, where the classification of beings was reflected in the order of colors, or from India, where each caste has its own color. We need only consider the forms of color prejudice at present existing among white men.

19   We have inherited from the Greeks and Christianity the two extremes of white and black, representing purity and evil. There is the example of Theseus using the black sail to symbolize failure, and the white sail success, when he returned from Crete to Greece. In Christianity, the chosen ones wear white tunics, and devils are black. And this dualism can be seen even in our playing cards!

20   Although we do not realize it, this association of black with hell, death the shades of night, and sin, inevitably influences the European view of Africans, as if the color of their skin had laid a curse upon them. This is so true that when someone white is speaking of a Negro whom he admires or of one who has become integrated into the white civilization, he may say that though the person in question is Negro, he has the "soul of a white man" as if, in order to make him acceptable, he must at all costs discover something white in the Negro.

21   Similarly, in the system of color symbols, gray is to some extent ambivalent, being regarded either as white tinged with black or as black tinged with white; and in the same way attitudes toward half-castes tend to be unfavorable or favorable, according to whether they are seen as a travesty of white (white tinged with black) or as an approach to white (black tinged with white). Hence there exist two contrasting forms of prejudice among white people who thus may be prejudiced to a greater or lesser extent against half-castes than against Negroes.

22   It certainly cannot be said that color prejudice is based solely on such symbolism, but the latter definitely has an influence, even among well-meaning white men. To recognize the relativity of systems of symbols may therefore be an effective aid in eradicating race prejudices (both against Asians, whom an Occidental may tend to consider untrustworthy or hypocritical because he has been told at school that they are yellow, and against Africans) and of doing away with ethnic stereotypes.

Apparatus for: The Language of Colors, Myths, and Symbols

Vocabulary:

1. What does *libido* suggest? (¶ 4)
2. Who is said to have a *psychosis*? (¶ 5)
3. What kind of feelings are *ambivalent*? (¶ 6)
4. Who is a *cuckold*? (¶ 6)
5. Why should a warrior smear his body with *annatto*? (¶ 9)
6. What subjects and topics would you investigate as a student of *ethnography*? (¶ 10)
7. What are *ethnic* stereotypes? How do they differ from other kinds? (¶ 22)

1. _____

_____

2. _____

_____

3. _____

_____

4. _____

_____

5. _____

_____

6. _____

_____

7. _____

_____

Discussion: *Rhetoric*

1. Why does the essay begin with a question? Is the answer to the question the central idea of the essay? Would the selection have been clearer had the author stated his thesis in clearer and more specific terms?
2. The first paragraph cites some familiar colors and their associations. Why does the author choose this method to focus our attention on his subject? Can you think of any other beginning which might have been more effective?
3. Notice the use of *furthermore* in paragraph 3 and *however* in paragraph 6 as transitional aids. Find several other such devices.
4. Paragraphs 18–22 comprise a complete section within the essay. What contributes to this being the strongest section of the essay?

1. _____

_____

2. _____

_____

3. _____

_____

4. _____

_____

Apparatus for: The Language of Colors, Myths, and Symbols

Discussion: *Theme*

1. What answer would *you* give to the first question in the essay, "What's in a color?"
2. Are we really motivated by color arrangements? For example, does red in a plush restaurant make you want to eat? Does the décor of physicians' offices suggest their belief in the psychological effects of certain colors?
3. In terms of human behavior, what do you associate with black, white, and yellow? Why?
4. How do you account for the fact that certain colors, such as black and white, seem to have a universal symbolism? Do cultural differences have any effect on our reactions to various colors?

1. _____

   _____

2. _____

   _____

3. _____

   _____

4. _____

   _____

Writing Suggestions

1. Colors as Symbols
2. Analyze the colors associated with courtship and marriage, with patriotism, or with some other institution familiar to most of us.
3. Use one of these phrases as the basis of a theme:
   "He's green."
   "I'm so mad I see red."
4. Consider the symbolism of colors in literature; for example, the use of black to portray evil, green to represent fertility, and so on.
5. Comment on the implied racial overtones of the statement, "That's white of him."

35. WHY WE REBEL *

Saraswathy Ganapathy

Himmat, *a Bombay weekly magazine, asked a number of college students throughout India to write on "Student Unrest—Its Causes and Cure." The first prize went to Miss Saraswathy Ganapathy, a last-year medical student at Madras University. Here is what she wrote:*

1 Everywhere youth in rebellion is hitting the headlines: Mods and Rockers, juvenile delinquents, *stilyagi, blousons noirs.* All over India, youth is striking, protesting, and demonstrating. And everywhere our "elders and betters" are throwing up their hands in horror and asking "Why?"

2 We have heard words like *God* and *country* used to whitewash some of the vilest deeds in history. We have been exhorted to honesty by crooks, to patriotism by near-traitors. We have heard sexual license extolled and advocated by those who should know—and then seen what havoc it can wreak in us, in our homes, in our societies. We "know the price of everything and the value of nothing" because all values have been carefully and efficiently destroyed before our eyes. We pin our faith in men because we have not been given a faith in anything bigger—and when men fail, as fail they must, we are left bewildered and hopeless.

3 We rebel because we want a new order in which man can stand up in the decency and pride that are his birthright—an idea occasionally so unfamiliar to us that we do not even recognize it as the cause we are fighting for, but this is why we rage and smash and destroy.

* Saraswathy Ganapathy, "Why We Rebel." Originally published in *Himmat Weekly*, Bombay; then in *Good Housekeeping*, New York. Reprinted here by permission of both publishers.

4 Enlightened self-interest seems to be the guiding principle in the lives of many of our elders—and you want us to sweat, to fight, to live for this? Thank you, but we are not interested. Give us a cause big enough to challenge and demand all our energy and spirit—dare us to take on humanity, to change the world—and then come and help us remake it.

Apparatus for: Why We Rebel

Vocabulary: *What do the following words mean?*

1. *stilyagi* (¶ 2)   _____

2. *blousons* (¶ 2)   _____

3. extolled (¶ 3)   _____

Discussion: *Rhetoric*

1. Comment on the fervor of this small selection. How does the author project
   the feeling of intensity?
2. Although the selection is short, the writer has dealt with many of the major
   issues of the day. How many significant topics has she covered?

1. _____

   _____

2. _____

   _____

Apparatus for: Why We Rebel

Discussion: *Theme*

1. Why do young people rebel?
2. Has this young lady touched on issues that affect you?
3. Do you agree with this writer? How do you differ?

1. _____

_____

2. _____

_____

3. _____

_____

Writing Suggestions

1. Why I Must (or Must Not) Rebel
2. Exhorted to Honesty by Crooks
3. Dare Us to Take on Humanity
4. Analyze a demonstration that you know about and account for the causes that lie behind it.

36. MAN'S GENETIC FUTURE *

Curt Stern

1   Assuming the human species is here to stay, what is likely to happen to us genetically? Will the stock improve, deteriorate, or remain the same? Is the future predestined, or can we direct it?

2   To answer such questions we must consider mankind's hereditary endowment as a whole and the distribution of this endowment among individuals. Let us assume, as we may for the purpose of this discussion, that the human germ cell has exactly 20,000 genes. That means that every one of the more than two billion people on earth today has acquired a set of 20,000 genes from the father and a similar set from the mother. These are shuffled like two decks of cards to produce new sets of 20,000 genes in the individual's own germ cells. Everyone has the same 20,000 kinds of genes but some genes appear in more than one form. Many probably occur in only one variety and are the same for everyone; others may show two, three, four, and up to 100 varieties. In any case, the total pool of genes in the earth's population at present is some 80 trillion (two billion people times 20,000 pairs of genes each). This is the storehouse from which the genetic future of man will be furnished.

3   The number of different possible combinations of the varieties of genes is huge, so huge indeed that of the hundreds of billions of sperms one man produces during his lifetime, no two are likely to be identical in the combination of genic varieties. The shuffling of the genic cards makes it unlikely that any person on earth (with the exception of identical twins) has ever exactly duplicated any other person in genic make-up, or will in the future.

4   This does not mean, however, that our inheritance is an entirely random affair. If men and women were completely promiscuous in mating—socially, racially, and geographically—then one genic combination would be as likely as any other, and people might vary individually much more than they actually do. There are times and places where man does approach such random mating —for example, during great migrations and large military occupations, when one group may sow its genic varieties among those of another group. As a rule, however, a potential child within a given group does not draw on the whole storehouse of mankind's genes. Usually his genes will come from a socially, nationally, and racially segregated part of the store.

5   Yet for thousands of years the barriers separating the store of human genes into compartments have been progressively lowered; and with the increase of human mobility in our era of world-wide transportation, many barriers will undoubtedly disappear. Tribes, minor races, and other subgroups will vanish. A diffusion of genes from one group to another is bound to occur, however slowly and gradually, and in time it will tend to eliminate all partitions in our storehouse.

6   Will this be good, bad, or immaterial for mankind? We cannot answer this question without evaluating the racial differences of the present. Have the present combinations of genic varieties originated in a haphazard way, or are they the result of selective forces in the earliest prehistory of mankind which adapted the different races to specific environments? It is probable that both chance and design have played a role. Thus the racial differences in blood types (Rh and so on) seem to be just accidental and of no adaptive significance. On the other hand, it is likely that the differences in pigmentation and breadth of nose between the Africans and the Caucasians were evolved to fit the differing climates in which these peoples lived. Does this mean that the leveling of the genic partitions will make the world's people less fit to cope with their respective environments? Such a conclusion might be justified if we could assume that the originally adaptive traits have the same significance today as they had 100,000 years ago. But has not man created new influences which effectively alter his environment in such a fashion that the external physical factors continuously decline in importance? Housing and clothing, food and medicine, occupation and training have changed radically, and it may well be that these new factors have superseded the old ones.

7   What of mental differences among races? Whether or not such differences exist has not been established; exact knowledge of the genic distinctions between groups is most lacking where it most matters. This is not only because psychologists have found it difficult to invent standard tests to measure the inborn capacities of different races but also because there is great variability in mental traits within any one group.

8   The 20,000 pairs of genes in the fertilized egg control a multitude of inter-

actions whose full complexity far transcends our understanding. In every trait of the individual, numerous genically induced reactions are involved. There is no absolute, one-to-one relation between a specific gene and a specific trait; it is necessary for the process that results in the specific trait, but it does not invariably produce the trait in question. A gene for clubfoot, for instance, makes for an inclination, a potentiality, toward the appearance of clubfoot; but whether this potentiality will become reality depends on the interplay of life processes. A slight variation in timing or in the environment may decide one way or the other. The clubfoot defect may appear in one foot, in both feet, or in neither.

9   The amount of variation in some life processes is small, in others large. A man's blood type, for example, remains the same throughout his life, but the color of his hair changes. Are the traits that distinguish different races variable in expression or invariable products of their genic endowments? It seems as a first approximation that genes for physical traits are more rigid in expression than those for mental traits. The Caucasian's hair remains straight or wavy and the Negro's kinky, regardless of any change in environment or training. It is otherwise with mental traits. A normal man's genetic endowment provides him with a wide potential for mental performance, from very low to very high. As with a rubber balloon, the state of expansion of his mind at any given time is hardly a measure of its expansibility. In human evolution those genes that allow the greatest mental adaptability, that possess the greatest plasticity of expression, seem to have undergone preferential selection in all races. If this is actually so, then the different genic varieties for mental traits may be comparably evenly distributed among all human groups, and the disappearance of the present barriers subdividing man's genic storehouse would not greatly affect mankind's mental potentialities.

10   What role will differences in reproduction play among the various socio-economic groups within populations? It is well known that the lower socio-economic layers of Western societies have higher birth rates than the upper ones. Do these layers differ in their stocks of genes? We cannot say with any certainty. The difficulties of research in this important field are great. We do not know, for instance, to what extent intelligence scores reflect true genetic factors in addition to education and environment, which they certainly reflect to a large degree. Nevertheless, the evidence strongly suggests that hereditary mental differences between socio-economic groups do exist. The mean intelligence scores of children at the higher socio-economic levels are consistently higher than those of lower groups, whether the tests are made in the U.S., in the U.S.S.R., or in any other country. That environment is not the sole reason for such differences is indicated by comparative studies on comparable groups of children, particularly twins reared together and separately. It is hard to avoid the conclusion that there are mean differences in the genetic endowment of different socio-economic groups, although the individual endowments within

each group cover the whole range from very low to very high. Since the groups that seem less well endowed intellectually produce the most children, a deterioration of the genetic endowment of the population should result.

11   This large-scale difference in reproduction rates is a rather recent phenomenon. It is primarily the result of birth control, which did not become an important social practice until the second half of the 19th century. So far the upper and middle groups of Western countries have adopted birth control much more widely than the lower ones. But there is reason to believe that the use of contraceptive measures will spread through the whole population, and that the group differentials in fertility will be diminished, although perhaps not obliterated.

12   Before we become too alarmed over the possibility that the genetic stocks of Western peoples may deteriorate, it would be well to obtain an estimate of the rate of this suspected deterioration. Such analyses as have been made suggest that the decrease of valuable genic varieties is probably much smaller than a naive consideration would suggest. High intelligence undoubtedly is based not on single varieties of genes but on the cooperation of many genes. The valuable varieties must be present, singly or in partial combinations, even in the great mass of individuals who score low in intelligence. From there they can, in the course of a single generation, reconstitute an appreciable number of the "best" combinations. In other words, the population at large constitutes a great reservoir, and the possible loss of valuable genic varieties possessed by the small upper layers of the population tells only a part of the story.

Apparatus for: Man's Genetic Future

Vocabulary: *From the list of synonyms below, select a word for each of the italicized words in the following sentences or phrases.*

_____ 1. Will the stock improve, *deteriorate,* or remain the same? (¶ 1)

_____ 2. . . . we must consider mankind's hereditary *endowment* . . . (¶ 2)

_____ 3. If men and women were completely *promiscuous* in mating . . . (¶ 4)

_____ 4. . . . these new factors have *superseded* the old ones. (¶ 6)

_____ 5. . . . far *transcends* our understanding. (¶ 8)

_____ 6. It seems a first *approximation* . . . (¶ 9)

_____ 7. . . . differentials in fertility will be diminished, although perhaps not *obliterated.* (¶ 11)

_____ 8. . . . a *naive* consideration . . . (¶ 12)

a. replaced
b. erased
c. casual or nonselective
d. credulous or believing
e. legacy
f. estimate or guess
g. degenerate
h. exceeds or surpasses

Discussion: *Rhetoric*

1. Find the one sentence in the selection that you think best describes or summarizes the contents of the essay.
2. What organizational pattern does the author use? Is it effective for his subject?
3. What is the purpose of the questions in paragraph 1? Is this an especially good way to begin an essay?
4. Does the essay end on an optimistic note? In answering, consider the author's attitude toward his subject.

1. _____

_____

2. _____

_____

3. _____

_____

4. _____

_____

Apparatus for: Man's Genetic Future

Discussion: *Theme*

1. Based on your knowledge of man's genetic future, will the separate races and divisions of men continue for only a few hundred more years? Explain.
2. Should birth-control methods be made readily available to poorer countries? To all countries?
3. If illiterate people have more children than do college graduates, what will happen to our civilization when there are more of the illiterates than educated persons? Or will this ever happen?
4. What do you consider to be the most startling discovery in terms of man's genetic heritage?

1. _____

_____

2. _____

_____

3. _____

_____

4. _____

_____

Writing Suggestions

Develop one of the following statements into a well-organized theme:
1. The best biological specimens should (or should *not*) mate.
2. Evidence for evolution can be found in the world about us.
3. New discoveries concerning man's chemical make-up will have effects on his concept of free will.
4. LSD: the trip to nirvana or despair?

XIII. USING THE DICTIONARY

Dictionaries have had a long and turbulent history. They probably began about seven centuries before the birth of Christ in the form of word lists; the Greeks, more than a thousand years ago, prepared similar lists, which they called *lexicons*. The early English dictionaries (the actual term was not used until 1623) or *glosses* (explanations of difficult terms) contained native English or Anglo-Saxon equivalents for Latin terms. These English-Latin or Latin-English books were most often used to make the Scriptures more easily understood. Following this meager beginning, the English dictionary did not expand greatly until the 1500's, when English involvement with scores of other countries in trade and commerce led to demands for various foreign-language dictionaries. The result was a series of English-French, English-Italian, and English-Spanish dictionaries. In 1565 a great classical dictionary appeared: Cooper's *Thesaurus*. Cooper's book was published five years after it was written because his wife burned the first draft, fearing that too much lexicography would kill her husband.

More than 150 years later another great dictionary was published, capturing the ideals and literary achievement of the age. The year was 1721, and the book was Nathaniel Bailey's *Universal Etymological Dictionary of the English Language*.

This, one of the most revolutionary dictionaries ever to appear, was the first to feature etymology, the first to give aid in syllabification, the first to give illustrative quotations (chiefly from proverbs), the first to include illustrations, and the first to indicate pronunciation. An interleaved copy of the 1731 folio edition was the basis of Samuel Johnson's *Dictionary* of 1755; through Johnson, it influenced all subsequent lexicographical practice. The position of dictionary pioneer, commonly granted to Johnson or to Noah Webster, belongs in reality to one of the few geniuses lexicography ever produced: Nathaniel Bailey.[1]

[1] *Webster's New World Dictionary of the American Language*, p. xxxii.

In his two-volume dictionary published in 1755, Samuel Johnson attempted to set authoritative standards for proper usage and meaning. His dictionary was to dominate the field of lexicography for a hundred years, and was to give us the notion that the dictionary is the supreme authority on all matters concerning words. Johnson's definitions are sometimes amusing because we see so clearly his personal judgment reflected in them. Below are some examples.

coffeehouse: A house of entertainment where coffee is sold, and the guests are supplied with newspapers.

corn: 1. The feeds which grow in ears, not in prods; such as are made into bread. 2. Grain yet unreaped, standing in the field upon its stalk. 3. Grain in the ear, yet unthreshed. 4. An excrescence on the feet, hard and painful.

gossip: 2. A tippling companion. 3. One who runs about tattling like women at a lying-in.

oats (Saxon): A grain, which in England is generally given to horses, but in Scotland supports people. It is of the grass leaved tribe; the flowers have no petals, are disposed in a loose panicle: the grain is eatable. The meal makes tolerable good bread.

Tory (a cant term, derived, I suppose, from an Irish word signifying savage): One who adheres to the ancient constitution of the state, and the apostolical hierarchy of the Church of England, as opposed to a Whig.

Whig: 1. Whey. 2. Name of a faction.

Although many of his definitions are erratic or inaccurate, Johnson had a remarkable ability to reduce a word to the many areas and ways in which it is used. All subsequent lexicographers owe him gratitude for his ageless work.

Persons who say, "Webster says . . ." are paying oblique tribute to Noah Webster who, in 1828, published the first important American dictionary, *An American Dictionary of the English Language.* This dictionary, which insisted on American spellings and American definitions, gave this country its first native dictionary that was equal in scope to Johnson's.

The collegiate dictionary, one which contains about 125,000 words, is a twentieth-century development. Portable and relatively inexpensive, the collegiate dictionary is a necessity for the serious college student. The following dictionaries are particularly useful:

American College Dictionary (Random House, 1965)
Standard College Dictionary (Funk and Wagnalls, 1966)
Webster's New World Dictionary (World, 1964)
Webster's Seventh New Collegiate Dictionary (G. and C. Merriam, 1963)

A good dictionary is a record of the usage of words—of their forms, histories, pronunciations, and meanings. A dictionary builds definitions of words from the study of illustrations of their use. The greater number of illustrations examined in the preparation of a dictionary, the better it will be. A dictionary is not intended either to prescribe or proscribe words, forms, pronunciations, or meanings; it is designed as a record of usage. Its purpose is to inform you how words have been used by others and not to tell you how you should use them, although generally following past usage is a safe procedure. . . .[2]

The point is well taken that a dictionary does not prescribe the usage of words but rather reflects how words are used; hence, it is descriptive, rather than prescriptive. This sounds more simple than it is, however, because a dictionary is a complex set of materials about words. An anecdote by Mitford M. Mathews illustrates the sophistication of a good dictionary.

> When I was a small boy, a carpenter once said in my presence that a few work-men, even among master mechanics, knew more than a fraction of the uses of an ordinary steel square. The remark amazed me, as at that early age I thought a carpenter's square was a very simple tool. It certainly appeared so to me— nothing more than two flat pieces of metal forming a right angle, and useful in marking a plank that one wished to saw in two in something like a workmanlike manner. True, the instrument has numerous markings and numbers on it, but I had never seen anyone making the slightest use of these, so I had concluded they might be ignored.
>
> When I became older and found that large books have been written on the uses of the steel square, I changed my mind about the simplicity of the tool and the limited range of its usefulness. For many years, as I have observed the use made of dictionaries by even good students, I have been reminded of that remark by the carpenter about steel squares.[3]

The dictionary can be thought of as many books brought into one volume. Following the suggestion of Mathews, we could list the titles to ten different books, all contained in a good dictionary:

1. How to Spell English Words
2. How to Capitalize English Words
3. How to Divide English Words into Syllables
4. How to Pronounce English Words
5. A Concise English Grammar
6. A Dictionary of English Etymologies
7. Levels of English Usage
8. The Meanings of English Words
9. A Dictionary of Synonyms
10. A Dictionary of English Phrases

The following exercises will help you to become familiar with the rich resources of the dictionary. Because the dictionary is an invaluable tool for acquiring a vocabulary, additional exercises will be provided in the next chapter.

[2] Donald W. Lee, *Harbrace Vocabulary Guide,* 1956, p. 1.
[3] Mitford M. Mathews, *The Freshman and His Dictionary,* from College Composition and Communication, December 1955, p. 187.

EXERCISE 1: Writing Suggestions

1. Choose any one page from your dictionary and read the entire page; then write a short paper on the interesting items you found.
2. Write a short paper (500 words) on the special features of your dictionary. Consider such items as arrangement of definitions, special tables, and supplementary material.
3. Write a paper on the proper use of a good desk dictionary.
4. Write a report on one of the early dictionaries mentioned in this chapter.

EXERCISE 2: Spelling

A dictionary records the acceptable spelling of words. If there are two accepted spellings, both are given. In the following list, some words are misspelled; others have alternate spellings. Using your dictionary, correct the misspelled words and supply variants.

1. pajamas _____

2. raccoon _____

3. grey _____

4. wiskey _____

5. programme _____

6. mispell _____

7. lustre _____

8. sacrilegious _____

9. cigaret _____

10. saviour _____

EXERCISE 3: Capitalization

Give the meaning of each of the following words—first, when it is capitalized; second, when it is not capitalized.

1. Scotch _____

   scotch _____

EXERCISE 3: Capitalization (continued)

2. Marathon   _____

   marathon   _____

3. Derby   _____

   derby   _____

4. God   _____

   god   _____

5. Exodus   _____

   exodus   _____

EXERCISE 4: Syllabication

Place a hyphen between the syllables in the following words.

1. a t m o s p h e r i c
2. m a n u f a c t u r e
3. s p a s m o d i c a l l y
4. e q u a n i m i t y
5. a d u l a t e
6. f i s s i o n a b l e
7. l a s s i t u d e
8. s p a s m o d i c a l l y
9. f o r m i d a b l e
10. g e n e r o s i t y

EXERCISE 5: Pronunciation

Using your dictionary, rewrite the following words, marking them with the appropriate pronunciation (diacritical) symbols.

1. gnome   _____

2. beret   _____

3. victuals   _____

EXERCISE 5: Pronunciation (continued)

4. posthumous   _____

5. dour   _____

6. mischievous   _____

7. Mao Tse-tung   _____

8. Vietnam   _____

9. intrepid   _____

10. rationale   _____

EXERCISE 6: Parts of Speech

Copy all of the grammatical information given in your dictionary for the following list of words. Be sure to notice whether or not the words can be used as more than one part of speech.

1. run   _____

2. record   _____

3. insult   _____

4. object   _____

5. protest   _____

6. mumble   _____

7. fast   _____

8. fail   _____

9. mail   _____

10. pipe   _____

XIV. VOCABULARY BUILDING

How many times have you said, "I know what I mean, but I can't put it into words"? The fact is, if you *really* have an idea, you *can* find the words to express it. Psychologists tell us that thought is impossible without words. By adding to your vocabulary, you are also adding to your storehouse of ideas, interests, and understanding. This is why it is so important that you, as a college student, constantly add to your vocabulary.

Success in the business and academic worlds is directly related to the size of your vocabulary. Employers are aware of this, as evidenced by the number of companies that give vocabulary tests to prospective employees. Colleges, universities, and the armed services, almost without exception, administer vocabulary tests to evaluate their applicants. They have found that the size of one's vocabulary usually indicates one's ability to think clearly and to communicate successfully with others. Finally, a large vocabulary is a social asset. Just as we judge others by the way they speak, so too are we evaluated by our own speech. If our vocabulary is limited, we create the impression—probably justified—that our education and interests are equally limited.

How large is your vocabulary? If you are a typical college freshman, you recognize about 50,000 words. Your *active* vocabulary, however—the words you actually use—is much smaller: from 10,000 to 15,000 words. Most new words that we encounter become a part of our recognition vocabulary. Later, after we become more familiar with them, we transfer them to our working vocabulary. The job of building a vocabulary, then, is twofold: Not only must we constantly acquire new words, but also we must make them a part of our active vocabulary.

The surest way to develop your vocabulary is through wide reading. By reading the best magazines and books (including textbooks), you expand the resources of both your mind and your vocabulary. Other sources for new words include newspapers, conversations with educated people, the lectures of your instructors, the special vocabularies of various academic subjects, and instructive radio and television programs. But none of these sources will be effective if you are not curious about words—curious about their origins, spelling, pronunciation, and meaning. By being inquisitive, you will not only learn many new words, but also gain new experiences, ideas, and knowledge.

The meanings of most new words you encounter will be found in your dictionary. However, many new words you will learn from context. The *context* of a word consists of the other words and phrases used in connection with it. Because the reader usually knows these other words, they serve as clues to the meaning of the unfamiliar word. Notice how the context helps to make clear the meaning of *umbrage* in this sentence: "Do not take *umbrage* at his thoughtless remarks, since he means no offense." What clues do you have to the meaning of *umbrage*? The fact that his remarks are thoughtless and capable of giving offense suggests that to "take umbrage" at such remarks would be to react with disfavor or resentment. By thus deducing the meaning of the word, you can continue your reading and infer the meaning of the sentence. Later, however, you will want to look up *umbrage* in the dictionary to confirm your notion of its meaning. In this way it can become a part of your speaking and writing vocabulary.

One of the features of modern English is its immense vocabulary, drawn from almost every known language. The basic words—most of our simple verbs, our articles, conjunctions, prepositions, and pronouns—are derived chiefly from the speech of the Anglo-Saxons. In fact, of the one thousand words that recur most frequently in our speaking and writing, at least 60 per cent come from Anglo-Saxon, about 30 per cent from French, and less than three per cent from Latin, with the remainder coming from various other sources. Examples of Anglo-Saxon (or Old English) words commonly used today are the following: *a, an, the, have, man, woman, child, father, mother, brother, sister, week, day, month, house, farm.*

Our borrowings from Latin extend over a period of some two thousand years, beginning even before the migration to Britain, when the ancestors of the Angles and Saxons were still in continental Europe. It has been estimated that about 50 per cent of all the words in the unabridged dictionary are ultimately Latin in origin. From the Romans we received words pertaining to government, religion, law, diplomacy, and medicine. Other Latin words come to us through the Romance languages, especially French. Some common Latin borrowings are the following: *chaplain, saint, street, minister, premise, deduction, conclusion, curriculum, insignia.*

EXERCISE 1

How many of these Latin words and phrases do you recognize? Match the first column with the meanings in the second column.

_____ 1. status quo   *a.* in good faith; genuine
_____ 2. per se   *b.* "by heads"; for each one
_____ 3. ad hoc   *c.* "for this purpose"; temporary
_____ 4. ad nauseum   *d.* "with praise"; with honor
_____ 5. bona fide   *e.* "foster mother"; one's school or college
_____ 6. cum laude   *f.* another name
_____ 7. per capita   *g.* by itself
_____ 8. alma mater   *h.* exact copy
_____ 9. facsimile   *i.* "to seasickness"; to a sickening degree
_____10. alias   *j.* the existing state of affairs

Modern science and technology derives much of its vocabulary from the Greeks. The following words, both scientific and nonscientific, illustrate the Greek influence in our language: *television, automobile, atomic, cinema, catastrophe, drama, psychology, philosophy, telephone.*

EXERCISE 2

How many of these Greek words and phrases do you recognize? Match the first column with the meanings in the second column.

_____ 1. chaos   *a.* something accursed or detested
_____ 2. anathema   *b.* a paper submitted for a degree
_____ 3. hoi polloi   *c.* the common, ordinary people
_____ 4. metropolis   *d.* the end
_____ 5. stigma   *e.* a mark of shame
_____ 6. thesis   *f.* highest point
_____ 7. dogma   *g.* complete confusion
_____ 8. omega   *h.* large or chief city
_____ 9. acme   *i.* basis for judging
_____10. diagnosis   *j.* doctrine or belief

Of all modern languages, French has contributed the largest number of words to our vocabulary. Beginning with the Norman Conquest in 1066, English has been enriched by French words pertaining to the church, to fashion, to the court, and to chivalry. Some of these borrowings have become so intimately a part of our language that we often regard them as native English words. Some examples are such common words as *state, judge, place, large, rule,* and *change.* Later French words introduced into English include *blonde, souvenir, prestige, chassis, etiquette,* and *rendezvous.*

EXERCISE 3

How many of these French words and phrases do you recognize? Match the first column with the meanings in the second column.

_____	1. macabre	*a.*	a feat of skill or strength
_____	2. faux pas	*b.*	a trite or worn-out expression
_____	3. tour de force	*c.*	gruesome
_____	4. debris	*d.*	a bride's outfit
_____	5. protégé	*e.*	a good trip; farewell
_____	6. cliché	*f.*	one under the direction of another
_____	7. devotee	*g.*	rubbish
_____	8. bon voyage	*h.*	a clever saying
_____	9. trousseau	*i.*	a social error or blunder
_____	10. bon mot	*j.*	one devoted to a particular hobby or pursuit

Although Latin, Greek, and French have contributed the highest number of loan-words to the English vocabulary, other languages have also supplied thousands of words. The list below suggests the borrowing and adaptation of foreign words that has been a characteristic of English.

Italian: balcony, corridor, profile, miniature, opera, sonnet, casino, traffic, risk, magazine, bank, alarm, colonel, arsenal, pistol, pizza, umbrella, pastel, stanza, buffoon, piano, studio, solo

Spanish: stampede, alligator, cargo, vanilla, tornado, desperado, negro, armada, escapade, embargo

Scandinavian: skirt, geyser, saga, ski, skull, axle, take, call, hit, law, ugly, wrong, meek, both

German: kindergarten, seminar, semester, nickel, sauerkraut, frankfurter, waltz, plunder, quartz

EXERCISE 4

Below is a list of 20 words, each taken from a foreign language. Using your dictionary, give the derivation of each word.

1. tomahawk _____

2. bamboo _____

3. chocolate _____

4. yacht _____

5. algebra _____

6. whiskey _____

EXERCISE 4 (continued)

7. sputnik   _____

8. robot   _____

9. tank   _____

10. goulash   _____

11. tycoon   _____

12. shampoo   _____

13. silk   _____

14. taboo   _____

15. safari   _____

16. camel   _____

17. bonanza   _____

18. judo   _____

19. replica   _____

20. yogi   _____

Studying the etymology of words not only helps us to know their histories, but also contributes to our understanding of their meanings. It is not surprising that many words have undergone changes in their meaning and spelling. An examination of several words will illustrate this point. To *meander* is to go off course, to twist and turn, or to drift. This word is derived from the Menderes River in Asia Minor, which has been known since ancient times for its winding course. Why is the Galaxy called the "Milky Way"? The etymology of *galaxy* provides an interesting answer: It is from the Greek word *gala*, meaning *milk*. *Sideburns* were formerly called *burnsides*, after the Civil War general Ambrose Everett Burnside, who wore side-whiskers. *Sinistra*, Latin for "left hand," gives us *sinister*. *Silly* in Old English meant "happy," and later came to mean "harmless" or "innocent"; today it has taken on the unfavorable meaning of "foolish." Who would guess that *grammar* and *glamour* are related? A check of their etymology reveals, however, that *glamour* is a corruption of *grammar*. Our word *idiot* comes from a Greek work used to describe citizens who did not wish to hold state office. And all freshmen will be delighted to learn that *sophomore* is from two Greek words meaning "wise fool."

EXERCISE 5

Using an unabridged dictionary, look up the origins of the following words and write them in the blanks that follow.

1. sandwich _____

_____

2. panic _____

_____

3. tantalize _____

_____

4. bedlam _____

_____

5. titanic _____

_____

6. alphabet _____

_____

7. Halloween _____

_____

8. robot _____

_____

9. maverick _____

_____

10. scrooge _____

_____

EXERCISE 5 (continued)

11. maudlin

_____

_____

12. boycott

_____

_____

13. gamut

_____

_____

14. lampoon

_____

_____

15. vandal

_____

_____

16. watt

_____

_____

17. cereal

_____

_____

18. jovial

_____

_____

19. dunce

_____

_____

20. canter

_____

_____

XV. VOCABULARY BUILDING

Many of the words in our language, particularly those derived from Latin and Greek, can be divided into basic parts which reappear in numerous other words. By learning these basic parts, we can analyze the meanings of thousands of words. The basic element of a word—the "idea" part—is the *root*. Many roots are preceded by one or more syllables; these are called *prefixes,* and they serve to modify or make more specific the meaning of the roots. A *suffix* is a syllable or two added to the end of a word to change its meaning or grammatical form. As we will see, the analysis of prefix, root, and suffix will not always give the current meaning of the word. But by learning the elements, you will be able to deduce the meaning of many unfamiliar words.

PREFIXES

A knowledge of the most common prefixes can help you to understand many words you would not otherwise recognize. Listed below are frequently used Latin and Greek prefixes, together with their meanings and illustrations of their use.

Latin

prefix	*meaning*	*examples*
ab-	away, from	abduct, abnormal, absent
ad-, ac-	to, toward	acclaim, adequate
ante-, anti-	before	anteroom, anticipate
bene-	well, good	benediction, benevolent, benefit
bi-	two, twice	bicycle, bifocal, bisect
circum-	around	circumscribe, circumvent, circumference

Latin

prefix	meaning	examples
co-, col-, com-, con-, cor-	with, together	coauthor, collaborate, combination, concert, correlate
de-	down, from, away	deceive, descend, decline
e-, ex-, ef-	formerly, out, beyond	evoke, ex-convict, effect
extra-	more than, beyond	extraordinary, extract, extramarital
in-, il-, im-, ir-	not, in, into	infinite, illuminate, impotent, irrational
inter-	among, between	interlock, intercede
mal-	bad, evil	malevolent, malign, malady
non-	not	nonconformist, nondescript, nonsense
per-	completely, by, through	per cent, perceive, perforate
post-	after	postgraduate, posthumous, postscript
pre-	before	predict, prejudice, prelude
pro-	before, for, in behalf of	prohibit, proceed, proslavery
re-	again, back	recollect, restate, reduce
sub-, suf-, sup-, sus-	under, beneath	submerge, suffer, suppress, suspend
super-	above, greater, over	superhuman, superstructure, superb
trans-	through, across, over	transition, transfer, transmission
uni-	one	unity, unison, uniform
ultra-	beyond	ultramodern, ultimatum

Greek

prefix	meaning	examples
a-, an-	without, not	atypical, agnostic, anarchy
anti-, ant-	against, opposite	antitoxin, antipathy, antagonist
auto-	self	autobiography, autopsy, automobile
dia-	across, through, between	diameter, dialogue, diagnosis
epi-	outside, on	epigram, episode, epitaph

Greek

prefix	meaning	examples
eu-	well, good	eulogy, eugenics, euphoria
hyper-	over, above, beyond the ordinary	hypercritical, hyperbole
hypo-	below, under, less than ordinary	hypodermic, hypocrisy
para-	beyond, beside, alongside of	paragraph, parallel, parable
peri-	around, near	perimeter, periscope, periphery
pro-	before	prologue, prophet, program
syn-, sym-	with, like, together	synonym, syntax, symbol

By learning the above prefixes you will acquire an effective tool for analyzing unfamiliar words.

But let us consider two problems that you may encounter in the use of prefixes. To avoid awkwardness of pronunciation, some prefixes change their spelling to blend with the initial letter of the root. This process, called *assimilation,* is responsible for the double consonant at the joining of the prefix and root. The Latin prefix *ad-,* for example, becomes *af-* in *affect, ag-* in *aggravate, al-* in *allot, an-* in *announce, ap-* in *appear, as-* in *assign,* and *at-* in *attend.*

Another problem in the study of prefixes is the possibility of confusing one prefix with another, or mistaking the beginning letters of a word for a prefix. The Greek *anti-* (*against*) and the Latin *anti-* (*before*), and the Greek *pro-* (*before*) and the Latin *pro-* (*favoring, in place of*) are examples of prefixes that are similar in form, yet different in meaning. Beginning letters sometimes appear to be prefixes: *amen* is not *a-* plus *men,* nor is *union* merely *un-* combined with *ion.*

EXERCISE 1

Using a virgule (/), separate each of the following words into prefix and root. Then, with the aid of your dictionary, give the literal etymological meaning of each word.

Example: ante / bellum   before the war

1. admit   _____

2. interfere   _____

EXERCISE 1 (continued)

3. hypertension   _____

4. sympathy   _____

5. edict   _____

6. extravagant   _____

7. translate   _____

8. interregnum   _____

9. pentagon   _____

10. amphibious   _____

11. bicameral   _____

12. precaution   _____

13. autosuggestion   _____

14. unification   _____

15. subvert   _____

16. declare   _____

17. euphemism   _____

18. antithesis   _____

19. antecedent   _____

20. proclamation   _____

21. beneficial   _____

22. progenitor   _____

23. superimpose   _____

24. impart   _____

25. prefabricate   _____

EXERCISE 2

Using your dictionary, find three words containing each of the following prefixes. Do not use any words mentioned in this chapter.

1. ad- _____

2. com- _____

3. de- _____

4. in- _____

5. trans- _____

6. re- _____

7. dia- _____

8. eu- _____

9. para- _____

10. pro- _____

EXERCISE 3

By combining the prefix with the stem, spell correctly the following words.

1. in reverent _____

2. sub round _____

3. com motion _____

4. ad filiate _____

5. ob casion _____

6. dis ferent _____

7. sub plicate _____

8. ad breviate _____

EXERCISE 3 (continued)

9. dis appear　　　　　　　　　_____

10. ob posable　　　　　　　　_____

11. ad fect　　　　　　　　　　_____

12. ad vise　　　　　　　　　　_____

13. com rupt　　　　　　　　　_____

14. in legible　　　　　　　　　_____

15. ad sociate　　　　　　　　　_____

16. in luminate　　　　　　　　_____

17. a moral　　　　　　　　　　_____

18. mis spell　　　　　　　　　_____

19. syn pathy　　　　　　　　　_____

20. com lect　　　　　　　　　_____

ROOTS

The root of a word is its basic part. It cannot be analyzed further, and it has little or no variation in meaning. Because this part of the word determines the meaning, it is more important than its prefix or suffix. In the following list of Latin and Greek roots, look up the meanings of any examples you do not know.

Latin

root	meaning	examples
cap, capt, cept	take, seize	capture, captivate, concept
ced, cess	go, move, yield	procedure, concede, concession
cred, credit	believe	credible, credit, creed
dic, dict	say, tell	predict, diction, dictionary
duc, duct	take, lead, draw	reproduce, educate, conductor

Latin

root	meaning	examples
fact, fect, fic	do, make	facility, factory, perfect, sufficient
jac, jact, ject	throw, cast	ejaculation, objection, projectile
junct, jug	join, connect	juncture, conjugal
leg, lig, lect	read, choose	legend, diligence, lectern
mit, miss	send	emit, admit, missile, mission
pend, pens	hang, suspend	pending, suspense, dependent
pon, pos	put, place	postpone, positive, exponent
port	carry	report, portable, support
rupt	break	interrupt, erupt, disrupt
scrib, script	write	subscription, inscribe, scripture
spec, spect	look	specimen, inspect, spectacle
ten, tin, tent	hold	tenacious, tenable, attention
ven, vent	come	intervene, convention, prevent
vert, vers	turn	inverse, revert, divert
vid, vis	see	provident, advise, revision
viv, vict	live	revive, vivid, victuals

Greek

root	meaning	examples
anthrop	man, mankind	anthropology, misanthrope, philanthrope
arch	first, chief ruler	architect, archbishop, monarch
auto	self	autobiography, automotive, automatic
bibl, bibli	book, books	Bible, bibliography, bibliophile
bio	life	biology, amphibious, biography
chron, chrono	time	synchronize, chronological, anachronism
crat	rule, power	autocrat, aristocrat, democrat
dem	people	epidemic, demagogue, endemic
derm	skin	epidermis, hypodermic, dermatologist
gen	birth, origin, race	genesis, gene, genetics, genial
geo	earth	geography, geometry, geology
gnosis, gnostic	recognition	diagnosis, agnostic, prognosticate
gram	writing	telegram, diagram, monogram
graph	write	graphic, autograph, graphite
homo	same	homogenized, homonym
log, logy	speech, science, study of	prologue, etymology, analogy
meter, metr	measure	diameter, metrical, barometer
micro	small	microbe, micrometer, microscope
mono	one, single	monotone, monogram, monosyllabic
onym	name	pseudonym, anonymous, synonym

Greek

root	meaning	examples
path, pathe	feeling, suffering	sympathy, pathetic, antipathy
phil	love	philosophy, philologist, philanthropist
phon, phone	sound	phonics, telephone, euphonious
poly	many, much	polytechnic, polygamy, monopoly
psych	mind	psychic, psychology, psychiatry
scope	view	telescope, microscope, periscope
tele	far, distant	telegram, telepathy, television
therm, thermo	heat	diathermy, thermometer, thermostat

Two hazards in studying roots should be mentioned: First, roots, like prefixes, often undergo spelling changes. The root *fac* (make, do), for example, appears as *fac* in *facile, face* in *surface, fact* in *faction, feas* in *feasibility, fect* in *infect, fic* in *officer, fit* in *profit,* and *fy* in *unify*. Another possible source of confusion is the fact that some Greek and Latin roots are spelled alike; by learning the meaning of each, you will avoid confusing them in words you meet. The Greek root *nom*, for instance, means *law,* as in the English word *nomism*; in Latin, however, *nom* means *name,* as in *nomenclature*; similarly, the root *tact* means *arrangement* in Greek, as in *tactics,* but *touch* in Latin, as in *tactile*.

EXERCISE 4

Write three English words that use each of the following Latin roots. Do not use any words mentioned in this chapter.

1. cap, capt, cept   _____

2. duc, duct   _____

3. fac, fact, fect, fic   _____

4. leg, lig, lect   _____

5. mit, miss   _____

6. pon, pos   _____

7. port   _____

8. ten, tin, tent   _____

EXERCISE 4 (continued)

9. ven, vent   _____

10. viv, vict   _____

EXERCISE 5

Write three English words that use each of the following Greek roots. Do not use any words mentioned in this chapter.

1. arch   _____

2. crat   _____

3. dem   _____

4. gen, gony   _____

5. log, logy   _____

6. mono   _____

7. onym   _____

8. path, pathe   _____

9. poly   _____

10. tele   _____

EXERCISE 6

Analyze the following words into prefix and root, giving the meanings of each.

	prefix	meaning	root	meaning
Example: transcribe	trans	across	scribe	write
1. hypodermic	_____	_____	_____	_____
2. excision	_____	_____	_____	_____
3. suppress	_____	_____	_____	_____

EXERCISE 6 (continued)

Example: transcribe	prefix trans	meaning across	root scribe	meaning write
4. ultramarine				
5. introspection				
6. supersonic				
7. nonentity				
8. collect				
9. suffer				
10. aspire				
11. concur				
12. react				
13. propose				
14. transpose				
15. symphony				
16. pentagon				
17. extradite				
18. segregate				
19. illegible				
20. educate				
21. perspicacity				
22. diverge				
23. benefactor				
24. appendix				
25. antiseptic				

SUFFIXES

The following are some of the most commonly used suffixes with explanations and illustrations.

suffix	meaning	examples
-able, -ible	capable of being	adjustable, tangible, capable, edible
-al	having the character of, pertaining to	verbal, formal, annual, regal
-ance, -ence	action or process, condition of	assistance, obedience, abundance, permanence
-ant, -ent	one who, that which	occupant, solvent, servant, irritant
-ary, -ory	pertaining to, or a place for	military, advisory, aviary
-ate	to make	legislate, agitate, liquidate
-ation	act or doing, state of being	transportation, civilization
-er	one who	lawyer, teacher, farmer
-ful	full of	hopeful, pitiful, beautiful
-fy	to make, form	beautify, sanctify, solidify
-ible	having the quality or fitness, able	irresistible, credible, edible
-ic, -ical	pertaining to, resembling	democratic, epidemic, historical
-ion	act of, state of	fission, rebellion, recognition
-ism	act of, doctrine of	baptism, barbarism, Communism
-ist	one who does or believes	theorist, tourist, pianist
-ity	state, condition, degree, quality	equality, superiority, depravity, legality
-ive	having the quality of, pertaining to	active, productive, appreciative
-ize	to subject to, make, or practice	penalize, dramatize, verbalize
-less	without, beyond the range of	tasteless, pointless, countless, quenchless
-ment	condition, quality, or result	discouragement, amazement, pavement, sediment
-ness	state or quality of	gladness, blindness, illness
-or	state or quality of, one who	pallor, ardor, senator, actor
-ous	full of, having qualities of	joyous, courteous, vigorous
-ty	quality, state, condition	loyalty, liberty, veracity

EXERCISE 7

Using virgules (/), separate the following words into prefix, root, and suffix. (Check with your dictionary.)

1. u n p a l a t a b l e   _____

2. i n d u c e m e n t   _____

3. t r a n s f e r e n c e   _____

4. o b d u r a t e   _____

5. c o n s p i r a c y   _____

6. s u g g e s t i o n   _____

7. p e r f i d y   _____

8. d e l i n e a t e   _____

9. i n n o v a t i o n   _____

10. d i s s i m i l a r   _____

11. c o n s e c r a t e   _____

12. d e s t i t u t e   _____

13. a t t e n u a t e   _____

14. r e t r o s p e c t i o n   _____

15. o c c u r r e n c e   _____

16. a d j u d i c a t e   _____

17. a m o r p h o u s   _____

18. e m a n a t i o n   _____

19. i m m i n e n t   _____

20. c o n t i g u o u s   _____

EXERCISE 7 (continued)

21. s u b s i d i z e   _____

22. d e c e i t f u l   _____

23. p e r c e p t i v e   _____

24. a r r o g a n t   _____

25. d i a g o n a l   _____

EXERCISE 8

Add suffixes to the following words, thereby making nouns indicating action, state, or quality.

Example: bachelor bachelorhood

1. scholar   _____

2. ill   _____

3. jealous   _____

4. stow   _____

5. deduct   _____

6. alter   _____

7. adjourn   _____

8. coerce   _____

9. imagine   _____

10. certain   _____

11. free   _____

12. coward   _____

EXERCISE 8 (continued)

13. boy   _____

14. supreme   _____

15. inquire   _____

EXERCISE 9

By adding appropriate suffixes, form verbs from the following words.

1. familiar   _____

2. hyphen   _____

3. apology   _____

4. satire   _____

5. simple   _____

6. glad   _____

7. beauty   _____

8. brutal   _____

9. alien   _____

10. epitome   _____

Because words undergo change of meaning—semantic change—we should remember that word analysis is not always a reliable guide to the current meaning of unfamiliar words. An analysis of *manufacture,* for example, would disclose that it is derived from two Latin words: *manu* ("by the hand") and *facere* ("to make"). Yet "to make by hand" is hardly an adequate definition for "to manufacture." In such a case, then, we are learning the *original* meaning—not necessarily the *modern* meaning. Only by observing the context— the sentences and paragraph in which the unfamiliar word occurs—and by checking our tentative definition in the dictionary, can we be reasonably certain that our analysis of a word is correct. But learning to identify roots, prefixes, and suffixes provides an aid for learning and remembering many new words, as well as for using the words presently in our vocabulary with greater ease and facility.

XVI. IMPROVING READING SKILLS

Although films, tapes, and records are becoming important in the college curriculum today, the ability to read efficiently is still the key to academic success. In fact, reading is involved in 50 to 90 per cent of all your college studies. As a result, any improvement in your reading efficiency will be reflected in your subjects. And, of course, success in the years that follow your formal education will depend in great part on your ability to read and digest quantities of printed material within limited periods of time.

How fast do people read? According to studies, the speed of the average reader is about 250 words per minute. This rate is too slow, however, to allow most college students to complete their assignments on time. Such students need to be able to read from 400 to 800 words per minute. But rapid reading is only one side of the coin; unless you understand what you are reading, you are wasting your time. Comprehension, then, is equally important. For this reason, you should consistently maintain about 75 per cent comprehension, regardless of the difficulty of the material.

Fortunately, one's reading ability can be improved with conscientious practice. This chapter will give you some suggestions that can help you to read faster and with more comprehension—the two traits of the efficient reader.

SOME COMMON READING PROBLEMS AND THEIR CURES

From your knowledge of athletics you know that any attempt to improve one's performance in a particular sport begins with getting rid of bad habits. So it is in reading. Before you can hope to be a better reader, you will have to identify your reading habits and get rid of those that are holding you back. Listed below are the most common reading problems, with some ideas for their elimination.

1. *Regression.* The poor reader makes a habit of regressing; that is, his eyes backtrack when he is unsure of what he has read. Sometimes he will return to an unfamiliar word; at other times, he will re-read several lines. In this respect he is like a hobbled horse—he will never be able to travel with speed until he has broken his shackles. Of course, even the most efficient readers sometimes consciously regress. An unfamiliar word, an important idea, or a doubtful statement usually requires backtracking. But the poor reader makes many regressions, even for simple material. Such a reader is usually reading word by word. As a result, his mind wanders and he loses his train of thought. He constantly returns to re-read words or whole sentences. Another cause of regression is an inadequate vocabulary, which we have discussed in the two preceding chapters. Lack of concentration is still another cause.

To overcome the habit of regressing, you should think *ahead* of, rather than *behind,* the author's thought. That is, you should try to anticipate what he will say next. By thus looking for large units of thought, you will keep your mind active. And soon you will realize that the author will give you enough aids—such as examples, synonyms, repetitions, and summaries—to make constant regressions unnecessary. By consciously refusing to backtrack, you will increase not only your speed but also your comprehension.

2. *Vocalization.* A student who moves his lips or sounds his words in his throat is always a slow reader. Because he forms each word separately, he will rarely be able to read more than 180 words a minute, little faster than the average speed of a radio or TV announcer reading aloud. Conscious effort will do much to overcome vocalization. But some practical steps can also be taken to reduce movements of the lips and throat. By reading with your finger pressed against your lips you will become conscious of forming words. If continued practice fails to eliminate the habit, hold a pencil between your teeth while reading silently. This will virtually eliminate the habit. To break the habit of sounding words in your throat, keep your fingers lightly on your throat while silently reading. This will make you aware of the movement of your vocal cords, and discourage you from sounding words.

3. *Pointing with the finger.* The human eye can move over the words on a page at a rapid pace—far faster, in fact, than you can point to them. By underlining or following along a line of print with your finger, you may be holding back the movement of your eyes. The obvious result is that you reduce your rate of speed. If you are guilty of this fault, start right now to correct it.

4. *Eye trouble.* A common barrier to reading enjoyment and efficiency is weakness of vision. It is not unusual to find from one fourth to one third of a freshman class hampered by visual defects that interfere with proficient reading. Because many students have serious eye defects without being aware of them, you should have your eyes tested at least once each year.

The most frequent symptoms of eye trouble are: 1) blurred vision, 2) eyestrain, 3) headaches while reading, and 4) holding the page either very close or very far from the eyes.

Of course, not all eye fatigue is caused by poor eyesight. Inadequate lighting will cause eyestrain, as will reading for hours without a break.

5. *Distractions*. In this day of television and transistor radios, it is increasingly difficult to find a good reading environment. Even in the library one is often interrupted, and concentration becomes almost impossible to sustain. The best environment is one isolated from friends and other distractions. Your chair should not be too comfortable, or you may become too sleepy or relaxed to read. Your book should be placed on the desk or table before you, supported by a bookrest or another book so that the top and bottom of the page are approximately the same distance from your face—about 14 inches. You should have a pencil and paper at hand, as well as a firm writing surface. Make every effort to put personal problems out of your mind while reading. By taking these steps to eliminate distractions, you will find it possible to concentrate effectively.

Developing Concentration

Most of us are occasionally troubled by poor concentration. For some, however, it is a constant problem. If you find that you cannot keep your attention on the page for more than a sentence or two at a time, then you, too, are experiencing this problem. But unless you have a serious emotional problem, you can improve your ability to concentrate.

We have already mentioned one of the factors influencing concentration— the environment in which you read. Another factor is time. It is impossible to concentrate under the pressure of insufficient time. Try to allow yourself enough time to complete your assignment without interruption. Choose a time of day when you are alert; don't wait until bedtime to begin your assignments. And try to have a regular place for your reading and studying.

So far, we have been speaking of the external causes that make concentration difficult. But there is another, internal, cause which is more difficult to deal with: lack of motivation and interest. This problem causes daydreams and boredom, with the result that although you have been looking at the words on the page, you have understood and remembered very little.

By increasing your interest in your reading, you will be able to concentrate with much less difficulty. One of the best ways to develop interest is to recognize your purpose in reading. The *immediate* purpose, of course, will usually be to complete an assignment. But you should develop another goal: *think*. Try to determine the direction of the author's thought. To do this, ask questions as you read, challenge his statements, get involved with his message. By thus participating with the author in the subject, you will be less likely to be distracted.

Pre-reading is another technique that will increase your interest in what you read. Before beginning actually to read, notice how the author has organized his book or article within chapters, headings, divisions, or sections. In this way you will see not only his over-all plan, but also his main thesis, arguments, and conclusions.

Finally, sometimes there is no better cure for the inability to concentrate than to stop reading—that is, to take a break. By occasionally taking a rest period and turning to something entirely different, you can refresh your mind. When you return to your book, you should be more alert and ready to resume your reading with more efficiency.

Increasing Your Speed

There are several advantages to being able to read rapidly. The first is a practical one: You will save time. The second advantage is that you will come to enjoy reading more, and new worlds will open to you. The third advantage is perhaps a surprising one to you: In general, the faster you read, the more you comprehend.

As you learn to read more rapidly, your concentration will automatically increase. Speed has a tendency to generate a feeling of urgency and greater interest, because the mind is forced to pay close and constant attention.

Many students ask, "How fast should I read?" There is no stock answer to this question—it's like saying, "How fast should I drive?" In the latter case, the answer depends on driving conditions, traffic, weather, and the purpose of one's trip—one does not drive at the same rate of speed at all times. Similarly, your reading speed will be determined by your particular purpose. At times it will be very slow—perhaps between 100 and 200 words per minute when reading poetry, chemical formulas, charts, dates, and other material that requires the mastery of concentrated facts or ideas. At other times—particularly when reading a light novel or when skimming an article of only casual interest to you—you may read at 500 or more words per minute. In other words, your speed is determined by the difficulty of the material you are reading and your purpose in reading it. The point to remember is that the *correct* rate is the *efficient* rate. By developing flexibility in your reading speed, you will become a more efficient reader.

Your reading speed also depends on the movement of your eyes. Let us consider what actually happens as you read. You probably think that a good reader's eyes sweep smoothly over the page. But this is not the case; instead, they move along the line of print in a series of jumps and pauses to the end of the line, somewhat like the stops and starts one makes when driving in heavy traffic. The pauses, or fixations, occur when the eyes are focused directly on the printed words. The *length* of the pause depends on the amount of time it takes the brain to decode the printed symbols into meaning. The *frequency* of the pause is determined by the span of recognition—that is, the number of words that can be seen at one fixation. Beginning readers can see only a part of a word at each fixation. A good reader, on the other hand, will see several words at each fixation. It follows, then, that your reading speed depends greatly on your span of recognition—the number of words you can pick up with each pause or fixation. To read faster and to improve your comprehension, it is necessary to extend your span of recognition, thereby reducing the number of required pauses.

If you are a slow reader, you read just one word at a time; your span of recognition is too short. Think of the way you look at a word—the word *help*, for instance. You would not say to yourself "*h*," then "*e*," then "*l*," and then "*p*." Rather, by looking somewhere in the center of the word, your eyes see all four letters at once. Similarly, a good reader approaches phrases in their entirety, rather than word-for-word. The phrase *on the way,* for example, would be the object of one fixation, rather than three. If you practice handling phrases rather than single words, you will find that meaning comes more quickly and more clearly. This is because you will be dealing with meaningful wholes, rather than pieces, and receiving whole ideas, rather than fragments of thoughts. In practicing reading by phrases rather than by single words, start out on easy reading materials. Articles that are too difficult will have terms, ideas, and vocabulary that will cause you to regress and spend extra time on each fixation. Of course it will take practice for you to acquire this way of reading, but the result is well worth the effort.

Skimming

Skimming is an extremely rapid form of reading. You practice it every day in one form or another. When you read the newspaper, for instance, you glance at the headlines, ignoring some and reading others. You glance down the news columns looking for stories that interest you. And you check the advertisements, stopping to read the prices of those items you might be interested in purchasing. So, too, do you skim when you preview and review material for class, or prepare for a test.

Understand that skimming is never a substitute for reading in depth—the kind of close reading often required in your college work. Skimming is, in fact, the art of reading what you are looking for, and leaving out everything else. It saves you time and effort, and for this reason it is a valuable tool.

Skim with a definite purpose in mind. You will be able to skim rapidly only if you know what you are looking for—specific information or the answer to a specific question. One authority has compared skimming to scanning the shelves of a supermarket to find what you came to buy. You know why you're there, you know what you're looking for, and you look for that alone. This is skimming.

APPENDIX

A. A GLOSSARY OF RHETORICAL TERMS

Abstract Words: words that describe or refer to general qualities and ideas, rather than to particular things, viz., *democracy, admiration, envy. Concrete Words* name particular objects or things, viz., *book, Sue, radio.* Because abstract words are more general, they are usually less forceful than concrete words; for this reason, the overuse of abstract words should be avoided.

Analogy: a comparison of two dissimilar things for the purpose of argument or explanation. Such comparisons usually explain the unknown in terms of the known, the abstract in relation to something tangible, or the complex in terms of the simple. For example, life may be compared with a journey, death with sleep, etc.

Analysis: in expository writing, the division of a topic or subject into its basic parts, thereby showing their relationships and functions.

Argument: writing that provides evidence to support the author's proposition, thereby persuading the reader to accept that proposition. Good argumentative writing is characterized by objective evidence, persuasive proof, and controlled language.

Balanced Sentence: a sentence in which the phrases or clauses are grammatically similar, viz., "I came, I saw, I conquered." (See Chapter 3.)

Cause and Effect: a method of paragraph or theme development in which the relationship between a particular cause and its effects is analyzed. Some causes are readily discoverable; others are hidden or remote. Similarly, some effects can be easily determined; others are obscure or uncertain. For this reason, this method should be used cautiously.

Central Purpose: one of several terms used to describe the central idea of a composition, determining the selection and arrangement of ideas, language, and attitude in a piece of writing. (See also *Thesis Statement*.)

Chronological Order: the presentation of events in the order in which they happened in time. This method of development, commonly used in narrative writing, employs linking words such as *next, then,* and *when.*

Classification: a method of analysis in which subjects are placed into categories on the basis of significant similarities. Americans, for example, could be classified on the basis of their financial standing as low-income, middle-income, or high-income groups.

Coherence: the clear and close connection between the parts of a sentence, the sentences in a paragraph, and the paragraphs in a composition. Coherence is achieved through the presentation of one's ideas in a careful arrangement, and through the use of transitional words and connectives to show that arrangement. Coherent writing enables the reader to follow smoothly the flow of the author's thoughts. (See also *Emphasis* and *Unity*.)

Comparison and Contrast: a method of analysis in which similarities are pointed out (*comparison*), or differences are emphasized (*contrast*).

Concrete Words: see *Abstract Words.*

Connotation: the association or atmosphere suggested by a word as a result of its past use or context, rather than its dictionary meaning. Connotation may be pleasant or unpleasant, depending on that past use or context. (See also *Denotation*.)

Deductive Reasoning: in logic, the application of a predetermined generalization to a particular example. In rhetoric, deductive reasoning is a pattern of development which proceeds from the general to the specific. (See Chapter 8.)

Definition: in logic, the placing of the term to be defined in its general class (*genus*), then showing what qualities (*differentiae*) distinguish it from other members of that class. In rhetoric, logical definitions are developed into paragraphs and entire themes by the use of examples, metaphors, and details. (See Chapter 5.)

Denotation: the literal or dictionary meaning of a word. (See also *Connotation*.)

Diction: the word choice or level of language in a piece of writing (as used here; another meaning is "vocal expression"). The author's subject matter and attitude determine the kinds of words he selects. Good diction is exact and appropriate, communicating the author's intention as specifically and fully as possible. Poor diction is vague, inappropriate, and stale. (See Chapter 2.)

Emphasis: the arrangement of a phrase, sentence, or paragraph so that important words or ideas are placed in positions stressing that importance. Emphasis can be attained by several methods: by using active rather than passive verbs; by altering the usual subject-verb order found in most sentences; by repeating key terms or ideas; by placing less important ideas in subordinate clauses and more important ideas in main clauses; and by placing the most important idea in the final position. (See Chapter 3.)

Example: a method of development in which an illustration is given in order to explain or clarify the subject. Because they serve to make clear the author's thesis, examples should be appropriate, concrete, and vivid. (See Chapter 6.)

Figurative Language: language that goes beyond the literal meaning of a word. (See also *Hyperbole, Metaphor, Personification,* and *Simile.*)

Generalization: a conclusion or general statement based on specific instances or particulars.

Hyperbole: a figure of speech employing exaggeration in order to intensify the meaning: "My briefcase weighed a ton."

Inductive Reasoning: in logic, the formulation of a generalization or conclusion based on the observation of a sufficient number of particulars or instances. In rhetoric, inductive reasoning is a pattern of development that proceeds from the specific to the general. (See Chapter 8.)

Irony: a tone of writing that suggests that the intended meaning is different from —and often opposite to—the literal meaning. Example: "Here's bad news: You just won a new car."

Loose Sentence: a sentence in which the main elements and ideas are placed at the beginning, rather than the end, of the sentence. (See Chapter 3.)

Metaphor: a figure of speech based on an implied comparison between two objects. Good metaphors make writing clear, vivid, and concrete, as in the Biblical metaphor: "All flesh is grass." (See Chapter 2.)

Paradox: an apparently contradictory statement which may actually be true. As a rhetorical device, paradox can be used to attract attention or secure emphasis.

Parallelism: the placing of ideas of equal importance in similar grammatical structure.

Periodic Sentence: a sentence in which the main elements and ideas are placed at the end, rather than the beginning, of the sentence. (See Chapter 3.)

Personification: a figure of speech in which human feelings or qualities are given to inanimate objects or abstract ideas, viz., "Time's cruel hand" (Shakespeare).

Point of View: the author's relationship toward his subject. This relationship can be considered in terms of attitude (objective and impersonal, or subjective and emotional), speaker (first person, second person), or perspective (omniscient, or unaware, or partially informed). (See also *Tone.*)

Rhetoric: the study of developing ideas in language that will achieve the results the writer wants.

Simile: a figure of speech that compares two objects essentially unlike. Similes are commonly introduced by *as, like,* or *than,* viz., "I wandered lonely as a cloud" (Wordsworth). (See Chapter 2.)

Style: the personality of an author as reflected in his choice of diction, sentence structure, and paragraph patterns.

Symbol: a visible or concrete image that stands for something invisible or abstract, viz., the American flag.

Thesis Statement: a statement of the specific topic of a composition. (See also *Central Purpose* and Chapter 1.)

Tone: the author's attitude toward his topic or his audience. Tone can be established by diction and by selection and arrangement of facts; it may be neutral, authoritative, sentimental, mock-serious, arrogant, cynical, ironic, sarcastic, or sincere. (See also *Point of View.*)

Topic Sentence: the sentence, expressed or implied, that summarizes the thought of a paragraph. (See Chapter 4.)

Transitions: words and phrases that show the continuity of thought between sentences and paragraphs, thereby assuring coherence. (See Chapter 10.)

Unity: the development of one idea, impression, or event at a time. A paragraph or composition that has unity contains only those sentences and ideas that develop its central or guiding purpose. (See also *Coherence.*)

B. RECOMMENDED READINGS

Listed here are more than a hundred books, any one of which will be worthwhile reading for you. They range in subject from adventure to religion to nature to war. The advantage of this list over browsing in the library for a book is simple: This list has been made with your interests in mind; thus many titles have not been included because they are likely to be of little interest to the young college student. On the other hand, this list includes many modern works that will be of specific interest to you. Plan a program of reading for yourself based on these works.

Asch, Sholem
  The Apostle
Baldwin, James
  The Fire Next Time
Balzac, Honoré de
  Eugénie Grandet
Beach, Edward L.
  Run Silent, Run Deep
Bennett, Jack
  Jamie
Bowra, C. M.
  Classical Greece
Brontë, Charlotte
  Jane Eyre
Buck, Pearl
  The Good Earth
Burdick, Eugene
  Fail-Safe
Caidin, Martin
  Ragged, Rugged Warriors

Camus, Albert
  The Stranger
Carson, Rachel
  The Sea Around Us
  Silent Spring
Catton, Bruce
  This Hallowed Ground
Chute, Marchette
  Shakespeare of London
Conrad, Joseph
  Lord Jim
Cottrell, Leonard
  Digs and Diggers
Cousteau, Jacques-Yves
  The Living Sea
  Silent World
Crane, Stephen
  The Red Badge of Courage
Daly, Maureen
  Seventeenth Summer

Dostoevsky, Fëdor
The Brothers Karamazov
Duggan, Alfred
The Romans
Forbes, Esther
*Paul Revere and the World He
Lived In*
Gibson, William
The Miracle Worker
Gilbreth, Frank B.
Cheaper by the Dozen
Godden, Rumer
An Episode of Sparrows
Golding, William
Lord of the Flies
Greene, Graham
The Power and the Glory
Hamilton, Edith
The Greek Way
Hamner, Earl
You Can't Get There from Here
Hansbery, Lorraine
A Raisin in the Sun
Hart, Moss
Act One
Hayes, Helen
A Gift of Joy
Hemingway, Ernest
The Old Man and the Sea
Hersey, John R.
A Bell for Adano
Herzog, Maurice
Annapurna
Hilton, James
Lost Horizon
Hugo, Victor
Les Misérables
Jackson, Shirley
We Have Always Lived in the Castle
Joyce, James
*A Portrait of the Artist as a
Young Man*
Kennedy, John F.
Profiles in Courage
Killilea, Marie
With Love from Karen
King, Martin Luther
Why We Can't Wait

Kreig, Margaret B.
*Green Medicine: The Search for
Plants That Heal*
Knebel, Fletcher
Seven Days in May
Knowles, John
A Separate Peace
Kroeber, Theodora
Ishi in Two Worlds
Lamont, Lansing
Day of Trinity
Lea, Tom
The Brave Bulls
Le Carré, John
*The Spy Who Came in from
the Cold*
Lee, Harper
To Kill a Mockingbird
L'Engle, Madeleine
Camilia
Llewellyn, Richard
How Green Was My Valley
MacArthur, Douglas
Duty, Honor, Country
McGraw, Eloise J.
The Golden Goblet
MacInnes, Helen
The Venetian Affair
McKenney, Ruth
My Sister Eileen
MacLean, Alistain
Ice Station Zebra
Manry, Robert
Tinkerbelle
Mather, Melissa
One Summer in Between
Maxwell, Gavin
The Ring of Bright Water
Michener, James A.
Bridges at Toko-Ri
The Source
Miller, Arthur
The Crucible
Monsarrat, Nicholas
The Cruel Sea
Moore, Ruth
The Coil of Life
Murphy, Robert

The Golden Eagle
The Pond
North, Sterling
Rascal
Orwell, George
Animal Farm
1984
Pasternak, Boris
Dr. Zhivago
Paton, Alan
Cry, the Beloved Country
Pei, Mario
All About Language
Perrine, Laurence
*100 American Poems of the
Twentieth Century*
Petry, Ann
Tituba of Salem Village
Porter, Katherine Anne
Collected Stories
Rand, Ayn
Anthem
Remarque, Erich Maria
All Quiet on the Western Front
Richter, Conrad
The Light in the Forest
Rostand, Edmond
Cyrano de Bergerac
Ryan, Cornelius
The Last Battle
Saint-Exupéry, Antoine de
Wind, Sand and Stars
Sandoz, Mari
Battle of the Little Big Horn
Saroyan, William
The Human Comedy
Schaefer, Jack W.
Shane
Sherman, D. R.
Old Mali and the Boy

Smith, Vian
A Second Chance
Steinbeck, John
Travels with Charley
Stewart, Mary
Airs Above the Ground
Tey, Josephine
Franchise Affair
Thoreau, Henry D.
Walden
Toland, John
The Last 100 Days
Tuchman, Barbara
The Guns of August
Udall, Stewart L.
The Quiet Crisis
Van der Post, Laurence
Flamingo Feather
Vidal, Gore
Visit to a Small Planet
Wellman, Paul
The House Divided
West, Jessamyn
Cress Delahanty
West, Morris
The Devil's Advocate
Westheimer, David
Von Ryan's Express
Wheelock, John Hall
What Is Poetry?
White, Theodore H.
The Making of the President, 1964
Whitman, Walt
The Whitman Reader
Wilder, Thornton
The Bridge of San Luis Rey
Wolff, Ruth
Crack in the Sidewalk
Wolfe, Thomas
Look Homeward, Angel

C. 100 THEME TOPICS

Here are some additional topics for themes. Some are in the form of propositions to be defended or attacked; others are merely subjects, giving you a chance to sharpen your own central thesis. Still others are in the form of questions, provoking answers that will form the bases of interesting themes.

I. *College Life*
   Why students fail
   The reliability of intelligence tests
   Should Communists be hired to teach in American colleges?
   Why students cheat in college
   Why grades are (overrated, important)
   The morals of today's college students
   The educated man: a definition
   How much education should a woman receive?
   Should students marry while in college?
   Federal aid to education
   Everyone (should, should not) attend college

II. *Sports*
   Why men gamble
   Is prize-fighting an uncivilized pastime?
   The commercialization of college athletics
   Mistaken notions about motorcyclists
   Sports-car racing
   How to play _____
   Cards: the old man's game
   Should our state have a lottery?

Should the city provide drag strips?
Is hunting "for sport" civilized?
Should colleges abolish football?

III. *Folklore, Myths, and Customs*
Courting customs in other cultures
Status symbols in suburbia
Is chivalry dead?
Why people have prejudices
The American way of death
How significant are dreams?
Why teen-agers pursue fads
ESP: fact or fancy?
Unidentified flying objects
How the custom of _____ originated

IV. *Politics*
How honest is the typical Congressman?
Should loyalty oaths be required for public employment?
Why I am a (Democrat, Republican, other)
How to distinguish between a politician and a statesman
How the electoral college works
Is a world government desirable?
Should requirements for voting in national elections be changed?
The American jury system
Civil defense programs in the nuclear age
Should welfare programs be expanded or reduced in scope?
Should national political conventions be abolished?

V. *The Contemporary Scene*
The ethics of American business
Are Americans anti-intellectual?
The major causes of suicide
Is the common man too common?
Why capital punishment (should, should not) be abolished
Is the labor strike outmoded?
The fairness of the military draft system
Why I (believe, do not believe) in censorship
What's (right, wrong) with the American press?
Is television getting better or worse?
The reliability of opinion polls
Pornography and the law
Credit cards: blessing or curse?
Are the young people taking over?

VI. *Personal Beliefs and Relationships*
   Why I (believe, do not believe) in God
   How to get rid of a phobia
   Are women really more emotional than men?
   Does organized religion help or hinder morality?
   Is experience always the best teacher?
   Why people are superstitious
   Am I my brother's keeper?
   How to distinguish between infatuation and love
   Human progress (is, is not) inevitable
   Is beauty only skin deep?

VII. *Science and Speculations*
   The effects of heredity on behavior
   Is psychology a science?
   The natural (superiority, inferiority) of women
   Is there a conflict between science and religion?
   The effects of race on intelligence
   Is nature kind to man?
   The possibility of life on other planets
   Are scientists morally responsible for the consequences of their discoveries?
   All college students (should, should not) be required to take a year of natural science
   Why I (believe, do not believe) in evolution
   The causes of homosexuality
   Science: destroyer or creator?
   The effects of automation on our lives
   Why go to the moon?

VIII. *Controversies*
   Should abortion be legalized?
   The guaranteed annual wage for industry
   Is war outmoded?
   The Marine Corps: a critical view
   How effective is the United Nations?
   Should public employees be allowed to strike?
   How effective are mass public demonstrations?
   Is political conservatism dead?
   Is God dead?
   Can we co-exist with Russia?
   The union shop (should, should not) be abolished
   Why students revolt
   Sex on the campus

Pop art: authentic or fraudulent?
Open-housing laws
Should LSD be legalized?
How safe are American cars?
Should euthanasia (mercy killing) be made legal?
Pre-marital sex (should, should not) be condoned